## About the Author

Siân Phillips was born in Tŷ mawr farm, G.C.G., Wales. She won the National Eistedfodd aged 11 and started acting for BBC Radio Wales at the same age. She took a degree in English and Philosophy at Cardiff University, at the same time working as a radio newsreader and announcer, and TV presenter, and leading the Welsh Arts Council National Theatre Company. She then went to RADA where she became a Bancroft gold medal-winner.

Her many stage roles have ranged from classics, such as *Hedda Gabler* and *The Three Sisters*, to musicals such as *A Little Night Music* and *Pal Joey*. Recently, she starred in the West End as Marlene Dietrich in Pam Gem's play *Marlene*, which she has since taken to South Africa, Ireland, Paris and Broadway, and appeared in her own cabaret on an international tour and at the Firebird in New York. She is currently working on a new play in the United States. On television she has appeared and won awards in countless plays including: *Shoulder to Shoulder*, *I Claudius* and *How Green Was My Valley*. She was made a CBE in 2000.

For twenty years she was married to Peter O'Toole by whom she has two daughters. She lives in Kensington in London.

*Also available:*

Private Faces
Volume one of Siân Phillips' autobiography

*Siân Phillips*

# Public Places

*The Autobiography*

SCEPTRE

First published in Great Britain in 2001 by Hodder and Stoughton
First published in paperback in 2002 by Hodder and Stoughton
A division of Hodder Headline

A Sceptre paperback

3 5 7 9 10 8 6 4 2

A CIP catalogue record for this title is available
from the British Library

ISBN 0 340 71258 9

Angus McBean photographs: copyright © The Harvard Theatre Collection,
The Houghton Library.

Typeset in Sabon by Palimpsest Book Production Limited,
Polmont, Stirlingshire
Printed and bound in Great Britain by
Clays Ltd, St Ives plc

Hodder and Stoughton
A division of Hodder Headline
338 Euston Road
London NW1 3BH

To my daughters, Kate and Pat, who have helped me and to those who helped all of us; the people who 'lived faithfully a hidden life'.

# Acknowledgements

My sincere thanks to my editor at Hodder, Rowena Webb, and to my agent, Mark Lucas, for their good advice and support throughout. I would like to thank Peta Nightingale at LAW for the invaluable editorial suggestions and Stephanie Darnill, my copyeditor, who gave so generously of her time. Without Nina Humm, who not only can read my writing but has a firmer grasp of the chronology of my life than I, the book would not have come to completion. I owe her more than I can say.

William Corlett has been unstinting in his help and encouragement during a year in which he and Bryn Ellis have smoothed my path. In many ways I owe a huge debt to Thierry Harcourt for reading the book as it progressed and for being so candid in his opinions, as was Sarah Randall who may know more about some aspects of my life than I do.

Bob Willoughby has been more than generous in allowing me to choose from his magnificent collection of photography taken in South America. I am grateful to my theatrical agent, Lindy King, for her forbearance when I was obliged to steal time from acting in order to write. Above all, I thank the friends who have stood by me during the past year – in particular Fabi Waisbort, the best sort of friend with whom to travel a difficult road.

Private faces in public places
are wiser and nicer
than public faces in private places

*Orators* by W.H. AUDEN

They change their climate, not their lives, who rush
across the sea

Horace

# Public Places

# Chapter One

## *March 1975*

Naples Airport and I'm frightened. Coming after the black winter months in London and the weeks of filming on the icy Suffolk coast, the March light of Italy is blinding me. And the noise is confusing me. London and its airport must have been busy but I feel that we have emerged from near silence into this aggressive, lighthearted tumult. Years of disciplined dieting have left me stick-thin and as I shuffle the travel papers and passports and begin to worry about the baggage, I am aware that there's nothing much in the way of protection between my frame and the demands that are being made on it by this expedition. No ordinary journey for me or for the tall figure standing a little to the side, detached, aloof and rather grand but in fact carefully positioned so as not to be conspicuous and finding the place of maximum safety in this press of people. If I'm scared, he must be terrified. Not that he's showing it. Only a slight over-stillness and a too-studied air of relaxation betray him.

He is not supposed to walk more than a few steps, forbidden to lift anything heavier than a teacup. There is no certainty that he won't suddenly need the resources of a well-equipped hospital. I have on me the number of a helicopter ambulance service and the address of an approved hospital. His medical records are in my suitcase along with a letter from our doctor, Gerry Slattery. Don't leave London, they all said, the doctors who have become familiar to me these last months. And here we are in Naples Airport on our way to the San Pietro Hotel outside Positano. More importantly, we're on our way to Sr Carlo Cinque, the builder, architect and proprietor. We are the hotel guests from hell.

Left to me, we would still be safe in Guyon House, on Heath Street in Hampstead, just up the road from Dr Gerry Slattery and the Royal Free Hospital (the umbilical cord attaching me to Men's Surgical has yet to be cut). As usual, confronted with the prospect of O'Toole standing alone against expert opinion and common sense and people who know what's best for him, I crossed the line and stood with him against Them. 'He's not an alcoholic,' they told me. 'He just drinks a lot.' When he became aggressive they always made themselves scarce, I couldn't help but notice. 'See you tomorrow,' they'd cry, trooping out into Heath Street as the first glass shattered. They have been very present at the hospital, looking grave and concerned.

The sense of the folly of this adventure and awareness of the responsibility I've taken on myself have kept me awake for a week past. And this comes at the end of the worst time in my life; standing vigil while he hovered between life and death, returning to an empty house only to change clothes and deal with the journalists anxious to verify the show-business facts of a life that they believed to be coming to an early end. They didn't try to hide what they thought and offered sympathy. Only Jules and Joyce Buck, our partners in Keep Films – our 'family' – knew what was really going on. We spoke briefly at night. They knew too much, feared too much, to be interested in chatting or speculating. Night after night I sat, alone, on our bed in the big, gleaming house. Manolita, much, much more than the 'daily' and one of the few people to know anything of our private life, had been there all day, cleaning as though she were banishing fiends, conquering illness with antique wax. She brought from her house little plates of food and left them in the fridge and these small kindnesses were enough to tip me over into short, violent bursts of weeping, never a long, healing, outpouring of grief. There were too many moments every day when I had to assume a bright face; even the children and my mother, away in Ireland, and his parents, in a flat off Haverstock Hill, are not to be told how bad things are until the last moment – should the last moment come.

For a while I even fooled myself. 'All this is to be expected, I suppose,' I said to Sister in a sensible tone after a particularly bad night. 'It will get better, won't it?' Her eyes filled with tears and she looked away before leaving the room without speaking. Then I knew we were in more trouble than I had realised. 'Be prepared for the worst,' I was then advised and during the next few weeks I forced myself, alone at home, to come to terms with the fact that the person dearest in the world to me was possibly never going to return to himself but would slide from this comatose state into his death and I would never speak to him again.

I had never before felt such grief. When the worst thing in the world happens it seems incredible that one should be able to get up and bathe, get made up, phone for taxis, wish people good day and lie. Lie all the time. 'Oh, you're giving yourself a bad time,' said my closest friend, Ricci Burns, when we met in the street. 'Stop making a drama. He's going to be fine.' Oh Rick, if you only knew what it was like in that side ward.

Against all the odds one day, many weeks later, he opened his eyes in that side ward, ripped out his tubes and irritably demanded sustenance. The tubes were replaced and it was explained to him that he'd been 'really quite ill'. He didn't seem interested and quickly graduated to what we called 'flat' food – little pools of pureed who-knows-what. The family returned to London, the house grew light again, and not quite as gleamingly perfect. And he came home. 'I *told* you it was nothing too awful,' I said to everyone. Dr Slattery and the surgeons and Manolita and I looked at each other in mute fellow feeling. All our lies were coming true, but the shadow of death had come very close.

The question of drink was not broached. Gerry Slattery must

have explained the score to him. Large quantities of vitamins and packets of something new and helpful called Valium were deposited in the house. O'Toole insisted that the bar – just opposite his large leather chair – was fully stocked and the wine cellar kept full. He just didn't drink. No discussion, no help required. It was an extraordinary turn of events. He'd always been bookish and an easy, fluent writer. Now he became a slow, painstaking writer of sonnets. I could not even imagine what went on in his head as he embarked for the first time since his mid-teens on a life of sobriety. My admiration for him increased even as I found it difficult to keep up with his frantic intellectual curiosity; everything was considered and questioned down to the most trivial newspaper stories. It was exhausting. Admiration and respect struggled with resentment. In the past I and the girls, Kate and Pat, could have done with a sober, present husband and father but nothing that I could have said or done would have stopped him drinking. He stopped now to save his life – which is reasonable enough and thank God he has but – but, I wish he could have stopped for our sake.

My mother, who had come to live with us in London after my father's death in Wales in 1962, flung herself into the role of matron; cauldrons of beef tea were prepared in the kitchen and she mastered the art of flat food. The children, aged twelve and fifteen years, learned not to lean on his stomach but otherwise enjoyed having a father captive in bed instead of one that dashed in and out of the house, worked behind closed doors, surrounding himself with people. I never talked to him of the time in hospital but he must have thought I looked the worse for wear and after a few weeks he urged me to accept a job that I had thought I couldn't possibly take. Each night, scared, I called him from Suffolk and he, tucked up in bed which he referred to as his 'teapot', assured me that he was enjoying his life as a dormouse. Dressed as Mayflower pilgrims in a film made for American TV, we froze all day on

4

the desolate beach and I returned to long, dreamless sleeps in the hotel. I discovered a tiny brewery that made exquisite beer. That and the fresh air began to repair me. I went home to my beloved dormouse.

'I need to go somewhere nice to recuperate. Not too much sun. Quiet. Nice.'

'Go? Where? You're not even supposed to be *up*. Not for ages.'

'I'll *get* up.'

'Categorically, NO. We stay in London.'


'Oh. Hello. My name is Siân O'Toole. I'd like to make a reservation. Is your hotel suitable for a semi-invalid?'

'Is there total privacy in your hotel?'

'How far is it from your hotel to the nearest hospital?'

'What do you mean, you're not even open yet?'

'I see, sorry to have troubled you.'

O'Toole's partner, Jules Buck, and I looked at each other in despair. We'd been on the phone for hours. North Africa, France, Italy, Austria. Nothing.

Then suddenly, 'Oh, we have *total* privacy – a suite hanging over the Tyrrhenian Sea. No, we are not open but we will open for you and look after you like family. We will respect the ill-health and never make anything of it.'

Oh blessed, blessed Carlo Cinque. Just let us get to you quickly now. We are an odd little procession. I've got a porter and the bags are piled high on a cart and he wants it to be the fastest cart in Naples Airport. I want to slow him down so that the third figure bringing up the rear can seem to saunter as though his mind were on other things. Each step is painful, I know. Tapping the porter on the shoulder, I shake my head and apologetically pat my chest. I don't have the Italian to say, 'Feel a bit woozy'. But, hands raised in comprehension, he nods sympathetically and we proceed at a regal pace and he keeps a brotherly eye on me until we reach the waiting car.

Good as he is at 'disappearing' in a crowd, people are beginning to recognise O'Toole and as I'm carefully eased into the back seat I try not to look at him on the other side of the car, nonchalantly negotiating himself into the seat beside me. I can tell it's a miracle of small, self-controlled, slow movements. The half-smile disappears once he's seated and we're pulling away from the curious crowd. I'm so relieved I could weep. As for him, I think that in the last forty minutes he's done enough acting to last the year and now we're silent and grateful that the pressure is off. Well, I am. Who knows the state of mind of someone who has been in what doctors call 'unacceptable' pain ('torture', I'd call it) and who is now, after a close brush with death, biting all the hands that have helped and fed him because he *must* try to return to what *he* thinks of as normal living. O'Toole on the ropes is beyond sensible help. Only crazy people can lend him a hand. No, not that. He needs crazy people who are also rational. Madness has to walk hand-in-hand with common sense to be any use to him. And that's my talent. It would be nice to say only great love can help in these extremes but I don't think that's it. Fear and anxiety and grief have left me empty of soft emotion but I can't see this person without seeing my shadow behind him. And I don't feel I exist without his presence, informing my voice, my behaviour, even when he's there only as an irritating grain in my shell and I'm forming layers of disagreement along with the shiny, graceful insights I get from observing him at what I think of as his best. Even after all these years I'm not sure that I don't make up this state of mutual dependence, the 'oneness', this very special state that is never discussed. Maybe it only exists in my head and that has worried me in the past; now it doesn't matter. We're on yet another crazy, possibly doomed journey.

There's a tiny chapel – hardly that, maybe a shrine – on the roadside. In a less anxious state the twists and turns of the Italian Riviera road would have left me a wreck but today

I'm not worried about my skin. Steps! Damn! Lots of steps! No one said anything about steps. The hotel is out of sight below us. How far below? Very slowly we begin the descent. If there are hundreds of these steps we're not going to make it and this place will be impossible for us to stay in. So what do we do? There's a turn in the staircase and a lift door appears in the rock. We step inside and descend, emerging into a lovely room – a huge foyer looking out at the ocean. There seem to be seven people to help us to our set of rooms and the terrace, already flaming with bougainvillaea, does truly hang over the Tyrrhenian Sea (is this the 'wine-red' sea? It's lovely but about as wine-red as ink).

This feels like home. Are the Italians alone in their talent for purveying luxury in a way that has one reaching for words like 'simple', 'homely', 'unassuming'. Since 1970 I've spent almost five years building a house in Ireland and immediately I feel here much as I feel on the West Coast in Connemara. Even the ground under our feet is familiar; solid rock everywhere around, above and below. Who or what guided us to this place? I'm overwhelmed with a sense of good fortune. Maybe our luck has turned. Luck is important. O'Toole is lucky. Leaving him to potter around the rooms, I set about fine-tuning our life here. Breakfast quite early, big jugs of fresh juice mid-morning. No alcohol. The simplest of small lunches. More fresh fruit juice at the cocktail hour. Dinner as much like lunch as possible. The minimum of attention. Telephone calls only from my mother or Jules (and they won't ring unless there's an emergency). I unpack and within hours his books and papers (O'Toole never attempted to master the art of travelling light when in 'civilised' surroundings) cover the tables in the enormous sitting room. My books are piled high in the bedroom. Carlo has raised the drawbridge for us and we are alone.

I've stayed in some of the loveliest hotels in the world but never in one that met all the urgent needs and desires of the moment as did the San Pietro. As the weeks went by we began to tackle the corridors and the steps to the foyer and the dining room. At first we were the only guests and it *was* like being in the West of Ireland. Service was impeccable but running through everything was a streak of idiosyncratic joie-de-vivre that was peculiar to Carlo. There was a St Bernard (suffering in the warmth of Southern Italy) who came and yearned mournfully at the food on the table. Outside there were grumpy penguins living in and around the pool. The parrot in the dining room shrieked obscenities learned from the village builders. The builders . . . When we learned the story of the making of the hotel I knew that we were right to feel at home. In the West of Ireland, before you build anything, you buy gelignite and you blast yourself a flat space on the granite. The boys cycle out to you with a bit of 'jelly' in the basket and, fag in hand, survey the impossible terrain, then they lay their charges and murmur, 'Better get back there now, missus', before the ground explodes. 'Would ya like a little bit of that over there blown off?' 'Mmm, I think a terrace looking out at the—' 'Sure thing. Better move back a bit.' Pow! And there's your terrace – just where you wanted it.

Carlo Cinque, who ran a successful hotel in Positano, thought he'd like a quiet place just for himself and, having bought the San Pietro chapel, perched on the edge of a cliff outside the town, he and a few of the village boys 'jellied' a bit of a ledge and, having cut some steps down to it, he built himself a few rooms and a kitchen. His friends kept borrowing them so he blasted away another ledge and built a few more rooms and on it went. Most wonderful of all (and if he was proud to tell this tale he never found a more admiring audience) when he decided that this was now a proper hotel and maybe should include access to the beach, he decided to make a lift through the cliff to the sea shore hundreds of feet below. A couple of village boys came and surveyed the problem and quickly said they were ready to start. Carlo gave them the go-ahead and provided the explosives. (A less confident man might have feared for his hotel.) Off they went. One boy descended through the rock from the hotel ledge and the other ascended from sea level. They blasted away and one day they met – smack on target in the middle – and there was the elevator shaft. It's sad that this is an extraordinary story. People, understandably people in remote neighbourhoods, have talents and skills and don't question them. Closer to urban communities they lose their confidence and learn to bow to 'experts in the field', experts on building, parenting, meteorology, lift construction. Well, I hope nobody wages a guerrilla war in Southern Italy. Those men are invincible, natural engineers.

We were told that we were too early, alas, for the annual, month-long visit of the famous Welsh actor Hugh Griffith and his wife, Gwnda (one specially designated member of staff would tactfully head him off as he made for the edge of a cliff late at night, glass in hand), but a few guests appeared in the dining room as time went by – charming, quiet Americans mostly. Carlo and they and O'Toole and myself began to meet for 'drinks' before dinner. Innocently, they would urge us to have a glass with them. Carlo never betrayed his anxiety at these moments. Nor did I. O'Toole was a model of tact and sweetness, saying he'd 'not been very well' and would have a fruit juice. They, worlds away from the hells we'd inhabited, said, 'Well, when we get home, there'll be no more wine, Fanta only, so we're going to have a glass *every night*.' Oh God, they were so nice and I loved the glimpse into their nice, safe lives. 'Why *not*?' we chorused, raising our glasses of fruit juice and Carlo nodded, beaming.

Normally a sound sleeper, even in the most desperate of circumstances, I lie awake in this Eden. James Herriott's books are making me laugh in the wind-down part of the day. Siegfried seems to be such an O'Toole character; I read aloud to him and he recognises his own maddening habits and it makes him laugh also, before he falls asleep. After that, with the lights out, in the profound silence I lie awake, listening. When I was a little girl I would creep across the landing to see if my parents were still breathing but that was out of fear that I would be left alone in the world. This is different. I feel that if I don't stand vigil he might stop breathing after all. I fall asleep at dawn. Only the dark hours are dangerous. Exhausted, I fall asleep again after lunch. I think that my fears are concealed but one day we decide to take the famous lift to the deserted beach. Entering the cave below we look around, admiring the arrangements, the bar that would operate in season. We stand there looking out at the sea, which looks different at close quarters, more real, less like a set. Above us rises the press of hundreds of feet of rock. My feeling of dread is profound and when O'Toole says, 'Well, I think we've seen enough of this', I gratefully get into the lift and return to the familiar warm, sunny lounge high above the painted sea. In our suite I climb on to the beautiful ornate day-bed in a corner of the sitting room – and sleep, and sleep. When I wake, O'Toole is sitting there looking at me. 'You were afraid, weren't you?' I nod, eyes full of unshed tears. 'Don't fret,' he says, stroking my head. Does he mean that there's nothing more to worry about? Does he mean I'm allowed to feel nervous about rocks? Does he mean he's going to be all right? I nod and resolve to try not to fret.

We now have a lovely pattern to our lives. We've so rarely had patterns. Rising, we have breakfast in the sitting room. (Who brings breakfast? I see no one.) Then we prepare for The Walk. It becomes a little longer each day. The hotel car follows us and at first we're lifted the last kilometre into the town. There we buy the New York *Herald Tribune* and sit outside drinking coffee and doing crosswords or playing word games. There are few people about. Then the car takes us back to the hotel and we lunch in the dining room. Now that visitors are beginning to arrive the foul-mouthed parrot has been banished. Also the St Bernard (we know that he stands in the kitchen, drooling over the preparing of lunch). The penguins also have had to go. The hotel still doesn't look quite 'there' in brochure terms. It's the gardens, of course. Carlo and I go to Naples and buy hundreds of plants. (This time the road *does* scare me half to death.) Over the next week I spend a few hours a day digging and fertilising and planting and *voilà*! There we are. Every suite has a beautiful, planted, fed and watered garden. By now, I almost feel I'm on the staff and I'm happier than I have been for a long, long time. One day O'Toole and I walk *all* the way into Positano. Triumph! We peer at Zeffirelli's villa down on the beach and hear stories of the goings-on down there. Nureyev hurling heavy objects down from road level is one I particularly like to contemplate. Having been around during the time of Rudi's worst excesses it doesn't surprise me in the least that he should have been thrown out of the villa. Though frankly, by O'Toole standards he's not so bad and I, for one, would never have kicked him out.

Life is calm, a bit like our early days in Connemara when we first acquired a small cottage and a little land. It's not so much having a time to think and reflect, rather it's inhabiting a space in which not to think at all. There was a time in 1960 in the desert when I felt like this. Nothing happened. Living closed down to existing, getting through the day, like a tree. Or a cabbage. Maybe there's something wrong with me. I love life at its lowest level. One thing is clear: I have never felt such love for O'Toole as I feel now. I was all loved out, slumped like a boxer, beaten in my corner. I thought I knew all the turns in this maze he and I inhabited and there was nothing that could dismay or surprise or delight me. Wrong. Where did it come from, this huge, even surge of love? Not from pity. I could never feel pity for such a dangerous, disruptive human being. Sympathy? No. I've never almost died so I don't know what that feels like. Well, this is the place we've arrived at after so many exhausting twists and turns and stops and starts and ups and downs and false endings and I've learned one thing: to accept what comes my way. I'm not going to try to work it out, the reason for this intensely happy time.

# Chapter Two

Nineteen fifty-seven, when we first met, seems a whole lifetime away . . .

'Marry Siân and become a famous couple in the theatre.' Emlyn Williams talking over the supper table, Micheál MacLiammóir nodding enthusiastically. The two matchmakers smiled on us. We were in our early twenties and it was only a matter of weeks since, after a long estrangement following our first play together, John Hall's *The Holiday*, he'd appeared in the early hours of the morning at my window in Ladbroke Square and swung himself back into my heart and my life. No, he'd never left my heart.

Now, we were sitting in a dark night club arrangement that Clement Freud used to run high up under the roof of the Royal Court Theatre in Sloane Square. We raised our glasses though the subject of marriage had never been mooted before and I don't think either of us was keen on the idea, and I was still married to Don, from whom I'd run off to come to London and RADA. For now, it was more than enough to be together. I was dazzled by him (and I could tell that he was fascinated by me). We knew from our time together on tour that we got on very well. We were good company for each other and had no trouble adjusting our living habits to suit each other. I'd never stayed up late but I got to love it. He began to enjoy seeing the world in daylight hours – streets and parks as well as the dark interiors of bars. We shared erratic eating patterns, a love of music, singing, guitar playing, people watching. Our likes and dislikes chimed. The only slight difficulty was drink. Before I met O'Toole I had never even tasted beer or whisky.

On tour he had introduced me to Highland malt – single and blended – and I had liked small quantities of both. Beer and Guinness were utterly beyond my comprehension but I realised that an appreciation of draught Guinness was pretty essential in my new life and I persevered, sipping the hated drink slowly during evenings when O'Toole drank his own age in the stuff. Everyone we knew drank so much; incredible quantities of alcohol were lowered on every conceivable social occasion. I was cautiously intrigued.

Drink apart, it was easy living together and with wonderful sex thrown into the mix it was ecstatic. He was still in Willis Hall's *The Long and the Short and the Tall*, his first big London success, while I played lead after lead in live television plays, also successful and making a great deal of money. We would meet in his dressing room after my rehearsal ended, before his performance began, and eat high tea together; the same meal every day. Huge plates of anaemic scrambled eggs on white bread toast and mugs of tea, sent in from the workmen's café round the corner. While he did the show I would spend the evening watching bits of the play or looking after the new friends we were making, the people who flock to a new success. They were, on the whole, truly nice people, some of whom became part of our lives – people like Dr Slattery and his wife, Johnny, and R. D. Smith, the radio producer, and his wife, Olivia Manning, the novelist; but already I could distinguish between them and the people who came to devour, whose eyes lit up if he said something outrageous and unsayable, who became excited when he crossed the line between high spirits and being hopelessly 'jarred', as the Irish put it. I was made uneasy by them.

I became used to working really hard all day (fortunately I never had to sit down to memorise anything, lines sank in after a few readings) so that I was able to join O'Toole after the show, ready for whatever the evening had to offer. After the play the company would move back next door to the bar where a few hours previously they had been enjoying themselves as the 'five' was rung. Bowing to the inevitable, the theatre had rigged a line relaying the calls through to the pub – there wasn't much hope that the hard core of the company, Ronnie Fraser, Bob Shaw, Bryan Pringle, O'Toole, was going to leave the 'craic' and get into the theatre at the 'half' hour call which is given thirty-five minutes before the play is due to begin. The 'five' sounds ten minutes before curtain up and at that point they would straighten up and stampede for the theatre, pausing only to wipe their fingers under the hot-water pipes and rub the dirt on to their faces. It took them a matter of seconds to discard their clothes and pull on their 'distressed' army uniforms. A dab of Vaseline rubbed into the dirt and they were on stage, looking as though they'd spent a long time in make-up to achieve that diseased, desperate, jungle-damp look which the play demanded. They drove Lindsay Anderson, the director, mad. The expert on army behaviour brought in to make them look like soldiers had a nervous collapse and left. I don't suppose any of them behaved as badly ever again but they and author, Willis Hall, were unstoppable. Had they not been a triumph they would never have worked again. As it was – who argues with success?

A member of the company who did not racket around London was Peter's understudy, who was called Michael Caine. When O'Toole hurt his knee badly and was told he'd have to go 'off' for surgery, he refused flatly. 'What – and let Mick on stage?' he said. 'No chance, thank you very much.' It was a compliment from one good actor to another. Who knew what Michael got up to? He was focused, quiet and circumspect.

Observing the boys, I realised that in fact they'd all done a huge amount of work and that they were desperate to conceal the fact. I heard the story of the 'foreigner' in Dublin who suddenly realised to his nervous amazement that the men standing next to him at the bar were members of the inter-national rugby team he was about to watch playing England. 'And they played a *blinder*. *And* they *won*.' Playing a 'blinder' was crucial. So was winning. The company's behaviour was a pose, and none of them believed you could just stroll on stage without preparation and be wonderful, but that was the impression they liked to give – no one more than O'Toole.

There was something else to it as well. I think there was a revulsion against the 'actorish' English actor who went home after a quiet day of organised rehearsal, had a small sherry and settled down to a few hours of 'study' after dinner; the sort of actor who appeared in well-made plays and led a middle-class life, as respectable as a banker, who, after the show, tied a silk cravat around his neck to protect his white shirt against the remnants of Leichner make-up, numbers nine and five. Plays were altering and the lads were going to show that they were the new breed of actor, born for the occasion; unconventional, bohemian, with no pretensions to belonging to the polite society of 'civilians'. No use expecting polite speech and middle-class behaviour from this lot. The Lord Chamberlain was being challenged to allow unheard of words on the stage and they were the guys to whom such speech came naturally. Stage make-up was considered 'poncy'. It was all very understandable and rather attractive. Exciting, certainly. It was over simple and no actor who cared about theatre would have maintained a prejudice against the great writers and actors of the Thirties and Forties, but for a while in the late Fifties it was no bad thing to seem to be rebelling against everything that had gone before.

It was a mercy that we were all so young and in possession of endless energy. When the pub shut there would be a muttered conference and then a large part of the crowd would drift into taxis and cars and find themselves in basement flats in Paddington and Bayswater. How did anyone know where the parties were happening? It was all a mystery to me.

These gatherings weren't recognisable parties either. 'It's just a piss-up,' explained O'Toole. I don't ever recall going further north than WC2. Hampstead was reserved for exquisite Sunday lunch around Johnny Slattery's kitchen table. She would feed at least six actors as well as her own family and it was often the only 'proper' meal that we found time to sit down to eat all week.

More or less the same fifty people found themselves together late at night several times a week; actors from the London shows. All the new Australian actors in town were there, arriving bearing crates of Fosters lager (Ken Warren from *Summer of the Seventeenth Doll* was a host several times a week). The actors were mostly young, those unencumbered by domestic life, and guilty young actors who *did* have families and went home at dawn to ruffle the sheets and take the children to school. There was always a sprinkling of actors from an older generation who were curious to see what was going on. Willis Hall was an enchanting leader of the pack. Describing a more sedate version of an actors' party he said, 'Oh awful. You know – white wine in cups and young girls being sick.' There were very few rehearsal rooms and companies moved from church hall to church hall – St Thomas, St Luke, St John. One day Willis, checking his diary for the next rehearsal, shook his head and said without looking up, 'If I get knocked over they'll think I'm the fuckin' Pope.'

Robert Bolt was another nightly companion. He used to like to visit the theatre where his first West End play, *The Flowering Cherry*, was playing. Anxiously eavesdropping, he usually heard good, enjoyable things about himself. Not always. (One of his favourite remarks was a grumpy, 'It's all right, I suppose – if you like a great play'.) I listened to his worries and didn't talk about mine, but I remember a night after I'd been to a party at the German Embassy (I did so many translations of German classics on television that I was on their guest list for years) and Robert and I were slumped,

I in full evening dress. Conveniently forgetting that, acting on advice, I'd turned down three film contracts in order to become what people in those days called a 'real' – a theatre – actress, I moped a bit and shed a maudlin tear and said, 'I was sent for by Mr Vidor for a big movie and he's just DIED!' Robert, who'd been going on about the problems of being a writer, wrenched his attention on to my life for a moment and tried to console me. 'Oh my poor girl. Sudden death *does* seem a bit hard. But cheer up.' We both started to laugh at ourselves at the same moment and reached for another Fosters.

There were after hours clubs. Jerry's, which I knew when Sean Lynch ran it (he later married the formidable and talented Annie Ross and they opened Annie's). There was the Kismet run by Raj and his father, just off St Martin's Lane. Jack's near Orange Street was approached through an unmarked door alongside a plain black window. This seemed to be harder to join than the Garrick; only death left a membership place open. Joan Littlewood of Statford East held court there and as far as I could make out they served only steak and baked potatoes. The Buxton was the jolliest place, situated in a quiet street behind the Haymarket across from the stage door of the Haymarket Theatre. I liked it because it was the only place where I ever got to eat anything (a lunchtime sausage and a scrambled egg high tea left me ravenous by midnight. Tough, over-cooked steak and frozen peas were the staple diet and so good.) The Buxton was a bit more like an actors' restaurant of today, but there were no customers outside the profession and it had an illicit air about it. One memorable night in 1953, John Gielgud, newly knighted, and newly convicted of soliciting, squeezed his way through the crowded club. John was loved and revered in the profession but few knew how best to deal with what must be an embarrassing time for the great actor. Stumbling, he put a hand on Emlyn Williams's waist to steady himself. Without looking round, Emlyn in ringing tones cried, 'Four months!' When the laughter subsided, relief and comradeship pervaded the room. Some time afterwards, looking up from his mail, O'Toole said, 'This is ridiculous. I've been thrown out of the Buxton for bad behaviour and someone wants to put me up for the Garrick – oh, sod them all.' And he binned both letters.

The fag end of the night was my favourite part. Often still hungry, the two of us would walk down to the all-night tea and sandwich stand in Covent Garden and order huge white china mugs of tea and hot sausage sandwiches which we ate sitting opposite Lloyds Bank, alongside Boulestin's great restaurant. Fortified, O'Toole would say, 'Okay. Now for a little climb', and he would scale the wall of Lloyds. The first time he did this I was terrified and tried to dissuade him. I was upset by what seemed to be mad, dangerous behaviour. In a remarkably short space of time I came to accept the behaviour as fairly unremarkable – what did that say about the state of my mind? – and I sat nursing my tea, sitting on the low wall with the tramps who liked to hang around near the cheerfully lit stand, watching him as he negotiated the familiar footholds. He was sure-footed. And lucky. The regulars at the stall knew him as 'Pete' and gave him a little cheer as he finished the descent.

When it was time to go home, we would retire to our tiny room in Ken Griffith's flat in Belgravia, facing the side of the National Coal Board building. Ken Griffith and Doriah Noar were like guardian angels to us and we lived for next to nothing in SW1. If Doriah caught us standing still for ten minutes she fed us nourishing meals. We slept in a double bed which rested on about £75,000 worth of stamps ('Covers', as I learned to call them); part of Kenneth's passion for the Boer War. He adored and admired O'Toole and the feeling was mutual. He made me welcome, partly because I was a fellow countrywoman, but he had grave doubts about the union. When we were filming in Cardiff, he walked me round the Temple of Peace saying, 'You cannot marry this wonderful man. Understand, he is a genius but he is not normal.' I replied, 'He is the most normal man I've ever met.'

I meant it but what did I know about him, this super-normal man? Something and nothing, and everything. He was Irish and he came from Leeds, from the same neighbourhood as Keith Waterhouse and Willis Hall and Albert Finney. His father was an off-course bookmaker – feckless, a drunk and occasionally violent. His mother struggled to keep the family afloat. A Scots Presbyterian, she loved the Catholic Church, its kindly priests and candles. Beautiful, with a low husky voice, she was given to quoting Robbie Burns and loved to stay up drinking tea – or preferably whisky – and exchanging stories with her children, O'Toole and his sister, Patricia. I could tell that both children were bright and I was baffled by parents that wouldn't have fought to keep their children at school. O'Toole's sister had made an early exit from the bosom of the family and set about making up for their lack of education by joining the Wrens. Later, having achieved a coveted job as an air-hostess, she had just made a brilliant marriage, and here was O'Toole, one of the brightest young stars on the London stage, via National Service in the Navy and two years' training at RADA. I had never been to the north of England, except on tour, and couldn't quite make out what his upbringing had been like. His father had come to visit when we were on tour, playing *The Holiday*. He'd arrived, looking dapper in a good suit and a sharp trilby, no overcoat against the cold, long Irish face like a fiddle, a lop-sided half smile and a permanently raised right eyebrow.

'Where are you staying?'

'I don't know – I don't know.'

'Any luggage?'

'No. Stop fussing. Don't spoil everything with *details*.'

He sat in the front row of the stalls and when O'Toole entered he raised his hand in salute. Outside the theatre as we made off for a drink after the show, he didn't refer to the performance but he pointed to the front of the theatre, at O'Toole's name featured prominently. 'Look at that,' he said. '"O" as big as a cartwheel.' He wasn't much of a theatregoer.

I don't know what he thought of me. O'Toole's friends saw their free spirit being sucked into a conventional relationship and, with no special ill-will towards me, they tried to put a stop to it. I didn't mind. They weren't to know that we had a *new* kind of equal partnership and that the last thing I had in mind was domesticity – as alien to me as it was to him.

*My* friends, advisors, employers were equally appalled and bluntly said that he would destroy my career, that I needed taking care of and bringing on and that O'Toole would trample all over me. They must be mad, I thought. We both love the theatre above everything. What can go wrong? For the first time in my life I am living with someone who respects me as an equal and he *will* look after me. Gradually, I lost my support system – the older actors and the directors and producers who were good to me dropped away. But work was still plentiful.

When I left RADA, MCA was the agency I went to, but, with their approval, I had signed an exclusive contract with Douglas Uren, a businessman who was interested in the theatre and chose to make an investment in me. He guaranteed me an income whether I worked or not. But I liked working – all the time. I realised that my private life would have to alter now and I was willing to adapt – sometimes in unexpected ways.

O'Toole looked at my wardrobe of good clothes and said, 'You look as though you're in mourning for your sex life – all this black and violet. Give it here.' It was late at night and it was raining as he gathered up armfuls of organza and wool, bags, shoes, gloves, frocks, hats, suits and, opening the window, flung thousands of pounds worth of clothes on to the wet cobbles below. I had a momentary pang of regret but spoke only to say, 'But what will I wear?' '*My* clothes,' he said grandly, gathering me into his arms. I would have liked to retrieve my things but the new woman in me thought, 'Maybe he's right. That's an old-fashioned way of dressing.' So we became the only couple in town who shared a wardrobe. Winter and summer we wore coloured cotton trousers and canvas shoes and lumberjack shirts and big, thick, knitted fisherman sweaters. I had to roll his trousers up, of course, which made me look like a waif (he looked like a handsome pirate). My next TV role was that of a sexy publican's wife who was no better than she should be and after the show they gave me the skin-tight frocks and six-inch heels. So for months I veered between looking like a tart with a heart and the shrimp boy. I was so deliriously in love I couldn't understand why everyone around me was worried. 'You are going to ruin your career' was the constant warning. Indeed, it was as though he wanted to eradicate my life before I met him, but I was a willing accomplice.

*The Long and the Short and the Tall* ended, not having transferred well to the New (now the Albery) Theatre in St Martin's Lane and while O'Toole began to figure out his next move I went on from TV play to TV play. It was the time of the single play when the writer was still king, so working in television was not unlike working in the theatre. Many of the plays were written specially for TV, otherwise we did stage plays barely adapted for the screen; three acts with thirty seconds in between to change clothes and re-dress the set. Everything that went out on the screen was live. It was pandemonium in the studio. If anyone got injured they were dragged out of the way. During a flu epidemic I watched a sound engineer faint and fall off his seat high above the studio floor and since I was carrying around a bucket into which to throw up, I didn't have much sympathy to spare. In one play at this time an actor died on a set of a mine shaft and the rest of the company had to crawl over him, sharing his lines amongst them, until someone managed to extract his body. There were no rules to speak of. It was like travelling without a map.

We would rehearse for four weeks and after three weeks we'd get into costume and pop into a small studio, pose for stills and play the 'trailer' – live. Then we'd do the show and, having done it once, we'd have a few days off and then we'd go back into the studio and play the 'repeat' – live again. Prompting was out of the question. There was very little anyone could do to help. Being on screen alone when an actor was 'off' was a nightmare and we became used to ad-libbing – not very well in my case. I doubt if the watching audience was fooled as I sat there one night saying, 'Well, I thought that *GEORGE* would be here now. *GEORGE!* Is that you I hear on the path? Well, my goodness, there's no one there. I could have sworn that was *GEORGE's step*. Oh, *GEORGE* there you are – darling, you seem out of breath.' (You bastard.)

Only people who never lived through these experiences talk of the 'wonder' and 'immediacy' of live TV. Immediate coronary, more like. But it was all we were used to and very early on I began to see that television was going to be the most powerful and influential arm of show business. Many actors were snooty about it for a long time. Some of the directors had moved over from radio or the theatre and were pretty pedestrian, but there were also wonderful directors who were devoted to the new medium. When Sidney Newman joined the BBC he galvanised everyone and kept agitating for more boldness, more close ups; he didn't want to see any more 'photographed plays'. 'Get *in* there,' he yelled at cameramen. 'This has to be a close-up.' When you think about it, it stands to reason that close-ups come in ones or twos. At that time I was doing a rather 'sensitive' play for a sensitive director who was petrified when Mr Newman came in to watch our final rehearsals. He looked at the five actors in the scene and, feeling he should be moving in, he whispered desperately to the camera crew, 'Come on boys, in you go. Make this shot – a *close five*'. The fallout was awful.

O'Toole was offered three short films made for television. *End of a Good Man*, *Once a Horse Player* and a little aeroplane drama with Patricia Neal who had quit Hollywood and stardom for life as Roald Dahl's wife in Great Missenden. (I'm not sure that he explained to her where Great Missenden was. She was a little non-plussed and, unbelievably, she was finding it hard to find work and quite glad of this tiny film.) When we went to stay at her house we had to pretend to be married or her housekeeper would have resigned on the spot. Oh, the Fifties.

One of these short films was chiefly remarkable for introducing into our lives a woman who helped provide the glue of our relationship, the Abbey actress, Marie Kean, who was moonlighting in London for her chum, director Charles Friend. Immensely struck by O'Toole, it seems she'd tactfully nudged him so that his acting might be rather more than less visible to the camera whose existence he didn't appear to notice much. He in turn was hugely impressed by her. He knew all about her work and the Abbey Theatre, Dublin, was of course almost a holy place to any theatre-lover, let alone an expatriate Irish actor.

He introduced me to her at dusk near Victoria Station and before the evening was over we were a family. Older than we were, she was like a big sister, a big sister who didn't pull rank. A voracious reader, she had a prodigious memory for books and for people and a humorous outlook on the world that was to make my life possible and was at the same time the undoing of me. I learned from her not to take personally the abuse uttered in drink. 'Sure he was drunk at the time' was supposed to wipe out all hurt. Men, I learned, were given to excess and behaved like children 'when they had drink taken'. In *vino* was never in *veritas*. Drunken talk made no sense. Had no relevance. Women shrugged tolerantly and loftily in the face of masculine stupidity. Clever women never nagged. Clever women dodged the flying crockery and went away where they could get some peaceful sleep and never in the morning referred to the excesses of the night before. Clever women never made men feel guilty. I tried to learn these lessons. Up to a point they made my life tolerable. In the long run? I don't think the deception could be sustained.

A wonderful actress, Marie had a great love of food and drink and good company; something of a fine disregard for clothes and interior decoration (the minutiae of housekeeping passed her by completely). Shrewd brown eyes missed nothing and the lips could assume a threatening curl. I realised at once that we had come by our best friend. Somehow, then and ever after, she managed to love us both.

# Chapter Three

Each Sunday for three years, I would take a train or fly to Wales from wherever I was acting in the theatre or rehearsing a TV play and present *Land of Song*, a programme of light music with links which I wrote and delivered in Welsh and English. English was not allowed in the charter for TV Wales and the West but my bits of inserted English meant that we were taken up by the network and I spoke fast, hoping no one would notice which language I was speaking. The ratings were high and I was extremely well paid. That sort of job brought in a great deal more than I could earn playing a star part at Stratford, for example.

One Sunday O'Toole decided to come to Wales with me. As usual the journey became complicated. I think we went by way of Bristol – never a good idea if one wanted to arrive anywhere on time. I managed to mislay my presenter's dress and did the show, after racing against time to write it, in my trench coat, hoping it looked more Left Bank French than desperate. O'Toole mingled with the extras for fun and everyone was charmed, at which point he said, 'Let's go to Dublin', and we adjourned to the small, almost deserted airfield that was Rhoose Airport until we found a plane that would go to Ireland. We were due to go West, the mythical West I'd been hearing about since I met O'Toole.

In Ireland we hired a car and set off – O'Toole confident, although he didn't have a driving licence and had learned to drive on holiday in the Swiss Alps. (Kenneth Griffith to O'Toole on a vertiginous road, 'I say, old son, you're doing very well but should you be trying to change gear with the hand brake?') First we called in to see Johnny Slattery's brother, Dick Wilkinson, and his wife, Bridget, in their farm, Balcorris House at Santry. A day and night later we were still there. It was my first experience of Irish country house life and it was like being in a Chekhov play: the beautiful house in some disarray, a house full of drifting people (some never identified), rain, large meals with no discernible beginning or end, sad old dogs, cheerful old people, melancholy conversations and bursts of wild hilarity. Drink.

It was O'Toole who decided that we should move on. Too late to go West. (This was to become the first of many abortive attempts to go West.) What about going to Marie Kean's flat in Dublin? It was spring and the fields outside the farm house were yellow with thousands of daffodils. (Very un-Welsh that sort of farm crop. Could it be an Irish custom to farm daffodils among the cows?) We were given a carload of daffodils to take to the city. Arriving at Marie's, we hauled the flowers up five flights of Georgian stairs in the house in Lower Baggot Street. Marie had the ham and cabbage almost ready. She went back to the kitchen and, surrounded by daffodils, O'Toole clutched me and said 'Have my children'. Without pausing for breath I said, 'Yes'.

Thank God for contraception, or I could have become one of those women with nineteen children clutching at their skirts. Our first child was no sooner suggested than conceived. Marie, the witch, claimed to know this the following day. Never having given obstetrics so much as a passing thought (I'd never held a baby or particularly wished to) I forgot about the consequences of the long, joyous spring night – illuminated, it seemed to me, by the shine of scores of daffodils, pungent with the smell of bitter vegetation, remembering only that I'd – well, what had I done? Plighted my troth were words that seemed to fit the bill. Thrown my bonnet over the windmill. Cast my lot with. Now, had he said 'Marry me' I would have shuffled a bit and said, 'Oh I don't think you really mean that' and 'I don't really know about that' and we would have moved on to bacon and cabbage and Guinness and conversation and a simple, lovely night like any other, but the unwanted proposal didn't come. Not then. Not ever. And I began the one great journey that underpinned all the hilarious, foolish, reckless journeys that characterised our life together.

Five weeks later it dawned on me that I must be pregnant. I didn't tell anyone, especially not my agent at MCA, who grew restive as I turned down a long-term project. To do her credit, she was very satisfied with my contract with Douglas Uren which freed me from the necessity of taking job after job but I felt guilty now and booked myself up with a great deal of highly paid TV work and, as a nod towards what I should have been doing – theatre – I agreed to do a play for the reopening of the Hampstead Theatre Club with a translation of *Siwan* by Saunders Lewis, the great Welsh writer who had written for me and befriended me and helped to change my life by leaving Wales for London and RADA. James Roose-Evans was to direct this limited run and I figured the thirteenth century costume would conceal my interesting condition. Someone would have to be told. 'Someone – sometime, please – soon,' nagged Marie. Yes, but not yet. O'Toole and I were both pleased but I could tell that no allowances were to be made for this happy event. Life went on exactly as before and I was lucky that so far I wasn't visited by any of the inconveniences of pregnancy. Rude good health persisted, unmarked by fancies, moods and morning sickness or, should I say, rather there were no symptoms which I was able to identify, but what power was it that made me so blessedly, stupidly unworried about tomorow if not some kind of hormonal change? Any fool except me could see that it wasn't going to be possible to continue my present way of life; getting up early, working all day, staying up late, sleeping too little, eating when and if the opportunity arose. I didn't have to worry about smoking because no one suggested that it might be better to cut down, let alone give up. 'Relax, have a cigarette!' we all cried to each other; 'Have a drink!' And where were we to live? *How* were we to live? Would O'Toole help me with the baby? (That didn't seem likely but one never knew.) When would I have to give up work? (Last minute, I thought.) When could I resume work? (As soon as possible.) What did having a baby cost? Did we make enough money? The months went by and few of these questions were formulated, let alone addressed, except for one. O'Toole took a short lease on a fourth-floor flat in Bryanston Street.

Before we moved something happened that was to alter us both completely. 'People don't alter,' said O'Toole, 'they adapt. Or die.' Maybe. But make a huge, major adaptation and you end up pretty altered. Or so it seems. And if you *seem* altered then you *are* altered.

O'Toole's agent asked him to go and see a film producer called Jules Buck. I knew who he was because my agent had asked me to come and meet him at the MCA office near Hyde Park Corner. I couldn't confess that I was going to be too out of shape to be in the film so I went along half-heartedly, wearing a really boring 'good' dress that I'd just been given after playing a middle-class character in *The Tortoise and the Hare*. (Already it didn't fit properly around the waist.) Mr Buck, very American, smoking a big cigar, wasn't mightily impressed, I could tell and my agent was willing me to snap out of my lethargy and sparkle a bit. For the first and only time in my life I was asked to 'turn around'. I couldn't believe my ears. I turned on my sensible shoes, and felt the first spark of interest and amusement which lasted for the short remainder of the meeting. (It was a dull part anyway but I knew I'd never have to worry about how to play it. The part went to a sensible English Rose with a small, unpregnant waist.)

And now O'Toole was going to be seen for the same film, *The Day They Robbed the Bank of England*. Would he have to do a twirl as well? Or was it just girls? When he'd been gone for about an hour – just round the corner to Groom Place – the phone rang and Jules asked me to pop round as well. Jules and his wife, Joyce, were enchanting. I was ashamed that I had written him off in MCA as a crass American mogul. He was very funny and very Jewish. Joyce was the most beautiful and elegant woman I'd ever seen; sophisticated, witty and with such stories! Everything was going swimmingly, I could tell, and I was sure that O'Toole would be offered the quite nice part of the Irish 'boyo'. They were talking about Hollywood, telling hilarious tales about people who didn't seemed quite real to me, Olivia (de Havilland), John and Walter (Huston), Sam (Spiegel), Marilyn (Monroe), Dmitri (Tiomkin), George (Axelrod), Joan and Eric (Ambler), it went on and on.

Jules was part of the exodus from Hollywood to Europe as the studio system broke down. He and Joyce had just moved to London from Paris where they'd been working and sharing a life with Jacques Tati and his wife. This was almost too much to take in at one sitting. Hours went by. Joyce, ever the good hostess, provided a picnic dinner. Drinks came in huge, beautiful tumblers. The drawing room was the most lovely domestic drawing room I'd ever been in; clean and fragrant, dark walls, gleaming walnut and mahogany furniture, blissfully comfortable chairs, softly gilded picture frames and drawer handles and bits of ormolu glowing here and there in pools of light. Joyce noticed my look. 'Twenty-seven sources of light,' she said. (It was the first of many lessons I was to learn from her.) I marvelled and settled down for more delicious small eats and stories.

It seemed a shame to come back to the present and O'Toole's part in the film. And it seemed a *real* shame when O'Toole, who didn't have any other decent options, grandly said that he didn't want to play the part under any circumstances. Horrors. Dismay. He would, however, consider the part of the upper-class English officer. Jules, who was very taken with

the Irish Irishman who reminded him of a former business
partner, John Huston, was severely jolted. I nodded off but
at five o'clock in the morning I was nudged out of my chair
and joined the other three in a toast to a new company,
Keep Films – directors Jules, Joyce, Siân and Peter – and we
toasted O'Toole's coming appearance as an English officer in
Jules's movie.

# Chapter Four

I settled into the flat O'Toole had found – a fourth-floor eyrie in Bryanston Street. Doriah helped me move. Before he began Jules's film, O'Toole had a good part in another film, *The Top of the World*, which was to be directed by Nicholas Ray. We expected a great deal as we went to meet him; he'd been married to Gloria Grahame and he'd directed *Rebel Without a Cause*. Like all visiting Americans, he was installed in a sumptuous flat in SW1 (they didn't seem to consider living anywhere other than Mayfair or Belgravia). He was oddly disappointing; distracted and unfocused. But he wasn't drunk – maybe he was ill? O'Toole met his director at the fag end of an interesting career.

What had seemed a wonderful opportunity, playing opposite Anthony Quinn, quickly turned into a farce and O'Toole's mood blackened. Anthony Quinn was very honest with him. When O'Toole pointed out that his balaclava came down to his eyes and the frozen dirt covered the little bit of face visible between the cap and his beard, Quinn said, 'Listen kid, it's taken me twenty years to get to be first over the title. If you think I'm letting you loose on the screen with me think again.'

It was a disaster of a job. O'Toole turned to Jules to get his name off. More and more we were turning to Jules. He was beginning to regulate our lives. For instance, income tax was something O'Toole intended to think about some other time. While we were living with Ken and Doriah in Dorset Mews Douglas Uren and the accountants at my agents, MCA, saw to it that *my* affairs were in order and I was half horrified and half impressed by O'Toole's cavalier attitude towards law-abiding existence. His attitude towards most of the practicalities of life was nonchalant, to say the least, and Jules had a great deal to contend with. He urged O'Toole to acquire a driving licence for his car and on a wet morning in 1959 the newly hired instructor drew into the Mews and off they went, O'Toole a little hung-over but in great high spirits, brimming with confidence. He had, after all, driven in France and Switzerland, and London traffic held no terrors for him. Ken Griffith was apprehensive, and he was justified; in the few minutes it took to do a three-point turn and head out of the Mews into Wilton Street, connecting with one of the pillars on the way, an executive decision was taken inside the car and the BSM official requested that he be brought back to the mews. O'Toole obliged and as he got out of the car the shaken instructor wished him a firm 'Goodbye', adding mysteriously, 'a wink is as good as a nod to a blind horse, sir'. O'Toole seemed surprised by the man's attitude and promptly forgot all about taking lessons. Instead he bought an Irish driving licence for thirty shillings. Decorated with harps and shamrocks it was, surprisingly, valid in the UK. Then he made plans to buy a sports car he rather fancied. Jules was not happy but for the present he turned a blind eye to motoring and set about dealing with the Inland Revenue and its neglected place in O'Toole's life and he also turned his attention to the matter of my divorce.

In 1959 it was not possible to live in sin, as we were doing, and conduct a reasonable public life. Having a child out of wedlock, which we were about to do, was asking for trouble. Urgency was therefore in the air; but divorce was no easy matter. Three years of separation had to elapse before we could apply for a divorce. Before that, there had to be proof of infidelity or unreasonable behaviour. Private detectives did a roaring trade; men and women were made to sit in bed with each other while a prearranged photographer burst in upon the bedroom scene, after which they accepted the cheque, donned their clothes and left, breakfast uneaten. My husband wouldn't (why should he?) give me grounds for divorce, nor would he prosecute me, so I was stuck with another year to go. A year too much, Jules decided, assuming, correctly as it turned out, that we would shortly be the subject of public curiosity and scrutiny. Having something to hide would make life impossibly difficult. I maintained a kind of lunatic calm and didn't worry about the arrangements. Jules's (now 'our') lawyers got me divorced by proxy in Mexico. The papers were signed and O'Toole and I were free to marry – in secret, of course – and we chose to be married in the only registry office in Dublin.

As usual there were cliff-hanger moments on either side of the ceremony. Fog at the airport and over St George's Channel meant that we only just made it to the registry office. One of the requirements made at the office was that we should have been, for some weeks, resident in Dublin – O'Toole at the Wilkinsons' house in Santry and I, care of Marie Kean in Lower Baggot Street; (Marie was our best man and Joyce gave me away) so when I launched into a breathless apology and, finger pointing heavenwards and circling, began, 'I'm so sorry – there was terrible fog –' O'Toole grabbed my raised hand, turned my index finger down and, rotating it, finished the sentence '– around St Stephen's Green'. He had the nerve to wink at the registrar. Too late I remembered the Irish method: be seen to observe the proprieties and do what you damn well please.

I had never enjoyed a wedding; this one didn't seem any better than most but it was, at least, full of incident and quite wonderful in the early stages of the day. As far as I was concerned, O'Toole and I were indivisible. There was nothing I wouldn't do for him and he said as much for me. But a wedding? It seemed irrelevant and brought out the worst in both of us.

\*     \*     \*

Three o'clock in the morning in a Dublin shebeen. O'Toole, great, diminutive actor Harry Brogan, Marie Kean, Joyce Buck and myself and the host sit around a scrubbed wooden table in a first floor back. A child in his pyjamas sits half asleep in an armchair next to the fire. The lino is worn but was once patterned to look like Axminster carpet. No two walls are papered alike and any one of the patterns could easily be said to dominate anything near it. The ceiling of the beautifully proportioned Georgian room is papered blue, studded with gold stars. A sheet hangs on one window and a flimsy curtain gathered on a wire covers the other. The table has disappeared under Guinness bottles and there's a bottle of Jamesons whiskey as a nod towards Joyce Buck's superior status as an American. Harry Brogan loves Joyce Buck. I may be the bride but the early morning wedding is already forgotten and the star of the shebeen is Joyce.

We've just seen Harry on the stage of the Abbey. The moment we sat in the Circle we all fell asleep; the four of us waking in terror in that awful silence when there's a 'dry' on stage. Once they were back on track we all fell asleep again. (What would you do on your wedding night but catch the show at the Abbey? It seemed reasonable to me at the time.) The party had been moving around the city since curtain down. There had been Breakfast at the Dolphin where the Irish gourmets were said to order 'Four tomato soups, four mixed grills, four large Irish and hurry up with the Irish'. God, I was hungry and glad to be in the Dolphin. From pub to pub we crossed and criss-crossed the city, gathering well-wishers, famous or just entertaining. Liam O'Flaherty recited a poem for me. For me? Not at all. This wedding ceremony didn't signify. It was just an excuse for a piss-up, but I didn't feel done out of anything in the way of ceremony.

Now there are just the five of us left standing – or rather, sitting around the table. O'Toole and I have to be back in

London in the morning and it's decided that we really should go to bed. Harry, looking older with each glass of stout and not wanting to be parted from Joyce, says, 'Would ya like to go to the Ladies now? I'll take ya. My aould mother told me how to look after a lady.' 'I'm just fine,' she says firmly (what a test for a Jewish Princess and how brilliantly she's doing). Attempting a different tack, he says, 'Have ya ever read *Ulysses* by James Joyce?' 'No,' she says faintly, 'but I think I'm in it.'

We acquire two taxis. Marie and Joyce sweep into the night and we set off to deliver Harry Brogan home. We aren't to know that, great actor that he is and fully deserving to be the centre of our attention on our wedding day, his party piece is to refuse to say where he lives. We drive around for what seems like hours and he grows more and more skittish and it becomes harder and harder to maintain the respect due to great actors, *'even when they're drunk, Siân'*. Finally, I think we may have tipped him out and returned to Lower Baggot Street. None of us can be called sober but I develop a disdain for the tone of the evening and adopt a dignified *froideur* towards my bridegroom. Marie opens the door and I sweep in without a word. O'Toole follows, laughing sheepishly. 'I think she's a bit cross with me.' The phone rings.

Joyce: 'Siân, please, dear – come over to the Shelbourne and get some *sleep*.'

'No, I'm fine – really. Thanks. Goodnight.'

Putting the phone down, I turn into the bedroom saying (according to Marie), 'I might as well go on the way I'm going to start.'

Where is Jules? Back in London planning deals. Wise in the ways of our business, I doubt that he thought it worthwhile interrupting business to attend a wedding that, to outside eyes, seemed unlikely to last. Volatile young actor takes up with young actress. Same actor becomes an international movie star and *stays married* to the same young actress? Hardly.

\*        \*        \*

Back in London, a married woman. Oh, this is good. Proxy divorces made in Mexico are not recognised by English law. I don't want to be finicky but it seems to me that I may be bigamously married and there are those who have been known to take a dim view of bigamy. I don't like to complain; it seems mean-spirited after all the trouble people have taken over the arrangements. All the same, the sooner I'm properly divorced, the better. Getting divorced after the marriage ceremony could arouse comment, so how on earth are we going to manage that without attracting publicity? We manage it! I dress in a voluminous raincoat of O'Toole's and my mother's riding hat and use a Christian name, long abandoned but legal. We drive at dawn through the fog from London to Shrewsbury, missing death by inches as a four-ton truck screams to a halt in front of our wrongly overtaking bumper. It's so early and so foggy and so horrible that there's nothing to do but look each other in the eye and thank God that we're all alive. In court, the judge implies that Don is well out of this irregular situation and he's right. We drive away and I am now legally an O'Toole person. It feels astounding and enlarging. O'Toole – '"O" as big as a cartwheel', as his father had said.

If you put your mind to it, the press is easy to evade. Every so often we fail. When I was being made a Druid of the Gorsedd of Bards we had to take a taxi from the National Eisteddfod in North Wales all the way to London, I didn't mind the aggravation so much as the expense. I'm no longer sure how well-off we are. Media attention is pushing us into living like film stars – a taxi from North Wales, I ask you!

Finally I've given in and bought two maternity outfits. One dress – pillarbox red. One red and black suit and a present from O'Toole, a silk shirt covered in a design of playing cards. Nothing more eye-catching could have been devised. And I'm trying to lie low.

The fourth floor of Bryanston Street is lonely; horribly lonely. And the décor is pure Peter Jones – nicely painted or reproduction furniture, well-made shiny curtains. Blameless. Dull. If I hadn't observed Joyce's living arrangements I might have rather liked it. Now it's lowering my spirits. O'Toole goes off early for a gloomy day of filming in his balaclava with his back to the camera. He says he's learned from Quinn – they quite like each other – how to upstage on a film set. (Quinn is upstaging *him* of course at this point, but who knows when that little skill might come in handy.) There are polar bears who are dangerous and can't act and a Japanese actress who can't talk – or act. At night he comes grumpily home and sometimes he goes straight out again. Some nights he doesn't come home at all after work. I know what he's doing. He's leading the life we used to lead together but now I'm the wife and not really eligible. Anyhow I can no longer stand about in bars; it would look irresponsible and inappropriate. I acknowledge that I never much liked pubs and clubs anyway. I've given them a try and now I shan't bother with that life any more. But I don't mind O'Toole living it because it's what he's used to and he *does* love it. Occasionally after work, I call him a taxi to go to the Salisbury. Discomfited he says, 'I can't have you getting me a *cab* to go on a batter.' Well, I can and I don't know why he should find that so hard to understand.

*The Top of the World* was to be followed by *The Day They Robbed the Bank of England*.

The question of his nose came up, and was dealt with very casually. Little did we guess the furore that would follow. The nose was kicked in while he was in the Navy playing rugby against the Swedish police team and every cameraman who had to photograph him had complained of the time involved in shooting around the bent gristle, lighting it out. So much easier to push it back and straighten it to where it was before. It didn't take a minute to do. The media outcry was incredible. I was disbelieving when I read that his 'character' had disappeared. His nose was now 'retroussé'. He had 'sold out'. His so-called 'friends' said it was symptomatic of his changing life. I was so sorry for him. I think he found it very hard to recover from this ill-considered cruel stupidity. What, I thought angrily, had two-tenths of an inch of gristle to do with talent? Other actors might have insulated themselves by moving into the company of equals only; O'Toole obstinately refused to do that. His obstinacy was ill rewarded. I felt nothing but contempt for those smart-asses who saw psychic value in a rugby-bent nose.

Left alone in the flat I have time to take stock. I can't see the way forward at all. My agent isn't speaking to me, she's so fed up. There are jobs I want and I can't accept them. There are jobs I need and I can't go after them. Jules talks of a future framed around O'Toole's career, whatever that might turn out to be. It isn't acknowledged any more that I am an actress. I'm depressed and completely cut off from everyone I've ever known in my working life. I'd thought I'd show them how well this was going to work. Now, I have my doubts. But I don't want blame or sympathy.

When I see the stills of O'Toole in *The Day They Robbed the Bank of England* looking every inch an upper-class officer, I know he's made the right choice of role. It's not going to be a great film but he's obviously going to be very good in it, and the film won't be bad either. I'm ignobly happy to note in the rushes that the girl's part is hopeless. O'Toole is behaving himself. His new partner is pleased. So am I.

I may be worried and confused and depressed but I do love this man, that's the only thing I'm sure of. He comes home one day with a lovely red MG motor car, bought with his film money. 'Get your passport,' he says. 'We're off.' He's going to show me his favourite city in the world – Venice. We leave at once. The problems are left behind in Marble Arch in W1.

# Chapter Five

Two weeks of refuge from London. The November weather was foul but neither O'Toole nor myself much minded the cold and the wet. We arrived in Mestre, outside Venice, and it was hideous. 'Just you wait,' said O'Toole gleefully 'you won't believe what you see.' Then, more purposefully, 'Wait here.'

'Why?'

'Just wait here.'

There was a limit to the amount of money that could be moved from country to country but there was some kind of illegal scheme – something to do with petrol coupons – that enabled one to augment one's foreign currency and O'Toole had been told about it and was about to give it a try (I suppose). One of the things I most liked about O'Toole was that a great deal of the time I didn't know what he was up to. He didn't expect help either – just non-interference. I read my book while he trawled the bus station.

After a few hours he was back looking jubilant and I assumed we were in funds as we set off down the Grand Canal. Yes, it *was* all the things I'd been told and all the things I'd read but O'Toole loved it so much and expected me to share his feeling that I soon became tired of enthusing and was hungry and cold, I began to feel a bit unwell and not a little grumpy. Naturally, we didn't have hotel reservations. 'Wait here with the luggage.' He was soon back having found us a lovely room in the Gabrielli Sandworth on the Riva degli Schiavoni. It was dark and wet but I realised that the window had the loveliest view I've ever seen, across the water to the campanile and cupolas of Santa Maria della Salute.

This should have been such a lovely night and it wasn't. I was six months pregnant. My body was letting me down somewhat in that I suddenly felt I'd like to go to bed but O'Toole was so anxious that I should see and love everything that we walked and walked and walked in the rain before subsiding into a restaurant where the warmth and the food and the wine finished me off and I fainted away. I could hardly believe that we were scurrying 'home' through the rain, up and down slippery steps and I was actually crying with irritation and we were having a row about Hy Hazell's *legs*! Best he'd ever seen. How could he be so brutal as to prefer Hy Hazell's legs to mine? Grabbing a pillow and an eiderdown I flounced out to spend the night in the bath, where I slept like a lamb and woke feeling loving and happy and when I looked out of the window my spontaneous reaction of wonder and admiration would have satisfied the most demanding lover of the *serenissima*. We didn't refer to Hy Hazell or her wretched legs.

My great, abiding love for Venice didn't catch fire for years but from that first visit I was over-awed and over-impressed and wanted more, much more. I was glad to have a respite from my problems. O'Toole was also escaping problems. After the huge impact of *The Long and the Short and the Tall*, and the film work that followed, he was restless. Now, after a few days in Venice he said 'Let's see if it's warmer down South,' and handing me the map said, 'Let's go to Rome.' I'd never been asked to map-read before. 'Turn right, here,' I said and by late afternoon we were heading towards Yugoslavia. (I think Rome was a left turn.) Soon it was dark and we were high in the mountains on a horrible road and when we came to a checkpoint where soldiers with serious-looking guns wanted visas (visas? What were they?) O'Toole reversed hurriedly and thought for a moment. I knew what he was going to say. Extracting a bottle of emergency brandy from the back of the car, he said, 'Wait here. It'll be all right,' and disappeared into the darkness.

When he came back he had a sheaf of papers and he was smiling. 'Off we go,' he said, accelerating alarmingly, and we shot past the waving, smiling soldiers.

'What did you do?' I asked.

'Just trust your uncle,' he said, smiling wolfishly.

What could he have been doing? Yes, I'd trust him to get us out of any mess, I thought, but the journey over the mountains was unremittingly awful. Although I was ready to trust him with my life in a crisis, I couldn't fail to notice that he was a terrible motorist. In the total darkness I could sense that we were perilously close to the edge of the road and that the darkness beyond the road was that different darkness of nothing but space. It stood to reason (I thought) that as we climbed, the drop on our right became greater. Every muscle tensed, I sat bunched up, stifling the squeals and whimpers that threatened to surface as we swung around the hairpin bends on that terrifying road. I longed for the drive to be over. Even more, I longed for it to stop for a bit.

My prayers were answered and O'Toole braked suddenly as, into the middle of the road, ran the first person we'd seen for hours. She was old and draped in black shawls which rose and fell like wings as she waved her arms up and down. Satisfied that she had our attention, she darted to my side of the car and launched into an urgent torrent of what I supposed to be Yugoslav – or Serb – or Croat. Apologetically, I shook my head and she immediately switched to a violent mime, holding her head and rocking from side to side and moaning horribly. 'Oh my God, help me get her into the back,' said O'Toole, catching the urgency of the moment. It took us a few minutes to realise that we were failing to get her into the car, not because she was infirm and hampered by layers of clothing, but because she was putting up a spirited resistance. Discomfited, we stopped being good Samaritans and stood back from the lively little bundle of shawls, still wailing, but now wailing with a note of irritation. There was something we weren't comprehending and she was losing patience with us. Clutching her head with one hand, she pointed into the darkness with the other and took a few steps, gesturing to us to follow her. I realised that any fears I entertained that we might be about to be set upon and robbed was an utterly inappropriate emotion at this point in a promising and developing adventure. I was learning to strangle at birth these petty feelings of caution and prudence. It also occurred to me that while I was exhausting myself during the white-knuckle ride O'Toole might very well have become *bored* as he flung the car around the turns in the road and to him this could well be an agreeable diversion. Briskly I brought up the rear of the little procession as it disappeared on to a rough path. Very soon we came upon another little group (more moaning) and I realised that the old lady wanted to load a child on to us. Obligingly, stumbling back to the car, we heaved the boy into the back seat and he was followed by a couple of men who got into the car, nodding approval and pointing at the road ahead. They wanted us to get a move on. O'Toole performed a racing start and we roared off, leaving the old lady in the darkness.

I couldn't make out if the boy had terrible toothache or acute stomach-ache. O'Toole concentrated on driving like a man possessed (I cannot begin to describe how much worse the driving became) and I kept an anxious eye on the passengers and they in turn kept nodding approvingly at me. We were doing the right thing. Whether more was required than making speed in the dark we had no way of knowing. As we approached a town the two young men leaned towards the front of the car, one head each side of O'Toole, and began to give directions, speaking very loudly and slowly in Yugoslav and making simple, clear gestures. The car was filled with a new smell – sweet and faintly rotten at the same time. What was it? We drew up at what turned out to be a very dimly lit, bare hospital and out hopped the men, half carrying, half dragging the boy. As they ran for the door they made expressions of gratitude, more simple mime and much pointing vaguely in the direction of the heart. 'It was nothing,' we mimed back, shaking our heads from side to side, 'glad to be of use' and we pointed at *our* hearts. We felt a bit flat now that we weren't an ambulance any more and when a couple of men in boiler suits carrying bags of tools (plumbing tools, I thought) indicated that they wouldn't mind a lift, we leapt on them as the most welcome of passengers and off we tore through the sparsely lit streets. I realised that we hadn't seen another car since we'd crossed the border. We were a novelty in our bright red MG.

The town centre of Zagreb was bleak; nothing much happening it seemed, not many people about, the few shops with lighted windows were uninviting (the window-dresser's art hadn't penetrated Yugoslavia). One of O'Toole's talents lies in his nose. Standing in a strange town he turns his head this way and that, picking up little smells and sounds, like an animal, then he sets off, making unerringly for the best place to eat and drink or the only place still open after hours. Zagreb, however, had him nonplussed for a moment. Beaming, our plumbers directed us to what looked like a grand town hall. Entering from the gloom and cold outside was like entering paradise. There was no food in evidence but I felt there must be some, somewhere. Not having eaten since breakfast, I was ravenously hungry, but I forgot my empty stomach as I took in the extraordinary scene.

We were in what had once been the ballroom of a grand baroque hotel which the People had taken over with a vengeance. Figures still in drab working clothes filled the huge, brilliantly lit room, drinking, dancing to fiddle music, having what could best be described as a knees-up. The story of our adventure as an ambulance and taxi service was told at once and we were immediately the centre of a large, noisy, extravagantly friendly crowd of workmen. An old lady in long skirts appeared and, clucking at my interesting condition, took me off for a much-needed toilette, shrieking with mirth as she showed me how to negotiate the hole-in-the-ground loo. It seemed rude to ask her to wait outside so I pee'd as best I could to her accompaniment of more gales of laughter. 'Please, I have to be alone. I'm an only child. Intimacy doesn't come easily to me.' No. Instead I nodded at her toothless smiling face and, having washed my face and hands, launched into more 'How can I thank you?' behaviour. Bereft of a single word of Yugoslav, I developed a kind of Japanese mime; a little bow from the waist while indicating my heart. Rock-hard sausage appeared just for me. Delicious. I identified the sweetly corrupted smell which hung in the air everywhere as the smell of ingested slivovitz, divine corrupted apples.

A few hours later, excusing myself on the grounds of my advanced pregnancy – this time my bow was accompanied by a triple hand gesture; tummy to heart to tummy – I went to bed. O'Toole stayed behind to explore the true nature of slivovitz and to do a bit more taxiing while I was shown to a room high above the celebrations which looked as though they might well continue 'til morning.

Lying flat – *not* hurtling through the night, *not* expecting every moment to be my last – was negative pleasure enough but it was augmented by the sign above the table, 'Your commands by telephone will be obeyed instantly'. I didn't want anything but I picked up the Bakelite receiver. Dead. I went to sleep smiling. This wasn't Rome, where we'd meant to go, but I felt very lucky to be here alive, lying flat in Yugoslavia.

Walking around town in the morning we saw that the theatre was as grand as the hotel. 'Better go and make ourselves known, then. They may give us "comps" for the show.' (Like all tourists we were short of money, in spite of the petrol coupon scam.) All we said at the theatre was that we, like them, were actors. There was someone who spoke a little English and he believed us and may even have thought that we were important actors (it could have been the effect of the car, which was still attracting a good deal of friendly envy) and with much hand-shaking (and bowing from me) we were told to present ourselves at the theatre and we would be 'passed' in to see the play that evening.

We felt under-dressed when we were shown into a prominent box at stage level, but it was clear that no one was dressed to suit the splendour of the theatre and we settled down to enjoy the performance. Four and a half hours later we were still there, hanging on to the arms of our chairs, glassy eyed, stupefied with boredom. The play wasn't even in Yugoslav, it was in an obscure Serbo-Croat dialect. It looked faintly fifteenth century. There were lots of children in the audience and they also looked a bit glum but I could tell that the play was meant to be a comedy. 'I know what this is,' hissed O'Toole viciously. 'You know that one performance of some ancient bit of culture you have to give every year to justify the Arts Council grant? Well, this is *it*. The Serb equivalent of *Gamma Gurton's Fuckin' NEEDLE*!'

During the ensuing week, hurtling from country to country, we saw four plays. Three times the offering was *Boeing Boeing*, the most popular play in Europe that year. Probably the most popular play in the world. We didn't see any German theatre because O'Toole suddenly took against the thought of being in that country and we drove across it without stopping. Never in my life have I been so glad to see a veal escalope as I was when we got to Linz in Austria late at night. (Hunger was one of the leitmotifs of this breathless trip.) In Switzerland I developed violent toothache and O'Toole decided that the best dentists in the world were to be found in Italy and only the best would do for me. (I fancy he was thinking of barbers' poles and a long operatic tradition.) Useless to say that any old dentist would do, so after an evening of *Boeing Boeing* in Schweizerdeutsche, off we set for Milan. I held brandy in my mouth for hours until it grew hot and O'Toole drove and drove like a demon along these frightening straight Autobahns. (He had never before encountered big, straight roads.) He got me to Milan in record-breaking time, slightly drunk, the pain all but banished by fear. After a lot of '*porco misere!*' and '*Bruto!*' and no anaesthetic because I was pregnant, the Professor of Dentistry put his knee on to the arm of my chair and pulled and pulled, encouraged by shrill cries from two admiring young assistant dentists. Finally, he reeled backwards across the room triumphantly, holding aloft a large back tooth.

O'Toole finished off the brandy – well, it had been a gruesome experience – and we turned the car towards Holland where Hélène (Van Moeurs, my old friend from RADA) lived and where she was playing Molière at a theatre in The Hague. Apart from the terror I experienced all day in the car I was loving the trip. O'Toole was loving the trip. He was the perfect travelling companion; each day was a challenge and a hilarious adventure. He was like a Pied Piper, collecting people wherever we went. No one knew who he was but everyone wanted to spend time with him and I was content to look on, but I was beginning to weary. The pace was gruelling and I wasn't making concessions to my pregnancy. I had never had many close women friends and now I thought that it was a good moment to have Hélène look over my new life, my new state.

The theatre at The Hague is so beautiful – like a meringue. It was, I was told proudly, 'the Stradivarius of Europe'. I was glad that we weren't seeing *Boeing Boeing* yet again but even Hélène had to admit that Dutch is not the ideal language for Molière. The play sank heavily like unleavened dough and lay expiring on the beautiful stage.

We got into the car and (a by now exhausted) O'Toole drove from The Hague to Hélène's home in Amsterdam. Hélène – sturdy, strong, fearless and practical – silently climbed the stairs to her flat. 'Does he always drive like that?' she asked as I joined her in the kitchen. 'Ye - es,' I replied guardedly.

'He should never drive *anything*', she said. 'He's *lovely* but I thought we were going to die on that journey.' In a way I was relieved that she felt as I did; I had begun to think that I was being feeble minded and wimpish out there, on the road. On the other hand, her reaction told me that I had a genuine problem on my hands. I didn't drive and I was terrified of cars and now was at the mercy of a terrible driver. 'You put a stop to all this,' she said briskly, chopping vegetables. I looked at her – so reasonable – and thought I couldn't begin to explain that it was completely outside my remit in the relationship to 'put a stop' to anything. 'And another thing,' she said. 'You should be resting and eating properly.' 'Oh it's okay. I do normally,' I lied.

After supper I went to bed, uneasy. Our life together would be lived very much at O'Toole's pace. I had played fast and loose with so many men that it was a huge relief – and a lifting of responsibility – to be involved with a man whom I could not hoodwink. There is something so attractive about being wholly known with all one's faults and vices and now it was a huge relief to be seen through. I couldn't at the time see how childish and truly irresponsible I was being. The idea of female service and support to men had been taught only too well in Wales and the childish part of me felt this to be right and proper. The Ireland I was beginning to know was male dominated as well. The idea of a wife with a career, demanding rights, was laughable in the Fifties.

I lay there in Amsterdam and saw that if things went awry over the birth of the baby and my ensuing life, then the problems would be largely of my own making. Hélène made a supper dish which I have never forgotten. Here's how she prepared it. Chop and cook every root vegetable you can lay your hands on (making sure you have carrots and swedes to make the final mixture pink). Vigorously mash the whole thing and pile it high in a large shallow dish. Make an indentation at the top of the pyramid and into it place half a pound of butter . . . eat.

Then go to bed and try to worry about your life and career. Sleep will soon take over.

# Chapter Six

Safe in London again, A mere two weeks have elapsed. So much has happened but the wonderful journey has done nothing to solve our problems. There's a Welsh poem that ends '*A groeso fôr, Ni newid onid air.*' ('Crossing an ocean only gives you a change of air.')

I sense O'Toole is profoundly dissatisfied with almost everything that has happened since Willis's play. The movies he's made have proved mildly interesting, profitable in a moderate way but they were not what he wanted. The ones he did want have not come his way. There isn't a good play on the horizon. We have a rare council of war and decide that the best thing would be to go back to the beginning and restart in the theatre. Almost at the same moment there's an offer from Stratford for him to play Shylock and Petruchio and Thersites in Peter Hall's new company. It's so obviously the right thing to do that I can hardly believe our luck. I don't know what Jules thought of his partner's decision to disappear to Warwickshire for six or seven months but he's extremely graceful when we all meet for dinner. About a week after the offer is accepted I do a very delayed double-take and think, 'But how will *I* manage in Stratford?' The baby will be born at the end of February before the opening of *The Merchant of Venice*. I would hope to go back to work in the spring but Stratford? Notoriously difficult to live in, I'm told. How will I manage? And O'Toole's salary will be low – but then I have an income and a reasonable bank balance. But is having a baby within the terms of my contract with Douglas Uren? My agent is already cool towards me and I no longer have a single friend or advisor to turn to. And where will we live? Pregnancy is making me feel completely powerless. My body, which has never let me down, seems to belong to someone else. And I'm lonely. I'm not accustomed to being isolated from people but my life with O'Toole is absorbing all my energy and excludes everyone I've ever known. There is no question in my mind that my loyalty should lie with him but it does seem hard to have to cut my ties with everyone else. I see no one. I begin to draw close to Jules and Joyce Buck. They are my new family. Denise Sée, the company lawyer becomes a valued advisor – but she's not principally *my* advisor. Nyman Libson is to be our accountant. He and his wife and family, Sue and John, are to me the impossible-to-attain perfect family. Again, they are to be O'Toole's advisors, not mine, but I like them all, on sight. When I'm with them I admire them so much that I lose all confidence in *my* family life. Brutally, I don't have a family life. It's fashionable in our circle to despise uxoriousness, domesticity, bonds, ties, fetters. We're standing in some kind of no-man's-land, me and my unborn baby, because motherhood is suspect as a shackle on the masculine genius/worker/provider. Cyril Connolly's 'sombre enemy of good art – the pram in the hall' is familiar to all of us.

Before Stratford I do Saunder Lewis's play in Hampstead. It's well received but in translation it just doesn't work as it does in Welsh. 'Lovely Siân recalls the days of Mrs Pat,' says one big headline but I know that Mrs Patrick Campbell played Hedda at the Hampstead Theatre when she was fat and truly past being convincing! (Still, no one seemed to notice I was pregnant.)

One television play and then we're off again! Where? O'Toole wants us out of the flat in two hours. It's late. Why? Never mind. It's an adventure. I never really liked this flat. But where to go? My mother's brother, Davy, newly widowed, has a house near my old family home, Tŷ mawr farm. We can go there. I call him and he seems glad of the prospect of our company. Another journey through the night, this time from London to West Wales. No Autobahns, thank God. As we climb in the dark towards the Black Mountains, I roll down the window and take deep breaths of the air which is different from any other.

Gwaun-Cae-Gurwen.

This is going to work out very well. O'Toole in preparation for *The Merchant of Venice*, is reading the whole of the Old Testament – two fields away from Tŷ mawr farm, where I was born, where my grandmother, Mrs Thomas, Tŷ mawr, read the Good Book every day and was said to be able to write out the whole of it from memory. I'm not a good cook but neither Davy nor O'Toole are gourmets so I make very ordinary meals and sit reading at the table in the house on the Betws Mountain and watch Davy dealing with school and local government work and O'Toole in the other armchair, burying himself in the family Bible. Our evenings are long and silent and agreeable.

The best bits of our life together, like these months in the country, could not be imagined and would not be credited by people who see us out and about in London. O'Toole's friends wouldn't believe the sort of life we lead when we're alone. We keep it to ourselves, like life in a Persian garden – secret and unseen.

My tutor from university days, Moelwyn Merchant, is free to discuss *The Merchant* with O'Toole. We visit him near Caerleon and the men talk Shakespeare line by line and we women talk obstetrics. Is it being pregnant that excludes me from everything interesting? I hate Women's Talk. I'm sure that having a baby will be a breeze and there's nothing to talk about. I want to talk about Shakespeare. I feel mutinous.

And yet I have more fun with this Irishman than I've ever had in my life. One night he decides to cook dinner – he's never been known to cook anything. 'Oh yes. I can make French toast. The best French toast. Just leave me to it.' As the stove explodes into flames and we wrestle it, covered in blankets, out of the house on to the mountainside and the entire kitchen needs repainting and we have no supper, the three of us stand in the flame-lit cold garden and rock with laughter. It's been sad in this house since my Aunt Maya died. It took this conflagration to restore life and ordinary happiness and it took O'Toole to light the fire. He has an invincible drive towards joy and life.

My uncle has to go to Westminster on Council of Wales business and we volunteer to drive him to the station in Neath and pick him up a few days later. We set out after dark to collect him and on the hill to Rhyd-y-Fro the car goes out of control on black ice. This is it. We're in an uncontrollable spin. I remember from my schooldays that there's a big drop on the right. For what seems like miles we career from right to left and I pray that we shan't meet another car. Finally, we crash into a bank and come to a halt. When we pull out we have a young sapling embedded in the back door of the car. 'Whew! That was close,' says O'Toole, cheerily, 'but if we get a move on we'll still be on time.'

Through the moments of danger O'Toole said, 'Put your feet on the dashboard. Keep calm.' and I said, 'Don't worry about me, I'm all right. I'm prepared.' And I *was* prepared and I was not frightened. And he *did* get us out of trouble and we *were* in time for the train.

Davy, when he get into the car along with the young tree, splutters, 'What—?' 'Oh, just a little tap,' says O'Toole and Davy beams, reassured, as he leans away from the buckled door. How does O'Toole do it? Davy would have wanted an explanation from anyone else. He also is under the spell. It's no wonder that my family feels about O'Toole much as I do. Who wouldn't? He says the awful, confronts the impossible and shrugs it off as though it were nothing. He doesn't *care* that his car is ruined and that he can't buy a new one. His priorities that night of Davy's return were to avoid getting us killed and then to meet the train on time. Both were accomplished and he was contented. And so were we.

The family has moved away from Tŷ mawr on the Betws Mountain to the richer lowlands further west. My parents now live in East Glamorgan at Dyffryn House. It seems odd to look up the Betws across the meadows at the farm where I, my mother and my grandmother were born and to think it belongs to someone else. I don't mind that. It never was technically *mine*, but it is mine no less now than when I inhabited it. Property is a mystery. There are things I own that don't feel mine at all but some things are mine for ever.

The new farm is in Whitland. When the proposal to move was put to my grandmother, John and Meriel, my uncle and aunt, expected it to be the beginning of a long period of persuasion, emotional and painful. Elizabeth – Mamgu, my grandmother – sat in the house that her grandmother had built and looked at the business proposal and having thought for a bit said, 'So, when do we move?' When she drove away, almost ninety years of age, she looked straight ahead.

O'Toole is taken down to Whitland. The farm is set in beautiful countryside, gentler, easier, more profitable than the slopes of the Betws above Gwaun-Cae-Gurwen. The house is a traditional long house, at one end is a room with a deep and high inglenook and that is where my grandmother sits. O'Toole and Uncle John and some of the boys sit up late in the 'top room', drinking whisky. John and the boys are up and about early, back at work. So is my grandmother whose life is geared to six o'clock milking by hand (days long gone). When O'Toole descends at ten o'clock she greets him in that intimidating way, each English word weighed and considered, 'Good day to you'. She's slightly wrong-footed by her lack of English which is lucky for him, and never having encountered suede, she has spent quite a while trying to get a shine on his desert boots. Almost blind, there is very little she can do that is useful but she has to do something – something now reduced to washing up and cleaning the seventeen muddy pairs of boots and shoes in the kitchen corridor every morning. While O'Toole sits at the table I quickly cook us a Welsh breakfast and put both plates on a corner of the big table. I'm about to sit when her voice emerges from the semi-dark of the inglenook. 'Siân! *Tend* to Peter.' I realise that she expects me to serve O'Toole – pour tea, cut bread and wait on him before I give myself breakfast.

His eyes light up with amusement. It is inconceivable that I should disobey her, nor would I wish to challenge that touching certainty in her voice. She knows how things should be done. But this is a woman who ran a farm while her husband gossiped, and whose mother knocked her drunken husband down the stairs to his death. They are fearless and frightening these women but part of their strategy seems to be that lip service should be paid to the god-like quality of Man. As I stand between Mamgu and the table, I can see the funny side of this breakfast ceremony but I don't want to carry her teaching into my life and times, not even as a joke. I don't want to bend the knee – but then, I can't run a farm either. I feel lost between two worlds.

# Chapter Seven

January 1960 and I was almost at the end of my pregnancy. O'Toole and I finished taping the Saunders Lewis play, *Siwan*, this time for TV in Wales, and then we moved to Stratford-on-Avon. Dr Slattery had referred me to a doctor in the town. I made myself known to him and I liked him. He was reserved and quiet. I had been booked into a cottage hospital. We were to live in 'Mount Pleasant' (promptly re-christened 'Mount Unpleasant' by O'Toole). It was the house occupied during the 1958 season by John Osborne and Mary Ure (and a right nasty time *they* had there, I was told). We hoped we would have better luck with it.

It looked all right; a big double-fronted Edwardian house, two storeys high with a grand porch, almost a porte cochère. There was a lawn at the front and a rough private lane that led down through the fields to the road into Stratford. At the side, the drawing room side, there was a huge dilapidated conservatory. I loved the drawing room – big, with huge, comfortable neutral coloured sofas and armchairs and a large stone fireplace. There was a big dining room (the table seated about twenty people), a somewhat gloomy morning room furnished with reproduction oak furniture and at the back a big 1950s kitchen. The master bedroom and its bathroom were lovely – windows south and west like the drawing room below. There was another bathroom and two bedrooms and out at the back there was a stable wing which would be taken by someone else in the company. I wondered nervously who my close neighbour would be. I didn't notice the door at the back of the big front hall. Fool that I was, this was the door leading to the most important object in my life for the next six months. The door led to the cellar, and the cellar contained the Boiler, the monster which had to be fed with coke before we had heat or hot water in the rooms above.

We didn't have much in the way of possessions so I called a taxi and went into town to buy extra china, linen and cutlery. Meriel, my mother's sister, had sent me lovely bed linen and my mother sent me a superb Welsh throw. I looked at the immersion heater in the bathroom and wondered how to live economically in what was a very big house. What did it cost to run a house? Damn it, why didn't I know these rudimentary things? I was heavy now – and resenting it – but, finding the cellar, I started shovelling coke. O'Toole was going to start rehearsing at any moment. He had discovered that there were two or three more possible Shylocks standing by in the wings in case the wild Irish boy didn't come up to scratch. Could this be true? If so, the pressure on him was awful and I decided he didn't need to know about the coke boiler. (But *was* it true?) Now I was alone most of the time. The boiler was a monster and all my worries about the impending birth and my inability to run a house were centred on the problem of getting the elderly central heating system to work properly. I didn't know anyone here in Warwickshire – and there were no neighbours. My family was a long way off and anyway, I wanted to be able to stand on my own feet. There was no one to help with the cleaning. With the confidence of the healthy and ignorant I was not in the least worried about giving birth but I was terrified that I would not be able to run our lives once the baby was born. Would I get the food right? How did you tell the difference between a cry of hunger, a cry of pain or a shriek of bad temper? I was painfully aware that I had never spent *five minutes* in the presence of a baby. Would I be able to keep the heat and water going? Would everything come naturally?

Feverishly I read my Dr Spock over and over again. We

didn't have any prospect of help with the house or the baby and I tried to give myself a crash-course in housekeeping. Marie Kean in Ireland sent me a large hard-backed manual on domestic science and it quickly became dog-eared and dirty with furniture polish, detergent, cooking fat and blood. My hands were covered in small cuts. Apprehensive and clumsy, every time I began a simple task I cut myself – on sardine tins, chopping knives, the shovel in the cellar, blades of grass.

Alcohol had always been a major factor in our life together and, coming from a non-conformist, teetotal Welsh background I had been charmed by the guilt-free, amusing nature of drinking-to-excess as practised by the Irish. There was something so wonderfully un-English, un-Welsh and un-Scots about Dublin society where if you needed to see your MP you called round to his favourite bar, after hours, where he was busy getting very drunk. Everything functioned but there was a refreshing absence of bureaucracy and a totally un-British attitude towards life. And how merrily I laughed when I learned that the process of casting a play in Ireland began with the question 'Is he all right', 'all right' meaning back in circulation after a spell in hospital, drying out. The funny stories about drink were legion and no one enjoyed them more than I.

From being only a part of life, enjoyed in an endless festive atmosphere, drink became a dominant factor in my daily life. And I was alone now, no partying friends making jokes, and suddenly I was vulnerable and afraid. I was surprised but not shocked to find that my free spirit, my equal partner, expected me to take care of myself, clean the house, wash and iron and provide meals and be on parade when needed. This was the standard male expectation at that time. And I was faintly ashamed that I was so ill equipped for the job. I *was* taken aback however when I was told that the baby, when it arrived, was not to interfere with my husband's work. That *wasn't* what I'd expected at all; I think I'd rather hoped that I and my baby would be the centre of admiring attention (it's possible that a cradle with muslin drapes featured in this fantasy). Now our roles in life were made separate and strictly defined and I mentally revised the scenario of my life within wedlock. I couldn't begin to think where *my work* fitted into this and there were no discussions on that subject. I made meals at night and threw them away uneaten before I went alone to bed. Sometimes there'd be a dawn demand for something to eat; more often I would wake to find O'Toole asleep in an armchair, an overturned glass beside him. I looked out to see if the car was all right and wished I could take an axe to it. His driving when drunk had become my chief worry and source of fear. I tried not to think of the journey from Stratford to Mount Unpleasant. Every night I tried and every night I failed.

Stratford, the marshy graveyard of showbiz relationships. On Monday mornings the platform at Leamington Spa was damp with the tears of furious actors' wives, returning to London tight-lipped and red-eyed after a ghastly weekend. I couldn't leave. And I didn't want to. I was damned if I was going to join the list of Stratford casualties. Stubbornly, I resolved to find a way of living through what was shaping up as a testing time.

What happened next would have defeated me utterly had I not been so near to the birth of the baby and had I not thought – rightly or wrongly – that O'Toole was beside himself with nerves and worry. I was aware that his professional future depended on this performance as Shylock. There had been a few setbacks and missed opportunities and his drinking habits had led to a few hilarious and possibly damaging episodes. The bottle of whisky that fell out of his overcoat pocket as he sat down to talk to a producer, Cubby Broccoli, who wanted to see if he might replace someone with a 'drink problem' (at that time only Americans talked of drink as a 'problem') had added to a burgeoning legend. Now, he needed this job and needed to do it well. He was prepared, maybe over prepared, but he was still unconvinced that he had the confidence of the management. His moods became darker and his drinking became more dangerous. Every morning he pulled himself together. Doubtless the knowledge that he believed he was being watched made matters worse. I was completely on his side even as he tried to push me away. My admiration for him as an actor was enough to withstand the anxieties and miseries of this life of insecurity.

When drunk he was savagely critical of me and my ego was taking a severe beating. When he imitated me, I could see there was some truth in his cruelty but I recalled Hélène Van Moeurs at RADA, out of patience with the psycho-babble of the day saying, 'Ego? Little ego? To hell with ego! If my ego is so little and so feeble, it can go and take a running jump. I'll do *without* my ego.' I resolved to banish *my* ego, batten down the hatches and sit out the storm. Is it possible that you perversely push away your support just to test how sound it is? I felt he was doing that to me, trying me to the limit. That was the only interpretation of events which made sense to me but this may have been my way of justifying my acceptance of a situation in which I was learning not to answer back, not to argue, not to defend myself. Sobriety brought wonderful interludes of repentance and irresistible charm, when I believed myself supremely loved and needed, but when I was made to feel like a useless encumbrance I believed that just as fervently. I was living with the good cop and the bad cop in one person.

Meanwhile O'Toole justified his erratic behaviour towards me in the most unexpected way imaginable. He was the last person I would have expected to take the high moral ground over anyone's behaviour, let alone mine. Now he did just that. I had never made a secret of my past or made anything much of it either, never having had to live among people who subscribed to the Fifties double standard for men and women. The thinking of the time was that nice girls 'didn't'. Girls didn't really enjoy sex. Casual sex was fine for men but out of the question for women. Women were, by nature, monogamous and men were naturally promiscuous. Lest all this should seem to be something left over from Victorian times, biological arguments were produced to show that women were chaste in order not to become accidentally pregnant and men were promiscuous in order to ensure the continuation of their genes. Women were either Madonnas or Whores of Babylon. The idea that girls might have sex because they liked it, or for affection, or for fun, or for company, or out of boredom or loneliness was not entertained. If they did it they were Bad. I had lived a life of carnal pleasure outside wedlock, completely guilt-free. Now, as the weeks went by I came to accept the fact that my position was fairly untenable – in fact I had no position at all. In between whiles there were passionate reconciliations but I lost my spirit and doubted that I would get over this. I was disenfranchised and very little trouble to live with. A quiet girl.

This is how I saw things in early 1960, but I was pregnant and I was living – trying to live – a new, different life and perhaps my view was distorted. Even then I could see that my wish to keep up appearances *was* ludicrous and O'Toole was right to despise my petit-bourgeois desire to keep our problems secret. When he was drunk he publicly exposed his view of my character and at that time I couldn't endure the humiliation. The best I could do was to remain impassive but it was a very long time before I learned not to care what people thought. At that time I cared desperately – I wanted a private life, lived privately.

February was the longest month that year. I saw no one, spoke to few. My parents occasionally telephoned and we talked about immersion heaters and heat conservation and the boiler. O'Toole's big sister, Pat, who lived in a rich suburb of Birmingham, called and offered to help. She had married well and was living the most comfortable and orderly of bourgeois lives; a life I wouldn't have admired or wanted until now when, insecure and adrift from the certainties of my life, I envied her the calm, the certainty, the regular meals, the rock garden, the rose beds, the expensive reproduction furniture, the dogs, the housekeeper, the attentive husband who left the house and returned at the same time each day. I didn't want her or anyone else to visit me and see or hear what my life was like. It hadn't taken long for my Celtic guilt and pessimism to rise to the surface and I now felt that I was to blame for everything that was happening to us. All the attitudes I had despised as hypocritical or retrogressive reared up to mock me. I had been wrong all along about everything – especially my instincts. Seeing that I was low in spirit, Pat took matters into her own hands and in a rather feudal manner drove her housekeeper over to Stratford and left her with me for a few days.

Austrian Gertrude quickly took charge and for a while all was quiet and the smells of comforting middle-England meals soothed me more than any kind words could have done. I watched her moving around the big house, taming it and felt admiring and inadequate. After she left, I found myself alone again but now the house was orderly and well stocked with food and cleaning material.

Before I had time to become anxious again – the baby was due in a week's time – I fell ill with influenza. I didn't know where O'Toole might be and I could no longer climb the stairs to bed or descend to the boiler so I made a bed on the couch in the drawing room and lit a fire. I don't know how long I lay there, alternately shivering and perspiring, but one night after dark fell I awoke to find my doctor in the room re-kindling the fire. He'd become worried because I hadn't kept an appointment and, failing to reach me on the phone, he had driven up to the house and when no one answered the door he'd peered through the drawing room window and, seeing me lying on the couch, had broken into the house through the crumbling conservatory. I was too ill to eat and he left me with plenty of water and a roaring fire and went away, saying that he would be back in the morning. In the morning, miraculously the flu had gone away as abruptly as it had arrived and slowly I got up, bathed, washed my hair and began to tidy the makeshift encampment in the drawing room.

Unexpectedly, O'Toole appeared after work and was sweet and solicitous and made me sit down while he cooked supper. I was astonished by his re-appearance and sat there meek and vacant in the morning room; a room I would not normally sit in, it was so dimly depressing. I was given an enormous over-cooked fry-up and it was one of the best meals I've ever eaten. Some things do come naturally to one and suddenly I knew that I felt different. O'Toole's timing had not deserted him. He'd come home just in time to drive me to the hospital to have our baby.

# Chapter Eight

I've always felt apologetic towards my daughter Kate, not least because her birth was one of the most humbling and in a way annoying experiences of my life. It was unlike anything I could have imagined and it *hurt* and my physical well-being, my athletic body was useless to me. I simply couldn't get the hang of what was going on. Whatever it was, it was out of my control and I didn't like it. Lying alone, cold and fractious on a trolley in a hallway, I grizzled quietly to myself, a passing nurse flicked my shoulder with the back of her hand and said sharply, 'Come on, come on. Pull yourself together.' She gave me the mouth-piece of a gas and air machine and left me to 'pull myself together'. And I would have done had I been able. Rubber nozzle over my nose and mouth, I breathed deeply again and again before I realised that there was nothing but stale air in the machine and that the situation was getting nastier very fast. I didn't really want to see Miss Brace-Yourself of 1960 again but she reappeared with a colleague and they wheeled me out of the sad, dark corridor into a warm room with a very bright light overhead. I lost track of time. The pain worsened, the light grew brighter, brighter and then became completely white until the room was all brilliance and the light made a loud buzzing noise in my ears and I fell into blackness.

Waking up in bed in a ward, I thought I must have had a baby and I waited for someone to bring me a cup of tea. 'The best cup of tea you'll ever have in your life,' I'd been told. Ordinarily I didn't like tea but I really wanted this cup of reward-for-having-a-baby tea. When it didn't come I thought,

'Well, that's just about typical of this whole experience.' As soon as I was able to sit up and look about someone came and I was told that there was nothing to worry about but there was some complication about the baby's blood, which had to be changed. It seemed as though that was a lot to worry about and I lay there miserably. There was no way of demanding information. Demanding anything was out of the question in a 1960 hospital, but one had no reason to fear that best efforts were not being made on one's behalf. After what seemed an age, they brought me my baby. I looked at her, completely separate, already getting on with her life, and I wished I could feel that I'd *done* something. I wished I hadn't fainted before she was born. I felt as inadequate as I'd feared I would. I didn't know how to feel or what to do next. I held her and she seemed pretty solid. Whatever happens, I thought, I'm going to rear you properly. I didn't feel emotional. Just very, very determined.

There was a gypsy girl in the ward (a gypsy with no husband; how low can you get?). She and I were the only ones with no regular visitors at visiting time. (Visiting times were strictly ordained and maintained.) I tried to sink down below the sheets and pretend to be asleep lest anyone should come over and be sympathetic. Roy Dotrice's wife was right opposite and I didn't even want Roy's pity at that time. Just once O'Toole came in at the right time bearing a white television set! Televisions were still out of the ordinary and we couldn't watch this one – there was no aerial – it sat in a corner, silent and glamorous. One night, when all the lights were out, I awakened to hear the sounds of drunken revelry from the grounds outside – O'Toole and a car full of actors had left the pub or the party to come and serenade his daughter. Hoping no one would wake up and complain, I lay silently in the dark, looking at the ceiling until they went away.

I didn't feel very well. Sister said I was to feed Kate, as we decided to call her, in a small side room where I could be alone.

Sitting there one afternoon, I overheard my doctor talking to the Sister. Referring to the gypsy girl and me, he said, 'Keep both of them in. Neither has a suitable home environment.' I'd read that tension was bad for breast-feeding so I tried not to tighten my grip on Kate as she lay there. I couldn't look at her for shame. I had no suitable home for her to live in.

A few days later in the ward, we were both in better shape. The breast-feeding – so important to get right – was on track at last and I felt notably less of a failure. Kate looked quite wonderfully normal and even amusing. '*Kätchen lumpen*', I called her to myself, little lump of a Kate. Child of Stratford, she's called Kate, not Katherine, for Shakespeare's Shrew, she is 'Kate, sweet Kate, the prettiest Kate in Christendom'. O'Toole was due to play Petruchio after *The Merchant* opened and Peggy Ashcroft would play the Shrew. Before that, in a month's time, I was going to play Kate in another *Shrew* at Oxford. Many of O'Toole's friends became fathers round about this time and the preferred names were Kate and Emma. As I looked at my Kate a ladybird flew through the open window and came to rest on her shawl. I love ladybirds and in my shaky state I took it to be an omen – she was going to be all right. I hardly liked to think 'What about *me*?' No matter where I turned, this was not a 'me' time. But it was my deep-submerged question.

My experience during our winter weeks in Stratford had been so unnerving that I was anxious to resume what was to me the security of working life. I was able to do television plays until four weeks before Kate was born and then, four weeks after her birth, I would go back to the theatre. I would start rehearsing *The Taming of the Shrew* in London. Kate would come with me. I didn't know how to organise this but Ken and Doriah were letting me stay with them during the week and I would return to Stratford at weekends until I was ready to open at Oxford, when I could commute by taxi each day. If anyone thought this was a mad plan, not a word was said. It was up to me to pull myself together again and I was silently determined to try.

The cry of all new mothers – 'What did I *do* with all the time at my disposal before I had a baby?' Mount Unpleasant has become a school where the sole subject is Reality. Indulgence is a thing of the past. Every moment is taken up with learning how to take care of another life and the demands change every week. Armed with Dr Spock's book, I am efficient and determined to prove I am when the nurse comes visiting. I pass the test; the breasts are working like clockwork, Kate is functioning smoothly like a little engine but there is something wrong here. I am so anxious to get everything right that there is little room for spontaneity. Housekeeping is still a monstrous, alien task. Now there are visitors to see to as well and even if they only want cups of tea, rushing between the sink and sitting room, cutting bread and making sandwiches, keeping my eye on the clock for Kate's next meal, exhausts me. Washing up, cleaning, tidying the sitting room against the next wave of guests, running down to the cellar to feed the boiler, hand-washing clothes (no washing machine), ironing (what is the secret of the knack of ironing? If I do it the *Good Housekeeping* way I shall have time for nothing else). All this is unwelcome activity and, try as I may, I don't like it. I don't like it because I'm not good at it and practice isn't making me better. I love Dr Spock because he makes me feel successful. I hate *Good Housekeeping* because it makes me feel a failure.

Meanwhile the tension heightens. Only a few weeks to go to the opening night of *The Merchant*. Occasionally, some of the actors roll in, ostensibly to see Kate, actually to settle down, drink and gossip or worry aloud about their jobs. One night I go up to her and someone has dropped hot ash on her foot and I'm so full of bile I find it very hard to be civil to these genial fellows. They seem to inhabit another world; carefree, joky. I'm jealous, of course. This was *my* world. Well, now it isn't. Maybe it won't ever be mine again. Soon I'll go away but I don't want to leave O'Toole alone here; it isn't much of a home but in my absence it could disintegrate completely.

My mother-in-law comes for a brief visit. We haven't met since I visited Leeds as the Girlfriend. I'm struck again by her good looks and her beautiful, whisky-soaked, 'Tallulah' voice. Desperately trying to be the good daughter-in-law, I go along with everything she suggests. It's really difficult not to react when she urges drink on her son. I can't understand why she doesn't know that 'Just one more small one, son' can be the beginning of the end of an evening. When it comes to breast-feeding time she sits in on what has hitherto been a private occasion. 'I worked in a hospital you know.' Beside myself with misery, I grit my teeth and submit as she seizes my breast and rearranges it. O'Toole, reentering the drawing room at that moment, sees this piece of intimacy and roars his revulsion. Doors slam and the car is heard roaring off. He won't be seen again for some time, certainly not until tomorrow. His mother shakes her head, disappointed to be left with me and an empty whisky bottle. Too late, she shrugs and backs off. Thank God for the beautiful white television set. We watch everything, including the 'Interludes', periods when a potter's wheel slowly revolves to the accompaniment of gentle music.

After a few days she leaves and O'Toole returns and we are reconciled happily. His mother thinks he doesn't care for me. He doesn't when she's around. When later, his father arrives we have an easier time but Patrick Joseph is not my cup of tea. We go on what is for me a mind-numbingly boring visit to Warwick races and I win money and he winks and says, 'Another sucker born.' (I don't think so, sir.) When I look at him I see the man O'Toole has told me about. The father sitting the little boy on the mantelpiece. Arms outstretched, he says, 'Jump, boy. I'll catch you. Trust me.' When the child jumps, the father withdraws his arms and as the child falls to the floor he says, 'Never trust any bastard.' O'Toole thinks this is an admirable story. I find it despicable, so I can't warm to the man. He *is* charming, in a way, but I would hate to be his wife or child.

Producing a baby has done nothing to improve my status at home. I don't know why I had been so sentimental as to think it would. Most people become embarrassed when my public trials begin, late at night. I'm not sure they believe what O'Toole says about me. Much as they like and admire him they think he has a 'bad' side, a side that creates chaos and confusion and madness and I, as the closest person to him, come in for the bad as well as the good. Only he and I know exactly what the dialogue is about and we do not fully understand the struggle between us. Those who don't like me rejoice. A childhood friend of his comes to visit and is hateful. Even at our worst O'Toole and I are close, and the friend feels I've usurped a special place to which I have no right. One night, when O'Toole has finished abusing me and collapses into a deep sleep, his friend looks at me across the drawing room and, picking up from the coffee table the big salad bowl full of uneaten, dressed salad, smiles as he slowly empties the oily contents on to the pale green carpet. I can't defend myself. I can't complain to O'Toole because I know he wouldn't dare to take my part against this free spirit – the 'poor' artist, from his past life – the person who belongs to a world that he may be about to leave for success and fame and money. The friend picks up the half-empty bottle of scotch and, still smirking, saunters to his bed in the guest room. I want to garrotte him. I am left to pick up the lettuce leaves and wash the carpet and fetch a rug to cover O'Toole, asleep in an armchair. I am not sad but full of loathing, loathing for O'Toole's servility towards his friend and for my own inability to jerk the situation into normality and reason.

# Chapter Nine

Kate was four weeks old and I was rehearsing the *Shrew* in London but was home in Stratford for the opening of *The Merchant of Venice*. The season had already opened with *The Two Gentlemen of Verona* which was not bad but no great success either, so a great deal depended on this second play of the first Peter Hall season. And suddenly the wild Irish boy lived up to the worst expectations and disappeared into the Warwickshire air. Where was he? It was very simple, though shamingly no one at the theatre thought to ring me at home in Mount Unpleasant. He did what few people would have expected, he went to bed. Knowing how tough he was under his somewhat ramshackle, airy-fairy manner, I didn't fear the worst. He'll play, I thought. Occasionally, he took a cup of tea, mostly he wanted to be left alone.

When the theatre did begin to ring the house he refused to take the calls. 'He's not feeling very well,' I said, unconvincingly. Undeniably, he was under stress – and he *was* only twenty-seven – but in the back of my mind I wondered whether or not this behaviour wasn't due to what he saw as a lack of support and confidence from the management. I had a faint suspicion that he might be thinking along the lines of 'You want to field someone else? *Four* someone elses? Go ahead. Do it.' The house was quiet. Kate, whom I was beginning to think of as a true theatre child, was amenably good-tempered in her cradle at the far end of the drawing room.

Opening day tomorrow. I have to arrange some kind of party here at the house. Jules and Joyce will come before the show and Mrs O'Toole will be at the performance. I'm working on the assumption that he *will* play and I wash my hair and look out an old pre-Kate frock and ask the Shepherds at the local pub, The Dirty Duck, ('The White Swan' to the Brewery) if they will look after Kate during the performance.

The day of opening night and by now the calls from the theatre are coming here thick and fast. O'Toole is still in bed, not speaking. I wish I knew what he was up to. I clean the house and see to Kate. No food is required in the bedroom. There are moments when I could take a club to him but the minute anyone complains about him I become his chief defender. Jules and Joyce arrive. It's teatime and the situation is becoming critical, to say the least. Now, thank God, Jules will take all the phone calls and we will take turns to visit the bedroom. On one of my visits O'Toole extends a hand and says softly, 'Come to bed, girl.' I do and we are reunited after the long arid weeks since Kate was born. I dress and go downstairs. Jules goes up and I hear him saying, 'Listen, kid, if you're not going down there *I'm* going to play Shylock and God knows, all I've got is the nose for it.' Suddenly, all is laughter and bustle and excitement and 'Where are my clean clothes?' 'How about a cup of tea?' 'Where's the car?' 'What's the time?' 'For God's sake everyone, get a *move* on.' And he's gone. It's almost time for the performance. We look at each other, Jules and Joyce and I. It's their first O'Toole experience. We're perched on a cliff edge, danger passed, giddy with relief. But what comes now? 'Let's go to the theatre,' says Joyce.

Theatre at its best, that April night, 'One of the great nights in the theatre' they called it. Those of us who were there in Stratford looked at each other, smiling, knowing that this was a night to cherish for a lifetime. At the wild curtain calls I sat in my unbecoming dress, tears rolling down my face. Whatever it cost, and now I had no illusions as to the price of life with O'Toole, I was going to do everything I could to help cherish this talent. Joyce nudged me. She was in full, beautiful, glamorous, first-night mode. 'We have to go back. He'll be *mobbed*.' Child of Hollywood, she was used to high excitement, not realising that by English standards this night was an extraordinarily heightened occasion. Backstage I had a brief moment with him alone. He was laughing. Clutching me with make-up encrusted hands he whispered in my ear, 'You're not going to believe this. Peter Hall was the first in here and he said, "We're going to be the youngest knights in the history of the theatre." Is he completely mad?' I went to pick up Kate from the Shepherds, got a taxi back to the house and settled her for the night before greeting the guests at the party I'd hastily organised.

I tried to put a brave face on it as they asked, 'When will Peter be here?' I didn't think he would be home for some time. This was going to be Hamlet without the Prince. His mother was inclined to make a drama out of his absence and I spent some time reassuring her, telling her lies she didn't believe and she didn't help me by pretending to believe. I was nonplussed and caught off-guard, had no answer when a guest, non-theatrical and a stranger to me, enquired, 'Aren't you jealous? He could be anywhere, with *anyone*.' It didn't seem to be the moment to unravel my feelings, not even in the cause of polite hospitality. I filled her glass and moved on, smiling. She was insensitive but I had to accept that she voiced a question that must have been present and unspoken by many of our acquaintances.

I would have been astounded to have seen him on this of all nights, handing round the canapés on his own Axminster, surrounded by admiring, well dressed guests. At the same time, I would have liked him to have wished to share the moment with me in some way but it was his moment with no obligation to share it. I knew him well enough to know that he had a need as keen as a need for food and drink to be abroad, alone, obliterating the tensions of the weeks of anxiety as he had geared up to prove himself in this great part and earn his place in the front line of actors. For all his bravado, the understandable doubts and misgivings of those around him had kept him on the rack. Knowing nothing of science, I imagined that his system must be poisoned and curdled with left-over adrenalin churning around him with nowhere to go. Eventually, he would reach the point of oblivion and collapse somewhere. That worried me only in so far as I was concerned for his physical well-being. I wasn't jealous. Unless I had made a massive misjudgement, there was nothing furtive or squalid in his character and however outrageous his behaviour he retained a certain style.

Standing in our drawing room with the party subsiding gently around me, Kate safely in her crib upstairs, I dealt with the smallnesses of opening night, passing food around, pouring drinks, promising to pass on congratulations, laying aside the presents and cards and when everyone was gone and the big house was quiet, I cleared up and washed up; tired, cross at being left alone at home, proud of his great achievement, glad to have got through the day and resentful to be the prey of so many conflicting feelings. '*Tout savoir est tout pardonner.*' Too much *savoir* puts one at a terrible disadvantage. It might be healthier to be able to look at things solely from one's own point of view. I put myself to bed and listened to Kate making small animal noises as she slept. I could hear her father's great voice in my head.

At this time O'Toole composed a song and would sing it, smiling. 'A sweet crime I sing you, a sweet, sweet crime. There's a dainty way to rape and a sweet way to kill but I know something still.' Love and destruction walked hand in hand that spring.

# Chapter Ten

For me it was wonderful to be at work again. I was lucky in Frank Hauser, my director, and even more so in my leading man, Brewster Mason. Large, good-humoured and self-assured, he had what was in those days an original approach to the relationship between the Shrew and Petruchio. Eschewing the paraphernalia of the war between them – the whips, the threatened violence which had characterised the famous 'wooing scene' – he said to me, 'Just establish yourself as a shrew – for whatever reason you choose – but when you come on for our first meeting, fall in love at first sight and I'll do the same and we'll see how we go.' I enquired nervously about the laughs, the funny 'business', and he shook his head and said, 'Trust me. No business. Let the play do the work. It *will* be funny.' Even Frank wasn't sure about this and I was only three-quarters convinced and very nervous. Only Brewster maintained his god-like calm, making time to put me in his car and run me home at lunchtime to breast-feed Kate in Doriah's flat in Belgravia.

My part was very active and after four weeks of vigorous rehearsals my milk dried up. Dr Slattery had wanted me to breast-feed for four weeks and now I'd done eight so I thankfully moved Kate on to formula feeding and life became a great deal easier when I returned to Stratford and prepared to open the play – which worked like a dream! As the wooing scene approached I suffered a moment of terror; no props, no business, nothing but the words and a rather bare stage. Almost immediately I heard the first big laugh – another line and a huge laugh – a riposte and a roar of delight from the audience. The play really does work on this 'straight' level. Who'd have thought it? Not I. Thank you, Brewster.

We came in for a good deal of admiring attention from the academics in Oxford and from the press as well. Full houses always. Bianca was the gorgeous Samantha Eggar who had the most exotic beaux imaginable (Graham Greene seemed to be one of them or am I dreaming this?). She wore tattered jeans and cowboy boots and her boyfriend (Dandy Kim, renowned in the gossip columns – or am I dreaming this too?) picked her up in a jeep. What chic! No one else drove a jeep rather than a racy car. We shared a dressing room and she was forbearing about my taste for vinegar and chips. O'Toole was wonderfully admiring, especially lovely to Brewster and asked if he could 'nick a few readings'. Brewster, charmingly flattered, said, 'But of *course*.'

It was great to be back on stage in a wonderful part. Ted Hardwicke, O'Toole's close friend from Bristol, was in the company. Sometimes he drove me back to Stratford in his Morgan, and even *I* could tell that this was a special car and that he was a wonderful driver. He was also a lovely man, discreet and tactful. Son of Sir Cedric Hardwicke, an international movie star, he must have been accustomed to the very grand side of show business but maintained an impeccable, unassuming charm. I would say that he was more talented than his famous father, but I don't think he'd be glad to hear that. He told me stories about his time at Bristol with O'Toole when they used to entertain the talented young cub reporter Tom Stoppard (not so long ago Tom Straussler) in their humble dressing room. They played the smallest parts in their first year and invented fantasies about their unimportant characters. The road sweepers or footmen or ostlers which they played were actually the true leading parts in the plays in which they appeared, they only *seemed* to be unimportant. Occasionally the fantasies threatened the balance of the play and they were threatened with suspension if the 'complex business' they invented for door opening or floor sweeping or coat hanging wasn't cut out – *at once*. They'd spent an enviable three years acting together in the same company.

The atmosphere at home had become difficult as we approached our opening of the *Shrew*. I think O'Toole got scared for me, maybe he feared I was not as good as he would have wished me to be. I turned up for rehearsal one day wearing dark glasses to hide my eyes, red from a night of wakefulness and weeping. Frank was cross and shouted, 'For God's sake, take off the glasses!' As I did, the company grew silent and looked away, embarrassed. Nothing was said.

During the run I experienced a disturbing and revealing incident. The night had been endless with accusations and inquisitions. When had these interrogations begun? Long after we'd first met, after our long months of exploratory conversations where we had told each other everything we could think of about ourselves! I'd never talked so much in my entire life and I'd never been as open and honest with anyone. Discovery, marriage, houses, cars, a baby; it was as though it had been too wonderful, too exciting, too fast, too easy. Within a couple of months of Kate's birth when we moved to Stratford, everything began to come apart. What price now my belief that I was right to throw in my lot with O'Toole? What price my self-confidence in my own way of running my life? What about my rejection of the narrow morality of my non-conformist upbringing and my self-belief as I did what I pleased on equal terms with men? Hadn't I been proved right as my behaviour led to this wonderful union with the unconventional, totally loveable man? It was as though one day my husband made a huge, delayed double-take and found my past behaviour no longer just appalling but utterly unacceptable. Gradually, I came to see myself in the same, poor light. I was completely alone in that house, in that town and ashamed and frightened and only occasionally moved to answer back or to apply reason to the situation. Part of me didn't believe in his change of heart but part of me was heartbroken to be the cause of such blackness in O'Toole and such unhappiness in both of us and also, after Kate was born, to be responsible for bringing her into such an agonised home.

On this particular morning in early May, when usually O'Toole would have been expected to fall asleep, the row continued until it was time for me to leave for the Oxford theatre to play a matinée. There was silence – maybe he had gone to sleep somewhere. Mindlessly, I set about packing Kate's luggage for the day. The taxi arrived and I began to load the boot when I saw the driver's eyes lift and his expression changed. Looking over my shoulder, I saw O'Toole on the leads of the roof. There was silence all around. I couldn't read his expression but he looked – well – spectacular and impressive. He swayed precariously. I was aghast but it didn't occur to me to stay. I *had* to leave within minutes or run the risk of missing the matinée. Running into the house I called the only person I could turn to, my doctor. He promised to come over immediately. I got into the back of the taxi with Kate and said, 'Drive off, please.' Sitting there, looking straight ahead, I began to close my mind to the happenings of the night and the nightmarish scene I had just left. I was conscious of my lack of a 'normal' response; it was as though the effort of living with extreme behaviour was numbing my reaction. I thought ahead to the theatre and the prospect of doing two shows. Kate would stay with me in the dressing room, as usual, until I would hand her over to the wardrobe mistress as I went on stage. I felt a flicker of anger against O'Toole. It just wasn't *fair*. Living from day to day was proving exhausting and almost impossibly difficult *and* I had a job to do. I needed help and felt sabotaged at every turn. I couldn't sustain my anger. 'It's your fault,' whispered a voice in my head and how could I ignore the fact that O'Toole himself was in torment. 'Life isn't fair' was one of his often repeated remarks and I was slowly learning the truth of it. But clear in my mind was the conviction that I had to do my job meticulously with no concessions to my hopeless state.

We gave two good performances and, briefly, unbelievably to an outsider, I was very happy. On my return home I found the house in darkness. I hadn't been to bed for two days and once I'd settled Kate for the night I fell into a long sleep. When I awoke, O'Toole was home. We didn't speak of what had occurred.

Kate was now approaching five months old. I was still nervous of child-rearing, had worn out one copy of Dr Spock and was into my second, but my life was transformed by the advent of Lonnie Trimble.

Our house in Stratford had become a kind of ramshackle hotel for people who wanted to see the plays and stay over. Working closely with the tourist industry, British Railway timetables made it impossible for people to see a play at Stratford and get back to London again on the same day, so our spare beds and couches were constantly occupied and once, in fine weather, there were makeshift beds on the lawns, as well. O'Toole was lavish in his offers of hospitality. More often than not he wasn't there to attend to his guests and very often I had no idea who they were and hadn't been warned to expect them. I muddled through the day from one nightmare meal to the next. His salary of £45 a week was going nowhere towards covering the cost of this generosity. The laundry alone was a major problem and I learned how to remake beds with roughly dried sheets, plugging the iron in at the bedside and ironing only the top of the sheet where it turned over. Fortunately I had my weekly income from my contract with Douglas Uren and had money left over from my pre-marriage days with which to help subsidise our life. Even so, it was a bit worrying.

Kenneth Griffith, most blessed of guests, arrived and solved some of my problems. He had made the acquaintance – I never discovered how – of a young, black, ex-marine from Atlanta, Georgia, one Lonnie Trimble who, having tasted life in the Navy, found it impossible to resume segregated life in the South. He was in England with no job, no work permit and needing some kind of humble employment for three years so he could become a legal resident and fulfil his ambition of becoming a chef.

Me: 'Well, Kenny, thank you very much, but I sort of thought that I needed a *nanny* right now.'

Ken: 'Yes! And *he's* your *man*!'

Well, why not? He could read Dr Spock as well as I and he could cook a great deal better than I could, so it had to be a good move. It worked well in another, more subtle, way. I suspected that O'Toole was feeling half-guilty about the changes in his life; acquiring a wife and child was bad enough, renting a big house was a bit worse, employing a *servant* was beyond the pale. Which is why Lonnie was perfect; he was no man's servant. In his head he was already the boss of a catering firm. He wasn't an early bird either and I took him a cup of tea to awaken him in the morning. Oh, but he was fearless in the kitchen; an unexpected twenty people to supper brought a happy smile to his face. Faced with the usual request for a 'cup of tea and something on toast' from O'Toole, he sulked. Possessed of endless patience, he played with Kate; she emptied a box of matches and he picked them up. She emptied, he picked up. She was in heaven. We did the marketing together (it had never occurred to me before that you *planned* your meals and bought everything in one fell, weekly swoop). He was six feet four and jet black and beautiful. In the crook of his arm he held Kate in her beautiful white shawl which Sidney Poitier had unexpectedly sent me after we'd met at dinner one night in the White Elephant in London. 'All very well,' sniffed a Stratford housewife in an audible whisper in the greengrocers.

'It's the *children* that suffer.' Lonnie loved the sun and spent hours lying in it on the lawn. 'What are you doing,' yelled O'Toole as he drove off to the theatre, 'trying to get a tan?' and sometimes, 'Get out the Leichner Five and Nine, I've got some really racist people coming for supper.' Lonnie looked at him from under half-closed eyes and shook his head with good-humoured disdain.

Under his easy, masterful control the house assumed a semblance of normality. Now at least there were two of us ranged against the chaos. When times were bad between O'Toole and myself, he became an invisible presence in the house; to all intents seeing nothing, hearing nothing. It must have been an outlandish solution to his immigration problem. I could only hope that it suited him as well as it suited me. We didn't discuss it. He arrived in time to prevent a total collapse on my part. The scenes and inquisitions that had murdered the weeks before Kate was born resumed after her birth and I sank deeper into despair. I had never heard of post-natal depression, my books hadn't mentioned it. Babies, as far as I knew, arrived bringing good cheer and happiness unconfined, but I was getting more and more unhappy.

One night after hours of more close, drunken questioning about my past – and yes he was now right to doubt my veracity, I was lying with a will about everything. My instinct to tell him the truth had brought me nothing but trouble, and pins under my nails would not drag more confessions from me. The table overturned, doors slammed and the car raced erratically down the long drive. I walked out of the house reeking with fear and suspicion and noise, lay in the wet, long grass on the untended lawn in my nightgown, unable to stay inside. It was almost dawn but I didn't feel the cold. My wish was to get ill and die. 'Let me just *leave*,' I wished. Even as I made the wish I was shocked by my cowardice. Incapable of killing myself, what did I want to happen? That the harmless damp should carry me off while I wasn't looking? Desperate as I was, I couldn't bear to be so feeble. I sat up. It was quiet; in the distance the lights on the road led to Stratford, the theatre, actors, my past life, the only life I knew how to live. As dawn broke I heard the country noises around me and I returned to my senses. I looked at the house, the scene of more misery than I could have imagined possible. Kate was inside, sleeping in her basket. What was I thinking of? So long as she was there, I would have to be there. Getting up, I returned to the house and sat on the floor, leaning against the wall, waiting until she woke. I might have forfeited my right to what I had imagined was my due as a wife and mother – protection, tenderness – but all her rights as a daughter shall remain intact, I swore to myself.

I don't recall O'Toole hurting anyone when drunk. He broke things and made a great deal of noise. I didn't fear for myself but the noise and the destruction terrified me. I hadn't quite acquired the knack of never answering back and sometimes unable to resist speaking up for myself I would add fuel to the flames. When he erupted out of the house, running in bare feet into the dark across the Warwickshire fields out of sight, beyond the lights of the house, I stood alone crying tears of rage and helplessness.

My nerve was gone; a raised voice, a loud noise – nothing much in themselves – these were enough to frighten me. Sitting alone, trying to find a solution to my helter-skelter home life I did the stupidest thing imaginable; for the first and only time in my life I called my parents in Wales and asked for help. My father had retired from the police force and he and my mother were running a further education house in the country outside Cardiff and enjoying the work and their pets and hobbies and generally living a more comfortable life than they'd ever had before. I had not lived with them since moving on to University but I visited as often as possible and they were completely charmed by O'Toole and impressed by his talent. Of course, they were ecstatic at the arrival of a granddaughter. The consequences of my phonecall were appalling. My father, realising I must be desperate, believed me to be seriously at risk and, hundreds of miles away and powerless, he collapsed. It was left to my mother to find a friend, Joyce (director Herbert Davies's wife), to accompany them on the long car journey from Wales to Stratford. When O'Toole, sobered, learned what I had done he was angry and appalled; it was the first time that an outsider had been allowed into our private torment. There was nothing to do but wait for them to arrive and for once he said little. He seemed contemptuous that I'd felt the need to lean on someone else. I didn't know what to think. I had lost all sense of self, all sense of pride in myself. I doubted my motives, my abilities. And yet, I was sure of my duty as a mother. And there were moments when I thought I couldn't be as bad as I had come to believe. Was *everyone* out there, in the world beyond the lawn and the field to the road, virtuous and good? I thought with envy of the Company in the town, going to work, going to the pub, having fun, misbehaving – and all in some way acceptable to O'Toole where I was not.

My parents and Joyce Davies arrived and there was a good deal of shuffling of feet and tea making. My father looked awful. I felt guilty all over again. For the first and only time there was a proper 'family' talk and I didn't much like it. I had to confess all over again bits of my past in order to explain why O'Toole was so angry with me. I remembered my friend's sister being expelled from Chapel for sexual irregularity and felt much as she must have felt. People went away in pairs, regrouped and whispered. I just sat there in a pool of shame. Finally all five of us sat together and the consensus of opinion seemed to be that 'We all make mistakes' – we now had to 'Go forward'. I wasn't too sure whose mistakes we were talking about but I felt it was better not to enquire. We seemed to have arrived at a measure of calm. O'Toole had some time off from work and he announced that my parents were going to take Kate to Wales for a week and he and I were going, at last, to the West of Ireland. This was the most unexpected outcome. O'Toole charmed them all over again. I would never be able to forget the events of the last few days. I didn't expect anything good to happen again but everyone was now smiling and making sandwiches and everything was behind us, it seemed. I was unbelieving but I was relieved to be out of trouble, even if just for the moment. O'Toole was adorable to me, as only he could be, and he was taking me to the West – the precious, mythical West he'd talked about so much, the home of the troublesome O'Toole clan, I was told, after they'd been banished by Cromwell from the eastern side of Eire. I was back in favour. I was forgiven. Why? For how long?

Jules's film, *The Day They Robbed the Bank of England*, was due to open in London in a few days and we were to go to that after our visit to Ireland and before I returned to Wales to pick up Kate and resume life in Stratford. I couldn't quite believe what was happening. Had I done the right thing after all by calling in my parents? My father's face was bitterly changed. I didn't know what he'd said to O'Toole but it was evident that the episode had cost him dear. His worst fears for me had almost come true. His expression haunted me. Even as he smiled and joked and said how pleased he was to be taking Kate to Wales and was glad to assist, I could see fear and defeat in his eyes. I recognised his look because I now had been taught fear and defeat. I was an unworthy wife, an uncertain mother and a troublesome daughter. My theatrical vows were neglected and broken. He never lost the look he wore that day and that was my gift to him, the man who would never harm me.

My mother, harder, more realistic, didn't address the problem, the discussion or the resolution. She took me aside, looked at me and said in Welsh, 'Understand, if you want this to work – and for Kate's sake you must make it work – from now on you're going to have to stand in a very small space.' The unspoken question, 'What are you going to do?' hung in the air. I knew she was right. I had seconds in which to think as bags were packed, the fridge was emptied, doors were locked, cars were loaded. I didn't look at my mother or answer her. O'Toole was looking at me, smiling. He held out his hand and I could no more resist him than stop breathing. I waved goodbye and with a lightness of heart that comes from doing the inevitable, if doomed, I took my husband's hand.

# Chapter Eleven

After all that O'Toole had told me about the Eire beyond Dublin I was nervous when we arrived. What if he'd exaggerated? What if I couldn't enthuse? But, like Venice, everything was just as it had been described and at the same time better. The weather alone was wonderful to me and assuaged a homesickness I never dared acknowledge. It was weather Celts are used to and love; damp, unpredictable, changeable, unreliable, enlightening. Jack Yeats, the painter, talking of the problem of painting in the West said, 'The light has legs,' and everything does change even as you look at it. In the West, the countryside is a mixture of the lush – the Gulf Stream nudges past the coastline, cabbage palms intrude exotically, fuchsia hedges riot around the brutally barren little fields – smaller than one could imagine – bounded by lumps of granite. Cromwell, consigning the native Irish to the West, sent them 'to Hell or Connaught'. Coming from farming stock I was appalled by the agony of farming this landscape which looked at times like the far side of the moon. And the people – this was a foreign land and it was home to me. As a Celt, I was used to listening to stories, hearing people sing for enjoyment, wasting time talking, but these people were something extra, something from a past I'd only been told about. The gift of story telling, now barely a memory in close-to-England Wales, flourished here from acknowledged spielers to your neighbourhood grocer or the bus driver. Language was supreme. I remember that in London O'Toole and I were one night trying to find the Stratford East Theatre. Hopelessly lost, we stopped a local East Ender who turned out to be an Irishman.

He directed us, 'You go down that road until you come to nothin' at all and you turn left.' Thanks for nothing. Going 'down that road' we came to a bomb site which *was* 'nothin' at all' when you think about it. So we 'turned left' and there was the theatre. At the time I thought that man was a poet. Now going West, I realised that he was just an Irishman.

Coming to a crossroads we saw two men, *not* hitching a lift – nothing so vulgar – they were looking expectantly in the direction in which they wished to go. We stopped and they got in, my first Irish countrymen: the tall, serious, thin one in the front with O'Toole and I hopped into the back with the small, cheery, fat one. (How did I know to give up my place to the natural leader?) We drove in silence for a while and O'Toole asked his passenger if he'd ever been in England. 'Yes,' was the taciturn reply. My small, fat friend dug me in the ribs. 'He was in Dartmoor and Pentonville.' Oh, gosh. 'Yes, he was trying to shoot policemen and needless to say, he missed.' We both heaved with merriment in the back. The tall, thin, would-be murderer asks, ruminatively, 'Have you ever been to Brighton? When I left Pentonville I went there. Beautiful. England is beautiful.' I didn't really know what to say to that. They got out, thanking us in a sprightly, somewhat Japanese way that I remembered from Yugoslavia – a touch to the heart, the head, and then open the palms and bow from the waist.

In the Great Western Hotel in Kerry, as we sat in the garden the bartender approached us unsteadily, tray tilting perilously away, he treading the lawn carefully as though he was negotiating very long grass. 'Bin and Binjer Jeer?' he intoned sonorously as we clutched at our falling glasses of gin and ginger beer.

I love, I love, I love this place. I want to live here. I think this is what Catholic Wales was like before Non-Conformism laid its hand on it. That's unfair. Non-Conformism has done so much to save us as a nation, made us remember we are different from a nation that has a ruler wedded to the Church of England, it's sent us underground, which produces another kind of strength and energy. But the joy of this place, the lack of shame, is overpoweringly attractive. It is with difficulty that I embrace my husband at times, but I unreservedly adore his country, the things that made him. He may not have been born here but he is a boy from Connaught.

Another time, we sit in Frank Kelly's pub, Kings, on the square in Clifden (the centrepiece of the square is a half submerged concrete public lavatory). As we drink our Guinness – 'Takes forever to draw, half a minute to drink' – a long faced man asks, 'Are you here for the funeral?' 'No,' I say. 'What funeral?' 'Peter O'Toole's daughter.' 'Oh, my God.' 'No, Peter O'Toole. Peter's daughter.' 'Sorry?' 'Peter O'Toole. Peter's daughter's funeral.' 'Oh, I see. Yes.' Looking around I see that I am surrounded by men who look exactly like Peter O'Toole, long faced, blue eyed, thin, almost skeletal, tall, beautiful in a Sam Beckett sort of way. This is O'Toole country. I want to live in it.

How could I have imagined a mere two days ago in Warwickshire that I would be sitting here in Ireland totally happy with my decision to stay married. I didn't just marry O'Toole, I married a country and I am ecstatically happy with my decision. This country is part of my child's inheritance, she is half Welsh and half Irish. I'm proud to have made her this.

And looking at these poor little abandoned farms – hearing stories of people's grandmothers found dead, lips stained green from eating grass – I dimly understand something akin to the Welsh experience, the fear of something beyond poverty, the total annihilation of one's right as a human being. Is the dread bred into his bones as it is into mine? If so, we have a difficult time ahead. How can the blind lead the blind? In a relationship, opposites are better. When he says, 'I'm done for', I think, 'Yes, of course you are'. What use is that? I think I see his truth and he knows more of my truth than anyone. We are completely 'suited', and we have such a chance of riches. He buys me a red-dyed bawneen jacket. If only we could stay in Ireland. This is the land of lost content for me, which is absurd because I encountered it only yesterday.

We lingered too long and now we had a wild race against time to get to London in time to change at Dorset Mews and get to the opening of *The Day They Robbed the Bank of England*. My hair was a windswept disaster and I didn't have time to get made up and I vowed I wouldn't again be such a good sport. I looked awful.

The film was very well received and O'Toole was first rate as the English officer, it wasn't a great part but playing it was a good move, I thought.

It was a better move than I could have imagined.

Back to Stratford. The trip to Ireland and the opening of the film have had a miraculous effect on our home life. We're happy. The days get longer, the elms and laurels round the house stop dripping, everything lightens. Lonnie cuts the lawns. Max Adrian has now taken the stable block and the moment I meet him I recognise a lifelong friend. He becomes Kate's baby-sitter or rather she shares his bed when he's resting. With Lonnie on board, I no longer dread the guests and the rickety domestic arrangements seem bohemian and amusing rather than desperate and slovenly. And what guests! Celebrities come and go. Sometimes Lonnie is the only person to see them. Anthony Quinn arrives for the weekend from America, the current girlfriend in tow. He dosses down in Mount Unpleasant very gracefully and more or less ignores his gorgeous companion who sits in the drawing room and sobs for the entire weekend. Tactfully we also ignore her, walking round her armchair and leaving cups of tea within reach along with fresh boxes of Kleenex. He decides to take us to dinner and as I call the only decent restaurant he hisses, 'Book it in my name.' I call this restaurant at least once a week but I oblige him. 'Who?' says the Warwickshire lad on the phone. 'Anthony Quinn.' 'Anthony what? Can you spell that.' 'Q-U-I-N-N.' 'Is that Siân?' 'Yes.' 'Well, why didn't you say so, girl.' I replace the receiver and he smiles across the room. 'Got a good table, huh? Always pays to *use* the name.'

Elizabeth Taylor wants O'Toole to be in a rather dubious version of *Anna Karenina*. We've read it and it's horrible and O'Toole has turned it down but now Eddie Fisher is dispatched to Stratford to woo him afresh. Just for the fun of it, O'Toole nips up to the Dorchester for talks, wins £100 from them at poker and buys a new set of clothes, and having thrown his old ones away comes home looking gorgeous like a peacock. No *Anna Karenina* of course. Everything is fun. He's inundated with illustrious visitors but the only solid job offer on the table after his colossal success in *The Merchant of Venice* is a schools' broadcast for the BBC. We both vow that we'll try to remember this. Huge successes are more often than not followed by absolutely nothing.

I am approached to be in a play with Gladys Cooper and that is hugely tempting but just for the moment I feel I have a chance to mend my life with Kate and O'Toole and I decline. O'Neill's play, *A Moon for the Misbegotten* at the Arts is more seductive still but now we are getting along so much better I will stick out what remains of the season in Stratford and fill in with radio and television. Now, unaccountably, life is good; I'm a good Irish wife; Marie is here; I feel useful in Mount Unpleasant. I'm living again with the man I married and he is the only person I can imagine living with.

Now most nights Kate and I are invited to supper after the show in one of the two restaurants in the town. She is an amazing child and sleeps in her basket under the dining table. (In the theatre at Oxford she slept in a skip in the Wardrobe.) I don't think she ever utters a sound when she's out for the night. We don't go to the parties, of course, but at least I hear about them now and I feel a little as though I'm part of the season.

Patrick Wymark comes calling and when he gets drunk he puts classical music on the record player and conducts an imaginary orchestra for hours on end. He reassures O'Toole, who at twenty-seven is playing Petruchio to Peggy Ashcroft's fifty-two-year-old Kate, that she will *give* him more than any other actress alive. She has a reputation for being predatory towards her leading man and I can't help but feel nervous that she will be *too* generous with her attentions. But I remind myself that, at fifty-two, she's ancient and past such follies. She invites us to tea at the lovely house she's rented outside Stratford – strawberries and cream on the lawn. Hanging in the hall is her Vita Sackville-West type hat and rain coat. 'I walk to work,' she declares briskly. I'm afraid she *does* look struck by O'Toole but I don't think it's anything for me to worry about.

Sam Wanamaker and his wife invite us to tea as well (I hate tea but I like these invitations – they're a Stratford institution). They have a wonderful half-timbered house and beautiful garden. There are young girls – daughters? – in the kitchen but they don't join us. Kate's Moses basket is placed on the lawn and when I turn to see if she's all right I see her covered in blossom from the tree above. Her arms are raised and she's smiling in the soft pink shower. No one remarks on the sight but we all smile and the picture is engraved in my mind as *the* picture of my daughter as a baby in Warwickshire.

These were the more sedate aspects of our intense social life. The parties I didn't go to sounded a lot of fun. Jackie McGowran was in the *Shrew* company. He was one of the most famous Irish actors working in England at that time and 1960 was the height of his excess, the watershed of his drinking life. (At the end of the season he checked into a drying-out clinic under our former flat in Bryanston Street.) In his apartment in Stratford there were two goldfish called King Lear and Cordelia. During a party, in the early hours of the morning, Jackie slipped out of the sitting room and got busy with the frying pan. He re-emerged, ashen, saying, 'Jayses – I feel like a fuckin' cannibal. I've just eaten King Lear and Cordelia.' He'd had them on toast.

Dinsdale Landen and his beautiful wife, Jenny, woke one morning (at her insistence, 'There's someone in the room, Din.' 'Oh, don't be silly, darling') to find a damaged car, *in* their very damaged bay window. There was an explanation for this but at the time it escaped a hung-over Dinsdale. There was so much bad behaviour during this season that people flocked to the town to see what this outrageous bunch of actors were getting up to. Mercifully, on stage, they were wonderful but it was touch and go at times. The Shepherds who ran the Dirty Duck were invaluable allies in times of crisis. One day Jackie McGowran before a matinée, blind drunk since the night before said in the Duck, 'I can't go into the theatre in this state – I'm a disgrace to my profession.' He was on a warning so it was imperative that he should play the matinée. 'Look, Jackie,' said Dinsdale, 'put your clothes on back to front and they'll think at the stage door that you're coming *out*, not going *in*.' 'Right, aould son,' said Jackie, beginning to take his clothes off. O'Toole mixed him a 'cocktail' of beer, mustard and tobacco from cigarette ends, guaranteed to make anyone throw up. Jackie drank it down, shook his head and said 'Great, aould son, great!' and proceeded to put his clothes on back to front. He played the matinée and never threw up.

The Stratford *Shrew* was a joyous production (Peggy carried Kate on at one matinée) and with other actors it went on to enchant London audiences, but it had had a difficult birth. John Barton's production was set in a winter-gripped Italy. The company was encased in furs and wools (a bit at odds with the text). There were endless revolves and the difficult part of Biondello was played by a child. Peggy had decided to play Kate as a stroppy, angry, militant suffragette (shades of the CND demonstrations of the time). Came a night when Peggy shut herself in the dressing room in tears of despair and refused to come out. Rehearsals were abandoned. The following day, the furs and wool were jettisoned and the wardrobe department raided for sunny Italian clothes, the revolves were halved, Dinsdale replaced the child and O'Toole persuaded Peggy to stop being Major Barbara and just come on and fall in love with him. She did and she was sensational. It was odd, seeing her do the 'gags' that Brewster had worked out for me but she did them so wonderfully that I was forcibly reminded that, in acting, it doesn't matter who *gets* the idea, it's how well you *execute* it that matters. She was heavenly and seemed younger than her Petruchio, who was more than young enough to be her son. The opening night performance was a great occasion but I didn't organise a party. The tense opening of *The Merchant* – the party without O'Toole – meant I never again expected an opening night, mine or anyone else's, to be pleasurable, or fun. But I was happy he'd 'done the double', as his bookmaker father would have said.

# Chapter Twelve

Ordinarily I would have been disappointed that the proposed foreign tour of the Oxford *Shrew* was cancelled but, given the volatile state of my domestic life, I recognised it as a piece of good fortune. I was far from giving up my efforts to redeem myself in O'Toole's eyes but part of me just wished for a miracle; a change of heart on his part. The likelihood that he would turn round and agree that he was over-reacting to my 'past' – which was no worse than that of most of the actresses he admired and respected and which had never been concealed from him – receded as the weeks went by. Every so often our bubble of normality was punctured by scenes of appalling verbal abuse and these were to continue at unexpected moments. I realised with regret that in his eyes I was not a woman deserving of respect. There wasn't a stage play on offer that would not keep me away from Stratford for unacceptable periods, so I began to consider television plays again.

Wilfrid Lawson was one of the greatest and most revered actors of the first half of the twentieth century. A driving accident in Hollywood had left him with a legacy of ill-health and he continued throughout his life to be a spectacularly heavy drinker. He was a great actor and it wasn't his fault that subsequent generations strove to emulate his drinking exploits and his outrageous behaviour as well as his talent. When I was considering a play by Kenneth Jupp, *Strangers in the Room*, O'Toole happened on the proposed cast list and said, 'You *have* to do this play. It's the chance of a lifetime to act with Wilfrid Lawson!' Richard Pasco, Donald

Houston and I were the leading players. Mary Ellis was going to appear and Wilfrid was to play the relatively small part of my grandfather. It was a good play but I went into it as a designated handmaiden to the great Wilfrid. 'Look after him,' said O'Toole sternly. 'Whatever it takes, DO it.'

I did. Wilfrid, playing a part that absorbed less than ten per cent of his ability, reined in his astounding talent and behaved meekly during rehearsal. The producers were on the alert for the smallest backsliding into drunkenness. Mary Ellis loathed him and his reputation, and *still* he was adorable. Remote and unfathomable – but adorable.

During rehearsals I had an urgent dental appointment and Wilfrid offered to look after Kate! (As usual I had her with me in her basket in London.) I couldn't believe this – I was so in awe of him and he was completely undomesticated. 'Where will you be?' I asked. 'At the Kismet,' he replied. The Kismet – the afternoon drinking place in Cranbourne Street, peopled by drunks in between licensing hours in the pubs, where the owner, dear Raj's father, cooked delicious but dubious curries in the rudimentary kitchen over a blackened stove. Never had a baby graced these premises. And a baby in the charge of Wilfrid Lawson? No. Yes. Why not?

I went to the dentist and rushed back to the Kismet and . . . Wilfrid and Raj's father had looked after her beautifully, so we stayed on for more convivial hours but even O'Toole was taken aback when I told him where Kate and I had spent the afternoon.

After that I was Wilfrid's willing slave and when we went to Manchester (without Kate) for the transmission I was the first person dressed, packed and in the foyer of our hotel when Wilfrid was evicted for roaming the corridors in the night shouting for 'Aggie'. I knew that 'Aggie' meant something to Wilfrid. She meant nothing to anyone else. There was a story of him going to Germany to do a television show. In his scene he had to say, 'Kneel, serf,' and then proceed with some faintly ridiculous speech. The lines escaped him. 'Kneel, serf,' he intoned then, searching around for a suitable continuation, he went on, 'I have fought with Aggie' – long pause – 'the one-eyed Dane' – pause – 'several times' – pause – 'recently.' 'Cut!' said the horrified director in hushed tones. Wilfrid turned to his equally shocked fellow actor and murmured, 'That was a close shave,' pleased to have got away with something. He wasn't aware of being dismissed from the show and sent home to England. Who was 'Aggie'? Now she was here in a Manchester boarding house. I wouldn't have dreamt of abandoning Wilfrid and we taxied around until we found an Aggie-proof boarding house. The landlady liked him on sight. He kissed her hand and we were given lovely rooms and special breakfasts.

He repaid me by trying to give me a few acting notes. One of them: 'That big scene – don't play it like Lady Macbeth, it won't stand it. Never impose more weight than a scene will take. That's showing off. Never show off.' When we came to transmission day for ABC television (the Aereated Bread Company, Wilfrid called it) he fell off the wagon. Chlöe Gibson, the director, was incensed. Mary Ellis was beside herself and Wilfrid stole every scene he was in; drunk but great. I sat on the arm of his chair (he was my grandfather) and acted away, laying down yards of text while he made holes in his biscuit with a pencil he happened to have handy. Even I was fascinated by this bit of business and I realised that my fascination with 'characters' and my slavish admiration for good actors was not going to be a help in my career. He was drunk as a skunk and all I wanted was for him to get through the show. As though he needed my help.

I was asked to join the Royal Shakespeare Company for its move to London and the first Aldwych season. I hadn't been on stage for a couple of months since *The Shrew* just after Kate was born and this seemed to be a gentle return. They were the dullest parts I'd ever been asked to play but I so wanted to be in the company. Events at home overshadowed this small decision. David Lean had seen *The Day They Robbed the Bank of England* and decided on the spot that he wanted O'Toole to play Lawrence of Arabia. Sam Spiegel – no admirer of O'Toole's – offered it to many other people including O'Toole's friend Albert Finney who, it seems, turned it down because he didn't want film stardom at that moment and Marlon Brando who turned it down goodness knows why. David's choice was always O'Toole. Sam desperately went on suggesting other actors, *any* actors. O'Toole went to London to do a test, the same test that Albert had done. His partner, Jules, an old adversary of Sam's, insisted that he test in uniform as well as robes. He looked great in both. David's instinct was confirmed and even Sam had to capitulate. O'Toole was undeniably Lawrence.

'It'll be a six-month shoot,' said Sam. Jules warned that movies on this scale took twice as long as scheduled. Sam insisted that it was a six-month job. O'Toole's contract with Stratford ended with the 1960 season, in the autumn with *Troilus and Cressida*, but he had expressed a wish to play *Becket* by Anouilh in London the following spring. He and Peter Hall went to the States to see Anthony Quinn in the play on Broadway. It was O'Toole's first visit to America and he fell in love with New York. For a city boy it was *the* city above all cities and it became his favourite playground. As a country girl, I wasn't sorry that he liked to visit it alone.

He was morally committed to *Becket*, five or six months away. Also on offer was the biggest film opportunity of the decade which should end in five or six months. When Sam Spiegel reluctantly gave in to David Lean's insistence and announced the casting of O'Toole as Lawrence, there was consternation at the theatre. O'Toole was characterised as a traitor to his profession. Life at home descended again into chaos. The brief interlude of shared days and meals eaten together was over. I lost my precarious happiness. Sadness, which I didn't think to characterise as depression, crept closer and coloured the days and nights grey.

I could still take my pick of the best television on offer but my confidence was at rock bottom. O'Toole despised radio and television, media in which I'd grown up. Welsh-speaking theatre was, to him, not theatre at all. The Welsh were completely outside the mainstream of 'real' life and art. I took him to meet Saunders Lewis in Cardiff. During lunch at the Park Hotel, he told Saunders this; Saunders took it badly and rushed out of the hotel to disappear from my life for five years. I thought that if he dared to treat our greatest Welshman in this way, there was nothing he wouldn't dare to do to me. At the nadir of my life at this time, the BBC came to Stratford to film a day in the life of one of the 'bright young hopes of the British Theatre'. My agent said I *had* to do it. I slunk out of the house and spent the day walking around Stratford being interviewed in scenic spots, smiling, looking confident, talking about my 'exciting life' and my 'glittering future' and wishing I were dead.

Peggy Ashcroft summoned me to tea and lectured me on O'Toole's folly in 'selling out'. Surely, she said, I could use my influence to make him see sense and play Becket for the RSC rather than Lawrence in the movie. Much as I admired her I felt unfairly invaded. She was so enviably in the right, and at the same time so comfortable, so successful, so middle class, so English. I wondered whether she had ever been asked to refuse the chance to become an international movie star, in a great part, written by a wonderful writer, directed by one of the best living directors. Given my training and inclinations, I agreed with her and, asked to choose, I would have accepted a play rather than a film. But the world had changed and was changing very fast and in my heart of hearts I feared that my recent choices and the one Peggy was advancing were mistaken. And I wondered if she had any idea how little influence I wielded. Aloud I said that I felt it would be wrong for me to try to influence events. We parted frostily. I didn't want to alienate the great woman but even at a time of resentment and fury with him, my loyalty to O'Toole was absolute. I couldn't discuss him. Not even with her.

Our life spiralled further out of control as his professional problems grew more oppressive. He was being made to feel guilty and unworthy by day and at night he had the responsibility of two major parts and was on the receiving end of a huge amount of adulation. I felt that I and Kate and the house were just too much for him to deal with at this time. Had there been no love, no need on his part, it would have been easy to turn aside and wait for his life to return to something approaching normality. As it was, there were times when he clutched at me as though his life depended on me. And there were times when he couldn't bear to look at me and I had neither the years nor the sense to know how to find a balance. All too often now I found myself accepting his view that my behaviour before I met him was something for which I had to atone. Marie Kean was the only person who was allowed to witness the worst of these scenes. On a brief visit she tried to make light of things for my sake. 'Look now. He can't have expected you to live like a NUN until you met him.' 'But he *does*!' 'Not at all. He's just having a bit of a bad time and it's up to you to put up with these Moments of Truth and it will all blow over.'

The Moments of Truth, as I learned to think of the hours when my character and morals were scrutinised and found wanting, grew more frequent and one night, more intense, more anguished than ever before, I decided that I could no longer continue to live in this fashion. As the car hurtled down the lane, I looked about me and vowed that I would never again spend the dark hours in this house which had become so hateful to me. I assembled Kate's things and packed a suitcase for myself. For the remainder of the night I restored the house to perfect order, working mindlessly until the sun was high in the sky. I bathed and called a taxi.

It was a couple of days since I'd slept but I wasn't tired. I fed Kate and took Lonnie a cup of tea. On a deep level and beyond expression, I was angry. I couldn't work out the consequences but I knew I had to leave Stratford, taking Kate with me.

It was a beautiful morning. I sat on the front step and thought I must be slightly deranged to be so happily affected by a perfect English summer morning, looking at a view Shakespeare might have seen. There had never been a moment in my life where my concern with my own affairs couldn't be entirely diverted into pleasure in my surroundings. That *must* be a kind of madness, I thought, not for the first time.

Barely more than a year since I cocked a snook at everyone as they predicted that I was embarking on a course that would ruin my life and my career and if I'd laid about with an axe I couldn't have made a better job of fulfilling their prophecies. The stupidest thing I'd done was to allow Keep Films, at O'Toole's urging, to buy me out of my highly unusual and good contract with Douglas Uren. I had hoped that ending the contract would help our situation but all I'd achieved was to place myself in a very vulnerable position. I had to take a job as soon as possible. I was short of money.

The taxi was late but the best imaginable house guest appeared. Gary Raymond, slightly taken aback to be given a pram containing Kate and asked to wheel her around the lawn for a while, obligingly fell in with the unusual social arrangements. He'd been at RADA with O'Toole and had made a name in movies almost immediately (he'd just appeared in *Suddenly Last Summer*). Much too gentlemanly to ask questions, he helped us into the taxi when it arrived and I left him in Lonnie's care to enjoy the delights of Stratford, a place I devoutly wished never to see again. I reminded myself that I shouldn't make too operatic an exit since I would have to return to rehearse *Malfi* and *Ondine*, the plays which would open the RSC season at the Aldwych in December. How

I would organise that was impossible to imagine. For the moment I should content myself with the mundane business of finding shelter and quiet and getting some sleep.

Ken and Doriah's mews in London provided all that. I saw no one except Jules and Joyce briefly. I had cut myself off from everyone I had ever known and now I was much too proud to look them up, admitting I'd made a terrible mistake. Jules and Joyce were sympathetic but I reminded myself that they were in business with O'Toole; the three of them were about to take off on the exotic journey that is the beginning of a great career. I would probably have no part in this; already I felt part of the past. I don't know how people like Ken and Doriah preserve their integrity – discreet and unintrusive, they found it possible to shelter me and Kate without for a moment taking sides or even wanting to know what passed between me and O'Toole in Stratford.

And what *had* passed? Nothing that made any sense. O'Toole found it intolerable that he was not the first man in my life and he found my past beyond pardon. I found it intolerable that I should be blamed for having a previous life and then I came to blame myself for it as well. Was that really what made our lives so dangerous and hideous? Looking back, the only reality was that we were hurting each other beyond reason.

# Chapter Thirteen

I spent a few weeks hibernating in London. Returning to Stratford to rehearse the new season was difficult. I found lodgings in a quiet back street and my landlady took care of Kate while I was at work. I ran home at lunchtime to feed her and returned home as soon as rehearsals were over, taking care that I was not followed. For two weeks I remained hidden. At night I sat in our room, reading, but inevitably in the end I was followed and found and O'Toole insisted that I be moved to his sister's house outside Birmingham. From there, I could commute to work every day and his sister's housekeeper would look after Kate. I felt like a Victorian serving maid who'd got into trouble and whose life was being organised by the Young Master. Had I had only myself to think about I wouldn't have agreed to any of this but I was now a mother and, good as my landlady was, my digs weren't ideal for Kate. I sat on my single bed and looked at her in her basket. What right did I have to subject her to this improvised existence which was the best I could muster? I had to admit that O'Toole's arrangement was better for her. I'd spent all my savings on that profligate season at Stratford and, my contract terminated, I now had no private income, only what I earned each week.

My brother-in-law, Derek Coombs, and his wife, Pat, were generous and tolerant. Their house and its comfort and security had an alarming effect on me. Arriving, I sat at the end of one of a pair of seven-foot couches and burst into tears. For two days I sat there and wept, rising only to see to Kate. I couldn't stop crying. The warmth and the comfort debilitated me completely. Derek and Pat looked in from time to time and just let me get on with it – whatever *it* was. Later, Pat said she thought I would never stop. She drove me to the train each day and picked me up at night and I marvelled at her kindness (I still do). She must have had better things to do with her time. I thought that my world had come to an end, but Derek and Pat didn't seem to understand this. I thought that if these good people understood how 'bad' I was and how my badness had led to the destruction of my life, they wouldn't want me under their roof. Sitting on the train to Stratford I wondered how on earth I had come through life before O'Toole with no carnal guilt. Now, I felt guilty about everything I'd ever done or felt.

Not only guilty but scared. Scared because not only was I heartbroken and sad, I was incompetent. All my life, through bad and good, I had been able to perform. Now, suddenly, at the beginning of this engagement with the RSC, I couldn't act. The prospect of walking on to the rehearsal set was terrifying. The prospect of 'doing it' in front of an audience was so terrifying that I couldn't entertain it. Was this the thing I'd only read about – stage fright – or was it life fright? To whom could I turn? There was no one except O'Toole and he was the prime 'fixer' and solver of acting problems. When he called me to see how Kate and I were doing, I slipped in an acting question. He responded immediately and effectively. Sensing I was in trouble, he told me to call him with a progress report. From that time on we talked acting every day. My tormentor had become my saviour. Wouldn't it be nice, I thought, if we could solve acting problems all the time? We seemed so hopelessly bad at everything else.

We didn't meet. I was informed by Jules that O'Toole had rented a mews house into which I and Kate were to move when the company moved to London. What did this mean? Did it mean that we would resume life with O'Toole? I couldn't ask.

One November morning weeks later we *did* meet. He met

my train from Birmingham and drove me to the theatre where I was rehearsing. Parking the car, he said. 'Bit of a problem. I'm to be taken to court because Anouilh is allowing *Becket* to be performed only on condition that I play Henry.' It was odd to be sitting so close to him. Reluctantly I acknowledged to myself, looking at his left shoe and his hand resting on his knee, that I loved him as passionately as ever. Focusing on his problem, I said, 'I very much doubt, saving your presence, that Anouilh has ever heard of you.' He looked at me for the first time, my conspirator, and an evil Irish smile suffused his face. 'Hmm,' he said. 'Maybe I'll just nip over to Paris.'

In Paris, it seems that John Huston's mistress at that time, the wonderful actress Suzanne Flon, also a friend of Jules and Joyce, took him to see Anouilh who said, 'I am enchanted to meet you but who are you?' Anouilh wrote a letter saying he did not care who played the part and by 10 November O'Toole was free to play Lawrence of Arabia.

We opened *The Duchess of Malfi* at Stratford while I was still living in Birmingham. Max Adrian, with whom I played my erotic scene, making love on a tombstone – he in Cardinal's robes – was a tower of strength. Stephanie Bidmead got me through the worst of my stage fright. O'Toole was wonderfully supportive on the phone (the house in Stratford had been given up and he was in London). I don't think I was very good but my sights were so lowered that I was grateful to be 'on stage', picking up my cues, making sense. It was the lowest point in my professional life but at least I was practising my profession – and that was something.

Why was I so passive about my living arrangements? The stuffing had been knocked out of me but I couldn't understand how I'd been brought so low, so fast. There must have been something in me – some infection at the core – that lay there waiting to be exposed, biding its time to spread through my system. O'Toole was the only person close enough to me to probe that core and his terrors happened to chime with my failings. We clung to each other like drowning people, incapable of helping one another, unwilling to let go. We both had an instinct towards health and we kicked away from each other, only to return for another possibly fatal embrace. But health lay in being together as well. Parting for good was inconceivable. It wasn't an option for me nor, it appeared, was it for him. I don't think I hoped for happiness but I couldn't stop trying for resolution. Ken Griffith's words came back to me: 'Do you really think you can sustain being Mrs Edmund Kean?' I loathed the romanticism, rejected the exaggeration of the notion of the wild, doomed genius. But, all the same, I *was* hitched to an acting genius, according to some and I *was* attempting the impossible.

When *Malfi* opened, the rollercoaster life at Mount Unpleasant had taken its toll and I was very far from being the healthy, optimistic, confident young woman who had arrived in Stratford at the beginning of 1960. I was doggedly following Helen's dictum, and managing without my 'wretched little ego' but it was hard to get through the days. I had no idea what life held in store for me. Was I to live in our London mews house alone? Sometime soon O'Toole was to go to Arabia to acclimatise; learn to ride a horse, a camel, stay with the Bedouin who were going to make a major contribution to the making of the film, learn some Arabic, get fit.

I was astonished to read in the newspaper that his contract stipulated that each month I, his 'cherished' wife, should be provided with an airline ticket to visit him in Jordan or wherever he might be filming during the making of the film. What did that signify?

We moved to the Aldwych Theatre and after *Malfi*, the company opened *Ondine*. Peter Hall's wife, Leslie Caron, was the water nymph and was ravishing but the play, like most of the French plays I was ever in, didn't travel well.

What a company it was, though. Peter Jeffrey, Ian Holm, Gwen Ffrangcon-Davies, Eric Porter.

So I returned to London to a little mews house in Hyde Park Gardens, a house rented for a year by our Company, Keep Films. O'Toole was in residence and charmingly anxious that I should approve the arrangements. Bemused, I settled in. It was as though the previous eleven months had not occurred. I was wary and faintly disbelieving as he took me out and we posed for magazine and newspaper features. My new helper – Swedish Marianne – was installed, Kate was promoted to a bigger cot and it seemed insane to embark on questions and recriminations. I wondered if I would ever lose the mistrust that had lodged in my system. I ignored it and faced forward, undeniably happy again.

Lonnie had moved on to a job cooking for the American boss of Pan Books just around the corner. It was a hectic job; he was all the help there was. He wore three uniforms in rapid succession each day. One for cooking, one for cleaning and one for serving drinks. On the evening of a dinner party, when the front door bell rang, he ran to answer it, tearing off his white cooking jacket and replacing it with a dark one as he majestically opened the door and took the coats. He served drinks wearing white gloves and from time to time hurtled back to the basement kitchen to keep dinner on track, tearing off his upstairs jacket as he ran. White gloves were replaced for serving at table. Occasionally, English food flummoxed him. One night the telephone rang at 7.00 p.m. and an anguished voice said, 'Siân! Siân! Hurry! Hurry! Tell me, what is this mint sauce they're talking about for the lamb. Is it meant to be hot or cold?'

Domestic life was sweet and calm. Even when Marianne dropped all O'Toole's precious 78 rpm jazz recordings and couldn't look up she was so horrified by what she'd done, O'Toole shook his head tolerantly and said, 'Accidents.' His behaviour was unnervingly benign. Then, a few days before

Christmas he went missing. I was upset but not as worried as I would have been a few months earlier. All our cars had been wrecked or abandoned and he was no longer driving so I had no fears for his safety. It was dismal preparing for a Christmas that might or might not happen. I trundled up the Edgware Road in the winter dark with Kate in her pram, assembling a small tree and coloured lights and presents and food. On Christmas Eve I said goodbye to everyone at the theatre and returned apprehensively to an empty house. Marianne left and Kate and I were alone. Obviously he wasn't coming home. Was it worth preparing a Christmas lunch – the first I'd attempted? Before I went to bed the front doorbell began ringing insistently. There was a great deal of noise in the mews and O'Toole was at the door, laden with presents for Kate, beaming with pleasure, so pleased with himself and pleased to be home that I didn't have the heart to spoil everything by pointing out that he'd been gone for days. After a bit he said, 'Have you looked out of the window?' 'No.' 'Why don't you?' There, sitting perkily outside the house was a powder blue Morris Minor car with a huge ribbon around its middle and a massive bow on top with a banner reading: 'Happy Christmas Siân, with all my love, your Peter'.

I struggled with a confusion of emotions; guilt for having thought that he wouldn't be home for Christmas, pleasure at being given such a magnificent present and fury at being given a present which he must surely know I wouldn't use. When I was at RADA I had been involved in a traumatic accident which had led to a spell of reconstructive surgery. My terror-soaked experiences in O'Toole's cars when he drove when drinking in Stratford, had left me with an abiding fear and hatred of the combustion engine. But it did look lovely, sitting out there, motionless. The atmosphere in the room became positively Dickensian as we hugged our good fortune to ourselves. The fire glowed, Kate beamed, my recipe book was open at the page reading 'How To Cope With Christmas'.

The days that followed were happy until O'Toole, deciding that he would like to bid farewell to Bristol before leaving for Arabia, borrowed my car and, while I went back to the Aldwych, drove west on his sentimental journey. In bed after the performance I was awakened by the phone. 'Is that Siân?' 'Yes.' 'Ah, well' – West Country voice – 'now I'm very sorry about this but I'm afraid we've had to lock Pete in the cells. We thought you ought to know.' 'We' was the constabulary. Jules, awakened in turn, promised me that he'd take care of things. He rang me back to say that O'Toole, much the worse for wear, had absently driven 'my' car, full of actors, into the back of a police car which in turn was full of dozing policemen, who weren't best pleased. He was processed through the court with the minimum of fuss and the maximum of dispatch and packed off home by train. I never saw the car again and I was pleased about that. On this occasion it truly was the thought that mattered.

# Chapter Fourteen

There was excitement in the small house as O'Toole prepared to leave England in the early part of 1961. The film company had set up an office in Amman in Jordan and another, the home office, in Mayfair in London and mail was sent to and fro in the company bag. Filming was not due to begin until May but the preparations were well under way. The King was firmly on board as an ally and had placed the army and his own Bedouin desert patrol at the service of Horizon Pictures. I was told that O'Toole would be sent into the desert and would be completely out of reach of the phone or letters for long periods. We had been enjoying a wonderful time and I didn't like the thought of being separated for so long but in a way it was fortunate that we had endured that time of misery at Stratford. Being apart was not going to be much fun but it wasn't as bad as parting unhappily or even living together unhappily. The alcohol consumption had already been reduced drastically; in Arabia drink would have to be banned completely except for the odd infrequent break in Beirut, the nearest fleshpot. The heat at times would be over 120 degrees and we learned that it is impossible to live and work in that heat encumbered by a hangover.

This piece of information was part of a comprehensive briefing that took in manners and morals as well as food, drink and hygiene. O'Toole was reading everything that had been assembled for him; Lawrence, his campaigns, the geography of Jordan, religion, the background history of the 'fertile crescent', and we were meeting people who were involved with Lawrence himself. Anthony Nutting had been appointed advisor; an expert on Middle East affairs, he was a wonderful source of information and good gossip. Lunch with Captain Basil Liddell Hart at his house in Medmenham brought home to me the scale and nature of this job. Even to me it no longer felt like a job; this was the biggest adventure of a lifetime. Making a movie on this scale was a bit like mounting a military operation. I was aware that, David Lean apart (his confidence in O'Toole was absolute), there were doubts again about the maverick Irishman. Would he be able to submit to the unrelenting discipline, the physical hardships that awaited him? Did he have the strength of character? How would he manage, hundreds of kilometres from the nearest water let alone a welcoming bar? Did he have the 'right stuff' in him? The whispers were incessant. It was Stratford all over again. I had no doubts at all. I knew how hard he drove himself when he was working. I also knew that he wanted this film and all that it would bring. Jules, knowing as neither of us could that O'Toole's life was about to change completely, asked O'Toole suddenly one night, 'Do you *want* this? *Really* want it?' There was no need to answer yes as their eyes met. In his words, he wanted it so much he could taste it.

I buried any nervousness I may have felt about our future and joined in the excitement. I was ashamed to admit even to myself that the future frightened me. I was not at all sure that *I* wanted all this. I was not even sure that I would have a part in it. I was not sure that I liked the film world. I didn't voice any of these doubts and braced myself against the trial of the coming months which Kate and I would spend alone. 'Months?' said someone. This picture is going to take over a year and then some. My heart sank. Smart restaurants, interviews, photo sessions, eight shows a week at the Aldwych for me, and too many people packing into our small mews house, an endlessly ringing telephone, happy noise – and then silence. He was gone. It was as though he'd taken all the colour and light with him. For a week I mourned and moped and grieved then

I began to look about and realised how very fortunate I was in my job, in London, in Hyde Park across the road, in the shops of Connaught Street, in my lovely bedroom in the front with Marianne and Kate tucked in at the back but I couldn't even imagine what the desert was like. What his new life was like.

Naturally, during the bad times at Stratford my eczema, which I had suffered since childhood, had raged out of control and I'd developed abscesses inside my ears. At the theatre this was a problem. I was getting over my bout of stage fright but many nights at the Aldwych I couldn't hear anything much; it was like acting in a thick fog. My friend in the company, Stephanie – Steve – Bidmead who, having had health problems of her own and overcome them, recognised a fellow casualty and took me under her wing. She made coping with the deafness into a game. On stage or watching me from the wings, she would raise an index finger a mere centimetre and that meant 'speak up' and lower it fractionally to mean 'stop shouting'. Once I had arrived at the correct pitch she'd give me a big wink and get on with her own performance. Gradually, I learned to tell if I was too loud or too soft by the feeling in the resonators in my face but without Steve I don't know how I would have survived the early months of 1961.

The first wonderful letters had begun to arrive from Jordan. I read them over and over again, sometimes I read them aloud to Kate who looked benign and indifferent. I pinned a photograph of her father near her playpen. This was foolish, I know, but I was not quite sure how to behave and I was also sure that Mr Spock didn't tell me everything about babies in general and Kate in particular. I sang her the song that O'Toole composed for her and used to play to her on his guitar (the only thing which had survived Stratford unbroken and which had now been packed and sent to Jordan).

> Why do I laugh? Why do I sing?
> Why is there music? Birds on the wing?

Kate is charming
Kate is charming

Who knows? Maybe she recognises it, maybe not. I'm not sure of anything. Looking back at my younger self a mere year ago I cannot believe that I was ever so confident, so sure of myself. Now I'm uncertain of everything and, in particular, unsure of my own ability. It seems that once one's confidence is destroyed, nervousness seeps into every area of existence. I look at Kate and she looks back at me and I wonder am I doing right by her? We're a bit like a couple of comfortably installed hostages. I've learned to organise and manage and we share an orderly life but a life lacking in spontaneity. There is nothing to indicate when my period of atonement for my past might end – maybe never. I have overcome the pointless fits of frustration at not being able to do anything to put matters right. My childhood dream of having done something so bad that it is unpardonable and unforgivable has come true and all I can do is to ensure that I lead a life which is, and is seen to be, beyond reproach. My old, pre-O'Toole life is as though it never was.

I have a few new, permitted friends and acquaintances; Jules and Joyce keep an eye on me, Derek Bowman, a journalist on the old *News Chronicle*, comes round and patiently picks the bits of ham out of the omelettes I absent-mindedly make for him. Tom Stoppard, an old friend of O'Toole's from Bristol, temporarily fills the space I like to reserve in my life for the person-a-million-times-cleverer-than-I and brings me out-of-print books. He's going to be a full-time writer. John Libson, our accountant's son, soon to be an accountant himself, rescues me from the ladies' seminary I've created for myself and takes me for spins and Chinese meals. He, also, is a lot cleverer than I am and solves domestic problems as well as fiscal ones. Stephanie Bidmead stays over sometimes and we talk about everything except my private life. I don't think that she knows O'Toole at all. If she does, she never mentions him. Then – heaven sent – Marie Kean arrives from Dublin to do some filming in London. Now we're four girls in this little house. Marie and I step out after the show at night and within days she raises my spirits. I doubt that I'll ever again be as high-spirited as I once was but this will do to be going on with and I thank God for Marie, the funniest woman I know.

As the season draws to a close, O'Toole begins agitating for me to end the engagement. Understandably, since the Royal Shakespeare Company took him to court over *Becket*, he's taken against Stratford in a big way. This is a shame and inconvenient for me. My natural 'home' is obviously in the theatre and my natural place in the theatre is obviously within a permanent company. It is equally obvious that to make my life in the Stratford company would be regarded by O'Toole as totally disloyal, almost grounds for divorce. I don't know how I'm going to proceed but I do know that I have to finish at the Royal Shakespeare, go to Jordan (which I want to do) and only then come back and worry about my future. The values of the Forties and Fifties still prevailed in the Sixties and it would have been unacceptably disloyal of me to have defied my husband and thrown in my lot with people whom he regarded as enemies at that time. My mother had told me that I would have to stand in a very small place to make this marriage work and I was prepared to do that but I was quite unprepared to give up my work. I would try to have it all.

I have changed agents and am now represented by John Redway & Associates but I am being held to my contract with MCA and am paying two lots of ten per cent on every job. O'Toole is going to be paid £13,500 for making *Lawrence*. The other actors will make a great deal more but Jules says this is all fine and all is going according to plan – whatever that is. He doesn't say. My RSC salary is completely swallowed up by the cost of employing Marianne, the nanny, and the cleaner who comes with the house. During the day I'm able to do radio work and I make commercial recordings of plays as well so I get by but I do have to keep working.

Alarmingly, people assume that I don't need to work now that I'm a 'film star's wife'. They also assume I might not *want* to work and that if I do, I'll want to do only very smart work. These are problems which I had not anticipated. Even more worrying is the attitude I detect in my own camp. Keep Films, our company, is establishing itself; accountants, book keepers, lawyers, secretaries are being assembled. Naturally, everything exists because of O'Toole and everyone's effort is directed towards his work and well-being. I am very much a willing part of this team and I can see that my co-operation is essential to the enterprise but I am mortified to realise that my work hardly figures. It's as though my life before Stratford is completely wiped out. I'm known as a wife on a difficult assignment, a mother and – oh yes – an actress. Sort of. (Nice for me to have something to do in my spare time now that O'Toole's away.) Jules, who is genuinely fond of me and whom I like hugely and depend upon hugely, is heard to say, 'It's all right for her to work so long as it doesn't get in Pete's way and so long as he isn't embarrassed by her.' This is crushing but this is my life now and somehow I shall have to find a way of surviving as an actress. To protest and to demand a toe-hold of my own would be perceived as grotesque and graceless. This is 1960 and women – wives – are meant to be help-meets not strident nuisances. And this *is* a great, important and testing time for O'Toole and I *do* want to help. In the back of my mind I harbour the hope that, when he is able, and if ever he is able to accept the fact that I was not a virgin bride, O'Toole will be my ally and help me out of this difficult situation. He may disapprove of my past but he does also love me, and to others – never to me – he is extravagant in his praise of me. Michael Langham says that when he was thinking of mounting a production of *Cyrano*, O'Toole, approving my casting as Roxanne, wrote: 'Her voice is a great bell that rings in my heart.' To Marie he said, 'I'm marrying the best young actress in the country.' This astonishes me. I feel like a goose girl with bare feet over whom O'Toole has thrown a beautiful cloak that hides the rags underneath. I may have to buy my own shoes.

*Ondine* at the Aldwych comes to an end. The parts I've played have not suited me much – or rather, I don't feel that I've been able to do anything with them. For many reasons the season has been an uphill climb all the way. I'm not sorry to come to the end of it but I am desperately sorry to leave the company. Two recent memories of the play; exquisitely beautiful Leslie Caron in the title part, and the night when, processing as part of the Court up from the orchestra pit, on stage right and moving diagonally up stage and off, stage left, I felt my fourteen-foot train (suede, trimmed with fur, designed to look like velvet – don't ask) to be more than usually difficult to negotiate. Looking back I saw my Mother, the Queen, in the person of Gwen Ffrangcon-Davies on her hands and knees on my train, myopically peering at it in a puzzled way and presumably wondering why the stage cloth was moving. I dragged her about thirty feet but she seemed none the worse for wear when she was helped up in the wings. (Not a titter from the respectful audience.)

Kate has been taken to Wales to stay with my parents who are delighted to have her all to themselves. With a few pairs of trousers and a lady-like divided skirt and a sun dress for private wear and a few pairs of long-sleeved garments so as not to offend anyone on the street, I'm heading for the Middle East. I've been reading all O'Toole's research books but I don't really know what to expect.

Travelling in a nice new American tweed suit, I walked into a wall of heat in Amman Airport. Exhausted and overpowered by the heat, I immediately fell under the spell of Jordan. The flight had been endless. Hungry, I looked longingly at a street vendor's tray of pungent food. 'Uh-huh,' said the Columbia official as he followed my glance, 'never. Not ever. Asking for trouble.' The car bumped along what was little better than a dirt road and we drove to the best hotel in Amman, the Philadelphia, a ramshackle affair with flimsy doors and furniture – but still those wonderful spicy smells everywhere. And the sounds! Chaos in the street below and on the radio, music that seemed to go on and on and on without a break. 'Ghastly din you can't get away from,' said my American escort. I looked at him in his beautiful jacket and slacks and polo-necked cotton shirt, shiny shoes, manicured hands and thought he must be having an awful time since he didn't seem to like anything about the country. I couldn't wait for him to leave. Before he abandoned me for the night – in the morning I was to be taken south to Aqaba where O'Toole was based – he pointed out the Royal Palace on the dusty hill, one of the 'jebels' I'd been reading about. It was an undistinguished, squat, sandstone house and on another hill there was a biscuit-coloured piece of suburbia where Columbia Pictures had made its home.

Left to myself, I leaned out of the window (arms covered in case anyone looked up) and marvelled at the scene below. There didn't seem to be a rule of the road, or if there was no one observed it. The men in their robes looked exactly like the men in every drawing I'd ever seen in childhood Bible classes. I'd never been in a place where everything matched up to my mental picture of it, but I couldn't have known what the sound would be like, or the smell. I don't know how long I hung out of my window before the muezzin began to chant and the wonder was complete.

Reluctantly, I withdrew into the spacious, ugly room and began the long struggle to summon room-service and, having eventually raised someone, to order some food – *any* food – and then to get it delivered. When eventually it came it was nothing like the delicious concoctions sold on the street. This being the best hotel, the food was a muddled attempt at European hotel food, but nothing could lower my spirits and I ate the grey meat and watery boiled vegetables, then bathed in tepid water and, lying on top of my artificial silk bedspread, fell into a deep, contented sleep.

In the morning I woke early, dressed and hung out of the window until the company car arrived to take me to Aqaba. Breakfast was a bit of bread left over from dinner. I couldn't face another struggle with room service. It became hotter and hotter as we descended to the southern coast. The heat in the car was almost unbearable. The heat outside was just as bad. We passed no other traffic, occasionally I saw a little cluster of small dried mud-coloured houses that looked as though they'd been assembled from a child's outsized building kit. When I saw a few Bedouin on their camels I swallowed hard and pointed. The driver nodded, bored. I almost burst into tears; I had never, ever seen anything that looked so totally *foreign*. Everything, every single thing that was happening was intoxicatingly new and unknown – maybe unknowable. By the time we drew into the tiny settlement that was Aqaba and bumped along the track to the Columbia Pictures encampment on the shore of the Red Sea, I already felt in some way altered just by being in this place. I wasn't concentrating on myself and certainly wasn't ready for what greeted me.

# Chapter Fifteen

Aqaba – a dirt track through a sketchy village then, slightly apart, a military-style compound; a dining mess, a few hastily thrown up rooms around a cement yard on a beach bordering the Red Sea, rudimentary lavatories, showers and a few un-smart trailers. The film was in pre-production, O'Toole was one of the very few actors present and he'd been installed in a trailer. There was very little room. The walls were completely covered with sheets of paper on which he'd hand-written useful Arabic phrases and a daily addition of ten words to a growing vocabulary. One end of the trailer was filled by the over-sized bed. There were no home comforts but there was Arabic, Arabic everywhere, then books, papers, and a little ledge holding soap, towels, toothpaste and brush and bottles of Ambre Solaire. I had very little luggage and I found a small cupboard where I could stow my things. O'Toole was wearing long boots, trousers, cotton shirt and a belted cotton robe, his camel-riding gear. We were both shy and tentative as we greeted each other. He looked extraordinary, a thousand times fitter and healthier than he'd ever looked, his eyes were clear and for the first time in his life he was tanned, his curly black hair had been straightened and bleached. He looked – I couldn't quite think what he looked like. Then it came to me. He looked like a movie star.

Someone brought us tea. The heat was stifling. He began to pass on to me the lessons he'd learned about how to live here and in the desert where he would take me soon. He'd been living with the Bedouin camel-patrol as they travelled around the desert and clearly he'd formed a great attachment to them and their way of life. It sounded wonderful to me. He described the nights sitting outside the black tents, grateful for the cooler air after the horrendous heat of the day. They would sit, leaning on their saddles, still holding the sticks they held in their right hands while riding. Total silence, except for the occasional noise made by a sleeping camel and no conversation, unless someone had something useful or amusing to say. I couldn't quite imagine the absence of small-talk. Silence in society makes me feel uneasy. They would draw meaningless patterns in the sand with their sticks and the patterns looked like exquisite Arab calligraphy.

Enthralled, I forgot the heat and my inappropriate clothes. When could *I* go to see The Boys, as he called them? The atmosphere changed at once. 'Maybe not at all' was the reply. It was a totally male society. Women were never seen. I began to wonder where I would fit, even temporarily, in to this new life O'Toole was experiencing. He continued to talk about these wonderful people, their skills, their hospitality, their code of honour and I realised with dismay that we were moving into the familiar territory of my *lack* of 'honour'. It wasn't possible, was it, that we were reprising the awful, circular debates of our wretched months at Stratford, debates that I had assumed to be behind us for ever. Exhausted and incredulous, I couldn't think of anything to say except 'Well, shall I go home then?' I sounded cheap and chipper. 'Maybe that would be best,' was the reply and O'Toole slammed out.

I sat there in the little oven of a trailer. I had loved the journey, I loved what I'd seen of the country, I longed to go into the desert, I longed to be reunited with O'Toole. A part of me had now become so accustomed to failed expectations, to finding that nothing turned out the way I expected it should do that I didn't waste time crying. I began to puzzle out whom I should talk to in order to get a car back up the length of the country north to Amman. The door opened, O'Toole entered and swiftly, without speaking, we fell into each other's arms and laughing and crying we started all over again. It was the beginning of one of the best times of my life.

I'd thought I was a brisk creature of damp and cold, changing skies, winds and mountains and now I'm gladly ravished by the baking, dry, unbearable heat, the cloudless skies, the slow pace one has to learn in order to survive the long day between dawn and sunset. O'Toole gets us both up at five in the morning and we drink sweet tea with mint and shower and dress and tidy our tiny living space before the heat begins. We lie in the sun for ten minutes only; the rest of the time we stay covered up like the Arabs. Nevertheless, very quickly, I become brown and my hair bleaches itself. I've never looked like this before.

Gradually I meet the huge unit. Phil Hobbs, the location manager, has built a large village here, some of the men already dislike the climate and the lack of comfort (with much more hardship to come when filming starts) and they begin to ask to be sent home. The airlines are doing a brisk trade. It seems to be the luck of the draw; hating this place or loving it. There are very few women here. Barbara is the continuity girl and she's already up to her eyes in work. The most colourful members of the unit, the property master and his brother, Eddie Fowley and Dave, live slightly apart from everyone else and Eddie has his wife, Doris, with him but she is never seen except at night when Eddie returns from the day's 'recce'. Leila Lean, David's Indian wife, is installed in one of the concrete bunkers, windows shaded against the light. She's brought over a hundred saris with her and a huge, stringed instrument irreverently referred to as the 'joke banjo'. She doesn't emerge during the day. David has already gone into the desert and doesn't return to base.

Eddie Fowley is an amazing man. Blackened by the sun, stripped to the waist, he's ready for anything. I'm told that he's the man who built *and blew up* the bridge on the River Kwai. He has a large truck and no matter what outlandish request is made to him, he lifts his head belligerently and bites out a command, 'DAVE! In the *TRUCK*!' He speaks in capital letters and he's never been known to be found wanting. David Lean rightly treasures him.

People in these early stages are still trying to shake down into some bearable kind of life together, getting ready for the long, hard haul. I've never been on a location like this (I don't suppose there *are* many movies planned on this scale). The problems are mind boggling; I listen in the mess as they begin to discuss the question of trucking water, daily, hundreds of kilometres into the desert, some of it uncharted. How much water is needed by each person daily? Canvas villages will have to be erected, latrines dug, field kitchens built at speed. Huge quantities of salt tablets are flown in and every table has a huge jar of them along with the HP and ketchup. If you forget to take regular handfuls, with no warning at all you gently keel over as you stroll along. Sweat dries even as it's produced and sometimes one is so dehydrated that three tablespoons of salt in a glass of water have no taste at all. Occasionally we walk into the village proper. There's nothing much there but there is a lean-to café and we begin to eat forbidden local food – it's delicious – much nicer than our British-style canteen food. Leila Lean accompanies us and is grateful for the change of diet. We suffer no ill effects. The unit doctor shakes his head reprovingly. There is a Mayor of Aqaba and he sits outside his run-down house looking across the bay at the Jewish settlement, another small village, Eilat, which seems to be full of builders and – especially – electricians. It changes daily and one can just make out that they're building and installing lighted signs. It's odd to be sitting on this side of the bay, one mile and three or four hundred yards away from the Jewish side. Barbed wire divides the two places, the divide is mined, I'm told, and the stretch of no man's land is patrolled by soldiers in long frocks and bandoliers. What is the Mayor thinking as he sits hour after hour playing with his beads and glowering moodily across the bay? He's a bit jealous, I'd say.

Sam Spiegel, the producer of the film, is, of course, Jewish and his yacht is moored in the bay. He daren't come ashore, which pleases David Lean no end (no interference). There's trouble when the rumour is put about that this is a Jewish film with a Jewish unit. King Hussein comes to the rescue and drives into the desert to address the army and especially the camel patrol – his special 'boys' – and says he is entrusting the safety of the enterprise to them. They adore him – this is like watching Henry V on the eve of Agincourt – they'll do whatever he asks them to do and it's pretty plain that he loves them, as well. It's very unlike home.

The King is sophisticated. Sam tries to be smart. When the concept of Ramadan is explained to him he nods sagely and says, 'Ah yes. Just like our Lent.' The King is kind enough to pretend he didn't hear.

O'Toole and I on a rare visit to Amman are invited to the Basman Palace. It's very, very modest. Not pretty. We sit in large British-style, uncut moquette armchairs and are mightily impressed by the King, who is small with a bass voice and a wonderfully handsome head. I reflect that he's lucky to be a king not an actor; it would be such bad luck to be so handsome and so much smaller than the most petite of actresses. People – not just the Bedouin – love him. Over and over I'm told how brave he is; recently he had his appendix out without anaesthetic and walked out of the operating room. I'm suitably impressed.

Not long into Operation Lawrence, the King takes a fancy to the chief telephone operator at the production office. John Sullivan, the charming, good looking head of stunts and O'Toole's stand-in and companion, steps out of the romantic frame and, within the year, Miss Gardiner becomes Queen of Jordan and the phones never really work properly again. It's a bit like Alice in Wonderland here. Anything can happen.

Finally, I'm to meet the Bedouin – not in the desert – on a piece of scrub behind the little town. O'Toole and about six Bedu are practising with their camels. Racing camels are called *thalools*. They go from zero to thirty miles an hour in under a minute. The motion, I'm told, is almost impossible to understand and being a horse rider doesn't help because the camel rocks forward and back and up and down and you don't know what to do for the best. We do a lot of greeting and bowing. I'm decently covered and wear a divided skirt and desert bootees and socks. They seem very jolly – full of jokes – and contrive to look blood-thirsty as well, hung about with guns and bullets. I understand as they gesture towards me and one of the camels that I'm being asked if I'd like to try riding. Shooting a glance at O'Toole, who is good humouredly non-committal, I say, 'Why not? Well, of *course* I want to try.' It seems polite. They show me how to lock my legs around the pommel, hand me a whip and up rises the camel.

Well, this isn't too bad. It's rather lovely, being so high up, trying to get the hang of the motion as the beast begins to walk on. I look at them for approval; they nod. We're all in a good mood. Stepping forward, the man who seems to be the leader lifts his whip and, smiling broadly, gives my camel a brisk crack along the backside. I can only just hear the beginning of merry laughter behind me. I'm rocking at speed forward and back, hitting the big wooden 'nails' of a pommel front and back with each horrible movement. Lurching up and down and sideways I land just to the left of the saddle, then to the right. This seems to go on forever before I fall off. Well, no, I *don't* fall off, I hang upside down, my legs and feet are locked and I know that so long as they stay locked I can't *possibly* fall off and no power on earth is going to unlock my legs. I thank God quickly for all those years of training at gymnastics. I may be hanging upside down but I'm staying calm. But where are we going? I lift my head slightly and see that we're heading in the direction of a lot of barbed wire. Land mines? No man's land? This is not good. I'm thinking what to do when I sense another camel tearing along and overtaking me. The rider begins to beat my camel about the nose and she begins to turn in a circle and turning, decelerates, eventually slowing down to walk. I'm able to hoist myself back up into the saddle. The rest of the company has caught up with us. They're still laughing! I nod and smile and roll my eyes to heaven. I can see that this is one of the funniest things they've experienced in days. Too late, I remember – they love practical jokes. Down goes the camel and off I get, very shaky in the legs. 'After all that would you like to go back to the trailer?' asks O'Toole solicitously.

'Mmm – maybe.'

'You all right?'

'FINE.'

'Okay, then.'

A small jeep is summoned and I bump back into camp. Blood is now seeping through my shirt front and back and I stand in the shower to peel it off. Half a bottle of Dettol and a tin of lint and plasters later I'm as good as new. And when after lunch O'Toole sees my torn midriff and back I'm able – truly – to say that I'm just fine. Actually I'm more than fine. I feel I've passed some kind of test. I'm having the time of my life.

Thanks to The Boys, O'Toole is now a really good camel rider. I'm overcome with admiration. No one prepared him for all this at RADA. He's learning to keep his eyes open in the blinding light of the sun. They're pale blue and sensitive to light and all he wants to do is scrunch up his face and close his eyes but that isn't going to do. I can see why he's so fit – this is like being in the army except the hours are longer and he'll have to wear a bit of make-up. The day arrives when I'm to be taken into the desert to the black tents. We pile into a jeep with enough cigarettes for us both, a shovel for going to the loo and a straw mat for digging out when we get stuck, a compass and off we head into the desert.

Hours go by. He's becoming used to this terrain; we're miles away from Aqaba and I don't see how he knows where to go, there isn't a road. Occasionally we get bogged down and have to lay down the mats in order to get started again. It's incredibly *clean* here. When we stop the silence is profound – no birds, no insects, hardly a breeze today.

Suddenly O'Toole nudges me in the ribs. There, ahead in the distance, is the most romantic scene imaginable: in the middle of nothing, the long, low, worm-like shapes of the black tents – woven wool with rugs hanging from the 'roofs'. Camels are lying alongside and they *do* look like moored boats, necks raised like elegant prows. As we approach Getaifan Abu Tai (the grandson of the great Auda, played by Tony Quinn) emerges, dropping the door flap behind him. The women are inside the harem and we won't see them. We're invited to sit, and leaning against the large camel saddles on the ground I fondle a pommel, exploring the large, flat head of the nail-like shape, which crashed into me not so long ago. Greetings are elaborate and take a while. Then small cups of tea are prepared, sweet, sweet tea with mint, '*shai ma nana*'. I've learned the basics, '*hamdilla*', '*shwkran*' and '*afwan*', and nothing else. We sit under a black awning, shaded from the sun and are joined by three or four men, all in full fighting rig.

The men have become fascinated by some of the paraphernalia of film-making. Mascara has become a favourite toy, little mirrors also. Laying down their rifles, they peer at their eye make-up admiringly and laugh with pleasure. Occasionally you see these fierce-looking soldiers stroll hand in hand past the tents where the wives and children remain out of sight until the strangers are gone. It looks unselfconscious and totally charming. And here's the famous social silence I've been hearing about. We smile at each other – the formalities have been observed and we lapse into quiet. They draw patterns in the sand with their canes. I find I'm doing the same with my index finger. At first I have a real compulsion to fill in the pauses but once the pause is beyond help there's scarcely any point. Occasionally, catching someone's eye, I exchange a smile. Intermittently, someone does say something – there isn't necessarily a reply and the silence continues. Once I've become accustomed to this I find a wonderful state, a state of wakeful relaxation. Nothing need happen, nothing needs to be said. Hours go by and we finally take our leave, return to the jeep and make for the long drive back to camp. I realise that now *we* are hardly talking to each other either.

Night falls and the sky above and all around seems to dip below the line of the earth. I've never been so aware of the night sky and the stars and I wonder if I might be able to stay overnight out in the desert some time. We have supper and I go to bed. O'Toole works on his vocabulary while I try to assimilate the experiences of the day. One thing I realise now is that the desert Arabs are a good deal more sophisticated and tolerant than their small-town brothers. In the heat I took off my jacket revealing a very short sleeved bodice. No one batted an eyelid.

This was the first of many visits to the black tents. Much later that year we sat for hours with Getaifan and his friends and after we'd made the long trip back to base camp by Jeep there was a flurry of activity and shouts in Arabic. Looking out, we saw Getaifan, who'd galloped after us on his camel. While we'd sat there with him, his wife, inside the tent, had silently given birth to a baby – a girl. He wanted to know if he could name her after me. Later, on a rare break, O'Toole and I made for Beirut and in the gold market we bought Siân Abu Tai, Auda's great grand-daughter, a gold chain and we hung a ruby on it. On our return we gave the chain to Getaifan to give to his wife and when we next visited him he beckoned to me to come inside the back tent. It was an honour to be allowed into the women's quarters; dark and cool and hung with bright carpets and shawls, Siân was produced and unwrapped from yards and yards of swaddling clothes and there was her necklace, fastened round her belly with the ruby nestling in her navel.

That was the only time I was allowed inside the black tent. I was however invited to a Mansaf. O'Toole, who was acquiring Lawrence-like status in the desert, was asked to settle a blood feud between two families. We sat for hours in the shadow of the ruin of a Crusader castle while our interpreter did his best to guide us through the byzantine complexities of this ancient family row and when everything was settled to everyone's satisfaction, as darkness fell, a huge fire was lit and a sheep was killed and cooked and we ate it – *all* of it. I was ravenous and it was delicious – *all* of it. Meat was a rarity and we felt very privileged to be allowed to share what was truly a feast.

The first day of shooting arrived. The long preparation came to an end around the time of my birthday in mid May. I accompanied O'Toole and the unit into the farthest reaches of Jebel Tubeiq. Here and there are faint traces of eighth-century settlements. It is vast; one of the most inhospitable, awe-inspiring places on earth and, on the face of it, a mad place in which to try to shoot a movie. We received a message to join Eddie Fowley, with rough directions as to where we'd find him. After a long bumpy drive we came upon the truck in the huge empty landscape. Eddie had produced a roll of plastic 'grass', a table and striped umbrella, yellow paper daffodils – the Welsh emblem – and he served us 'cocktails' of fruit juice in glasses with little parasols and glacé cherries, all produced from the famous truck. I had been there for a month and now, when filming started, I went home, riding with one of the unit members on an errand to Amman. We got lost, we got stuck again and again and eventually reached the road that ran north-south through the country. Amman seemed incredibly noisy. I spent the night there and when I started a rare headache, prompted by misery at having to leave, someone sent out for some pills. When I got home to London Jules called me and said he'd just got a bill from the production office: 'Mrs O'Toole – one packet Aspirin'. We paid up.

# Chapter Sixteen

Back in London I missed O'Toole terribly. Picking Kate up from my parents' place in Wales, where they'd all had a wonderful time, I brought her back to Hyde Park Gardens.

Jules had decided that we could now afford to buy a permanent home in London; our situation had stabilised to the point where we both wanted to put down family roots. Lying on my couch suffering from flu, towards the end of the Aldwych season, I'd received a visit from Henry Woolf, a friend of O'Toole's from Bristol. He had presented what must have been the first performance of any Pinter play at Bristol University so I credited him with impeccable taste. I couldn't stir myself to go house-hunting and play in the theatre at night and I asked Henry if he would mind taking the house agents' lists and begin looking for a suitable house. After a few days he came back saying, 'Now, I know your top price is £8,000' (that was the price of a house in, say, Little Venice) '– but I've found a house which is £14,000 and needs *everything* doing to it and you *have* to buy it.' I went to see it. It was inconvenient, big, needed years of 'improvements' taken out, but it was beautiful and Henry was right, we *had* to have it. It dated from 1740 and was built on five floors, all listing slightly to starboard. There were big cellars that ran under Heath Street and it had been one of the group of five Hampstead houses where felons could be 'secured' overnight, before police stations were established. Ownership would give us grazing rights on the Heath. The top floor was level with the top of St Paul's Cathedral and there was an uninterrupted view, almost unchanged since the eighteenth century, down past gardens and small suburbs to the City. The view decided me. Promising Henry that should he ever need it one of the bedrooms was his, I put in a bid for £13,500 which we didn't have and dumped the problem of paying for it in Jules's lap.

O'Toole wrote wonderful letters from the desert – I wished I were there (maybe I would never return, I thought). I had left the RSC, as requested, and got myself a West End play produced by Peter Bridge. It was called *Lizard on the Rock*, written by John Hall, and was due to open in the West End in seven weeks' time and who knew when it would end? It didn't occur to me to take time off. Harry Andrews and Anthony Oliver were my leading men and it was a lovely company throughout that pitched in to help me when we went on the road and Kate – eighteen months old and now walking – came along as well, as did Marianne.

Kate had a badly 'wandering' eye so she wore patches and thick pebble glasses and had to endure her daily eye exercises. All the actors were careful with their language when she was around, solemn and adorable-looking with her owl-eyes.

However, on our last week on tour we walked into our bedroom and the first thing she did was to go over to the bed and test it for the quality of its mattress. 'Good,' she approved and then, dropping her little toy satchel, said cheerily, 'Oh fuck,' as she picked it up. Not a very good start, I thought. I looked at her, busying herself with settling into the room, and thought regretfully that maybe we should abandon the 'born-in-a-trunk' existence and establish a more conventional life and vocabulary for her.

The house is bought! I don't even *ask* Jules how he managed it. Joyce will help me 'do' it while I'm in the play. O'Toole will come home for a break in September and I'd like at least a part of it to be ready for him. Meanwhile our lease is up at the Mews and Marie Kean, who is working in London, Marianne, Kate and myself move temporarily to an apartment in a large building on the Edgware Road. It's hot and the noise with the window open is deafening. We keep it shut and swelter. I tread a path between the Phoenix Theatre, Heath Street in Hampstead and this very strange building on the Edgware Road. It *looks* quite grand but there's something odd about it. The corridors are spacious, the elevator doors elaborately decorated, but one morning the whole of the front large elevator has been removed and is lying across the corridor. There *was* a bump in the night, but now there's no one about. It's a bit like being on a sinister movie set.

The play has not, alas, been well received. It's the tail end of a verse-revival that began with Christopher Fry and continued with T. S. Eliot. The action takes place in Australia and as usual I have to toil away extra hard to achieve a tolerably presentable accent. Australians who see the play say, '*You* are what we sound like! People always exaggerate the sound of Australians.' My friends with good accents seethe.

As Heath Street was built and lived in for a long time by a family called de Guyon I re-name it 'Guyon House'. The last owner was the writer, E. Arnot Robertson, whose best-known book was *Ordinary Families*. Happily married to her sailing husband for the whole of her adult life, when he died, it's said she lost her will to live and her death was unhappy. The price of the house reflected this sad event. The dining room and the master bedroom are lovely, the stairwell is beautiful, but every other room (and there are lots of them) is a bed-sitter with a Baby Belling cooker and a sink. I keep meeting actors who've lived in the house. It's a piece of old Hampstead and in a way I'm rather reluctant to start dismantling and clearing it out, restoring the fireplaces and making up-to-date bathrooms.

The kitchen which lets on to the garden has the same beautiful bowed wall that rises almost to the top of the house and every deep window ledge, three to each floor, is piled high with bundles of letters and I long to start reading them but don't. One day when I go up to measure something or other, Mrs Robertson's son is building a bonfire in the garden – a bonfire of letters. Now I wish I'd stolen just one bundle.

Restoring the house is going to be a massive job – expensive as well. I wonder how long it's going to take me. 'Six months?' I enquire. Joyce Buck, who is going to help me, looks at me pityingly. 'It takes about five years to do a house like this properly.' Five years? 1965 before I'm through? I can't believe it. I questioned my other mentor in matters of building and decorating, Ricky, John Huston's wife who has just spent an age 'doing' St Clerans near Galway, one of the most beautiful houses in Europe, where I holidayed before Kate was born. She looked at No 98 and said, 'You should be through in five years.'

As usual, I hadn't thought through the practicalities of what I was up to. Now I began to learn about plumbing – *American* plumbing, plumbing that *worked* – wiring, lighting, how to recognise a good bit of furniture at the bottom of a pile of rubbish, learning what needed to be fixed, who could do the fixing, who was best at making lined, interlined, weighted curtains, where to find the best lamp makers, lamp*shade* makers. There was a never-ending list of things to be learned. And if something wasn't right, whereas my inclination would be to say wearily, 'Oh, I'll put a plant in front of it; it won't show,' Joyce made me take it back and have it re-done. Ricky Huston even criticised the look of the forty door hinges I'd bought and I had to take them all back and start another search for the perfect hinge. I was grateful for all the help and all the lessons but I was completely exhausted all the time because I was acting, as well.

Marie, Kate, Marianne and I moved into the house in despair that it would ever get finished. There wasn't a window that closed or a door that locked but none of us felt nervous; NW3 was a civilised, safe place. The nursery was finished – a beautiful Vie Bohème apartment at the top of the house, furnished, carpeted and curtained with a new bathroom and kitchen and sitting room and balcony and the view to St Paul's. Kate and her nanny, Marianne, were installed in style while Marie and I put our beds in adjacent rooms on the floor below and camped out. The play was over but I was still busy, now doing television. One morning – having done a gruelling, taped performance of a Shaw play with Cyril Cusack and Alan Badel at Granada the night before (it cost a fortune to stop the tape so you had to try to keep going) – I was awakened in my empty room in Hampstead by Joyce saying, 'Come on, come on! We're supposed to be in the Fulham Road looking at dressers in forty minutes.' I moved in a daze from antique shops to little basements full of promising treasures to rehearsal rooms, to studios.

My best moments that summer were spent at the BBC in Portland Place. Martin Esslin was presenting modern European plays and I was in quite a few of them and made my first acquaintance with Genet and Ionesco and Marguerite Duras. I couldn't believe my luck when I read that I was to play *The Afternoon of M. Andesmas* with Ernest Milton. We had a wonderful time together and I couldn't get over that amazing voice which I'd heard imitated by so many actors. *There* it was in the flesh and I was talking to it! He'd taught O'Toole at RADA, where he was adored by all the tearaway, young actors. He was a wonderful actor himself and had been an exquisite young man but, old now, he was undeniably, incredibly 'mannered'. O'Toole had seen him outside RADA in Gower Street chasing after a bus, crying, 'Staap! S t a a p! You're killing a genius!' I was very nervous around him at first but in no time at all we were sharing Chinese meals – still a bit of a novelty for me – in a restaurant on the first floor of a building above Boots in Piccadilly Circus. I'd always been fond of the company of elderly gentlemen and he came high on my list of Fascinating Old Men.

Life was good in Guyon House. The fine weather meant it didn't matter that the whole place was in uproar. Kate had

With Brewster Mason in *The Taming of the Shrew* at Oxford Playhouse in 1960 (*Studio Edmark*)

At 'Mount Unpleasant', with Jackie McGowran and Jill Bennett

In the *Duchess of Malfi* with Max Adrian and Pat Wymark at The Royal Shakespeare in Stratford, in 1960 (*Angus McBean © The Harvard Theatre Collection*)

With Joyce Buck and Kate in a pub at Stratford

My first camel ride in Aqaba

Watching the filming of
*Lawrence of Arabia* in
Jordan

At a mansaf in the desert
with O'Toole

In Beirut during a break from filming

In Seville with O'Toole during the last stages of *Lawrence of Arabia*

On tour with Kate during *Lizard on the Rock* in 1962

With Michael Bryant and John Phillips in *Gentle Jack* at the Queen's Theatre in 1963 (*Angus McBean* © *The Harvard Theatre Collection*)

With Wilfrid Lawson in *Strangers in the Room* – a play by Kenneth Jupp – in 1960

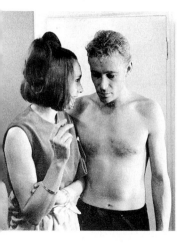

With O'Toole in his dressing room on the opening night of *Hamlet* at the National Theatre, Old Vic (*Jack Nisberg*)

The arrival of Pat in 1963 (*Independent Newspapers*)

In the film of *Becket* in 1963

With the family at Guyon
House (*Jerry Bauer*)

Marie Kean

My Father in 1961

Debbie Condon and Kenneth Jupp

Christmas in Venice, with (*from left to right*) Joyce Buck, my mother, Elizabeth de la Cour Bogue, Harry Craig, Joan Juliet Buck, Pat, Kate, myself and Shana Alexander

With Sam Beckett working on *Eh Joe?*
(*Michael Peto*)

With Mark Eden in *Night
of the Iguana* at the Savoy
Theatre (*Lewis Morley*)

Vivienne's portrait for her
exhibition during *Night of the
Iguana* (*Vivienne, London*)

her lovely flat and the rest of the house was an adventure playground for her – the garden was a wilderness and we began to explore the little streets behind the house. I bought a little boat for us to sail on Whetstone Pond. There was work to do at every turn but there was also calm, and Jules and Joyce saw to it that Marie and I saw a bit of high life as well. We were taken to the new White Elephant restaurant in Curzon Street – opened, so it was said, so a few prominent actors, Albert Finney among them, could dine in style *without wearing ties* (extraordinary in 1961). Life was changing; there was a wave of Italian restaurants. The owners and maître d's became as famous as pop stars, Leslie Linder at The Elephant, Mario and Franco in Soho and later all over the West End, were the top of the heap.

I was changing a little as well. I realised that my clothes weren't good enough for my social life. Marie laughed sardonically when she recalled how in the early days of our relationship with Jules and Joyce, I got 'decked out' as, she called it, in my only 'good' dress, a white shirtwaister from Jane & Jane with ropes of beads from a department store and high heeled gold shoes from Pinet. Arriving at the Bucks' front door, Jules greeted me warmly and innocently called up the stairs, 'Joyce, don't *dress*, honey.' I felt I'd better do something about my appearance but it wasn't easy. My head was faultless; my producer, Peter Bridge sent me to a new salon in Bond Street, owned by Vidal Sassoon, for a hair cut and colour job for *The Lizard on the Rock*. Vidal chopped off my perm and I emerged with dark red hair. (The author had specified smoky and I couldn't quite work out the connection but Vidal Sassoon was extremely confident and no one dared to argue with him.) I now had straight hair. Oddly enough, it looked just like that of my first form mistress, Miss Inkin, the person I'd most wanted to resemble when I was a little girl. (She *had* been ahead of her time in those days of upswept rolls and permanents.) Joyce Buck took me to a tailor who made me some plain dresses and jackets. I bought *plain* black and brown court shoes from Pinet. A *plain* black bag from Hermes, *plain* gloves from Harrods. Then, I discovered, at Liberty, clothes that I really liked; American clothes by a designer called Bonnie Cashin, wonderful, soft, unlined tweed, piped in coloured suede; canvas sports clothes, piped or edged in leather; swingy leather coats; cashmere sweaters with hoods; bean-bag caps in wonderful colours. I wasn't dressed '*up*' but I was *well* dressed in a way I liked. Evening clothes would just have to wait until I had more time and more money. Money was a bit of a problem. Every cent I earned was going into running the small household of women and dressing myself and taking taxis, a vice I wasn't to cure for many years to come.

One morning, as I was nervously setting out to make a recording of *Measure for Measure* with Eric Portman, I opened the morning post to realise that I just couldn't pay all the household bills that month. I stood at the top of the big house and was suddenly appalled by its size, and by the number of workmen scrambling around in it. Kate and Marianne sat at the breakfast table. How had I imagined all this was going to be maintained? I called Jules and, to my astonishment, he was completely unfazed and mightily reassuring and he said, 'And, of course, you should have an allowance.' Well! He – or rather, our office – would take care of the major building and decorating expenses and I would receive £60 a week with which to run our lives. I was completely enchanted and never thought to change that magic sum of unearned money which came my way henceforward. For the next twenty years I spent £40 on the house and each week I kept £20 of it for myself and thought myself very fortunate.

At work that week I was rather depressed. Eric Portman gave me his terrible cold. I *had* to show up but he didn't always show up and I lay under a grand piano nursing my temperature. Fortunately I'd played Isabella at RADA so I knew it quite well. When he did come to work he gave the impression of being overwhelmingly sad and I was glad when the job was over. Not for the first time I reflected that doing a part more than once was really difficult. If one had been – or thought one had been – good the first time round, one was very loath to alter the 'good' bits to suit a new production. If one hadn't been good in the part there was a feeling of desperation in the effort to get it right the second time around.

Months had gone by since I'd left Arabia. O'Toole and I had kept up an intense correspondence but we longed to see each other and he arranged my return. I took Kate down to my parents in Wales and left London as soon as I could. I was to fly out with Anthony Nutting and go straight to the canvas village in El Jaffre. El Jaffre, the huge, mercilessly hot plain, which made Tubeiq seem almost hospitable by comparison. My parents were overjoyed to be getting Kate again, the building works were coming along nicely and Joyce was spending a large part of every week in Hampstead overseeing the Irish team of builders. She never bought a spoon or a cushion or a table without taking me to see twenty spoons, cushions and tables and making me choose. I don't know where she found the patience. Slowly, I learned from her and soon my choices earned an approving nod from her. I was a good pupil but she was a wonderful teacher.

This time round the Middle East was even more enthralling than I'd remembered it to be. Many members of the unit had disappeared but the stalwarts were very much in evidence, thinner, more weatherbeaten and more determined than ever to see this film through to the end. O'Toole was more assured and he looked magnificent. He'd been having daily master classes in film-making from David Lean. (This job must be the equivalent of twenty ordinary ones.) Still there was A.G.Scott, (Scottie the Hair) successfully translated from Mayfair and in charge of the bleaching and straightening, still dapper and well-dressed; Charlie Parker, head of make-up, still cussing and feuding, being brilliant and impossible at the same time;

Eddie and Dave Fowley, indomitable, calm as though they were making a film on the back lot at Shepperton. Leila Lean was banished alas – her concrete bunker, never visited by David, was now occupied by an actor. We also were installed in a bunker at base and O'Toole had acquired a kind of 'body servant' Shwfti (what was his real name?). He would say, craftily, 'Shufti – *Mufti-Klefti*' (I see – I steal). It was hard to make life comfortable, even in a small way, and Shwfti would 'see and steal' little things to make our life cosier. He was a handsome boy, adept at killing vermin and keeping his eyes and ears open. Little happened in the camp that wasn't reported to O'Toole by Shwfti. He didn't travel into the desert and then I was glad of a reprieve from his constant twenty-four-hours-a-day presence, serving us, spoiling us, organising us, guarding our door day and night. O'Toole didn't seem to notice him but I was always aware of those inquisitive little brown eyes intent on interpreting our smallest change of expression. There were times when I couldn't accompany O'Toole to work and then to get away from Shwfti I would sit on the deserted beach reading or playing the guitar. If I was very still I would quickly become surrounded by hundreds of tiny sand-crabs. A deep sigh on my part was enough to make them disappear in two seconds. Eilat, across the bay, was pushing upwards; each night one could see more neon signs than before. The climate here on the Red Sea made life difficult so they must be spending a fortune on air-conditioning, unknown on this the Arab side of the barbed wire.

One day as I watched the filming, we were all crouched under umbrellas or in the shade of trucks while O'Toole, dressed in heavy khaki, sat mounted all day in the intolerable heat doing the same scene alone, time after time after time. No one knew *why* it was being retaken. No one could ask. The director was always God. I've heard that, great though David was, he liked to enhance his power by breaking down his leading actors, and when they were broken, build them up again so they became grateful or dependant. No one moved in this vast, silent landscape but I saw a few of the old hands exchange knowing glances. It did begin to look as though this was O'Toole's day for being broken down. I sat there under a truck knowing that O'Toole was *never* going to be broken down in this way. Calm and contained, he turned his animal and walked back along the camera track and waited patiently for the word 'Action'. Each take was faultless. Scotty looked pained. Even Charlie was subdued as he checked the make-up and walked slowly back to the unit, so far away from that solitary figure sitting alone in the hateful sun. Some eight hours later there was a simple word, 'Wrap'. It was the end of the day's work. O'Toole slid down from his horse and walked stiffly towards his jeep, parked in the distance. Everyone looked depressed. It had been a murderous day of unspoken conflict. Suddenly, I was compelled to run after David walking back to his vehicle. I didn't know him – I had hardly ever spoken to him. 'What in the name of God was all that about?' I demanded. His handsome face contorted as he replied, 'Actors! Actors! They have the easiest job going. Who gets here first in the morning? The technicians! And who gets the glory? *Actors!*' There was nothing to say to that and anyway I was now appalled by my cheek in ticking off a genius. We walked away from each other and I joined O'Toole in his jeep. He didn't ask what had occurred between me and David and I didn't tell him. I put my arm around his shoulders. Two things were clear to me suddenly. I couldn't bear to see him being badly treated, especially not at work where he was entirely correct in his behaviour and second, he had put me through so much that I had no fear of anyone. I had heard him say, 'I've been worked over by experts', well, so had I now. No one would ever be able to try me as he, the expert, had done. But now it was just a matter of getting through the evening quietly before he had to resume the fight tomorrow.

On the morrow, there was no fight. Work flowed enjoyably. David and O'Toole were sunny and the unit blossomed. Show business . . . When I was last here I was asked to help Maurice Ronet (the French actor who was to play Ali) with his English. David wanted him to play a scene on camera with Omar Sharif – newly arrived from Egypt. What no one knew was that Omar was to be looked at for the part Maurice had been engaged to play. David loved Omar and Maurice was dismissed (with $30,000, I was told. Seemed like a *lot* of money to me). O'Toole christened Omar 'Cairo Fred' and they were by now firm friends. They were the constant elements in the picture but all the big stars arrived to play supporting parts and O'Toole said he felt like a boxer waiting in the ring for the new heavyweight champ to show up. Anthony Quinn arrived and borrowed my eyelash curlers. He was on the run from a buxom blonde who pursued him all the way to Aqaba, God knows how she managed it. (I'm not sure that she didn't eventually succeed in getting him to the altar.) Things were altering at base. It was becoming clear in the film world that something extraordinary was going on and visitors began to arrive, never staying for more than a few days, with the notable exception of George Plimpton, who actually tried riding a camel.

Out in the desert everything remained inviolate – David saw to that. He and Barbara, the continuity, were, by now, living together. He and Barbara and Freddie Young, the brilliant lighting cameraman, formed part of a private nucleus in the huge unit. John Box, the designer, was another member of the closed circle. Every time I was around John I would pick up the crumpled drawings he discarded and threw away – wonderful drawings and watercolours which I straightened and ironed and packed away for framing at home.

There were wonders every day which I could hardly believe. In El Jaffre, the route to work was signposted by mirages, which never changed from day to day. The jeep travelled mile after mile over the chalk-white ground 'crazed' from the dry heat and when one saw 'Westminster Abbey' up ahead, one bore east until one came to 'The Lake' and turned north past 'Dickins & Jones' until one saw the real trucks and the real location. The landmarks remained constant, more real than reality. The silence of the movie set was always alarmingly wonderful. Everyone strained not to allow any of the detritus of our living arrangements to escape. A single paper cup rolling away across a virgin distant sand dune to be retrieved on foot was enough to stop work for hours. David and Freddie squinted at the sky and waited and waited for everything to be perfect while Sam Spiegel became mad with fury at the measured pace of filming. And, of course, he couldn't come into Arabia to see what was going on. David smiled evilly and sat in his chair happily waiting, waiting.

We took a short break in Beirut. The morning after we arrived in that most glamorous of cities, I leaned out of my hotel window and in the street below two men from the surrounding hills shot a young girl, a family member who'd brought disgrace on them by descending to a life of sin in the big city. 'What'll happen to them?' 'Nothing, it's their right.'

The Middle Eastern correspondent of the *Daily Mail* was someone O'Toole had known on *The Yorkshire Post* and we were invited to a drinks party in his flat. We passed a very pleasant hour or so and only afterwards did I have reason to remember a quiet chap we'd been introduced to that night – Kim Philby. It was unsettling, being in a city and I was glad to return to the desert. When I left Jordan this time I knew that I was unlikely to return. I realised that I'd rarely been happier, anywhere.

The month in the Middle East had gone by very quickly and I missed O'Toole but equally I missed the smells and tastes of the Middle East, and I missed the never-ending music incomprehensibly going on and on – and on. I didn't need reminding that if I weren't married to O'Toole and if he didn't wish to have me with him, I would never have experienced this adventure. I did however have an unexpected legacy from Arabia when I was suddenly presented with the ultimate in what I called Petruchio's servants, people who were undoubtedly good at something, but absolutely useless at what they had been engaged to do. When O'Toole finished in the desert, he determined to *do* something for Shwfti and contrived to send him to live with me and Kate and Marianne. To what end I had no idea. The house didn't suit him, our meals didn't suit him; he slept in Kate's small bedroom with a scimitar under his pillow. After the show I would return to find the small sitting room out of bounds to me as he lay, unsmiling, smoking on the hearth rug. His cigarettes smelled strange. One day, before a matinée when I'd cooked and cleared away lunch, I said, 'Shwfti, during the afternoon could you please wash the dishes for me?' He looked up from his favourite spot on the hearth rug and made no response. Holding the look between us, he slowly closed his hand on the wine glass he was holding and red wine and blood trickled down his wrist. There wasn't time to stop and discuss this new development in our relationship so I left for the theatre without another word. After that, mindful that to him I was a mere woman, I was tentative in my dealings with him. He began to explore London. I had no idea what he got up to but was relieved when a few weeks later he was picked up in Soho, arrested for drug dealing and deported. He was never mentioned again, the scimitar was tidied away and we repossessed the sitting room which smelled once again of Virginia tobacco.

The Hampstead house is progressing. Life is changing rapidly. People are taking an excessive interest in us as a family. One day I walk into an empty second floor room in Guyon House and find a journalist and a photographer poking about in a cupboard. The phone rings all the time with requests for photo sessions and interviews. The house, we are agreed, is not to become the subject of magazine layouts. For one thing,

O'Toole has begun to acquire art and the last thing we want to do is advertise to burglars that this might be a likely place into which to break and enter. Also, we want Kate to have a private life untroubled by publicity. Columbia Pictures' publicists are jumping up and down with irritation. I now have enough of the house done for O'Toole on his return to have a room in which to talk to people, a room with a bed where we can sleep, a front door that locks and for meals we'll just have to use the nursery kitchen or have picnics. Mercifully, food does not loom large on his domestic horizon.

On 28 September Sam shut down the production of *Lawrence* in Jordan. David was dismayed; there were many wonderful locations, Petra included, that would never now be used. And the charge at Aqaba would be the charge at – well, somewhere in Spain. The suspension of business was all to do with money and – contrary to popular belief – had nothing to do with screenwriter Robert Bolt's imprisonment; he was jailed in September 1961 after a CND demonstration in Trafalgar Square. It wasn't a horrible experience being jailed as he was in an open prison but they wouldn't let him write so it wasn't very convenient and, besides, Sam wanted Bob at his beck and call. He tried to persuade Jo Bolt, Robert's first wife, to cajole Bob out of jail. Little did he know that Jo had conceived a rich and abiding hatred of him and his way of life, and what it might do to their life (hers and Bob's). Finally, Sam convinced Bob that the entire unit would be thrown out of work if he didn't allow himself to be sprung. Shoulder to shoulder with the workers, Robert allowed Sam to secure his release and I don't think he ever got over the mortification of realising that he'd been 'Spiegalised'. His release was convenient for Sam and that was all. It earned him Jo's contempt and made him feel thoroughly guilty. Meanwhile the picture closed down in Jordan simply because Sam wanted it moved.

Activity at the house accelerates as O'Toole is expected home for a break. Everyone is feeling the strain. I desperately want him to be pleased with what I've done. This is our first real home and after a bad start our life together has moved, imperceptibly but surely into calmer waters. And I've made a friend. (Marie doesn't count. She is more like family.) During the run of *The Lizard on the Rock* throughout my visits to Vidal Sassoon I'm looked after by a young man; years my junior, still in his teens, but almost from our first meeting I sense that Ricci Burns is a friend – a potential friend anyhow. The changeable circumstances of my life make me slow to admit anyone beyond a certain point but I suppose only children always have their antennae out for potential brothers and sisters. Ricky feels like a potential brother. He seems to read my mind. He makes me laugh. He's smart where I'm naïve. He has a terrific sense of style. He's brutally honest with me but he's on my side. I'm immensely cheered to see him always. I think I'll keep him to myself for a while.

The homecoming is a stupendous success. The bags are laden with robes and coffee pots in three sizes and brass pestles and mortars for crushing cardamom seeds for future Arabic coffee (never made). There's beautiful, bad quality glass that breaks almost at once. O'Toole is bigger and handsomer than ever – he looks absurdly fit and if Kate doesn't really know who this is, like the rest of us she's fascinated and excited. We all want to touch him. The builders have stayed behind and share a glass of champagne with us as everything is inspected and admired. I have a feeling O'Toole at this moment is taking in little if any of the detail of plans for the rest of the house but we're all pleased and happy. What must it be like for him to be back in England after all these months and still only half way through this huge job. There's a break of at least four weeks and he'll have to keep everything bubbling in his mind in spite of the long pause and the inevitable distractions of London life.

After a few days' rest he begins to examine the house more closely and he falls in love with it; I can tell. Because of the complications of re-plumbing the old house, we've had to push many of the central heating pipes that festooned the dining room ceiling up into the room above and Joyce has had the notion of building a platform over them. This becomes the 'stage' and the room becomes the actors' Green Room. It's also known as the Marcus Luccicos room and there is a plaque on the door commemorating the character in *Othello* who is mentioned once, never appears and has no lines. Already it's the most used room in the house.

With one or two hiccups, he and I have been getting on better than I could have imagined during our Warwickshire life. I had not dared to hope that we could be as happy as this and the house seems to set the seal on this exciting, light-hearted phase in our life together. He runs up the ninety-seven stairs several times a day, revelling in the beautiful eighteenth-century stairwell. We have an uncomplicated month together, the three of us, and then it's time for him to leave again. I tell myself that this is no more difficult than the life of hundreds of servicemen's wives. If I want to work and let Kate have a settled life then I have to learn to deal with separations.

When he resumed it is in Spain and as soon as I am able I visit him in Seville. My mother takes care of Kate again. Now he's surrounded by actors – Claude Rains, Jack Hawkins, Alec Guinness. There are infantile, highly enjoyable unit jokes based on the 'th' sound in the Castilian dialect. They stay at the Alfontho Trethi and Alec Guinness, encountered in the street on Sunday morning and on being asked where he's been so early, replies sonorously, 'Confethione'. They're all happy to be acting in the interior scenes. The unit, after the rigours of Arabia, is ecstatic to be what they call 'ashore'. Sherry is a penny halfpenny a glass. For ten shillings (fifty pence) you can eat as many prawns as you are able and finish the evening blind drunk as well. There are a few catastrophes at work; men in the grip of ferocious hangovers fall off ladders and are sent home. Only the wild men on the unit regret the hardship and the beauty they've left behind in Arabia. I feel that David Lean is one of them.

O'Toole can see now that the film is going to absorb two years of his life. This is an unusually long time and the strain on him and indirectly on me is considerable. He is having to maintain concentration and immaculately good behaviour while coming to terms with the fact that his status is altering by the month and that the rewards – or recriminations – lying in wait are, in the world of entertainment, huge. I have a foot in two camps and make a quick adjustment to a way of life that will persist; one that combines the extremely ordinary business of shopping and cleaning and stripping and mending furniture and spending my hours in very unglamorous theatres and TV rehearsal rooms with occasional well-dressed, chauffeur-driven forays into a much grander sphere. Mrs O'Toole is treated very differently from Miss Phillips. I learn to take it as it comes. Ever a realist, I am not bothered either when people jostle me out of the way in their need to get near the rising star. I did object when little Gina Lollobrigida actually put her stiletto heel through the arch of my foot in her hurtling frenzy. Unrecognised and unacknowledged, some moments later in O'Toole's dressing room I handed her a quadruple single malt whisky and watched happily as, gulping unthinkingly, her eyes began to roll, and I took a malicious delight in reading that she'd been unable to turn up for work the following day because of a 'virus'. Ordinarily, I was all sweetness and understanding but she managed to get on my nerves.

I can hardly believe that, in spite of the unusual circumstances (or maybe because of them) our life has become so harmonious. Our times together are both hilarious and tranquil – not for a year had there been a mention of my Past. Did that mean it was forgotten for good? I didn't dare to relax my guard completely but nor did I allow the small fear to spoil the present. There is no one else I would prefer to be with. We talk and talk and talk again as we used to.

That was what I missed most during our estrangement, the interrupted conversation. Of course, now from time to time our conversations have to continue on paper and he writes such wonderful letters that I am almost reconciled to the separations. Some of the letters are written in pencil and the writing grows faint with re-reading.

No Christmas leave for the *Lawrence* unit. I have work to do and I take Kate to Wales and try to be cheerful for her sake. We do eye exercises daily but the eyes are not improving. It hasn't been nearly as much fun, working on the house in the cold and dark of winter. Marianne has left for home and I embark on a series of mostly awful nannies. Now that we're becoming famous, some girls come for the interview just to have a look at the house; one stays overnight and is gone when we wake in the morning. Because of the lack of good help leaving home is becoming a problem and much of my TV work is at Granada Manchester which has the most adventurous TV drama department in the country. I worry all the time and hurry home the minute work is over. All the young mothers I meet tell me horror stories about unreliable nannies. I don't really know how long I can go on like this and I think I am going to have to work only in and around London. Before that I solve the problem temporarily by asking my parents to take Kate to Spain to visit her father. They can all holiday and I can go on working without having to worry about child-minding. When they go south to Marbella my father, handsome still, has a lovely time at a bullfight with glamorous April Ashley, now Lady Rowallan. O'Toole didn't spoil everything at that moment by telling him – as April herself would have done, given time – that she had begun life as seaman George Jameson. April – a really good sort – was adorable and put herself out to entertain my unworldly father.

Later in the year I spent a few weeks in Almeria, where Columbia filmed the charge at Aqaba. O'Toole and Omar had rented a frightful house full of hideous religious objects;

there were figures of saints with seeping, lit-up bloody wounds, a sacred heart that pulsated. Every classical statue in the house had its sex organs removed. Living there was unnerving. Robert Bolt was the brightest presence. In spite of the rigours of working for Sam – and he did hate being 'Spiegelized' – he maintained his good manners and his good sense. His marriage was in difficulties, however, as was Omar's, whose sister had come to join us in Nightmare Towers. There was a strange mother and daughter duo there as well, the sort of people who trail around in the wake of film crews and one is never quite sure how they pitched up or why. The Twist had begun to sweep the world and everyone in the house practised it day and night. The noise was deafening and that and the lack of privacy made me long for escape, which we did briefly to a charming little place called Torremolinos. Sitting in a restaurant on a cliff we saw a British ship sail in. Taxiing down to the coast, we waved and waved until someone sent a boat for us and we had a lovely afternoon and evening in the bosom of the Navy. What is it about sailors that makes them the best of all hosts?

I didn't want to leave O'Toole but I was glad to leave the overcrowded house in Almeria. With the exception of the trip to Torremolinos and meeting April and catching up with the Navy, it hadn't been a successful visit. O'Toole had been distracted, or tired or worried or bored, who could tell? Any of these would have been understandable but I had not yet learned to stand apart emotionally and I was hopelessly affected by his moods. Now that we had become so close again I could not bear the occasions when we were not of one mind and heart. He was as bad as I was; absurdly possessive and jealous of my attention. My unthinking, polite response to another man, no matter how unprepossessing, caused him distress so I learned to tailor my behaviour to the occasion. It wasn't difficult.

I'm told that Columbia Films is spending millions of dollars on O'Toole's publicity. Can this be true? It seems an incredible amount of money. Jules is convulsed with mirth when we discuss this. 'What's so funny?' 'Never mind, kid.' I *do* mind. It's lonely once Kate has gone to bed. Marie has gone back to work in Dublin. Almost all the Irish actors I know have a cut-off point beyond which they do not care to stay in England and three months is the most that Marie seems able to endure. Alone in the building site at No. 98 I keep busy, acting in television. There isn't a commercial play I like and the Royal Shakespeare Company is now out of my reach. People say, 'You're always busy. You're so lucky.' No, I'm not. There is a world of difference between being courted, chased after, getting first bite of the cherry and keeping busy, mopping up the crumbs that fall from the big table. I think – no, I know that during the last year or two I've missed some big chances and have missed them because of my character, or a lack of it. Will I get another chance? I doubt it. Life isn't that sweet. The best I can do now is to persist somehow. Nothing will make me give up that first childhood resolve to be an actress, but I'm going to have to be a quiet sort of actress. It may be that I shan't succeed in being any sort of actress at all, but I'm going to try. I see clearly that all the career mistakes I have made I would probably make again, so I have to accept that my life is going to be problematical and the problems are of my own making. This doesn't make me feel better.

# Chapter Seventeen

Because of work and my need to be at home with Kate, I didn't visit O'Toole when the unit moved for a brief time to Morocco. I wasn't to see him again until he returned to England – we were reunited in the early autumn of 1962. The foreign locations are over at last. The remainder of the film will be shot in England. There's been a stupendous homecoming – the hall looks like a souk, he's been shopping in Morocco. There are piled up carpets everywhere, one of them so big it will only fit into the big, empty first-floor drawing room; there are robes from Ouarzazate, and Kate and I sit there covered in luxury, speechless. 'God has come home.' It is heavenly.

Joyce and I have made a ravishingly beautiful bedroom on the first floor back; walls upholstered in rough grey and off-white silk fabric, dim gilded lights, dull, gold curtained windows, a beautiful Louis XIV desk in the Georgian bay – she's made me walk all over London for six months before settling on this one. I've found there is a 'fair' price for a good piece of furniture. There's no such thing as a bargain but some pieces are marginally nicer than others, marginally cheaper too. I've looked at scores of desks including the supreme examples at the Wallace Collection and this is the best one going at £400 and I'm so keen on it I pay for it out of my most recent fee. It's almost an object of devotion for me; dark red wood inlaid with dull metal strips, the top pulling out to seven feet wide. I lie in bed and look at it and wonder at it, so plain and so beautiful. In a junk shop just off Gower Street I acquire a Louis XV chaise-longue in bad shape and have it done up and with a couple of plain English eighteenth-century night tables at the bedside and plain lamps and a huge, spectacular bedhead made out of a semi-circular picture frame picked up on a pavement in the Kings Road for £40, mended and upholstered with a pad covered with the wall fabric. I'm in the perfect bedroom business all right. Once inside that door there is total tranquillity. He's *got* to love it. He does.

Our bedroom sits behind the first floor drawing room which is a big empty shell. There's no money left to do anything to it at present. I can't mess about with the structure of this pretty house to produce an en-suite bathroom (so desirable these days), as it would destroy the proportion of the first floor, so our bathroom is on the second floor and it's quite beautiful – but it does involve a run up the stairs. O'Toole decides that he'd prefer his own bathroom which means running *down* the stairs to the newly made ground floor shower room. We've shared so little domestic life together and I realise that he doesn't see me getting made up and I don't see him shaving and this seems just fine to me. In many ways we're too close for comfort and this bit of apartness is welcome. The happiness of our time together in Jordan, in the Lebanon and in Spain was no illusion. In grey, damp Hampstead I can tell that we have turned a corner and we are truly happy.

Elated by our good fortune, we decide to have another child and I become pregnant at once. (Thank God for contraception, I breathe, yet again.) I am still unsure what the future holds. The film is not finished and already our life has changed utterly. We're invited everywhere but we don't go anywhere much. Every day there are requests for interviews, photographs; hardly any are granted. We lead a quiet life with very occasional forays into society. People come to us.

It was at home in Hampstead that I first met Rudolf Nureyev. He was presented to us by the writer, Eric Braun, as a brilliant, homeless waif. 'Not quite,' I thought as the slight figure pursed his lips dramatically and raised his hand to his heart and *retreated* a few steps, instead of advancing to take my hand, out-stretched in greeting. He struck a pose, standing in the Green Room with his back to the window overlooking New End Hospital's Men's Surgical. 'The kind of woman who gets me into trouble,' he said to the interpreter, throwing his head back and watching my reaction, which was to smile, shifting my feet awkwardly. I wasn't embarrassed for me. I was embarrassed for *him*; he was too theatrical by half. Nureyev swooped forward and kissed my hand and, at that moment, the door opened and O'Toole entered. Rudi dropped my hand like a used hankie and it was *his* turn to smile and shuffle and come over girlish as he fell under the scrutiny of a pair of eyes every bit as potent and confident as his own. We knew next to nothing of the ballet and meeting Nureyev was like encountering an exotic, amusing animal – a bit of a show off.

Nothing could have prepared us for our next meeting after he had rapidly become the huge star and partner of Margot Fonteyn. One didn't need to know anything about the ballet to realise that he was phenomenal. One didn't need to like ballet to love watching him, much as one could be enthralled by watching Cassius Clay in the ring while knowing nothing and caring less about boxing. Rudi conquered society as well as the theatre and the way in which he exerted his social power was a measure of a rapidly changing social structure. Young turks could get away with anything in the Sixties.

At a dinner given in Belgravia there was considerable excitement among the ladies because Nureyev was due to come on after a performance. It was a cold night of frost and snow. He arrived when we were still at the table, he swathed in woollen scarves and sweaters and carrying a duffel bag full of dirty practice clothes which he dropped in the dining room, making for the drinks tray and picking up a smallish bottle of plum brandy which he lifted to his lips. The large throat opened and relaxed like a singer's and he drained the bottle in what seemed like seconds while we all watched in silence. The room was, not exactly frozen – everyone was too delighted – but it was halted, wrong-footed; there were glad cries of welcome, some only half-uttered, people had begun to rise but didn't know if they should continue. Rudi's next move completed the confusion. He seemed to levitate on to the table and, slightly smiling, he danced down its length, sure-footed and dignified, extending his arms and deftly but forcefully lifting off a postiche here, a top knot of ringlets there. The cries of alarm and anguish were overlaid with uncertain laughter. The ladies were going to love and appreciate him no matter what he did to them. I wondered what O'Toole – no stranger to the outrageous – was making of this new Rudi. Margot had also arrived, perfectly groomed, smiling and imperturbable as though Rudi's behaviour was the most natural thing in the world. I was pregnant and wearing a heavy, green Dior velvet dress and jacket, trimmed at collar and cuffs with heavy jet beads. The heat and the excitement proved too much and as I stood chatting to Margot I knew I was going to faint, faint right on to her, squashing her flat. As I began to fall I felt someone catch me and when I regained consciousness I was floating in a stairwell and I realised after a moment that Rudi was carrying me above his head. He was drunk and I weighed a ton, what with the unborn Pat and yards and yards of expensive Christian Dior, lined, inter-lined, and beaded. There seemed to be a little procession. O'Toole and Margot followed us and they in turn were followed by a few ladies who, slightly unnerved, decided to leave us in a very pretty nursery, upholstered and curtained in pale, grey toile de jouy. I recovered and we chatted for a while until Rudi began to throw up violently. I don't think he missed a wall, a chair or a piece of carpet. Margot and I looked on while O'Toole came into his own. The great dancer was as drunk as a skunk and needed to be packed off home. Rudi wanted to curl up and sleep. 'Come on, mush,' barked O'Toole, 'you can't sleep on the town hall steps. Here we go,' and seizing him by the legs he began to bump him down the thickly carpeted stairs. Rudi seemed perfectly happy with this method of descent but in the hall below there were anguished cries of 'Be *careful* with him', 'Take care of his *feet*'. 'To hell with his fucking feet,' muttered O'Toole as Rudi giggled to himself, and louder, 'Just get us a cab.' As we negotiated the icy pavement, the assembled diners called out with more pleas for caution with the precious feet. Margot and I tiptoed behind the ungainly, slipping, lurching couple ahead. Rudi was angelic in the cab; smiling, well content with his evening, delighted to be looked after so glamorously, wanting to kiss us all.

O'Toole and he went out on the town alone sometime later when the Twist was still at the height of its popularity. In Al Burnett's club they were dancing with a couple of hostesses and O'Toole heard the rather bored girl, gracelessly twisting near Rudi say, 'Are ya Polish?' 'No!' growled Rudi, concentrating on a very muscular bit of twisting. 'I am *Tarrtarr*.'

Sam had ordained that the film be ready for public viewing by December! David was inclined to argue that this was completely impossible but Sam had craftily secured a Royal Première and since the Queen would attend, it had to be ready. A royal opening was important for the success of any movie. David was once a brilliant editor and he *had* a brilliant editor, Ann Coates, working with him now, but a large amount of the editing had already been done as he shot the film. He would, for example, cut in the camera to make it impossible for anyone to alter his concept. One day he asked O'Toole to casually move the cigarette to the 'wrong' hand during a scene which had been requested but which he didn't want used – the continuity was broken and the scene became useless. Even so, it was a mad rush and he moved a truckle bed into the cutting room and stayed there day and night.

I went to work on a modest TV film at Elstree, *This is not King's Cross*; Michael Craig was one of my leading men. He drove a Jaguar and, sensing I was under some pressure, he kindly named himself 'Radio Jags' and became my personal cab company, picking me up in the morning and returning me to Hampstead every night. O'Toole was now fully occupied doing press and publicity. Jules still seemed to be nursing some private joke as he organised O'Toole's busy days. I joined Jules and Joyce and their daughter, Joan-Juliet, and Peter at night after my rehearsals. I went home to bed alone. I wasn't really a part of the circus. Not yet.

December 1962 and the only London pea-souper I remember. There must have been others but I didn't notice them. When we worked in North London, I rose early and walked from Heath Street to rehearsals at Swiss Cottage, clutching at the walls, unable to see my hand in front of my face. Sound was so muffled that one collided with people before becoming aware of another presence. Cars veered dangerously and silently on to the pavement. It was frightening but everyone was imbued with the spirit of the Blitz. Mich Craig slowly, slowly drove me home at night. I had a beautiful brown woollen robe that O'Toole had brought me from Arabia and one night I went upstairs when it became obvious that he wasn't going to be coming home for dinner and lay on the bed reading until it was time to take off the big robe and go to sleep. No O'Toole. I was only a couple of months pregnant but I was thankful for quiet times. (A non-appearance at dinner and no phone call didn't rate highly as a bad time). I fell asleep and at five o'clock in the morning I was awakened by the telephone, always on my side of the bed. I looked around. Still no O'Toole. Picking up the phone I heard Uncle Davy's voice. In Welsh he said how sad he was to tell me that my father had just died in a hospital outside Cardiff. To my shame and surprise I realised that I was feeling a flood of relief, before it was followed immediately by acute grief. I put the phone down and sat on the side of the huge bed looking at the wall. Cold, I pulled on my heavy robe. As I sat there I realised that I had spent my life worrying about my father. He had probably done the same for me. Neither of us had been able to do much for the other. He may have heaved a sigh of relief when I married O'Toole and became his responsibility (as men of that generation would think) and now for a second I had breathed relief and release. I felt bad but I could understand why that feeling had come for a moment.

What to do now? I didn't know where O'Toole was and it was a measure of my acceptance of his need for freedom that I had no idea how I might reach him. He didn't carry identification, or keys and hated to be contactable. I wasn't sure if this was a pose or a genuine wish to maintain a measure of liberation in a life that was becoming more and more constrained by approaching fame. Whatever the reason, this behaviour was part of the rules of the house and I didn't have too much trouble incorporating it into my life, though I did have mixed feelings when roused to respond to his insistent ringing on the door bell in the early hours. But even then I thought there was something rather touching about his being so sure of his welcome. And I *did* always feel welcoming.

Now, calling Michael Craig, I left it to him to inform the company that I wouldn't be at rehearsals for a day or two and he volunteered to drive to Hampstead and get me through the fog to Paddington. I packed, went to the nursery to talk to the Nanny and make sure that she could cope for a while; played with Kate – she had been adored by her grandfather – and I felt sad for her, unknowing that she'd lost a great, tall, handsome supporter from her little corner in life.

Mich Craig picked me up. I wrote a note to O'Toole and left for Paddington, Michaël driving through the white wall of fog, to begin the long train journey to Wales. Oh those train journeys packed into claustrophobic compartments; no buffet, very little heat, no privacy. My father's death was such a shock I couldn't truly confront it. He'd been unwell and I'd brought him to London where Gerry Slattery had arranged a meeting with the Queen's heart specialist, a Welshman. 'Don't worry,' he'd said. 'Live normally, eat and drink whatever you'd like. Don't fuss.' 'There you go,' I'd added, briskly, willing him to be well and strong and willing him not to be ill, willing him not to die. 'Don't *fuss*.'

*Lawrence of Arabia* was due to open in a few days. Would I be there? O'Toole had bought me a dress in New York and amazingly it fitted; Joyce Buck had organised a coat to go over it. Ricky Huston had loaned me a reliquary to wear as jewellery and Ricci from Sassoon would do my hair. How? Where? I didn't care.

My mother was in black, observing the formalities, sitting alone while people came to pay their respects and talk of my father. I'd never seen the Welsh ceremony before and I was faintly and irrationally irritated by the formal demonstrations of grief. My mother *had* to look sad all day. There must have been moments when she would have liked to smile – but no – all was unrelieved gloom. Davy, her brother, was there, making arrangements and suddenly, out of nowhere, there was O'Toole. I was overwhelmed with relief. I adored him in the role of rescuing cavalry.

He'd found my note and, abandoning Columbia Pictures and the publicity machine, had hurtled down to Wales by taxi. His arrival changed everything and everyone for the better. My mother cheered up and resumed a little light cooking. Davy and O'Toole went to the pub and Davy looked uncharacteristically cheerful when he returned. Funeral arrangements speeded along, interspersed with little drinks (normally, unheard of) and then he was gone again to London. Before leaving he told my mother and Davy that I was pregnant and that also helped to alter the atmosphere for the better. I arranged with my mother that as soon as she felt able, she should come and live with us in London. I didn't doubt that O'Toole would be generous hearted enough not to question this decision and I was right to take his generosity for granted. He could be awful but he wasn't mean and at moments of crisis he displayed a shining grace that lightened all around him.

December 9 was the day of the funeral and I was overcome with grief afterwards. Icy cold, I went to the railway station in Cardiff and sat bolt upright during the three-hour journey to London and the première of *Lawrence of Arabia*. Jules had told me to go to Claridges and there I found him and Joyce and Joan-Juliet and O'Toole and his sister and Derek, her husband. My clothes were there in the suite and so, blessedly, was Ricci, who washed and fixed my hair, tweaked my dress and chivvied me into presentability. We went to the movies and in my sad state I didn't see an inch of the film. The Queen was there but as a wife I wasn't needed in the line-up so I was able to slump a little. Afterwards, it seems there was a party for about five hundred people. I don't remember it at all. But I do remember going to Tony Nutting's lovely house in Chelsea and sitting there until dawn when, leaving the group, I walked alone into the street and got a cab home. The fog was over. I bathed and changed my clothes at home and was picked up by Mich to go to Elstree to start filming.

I didn't see O'Toole for days; I was putting in long hours at the studio and he became the hottest young property on two continents. I knew that life had changed yet again but everything was happening at two removes from me – and anyway, there was a show to do.

# Chapter Eighteen

Guyon House is reorganised to accommodate my mother. She will have the second floor front as a bed-sitting room and her bathroom is almost en-suite. (This house is always going to be slightly cockeyed.) Kate is delighted she'll be one staircase away from her Mamgu (specially dear mother – the Welsh for grandmother) and I am delighted because now I'm going to be able to leave home and go to work without fear. (Since Marianne's departure to Sweden I've been glued to NW3.) On the other hand . . . I bid a mental goodbye to the kitchen, my mother will want to take over. But on the other hand, I can't cook well and don't much like it so why *not* hand over? On the other hand, am I going to enjoy resuming life under my mother's thumb? But we haven't lived together since I was sixteen – I'm grown up now and this is a big house, there's room for us all. On the other hand, she's never witnessed anything like O'Toole's drunken rages (no less alarming for being less frequent) but I don't intend that she shall, neither she nor Kate. (I add green baize-lined double doors to the list of work for the builders.)

Christmas is approaching, our first Christmas in Guyon House. My mother arrives. She's sold her furniture and almost all her possessions. 'Good!' I nod breezily and set about settling her in. She adapts to London life without missing a beat. Lying awake at night, thinking of her on the floor above – also lying awake? I wonder have I done something wonderful for her? Or have I asked her to do something incredibly difficult? I'm three months' pregnant and selfish and I don't dwell on the problem. There are no cosy chats. Not that we ever had any. The

Christmas holiday is here and we have immaculate Christmas and Boxing Day dinners and lunches – organised by Mamgu of course. The kitchen holds inexhaustible reserves for all who are invited or who drop in or pass by. The turkey is perfect, the puddings are my mother's vintage puddings made last year. O'Toole is not given to family occasions but even he goes along with this perfect festive regime. Kate bangs her turkey bone on her plate at the huge dining table. There's a massive fire in the newly uncovered eighteenth-century fireplace. The big tree shines in the hall. But I don't allow mourning. I miss my father so much and don't know how to express it so I don't allow *any* expressions of grief. I cannot bear to talk of him. My mother, still dressed in black, smiles and cooks and greets strangers and becomes 'Mamgu' to everyone. We don't speak of my father. And I know I'm failing her.

My pregnancy is beginning to show so I find a clever dress and do a television play with young Robin Phillips, feeling a bit too old to be his lover. It's the first time I've ever felt like that. Time is knocking on. I'm almost thirty and that seems so old. Robin wasn't very happy and it didn't surprise me to learn that he became a director shortly afterwards and directed Maggie Smith's glittering seasons in Canada. Just at the moment Maggie is involved with O'Toole and Marie Kean in London, preparing a reading of Sean O'Casey's *Pictures in the Hallway* (this is O'Toole's response to International Super Stardom). Arriving to rehearse at ten o'clock and finding the door open, Maggie drifts in past a builder or two and finds herself in Marie Kean's bedroom where the great Irishwoman is discovered fast asleep in a gold lamé evening gown. Maggie's day is made, I think. She's wreathed in smiles and Maggie, wreathed, spreads the smile over a half-mile radius.

When I am too heavily pregnant to work, O'Toole decides to do a play in the West End. *Baal* by Bertolt Brecht, his first appearance in London since the ill-fated *Oh Mein Papa* and

*The Long and the Short and the Tall* in the Fifties. And O'Toole is not going to take a fee. 'How good,' they say. I wonder about that. I feel that such a magnificent gesture really undermines people who have to make a living in the West End. After registering my protest and seeing it ignored, I shut up, but I'm disturbed. I suspect that O'Toole's altruism is tinged with guilt. Being a movie star is perceived in this country to be in some way a disgrace. Albert Finney turned down Sam's offer to play Lawrence because he didn't want to become a movie star. (He went on to make movies for Woodfall productions, nevertheless.) There's something about success that is regarded with suspicion and the received wisdom is that movies are not for 'real' actors. But I can see that our world is changing – it has changed. (And do these self-appointed critics have any idea how *difficult* it is to become a movie star?) I'm worried that Jules is being too accommodating when every fibre of his being must be screaming, 'No *Baal*! No dirty leading man in filthy rags singing dodgy songs in a not-too successful Brecht play.' Instead (and probably wisely) he says, 'Sure, play it until the next movie. Sure, do it for nothing.'

The next film? Finally, I see why Jules had been chuckling to himself at any mention of O'Toole's future. Wise, from their years at Fox, to Sam and his wiles, Jules has somehow slipped past Sam and Columbia an agreement for O'Toole's services that does not extend beyond *Lawrence of Arabia*. On the day when Sam tells O'Toole that his next four films will be X Y Z and A, Jules says, 'I don't think so.' Sam explains that over the next seven years O'Toole, like Omar, will play whatever he decides he should. 'I don't think so,' repeats Jules, softly. Lawyers and vice-presidents open files and scrutinise O'Toole's contract with Columbia Pictures beyond 1962. 'Hell let loose' is a mild way of describing what happened next. People were fired. People hastily resigned. Well into their million dollar campaign, they realised that they were promoting an actor they didn't 'own' and, what was worse, they had to go *on* promoting him for the good of the movie.

Jules and Sam were old hands at the game of dog-eat-dog but Jules had scored the revenge of a lifetime. Knowing the background, I couldn't do anything but salute Jules. I had never doubted his business sense but I was bowled over by his capacity to wait for his cooled revenge.

Jules and Sam had been partners in Horizon Pictures, which had produced *Treasure of the Sierra Madre*. As young things they had seen their furniture dumped on the pavement for non-payment of rent. John Huston (the third partner) had gone out hustling for production money. Joyce Buck's father had sent a cheque to ensure that Kate Hepburn continued on into the jungle for the shooting of *The African Queen*. Their association had been long and eventful. All the same, I was slightly worried that Jules – like all of us involved in the family firm – was over-charmed by O'Toole. Much as I adored him as a man and revered him as an actor, I was well aware that O'Toole could be horribly wrong about many things. It wasn't easy being the one person who would risk telling unpalatable truths and I had a feeling that no one would ever compete with me for that job.

*Baal* – well, worth doing, I suppose. I wasn't sure. It was, like all O'Toole's projects, fraught with dramatic incident. His dresser, on the night of the dress rehearsal, screamed, 'This show is cursed', flung the clothes on to the floor and fled into Charing Cross Road, never to return. The beautiful Jocelyn Herbert sets were changed by a gauze 'wipe' that traversed R to L and L to R and took for ever to move so the play lasted almost five hours. In the middle of it all O'Toole summoned George Devine to come and 'fix' it, ignoring the director's feelings. What a time they had! George Devine (who ran the Royal Court) and Jocelyn Herbert were lovers, the director had to be shunted sideways – it was exhausting just listening to the backstage drama. They opened and everyone fairly hated the play. A large portion of the audience slammed out each night crying, 'Disgusting'. But – was it all worth it? O'Toole looked awful on stage, which he wanted to be as a change from the beauty of Lawrence, but why, I wondered? The public isn't in the least bit interested or impressed by versatility. Marie and I went to the opening and nodded our approval of best efforts, but we both wondered, why bother? The play opened on 7 February and had to close at the end of April to accommodate the beginning of O'Toole's first picture as a co-production between Keep Films and a big outside company. The chosen film was *Becket*, based on the Anouilh play he had not done for the RSC.

May. *Becket* begins with Richard Burton. I haven't seen him or worked with him since I first took up with O'Toole after I left RADA. He's now involved with Elizabeth Taylor and against everyone's guess and wish has left his wife, Sybil. Of course, Elizabeth represents the great uncharted sea of superstardom and Richard has always wanted to be a superstar – a *wealthy* superstar. There's a story of him – a favourite of Daphne Rye, the H. M. Tennent Ltd casting director – at an all night party, sitting in a circle of young things who were asked to declare their ambitions. 'I want to be the greatest Juliet since Ellen Terry.' 'I want to play Hamlet as it has never been played.' 'How about you, Richard? What do you want to be?' The reply was simple. 'Rich.'

Thanks to Elizabeth, he is now going to *be* rich. Very rich. They both come down to the pub near Shepperton Studio and eat more food than normal people can imagine putting away. I'm a healthy eater (to say the least) but Elizabeth Taylor's food consumption leaves me standing . . . 'Those fat pigs,' snarls Kate Hepburn in disdain at such indulgence. I don't know. A part of me admires that kind of robustness. Another part sides with Miss Hepburn; such unbelievable self-indulgence *can't* be right – or can it?

Richard seems sheepish but rather pleased with himself, I

think. Not sure where he stands with us in his new role. Nor am I. As his wife Sybil's husband, he would have fitted perfectly into our life, but now? O'Toole senses that I am holding back rather and doesn't push to accept many invitations to the Dorchester or anywhere else.

Elizabeth and Richard are at the height of what is called the 'Scandale'. They seem to love the notoriety and the publicity. One night, Elizabeth wants to go to a theatre in St Martin's Lane. We arrange seats. Elizabeth is very small. She wears a huge, turquoise turban. Word spreads (how, I wonder?) that the Seductress is at the theatre. In the interval we arrange drinks to be served in the manager's office, front of house. 'No,' she cries to our horror, 'we're next door to the Salisbury. Let's go to the pub now!' St Martin's Lane is fairly heaving. Someone clears a path. All they can see is a turquoise hat. 'Oh,' cries a woman, 'the bitch! I'm so close, I could spit on her.' Unaccountably, Elizabeth finds this charming. She beams. 'It is so awful,' she says winsomely to O'Toole, 'not being able to go anywhere in peace.' 'It might help a bit,' O'Toole replies tartly, 'if you took off that fuckin' turquoise busby.'

There is something wonderful about her appetite for being noticed. Richard? No, I don't think so. He looks faintly embarrassed. But it's so obvious that he's willing to pay the price of fame. O'Toole may be disconcerted to be confronted by Stardom in its complete, unacceptable – but true form. He can have this, if he wants.

In 1967, very generously, they offered to take the children to stay on their yacht *Kalizma*. Over my dead body, I thought; it's hard enough trying to bring them up sane in NW3, never mind on a luxury yacht.

The same year, quite by chance, we flew to a film festival together, a beautiful festival in Taormina in Sicily where the Italian Oscars are given out. There was a confusion over tickets and Elizabeth snapped her fingers and got some boxes produced out of nowhere and the four of us cluttered up the front of the first-class compartment. We drank champagne all the way to Italy (I was right to avoid them, it was impossible not to behave excessively in their company). Elizabeth was very good natured. Richard was – Richard, and I remembered that even *reasonable* behaviour on the part of royalty or celebrities is translated into *wonderful* behaviour; the expectation is so much less, I suppose. When we got off, Rich and O'Toole and I looked dishevelled and blowsy. Elizabeth, who was royally drunk, looked stone cold sober and the photographs reflected this. 'Camera cleans her up,' said Richard philosophically.

At Taormina all the film stars were mobbed by screaming crowds. We stayed in a pretty and very uncomfortable hotel. Staying in the rooms (formerly monks' cells) was out of the question and in order to do some sightseeing and visit restaurants, we braved the boisterous fans who never left the front courtyard. After a day or two they grew bored with the stars and life was very pleasant for everyone. Richard and Elizabeth, on the other hand, remained closeted in two tiny rooms where they sat squashed in with their hairdressers and assistants. 'We're not going out till The Night,' said Richard. 'By then, they'll be MAD to see Elizabeth – it'll be a riot.' He was deadly serious, I realised dismally. He was right, of course; Elizabeth, the only star who hadn't been seen, was nearly killed by the pent-up enthusiasm as she left the hotel. On The Night, Richard said, 'Watch this, it'll be a sensation. The light will go on *there* but *she* will come in *here*.' We were in a Roman amphitheatre – rubble everywhere 'backstage' – the auditorium, beautifully lit by candles issued to the audience as they arrived and then sat with their backs to the ocean. O'Toole was suitably, sincerely grateful in bad Italian. My friend, Silvana Mangano, brought a loving house of fellow countrymen to their feet, striding on casually and exiting smartly, then Elizabeth was introduced and didn't appear – didn't appear – didn't appear – and finally she was picked up in a light in the wrong place, picking her way through the uncleared rubble to the podium. It seemed a lot of trouble for very little return.

Much later, Richard and I sang some Welsh songs. A minor princess who seemed to be setting her cap at him was not best pleased. Elizabeth suddenly summoned him and we exchanged a wry smile. 'Mabel calls,' he said. One thing I remember about Elizabeth was that she had a terrific voice, clear and incisive, always interesting, no affectation. Richard and I had other, sadder, meetings as he lost his robust constitution and the years of excess took their toll. But he got what he wanted: 'Take what you want and pay for it.' Didn't he just!

Kate is three and already, as my mother says, she is a 'bit of a character'. She wears her round, metal-framed glasses with a forbidding air, peering suspiciously at the world, pinning my mother to her chair with demands to be read to. We're heartily sick of *Ant and Bee* and *Janet and John* and I begin to read her poems and stories that I find entertaining. She tolerates almost everything – even the fourth leader of *The Times* – but remains loyal to *Ant and Bee* in particular. Between us, my mother and I run the house. Manolita, the daily help, comes every day and cleans and mends and helps organise our lives.

*Becket* is a long movie and is being shot at Shepperton. Peter Glenville, who has a sound theatrical pedigree, is having no trouble at all with his stars, O'Toole and Burton. The press tries to create stories of tension and potential mayhem but even they have to give up in the end. The journey from NW3 to Shepperton is long, so the weekdays are calm; O'Toole leaves in the early hours of the morning and returns late with barely time to greet everyone and have dinner with me in the Green Room before going to bed early. Saturday is a bit of a lost day when he sleeps and sleeps, but Sundays are enchanting and we all lunch in the dining room before O'Toole and I take a walk around Hampstead and then sit and read until it's time to prepare for another hard week. Quiet, dull and totally happy, those months.

However happy I am, I feel I cannot forget the circumstances surrounding Kate's birth and I make up my mind that I am going to protect myself and the next baby from the remotest chance of drama and over-excitement. How to contrive this? Marie suggests that I come to Dublin for the birth and everything falls into place. Having a child on Irish soil will compliment O'Toole and put me beyond his reach at the same time. It works! Everyone – except my mother – is happy. It's seen as a charming gesture, but it's actually self-preservation on my part. So, three weeks before Pat is due to be born in June, I fly to Ireland and move into a back bedroom in Marie's flat at Lower Baggot Street. She's booked me into the Stella Maris Nursing Home (staffed by nuns) and Declan Meagher, a friend of Dr Slattery's, will be in charge. I'm told to prepare a bag and the list includes a bottle of chloroform and a large pad of cotton wool; I find myself packing for myself a pair of white silk pyjamas of O'Toole's. I may be wanting to do this my way but I also need to feel close to him and wearing his clothes will help me, I know.

The June days are perfect and long. Marie cooks wonderful meals (the Irish potatoes in June are heavenly). I lie on my bed high above the Dublin rooftops and I think I may never have such a relaxed time again. Marie is at work at the theatre but her flat is lined with books so I read and read and read and look west out of the window. Joan Huet, a friend and stage manager, and Marie and a couple of the boys from the company decide that maybe we should speed things up a bit (I might sit there, reading and dreaming for ever). 'Into the car,' they cry. 'Off to the Wicklow Mountains.' Joan brings her stage manager's stopwatch. In the mountains we stop here and there. 'Small gin for the lady,' say the boys. I scarcely drink but gin and orange doesn't taste like alcohol at all. After a few hours of bumping around the country roads, I feel a twinge.

'Oh Jasus – great,' they cry, relieved, and we speed back to town, Joan recording twinges on her stopwatch. When we reach the Stella Maris, she confers with the nuns while Marie and the boys bring my little bag up to my very nice room – two beds (bathroom en-suite). 'Ouch,' I exclaim at the next small twinge. 'All right. Everyone away now,' says an adorable nun. 'Did you feel a little pain? Aren't you the good girl? Here!' And drenching a pad of cotton wool with chloroform, she plants it on my face.

I'm told later that Declan shot across Dublin for the birth and, as an ex-Irish Rugby International player, was non-plussed to hear the unofficial Welsh Rugby anthem issuing from the prone, unconscious body beneath him. '*Sospan Fach, yn berwi ar y tân, sospan Fawr, yn berwi ar y llawr.*' 'I didn't know,' he said, 'whether to pass the baby or score a try.' All unknowing, I woke up in O'Toole's silk pyjama top. 'You've got a beautiful baby girl,' said the saintly (I'd elevated her) nun. 'Oh, thank you. How nice,' I replied and looked at the perfect, pink happy bundle. Could anything be more perfect than this? This is the way to have a baby, I thought, as I drifted off to sleep again.

I woke up to find great excitement going on. O'Toole from England had ordered champagne and Guinness – enough Black Velvet for the city, it seemed, and the city was turning up. The bath was out of commission because it was full of ice and champagne. The room was full of Irish actors. I regarded the assembly calmly. I've done this my way. My baby was calm and untroubled and I was calm and untroubled.

So, Kate was born in Shakespeare's country but Pat has been born on Irish soil and I feel I've managed things very well. Jim Fitzgerald, a lively young director, drops in for a drink. Pat sleeps resolutely through the incredible din. Jim feels a little tired and says, 'D'ya mind?' as he rolls into the other bed in the room. He's still there twenty-four hours later. 'Ah, the craythur,' snaps Marie, irritably. 'Who cares?' I say. The nuns just smile.

O'Toole arrives. Jules and Joyce, also Peter Finch; various nobs. I'm concentrating on Pat. She is a miracle baby. I wonder if her manner reflects the way she was born, women only, no problems at all. She's easy. I'm easy. O'Toole leaves and returns to *Becket*. On my bed is the script of the movie. They need an actress who can speak old Welsh, find appropriate music, sing it and play the gittern at the same time. What kind of competition did I have to beat off to get *this* job? Yes. I'll do Gwendoline when I get home. But it's not a great part.

Robert Bolt sends me the script of his new play *Gentle Jack*. Again, it's not a great part but Edith Evans will be in the play. I have adored her for so long and nothing would give me greater pleasure than to sweep the stage so I could watch her – so, Yes! Of course I'll do it. Dame Edith . . . Can she be as wonderful as I think she is?

I feed Pat who is completely content and untroubled. Jim Fitzgerald wakes and says, 'Oh Jasus, where am I? I'm late for rehearsal.' He's a day late.

Marie makes me get up and get out to Bewleys for a coffee. I don't feel so good. Give it another day, she says, and then she puts us on a plane to England, where there's a *proper* Nanny. The first ever for me. Elizabeth de la Cour Bogue has arrived via Jack and Doreen Hawkins, almost snaffled by David Niven and then Lauren Bacall on the way, but she's OURS! Young, smart, upper-crust, great with horses as well as children. What have I done to deserve this? Doreen Hawkins, I bless you for ever. And Mamgu is in residence. And there's a crib swathed in pink. And there's a grim, cross-eyed, three-year-old sister. When she's seen holding a pillow over the baby's face with a pair of scissors in her hand, I think The Baby (even I can see 'The Baby' is a term of opprobrium) should be moved three floors down out of Kate's reach. Poor Kate, who had such a horrible birth and who has gone through so much already – has she any vague notion how she's been seized and rescued and re-seized and moved from pillar to post? And now here's this blissful creature who has never known a moment's trouble.

When Kate was born she was one of many children born to Royal Shakespeare Company members that year – all girls. Someone asked if my husband minded not having a son. I – so completely sure of my welcomed and treasured existence in my parents' lives – was amazed at such a question but, when I remembered it, much later, I put it to O'Toole. As I expected, he was as amazed as I and said that a houseful of women would suit him very well. When Pat was born, again I heard a sympathetic 'still no boy'. O'Toole and I looked at each other in mute amusement. What is this obsession with boys? Our friend Robert Shaw longed for a son and went on producing child after child until he succeeded in getting a boy. Such persistence was a source of wonder and amusement to O'Toole and we decided that two children was enough and so the houseful of women was established. When Pat was brought home from Dublin, Guyon House was up and running and it was much, much easier to ensure that O'Toole was not aware of the noise and tumult that a baby trails in its wake.

An infrequent visitor to the nursery on the fifth floor, he came up with me one night very late to see Pat in bed when she hadn't been too well. He was charming and she was charmed. Days later she asked me, 'You know that man – not the one with the beard, the other one who came to see me – who *is* he?' It had never occurred to us that his infrequent presence in London, coupled with the constant changes in appearance, could be so totally confusing to her. After that I made sure that I scattered around stills of their father in whatever new persona he had adopted for the current movie or play. These misunderstandings evaporated as the girls grew older but even so, Pat didn't exactly distinguish herself at her primary school by claiming that she knew the Bible *very* well and that it was a movie, starring her father.

# Chapter Nineteen

*Becket* continues without incident. O'Toole and Burton have both vowed to stay on the wagon. There's been no trouble and then one night they both fall off the wagon at the same time and meet up in some horrible dive (there are few pretty dives in 1963) and, partly appalled and penitent, go home for an hour or so and turn up on time for the first scene of the day, still drunk and hanging on to each other. They do a good day's work but the lapse has been noted.

I turn up to do my scene – quite complicated with all the music – but it goes smoothly and quickly. They incorporate my music into the theme of the movie. I go home to the girls.

Pat O'Toole continues to be the dream baby. Blonde, serene, she lies outside in the garden at Number 98. I, my mother and Liz, the daily, dote on her from a distance. She makes no demands. She smiles, the sun shines. Life is deceptively easy during the summer months. She's called Pat because I'd got it into my head that she was going to be a boy called Patrick and when they asked me her name in the nursing home, I couldn't think of anything different.

Soon it's time to start work again. *Gentle Jack* will now include Kenneth Williams, who is a great friend of Robert Bolt, and Michael Bryant, one of the best actors in England. It's a very classy show. Robert comes to stay with us while we rehearse. On the first day we're required to wear hats and skirts and gloves. Trousers are allowed on day two, thank God. Robert is conceiving a real dislike of the Dame. It's true that she hasn't read the play. It's true that she's demanding that Hardy Amies should design her a ball gown in stiff taffeta for all her daytime scenes in the City office. No one dares question her about this. They all moan in private. She sees that there will be rostra, six to nine inches high, here and there. 'I can't possibly act on those,' she cries. 'I'll have to wear slippers.' Carpet slippers and Hardy Amies frocks. No one dares comment. 'You seem very relaxed,' she accuses me in a cross voice. I'm petrified and I'm trying to *act* a relaxed, upper-class girl. I shake my head. She glowers. Gretchen Franklin learns that I'd like to improve my tap dancing. 'I'll teach you,' she offers. And does, until the Dame tracks down the source of the noise. No more tap. I have a passion for oranges. She hates oranges. No more oranges in the theatre.

But the Actress is everything I'd thought she might be. All day at rehearsal and every night during the run I stand and watch her and I can't see what she's doing. She gets laughs and I can't see how – there doesn't seem to be any preparation – no special light, no good place, no clean 'feed'. She just gets a laugh if *she* thinks it's a funny line. If she doesn't understand something she says it with no expression at all. She never 'helps' the dramatist, never papers over a crack in the script. Faced with a bit of bad writing she suspends her acting until the moment is over and then carries on. The behaviour is aristocratic.

Producer Binkie Beaumont is brutal to her when the play does badly on the road. In the broad alleyway to the stage door he barks, 'Come on, come on,' after a performance in Brighton. 'Do your magic! Pull the play together.' What a hope! He should know her better than that.

We play Brighton for a month. She and Kenneth Williams stay at the Royal Crescent, traditionally the stars' hotel. I stay in a suite at the Albion and have the girls there with me a great deal of the time. When Dame E. and Kenneth go home they share a miserable wilted salad and as they go up in the lift the friendly night porter nudges the Dame in the ribs and says, 'Enjoy your grub?' According to Ken, not once does she acknowledge his presence.

In the wings, at night, she stands, smoothing down her taffeta dress, making a horrible crackling noise and muttering to herself. She fairly *hates* this play. They told her she was playing a modern-day Elizabeth the First. Well, of course, her part is nothing like that at all and she hasn't read the other bits of the play. 'Remember *Nina*,' she says to no one in particular (*Nina*, a play few of us had seen, was a great failure and she left it on a stretcher), rustle, crack, rustle. Norah, in the prompt corner, hisses fearlessly, 'Please, SHUT UP, Dame Edith!' She smoulders a little and then resumes the crackle, rustle, crackle, mumble, mumble, until she has to enter in her carpet slippers and grand frock. I'm more enslaved by her than I could have thought possible. Robert cares for her even less than before. When she died, he happened to be staying with us and I said, 'Look who died!' Eulogies were pouring in. Robert looked at the tributes in *The Times* and delivered his own, terse, obituary: 'Well, she was no use to me.'

In Brighton – it being almost the Christmas season – there's a misconception that *Gentle Jack* is a children's show about Jack and the Beanstalk (grand managements like H. M. Tennent Ltd. don't think that they need to advertise or let the public know what to expect). When a dog is disembowelled quite early in the play the hatred wafting across the footlights is palpable. Occasionally people tut-tut at us in the street. This doesn't augur well for London.

While I was rehearsing *Gentle Jack*, O'Toole accepted an engagement in London which he'd be able to fit in before going off to shoot *Lord Jim* in Cambodia. It was to play Hamlet in the Laurence Olivier production of the play which was to open the National Theatre (housed at the Old Vic). Before we opened on tour in Brighton, I attended the first night. It was a huge occasion, a landmark in the British theatre. As I took my seat in the stalls I felt all the symptoms of acute stage fright. Bob Bolt took my hand and gave it a shake but I couldn't respond, my tongue had stuck to the roof of my mouth and I could only nod in answer to his encouraging 'Come on, girl, it's only a play.' It *wasn't* only a play (and he didn't believe it either). It could have been worse, I reflected. A few months previously Larry had asked me if I would like to play Ophelia. I was speechless and O'Toole had spoken for me, saying that they ought to cast someone really young (I was thirty at the time – no juvenile). For a moment, just a moment, I had felt dashed (and Larry looked quizzical) but within minutes I thought that I had probably been saved from myself. I was *not* a juvenile but would I ever have turned down such an opportunity? Now I sent up a prayer of gratitude that I was not backstage, coping with my own terrors and worrying about O'Toole as well. Even so, sitting out front was a nightmare; the play and the building were bedevilled. Buses thundered past the side of the unfinished building swathed in tarpaulin and this *Hamlet* was a pale shadow of the performance O'Toole had given at the Bristol Old Vic in the mid-fifties. Sean Kenny had made a lovely set that rarely worked. Only too often the company climbed down from the lofty bridge that hadn't met in the middle and continued the performance on the flat apron in front of the safety curtain. Since they were giving these performances uncut (nine hours on matinée days), some of the evening performances interrupted by technical glitches were interminable. The public didn't care. They flocked.

Larry seemed intent on making O'Toole look like a clean, well-dressed, young master. O'Toole went along with everything – pudding basin hair-cut, Lord Fauntleroy collar. Larry wrote him God-like notes and letters. 'My son, in whom I have such pride . . .' Some temporary cleaner swept these into the bin and I got the blame. I thought O'Toole was badly served by Larry and for once he was too obedient by half. But it's very hard *not* to be subservient around one's idol.

When we arrived in London the critics savaged *Gentle Jack* and Robert was terribly upset. He'd thought it was his best play. We played on while *Hamlet* closed and O'Toole prepared to play the lead in the film of Conrad's *Lord Jim*. Jean Simmons and her husband, director Richard Brooks, and their children had come to lunch at Guyon House to talk about the project before leaving England. 'No script to be seen until we've started shooting,' said Richard Brooks. The Conrad novel was a wonderful subject but I couldn't quite believe that O'Toole was breaking his cardinal rule: no script, no deal. Jean Simmons looked as harassed by domesticity as I. Our children got wet and dirty in the garden. My mother beamed at the Jean Simmons she saw in her mind's eye, not the tired mother scraping mud off small wellington boots.

It was time for O'Toole to leave (for 'the high China seas' I read in my atlas) and I would be able to join him there as soon as I was free. Pat was thriving, Kate was at kindergarten (and already her life was an endless round of parties). I'd grown to enjoy the long period of home life, only rarely threatened by alcohol owing to the daily pressure of work, and I didn't want it interrupted, but this was a pointless regret and I didn't even voice it. It was easier to deal with these separations if we didn't have farewell scenes.

While I was playing *Gentle Jack* I accepted, as a day job, my first 'real' movie, *Espionage*, albeit made for TV, and the first made for TV in the director's long and fascinating career. 'Oh, you'll have an *awful* time,' said his contemporaries. On the contrary, Michael Powell and I found ourselves working together extremely happily. The great Powell and Pressburger days were behind him but films like *The Red Shoes* and *Peeping Tom* were fresh in people's minds. He and Anthony Quayle, my leading man, between them gave me a month's seminar on movie acting and it was the first really interesting job I'd had in about two years. There was an actor in the movie whom I found dazzling. Marie knew and admired him also and we used to inveigle John Wood round to Heath Street for sketchy suppers, lots of drinks and tons of adulation which just slipped off his back unnoticed.

Michael Powell took me under his wing and began to make plans for a movie future for me. But he'd fallen on hard times himself and none of his projects for me came to fruition. I sensed that he was whistling in the dark, but I felt very privileged to get to know him and his wife and talk, talk, talk about films in his flat in Melbury Road.

Dame Edith, who wasn't good at names, usually addressed me as 'Mother-of-two'. I feel like a 'mother-of-ten' and I'm a full-time daughter again but finally I've had to learn how to run a house properly – even I can tell however that I'm very tense and over-anxious. There are lists everywhere; menus for the children, menus for us, notes to the daily, memos to myself and just about anyone I see who passes me on the stairs. And I feel I would like to be four wives – four separate wives: one, sleeves rolled up, seeing to the nuts and bolts of daily life, doing the odd bit of carpentry and furniture removal; one for dealing with the delicate, personal secretarial work that can't be handed on to an office; one for fun and one for going to the hairdresser, the dressmaker, the chiropodist, the manicurist and looking smart, and entertaining like a lady of leisure. Then, there's Miss Phillips, the Equity member, to accommodate somehow. I'm keeping a tight grip on things but every second of every day has to be accounted for and I'm losing even more weight and on my way to becoming 'thrillingly thin' as my friend, Debbie Condon, describes the emaciated, model-size figure I had never thought to possess. Deb is a beautiful American supermodel, married to our friend, playwright Kenneth Jupp and we spend what little time off we have with our friends and business partners, the Bucks – including daughter, Joan-Juliet – and Ken and Deb Jupp. I keep two diaries, one big desk diary and a small Hérmès agenda which I carry around. Ah, Hérmès . . . Yes, life is becoming very 'Gucci, Pucci, Cucci' as I heard a disgruntled husband mutter while he trailed up Bond Street behind his busily shopping wife. The diaries intimidate me at the beginning of every week. Kate's eyes require constant attention, the patches have to be moved regularly from eye to eye, so every page bears a note saying 'Left', 'Right', 'Both for a bit', 'Check-up, Mr Wybar' (Mr Wybar, the saintly oculist of Wimpole Street, is the man who features most regularly in my diary, accompanied by Mr Cuthbertson, the equally venerated dentist). The travelling is tiring even to read about. The lists read like incomprehensible gibberish within weeks of being written.

1964: Feb. Close play. Girls on holiday with my mother. Fly to Cambodia 26th. *Lord Jim*. Move to Hong Kong 28th. Depart to Japan by 3rd March, Kyoto on 5th. 11th opening of *Becket* in New York – organise hair and dress. Party P. Glenville. 13th March leave for London. Children. Kate to Mr Wybar. Work on drawing room. Learn lines. Be in Manchester 17th March. Film in Southport. Sleeper to London arrives 5.30 a.m. Dinner Ken and Deb. April 3rd *Tom Jones*. April 10th Bermans and Wig Creations. Costume pick-up. Ireland. Soup Bowl Restaurant, Molesworth Street today. Girls to Marie Kean – and so on and on unremittingly.

The circus moved on when O'Toole went away on location and life at the Ladies' Seminary settled into a quieter rhythm. There were seven of us, sometimes eight: my mother, Elizabeth the Nanny, Manolita, the treasured daily housekeeper, Pilar, the au-pair, Marie Kean, Kate and Pat and me. During the year I did more television and began another play for the West End. Out of the blue I was asked to do a play, *Hogan's Goat*, on Broadway and declined at once. I could see that there were several ways of organising family life, given our circumstances. More and more movies were being made on location and more Americans seemed to be based in Paris and

Rome, so the chances were that O'Toole would work away from home in Europe. Many actors liked to travel their 'homes' – wife, children, nanny, secretary, friends – with them. O'Toole firmly rejected this. Some mothers, when they travelled, took the children with them, travelling a tutor if necessary. My mother and I between us decided that the girls' life should retain in its own routine, regardless of our activities. I would try to work around their lives. They were not to go away to school and that way O'Toole would be able to see them whenever he was at home whether it was term or holiday time. My going to New York while O'Toole was in Europe was out of the question. The New York producers and my agent were put out by my continuing resistance. Finally they wrote testily, 'You know there is an actress in America who is *longing* to play this part.' 'Well, I'm afraid you'd better give it to her then.' So, Miss Faye Dunaway got her first Broadway break and very good she was, too, I was told.

Instead, I did a French play with my friend, Max Adrian. It was a fantastical work by Marçel Aymé, translated by Kitty Black, and it was the first of many French plays I was to perpetrate over the years – all flops – but I liked them and *Maxibules* was one of the most spectacular failures. No amount of work in rehearsal and on the road could make it acceptable to the English audience. After a faintly improper (for 1963) scene I had to say 'I'm disgusted'. 'So are we,' came a cry from the upper circle. 'And I'm going home,' I continued. 'So are we!' replied the self-appointed critic in the gods.

As the curtain fell on opening night someone hissed, 'Don't take the rag up again, for God's sake!' 'Nonsense!' barked Max – heart of a lion – 'Take it up!' He held my hand tight as we got the bird; my first experience of being booed and hissed. They threw money at the stage. Four days later we were off, but I'd had a lovely time working with Max and I *still* liked the play.

The television play was more successful. It was a very

interesting piece of work *The Other Man*, by Giles Cooper. I played opposite a reserved, young John Thaw and Michael Caine and Granada generously allowed us seven weeks in which to rehearse and film the play. On the long railway journey to Manchester, Michael – also quiet and rather self-contained – outlined his strategy for the next stage of his career, at the end of which he said, 'Within a year, I'll be in movies in a big way.' I nodded, doubtfully. I didn't question his ability but I didn't see how he could be so sure of a thing like that. Just over a year later I noted that he'd been absolutely correct in his strategy and in his prediction.

One night while I was doing a stage play on tour in Guildford, the well-known agent, Harvey Orkin, took the train to see the show and travelled back with me in our car. Before I dropped him off in the Fulham Road, he handed me a script and said, 'Read this, I think you'll find it funny and you'd be very good in it.' It was days before I got around to reading the screenplay and when I did I found it brilliantly funny. I'd never heard of the author. The part Harvey wanted me to look at was fine but the men's parts were wonderful. Harvey wasn't my agent and I didn't know him very well and I wasn't sure what he thought I could do with the script. When I showed it to O'Toole his eyes lit up. I was so pleased he agreed with me – it *was* brilliant. When he took it off to our office, which Jules had set up in Belgravia, I hoped that he would like it as well. O'Toole would be wonderful in the leading part and I wanted to be in such an original movie. The author was invited to London and I was intrigued and enchanted to open the door to a small, droll, shy character who settled cautiously into a corner of the big couch in the Green Room and was sufficiently moved to pull himself together to pay me a compliment on my dress as I brought him tea. Good. He liked me, and he warmed to me even more when I complimented him on *What's New Pussycat?* which is what he'd called the script.

O'Toole entered the room and the cosiness was at an end. 'All right – thanks,' O'Toole smiled and nodded affably but firmly at the door. Evidently I was dismissed. I said goodbye, hoping I looked as though I had lots of other interesting things to do and went up to the nursery. I was a bit put out but even more I was bemused. For someone to be flown across the Atlantic for a chat was wonderful and extraordinary. Less wonderfully, I never saw Woody Allen (for he was the short, shy American) or the script again and was never told what had been discussed over tea.

As the weeks went by I realised that our company, Keep Films, was actually going to co-produce *Pussycat*. During a meeting one day I gathered that 'my' part was going to be offered to someone called Capucine. I was mortified at first but I did appreciate that O'Toole loathed nepotism and it was a measure of his slightly cockeyed respect for me that he strenuously avoided doing me any professional favours. (I saw a photograph of Capucine; she was *incredibly* elegant!) We never discussed this development of casting and I confined my interest in the movie to events in the production office – drama enough.

Because of the attention of the paparazzi, and an attendant court case, O'Toole insisted that the movie he was shooting in Rome be moved to France and so began several years of filming in Paris. All the movies were co-productions with our company, Keep Films, so we kept an apartment at the George V and Jules and Joyce and I flew to and fro as though we were bussing to Putney. O'Toole built up his art collection and I bought my clothes from the big houses and there was much pleasure in our life but it seemed to me that my hold on my place in our life was so precarious that, like a mole in the night, unacknowledged even to myself, I began to build a little power. Rather pathetically, it took the form of making sure that I myself remained extremely thin; ultra-fashionably thin. Anorexia or bulimia was totally alien to my healthily greedy appetite but discipline was second nature to me and I now put myself on the strictest of strict diets. Eating only in the best restaurants in the world, I read the menu, looked at the elaborate food and ate a lamb chop or a piece of fish and a grapefruit every day for lunch and dinner. Sometimes I drank wine, mostly I drank water and I was so thin that I was much in demand by designers to model their clothes. I was flattered to be asked and, more to the point, bought my grand clothes cheaply at Dior because I was exactly the same size as their German house model, Christine and at the end of the season I could buy the clothes she'd been wearing during the shows. I don't think O'Toole even noticed my strange eating habits or my clothes; if he did, he never remarked on them, but being thin – never giving way to temptation – made me feel stronger and more in control than I actually was.

Of course, I was addressing the wrong problem in the wrong way, controlling the wrong thing.

# Chapter Twenty

During this period O'Toole found a way of 'remembering' my birthdays, our anniversaries and Christmas presents. 'Let me off the whole thing,' he said. 'I'll give you things to cover all occasions.' And he did. He'd begun to collect Etruscan jewellery – wonderful, intricate objects, unbelievably crafted before magnification. Most were things to look and wonder at but some were wearable – just. The gold was unalloyed so a chance bump in the night could seriously damage one's favourite bangle. I was happy with this arrangement; there was no suspense about one's birthday being forgotten, no marking of the anniversary to worry about – and Christmas? Well, one less thing to worry about at that time of year could only be to the good.

On Joyce's advice I took my Etruscan collection to Mme Claude de Muzak on the Left Bank in Paris who made beautiful, gunmetal-bound vitrines. I took a few of the more robust looking pieces to Boucheron to be fixed for wearing. The workroom there refused to touch them because they were afraid of destroying them. The man I talked to there asked me if I minded that he'd shown the collection to someone at the Louvre. 'Well, heavens, no, why would I?' I asked. 'No, you don't understand. This is something that should *be* at the Louvre.' 'Oh dear. Yes, I see.'

'O'Toole, do you want this to go to the Louvre – I don't mind, really?'

'Do I fuck? It's *yours*. Take it home.'

And there it sat in the drawing room for years and as the years went by there were more and more vitrines. They were so beautiful and they were *mine*. I couldn't quite believe my good fortune.

But those years in Paris were such a time of unbelievable beauty; beautiful things, beautiful places and acquisitions. The paintings were lovely: a quiet Bonnard for the wall opposite our bed, gorgeous vivid Brós for the entrance hall, a Braque for the drawing room. The drawing room at home was ravishing. Most of our Jack Yeats's paintings were hung there and we had seven big oils; the weakest of all (according to our friend, art dealer, Leslie Waddington) was the one I liked best, *False Morning Promise*, a clown on a raft sailing into heaven knows what sort of day. Milton Avery, the American, was the painter I best liked to live with. O'Toole bought a few, lone seagulls on a grey American coast. Jules and Joyce gave us a lovely grey bird against a blue sky as an anniversary present. I looked at it in the front study every day and loved it more and more. My only outright possession and my favourite painting was one that O'Toole gave me one Christmas when he had missed six planes from Orly to London (in all fairness the distance from the bar to the gates was, in those days, enormous). Lionel, the chauffeur, and I went to the airport at lunchtime and waited in vain – came home; went out again, came home – and so it went on all day and finally the children went to bed and so did my mother and dinner was thrown out and Lionel went alone to the airport. Late at night a very vague O'Toole was delivered to the front door, apologetic and not very well but clutching a smallish parcel which was my Christmas present. When I saw it all was forgiven. It was a painting by Paul Klee. Called *Little Hope*, it was a small, sad face painted on burlap in 1939. I couldn't believe that I could own anything so extraordinary. Every day after that I unlocked the drawing room door and snatched a look before locking up and going about my day.

Joyce Buck was a wonderful companion in Paris. She and Jules and her daughter, Joan-Juliet, had lived there for years – part of the time as neighbours of their colleague, Jacques

Tati, when Jules was producing *Mon Oncle*. (He introduced Jacques Tati to America.) Jules hadn't even got to the point of pronouncing 'Peugeot' properly, but Joyce had taken the whole thing very seriously and had learned French, and young Joan-Juliet to all intents and purposes *was* French. When we came to Paris at weekends Joyce took me around art galleries and antique shops and framers, restorers, carpetmakers – I saw aspects of Paris I would never otherwise have seen. At night we went to the smartest restaurants – lamb chops and grapefruit for me – the newest night clubs (hell on wheels) and one night, I cannot imagine why, Joyce and I – so correct, so controlled, so proper, so not wanting to get our hair messed up – went madly out of control, got drunk in a Russian restaurant, danced all night like dervishes, while our bemused husbands sat, mournfully patient at the bar, looking on. One of my (four) hair pieces fell off. I kicked it into touch without missing a step and cried, 'Leave it! The waiter will get it.' 'Is she often like this?' asked a tired out and sympathetic Regine, queen of the night-club scene. 'No,' said O'Toole, puzzled and truthful. John Shepbridge, the producer, danced with Joyce – watched by an unbelieving Jules. 'Oh John,' she said the following day, 'was I dreadful?' 'My dear,' said John, 'I don't remember a thing.' Joyce, who did remember dancing lewdly, said to me, 'There *are* good guys. They're the ones that say they don't remember a thing.'

During the late Sixties especially, O'Toole spent a great deal of time filming in Paris but my attention was mainly on life at home with the girls and my work in London. I do remember learning that my hero, Hugh Griffith, had been fired off *How to Steal a Million Dollars*, one of the films we co-produced during this period, after persistent bad behaviour, culminating in a naked stroll down the corridors of the George V with 'Don't' struck out and 'Do' substituted before 'disturb' on the card he held in his hand. What is the matter with these film people? They themselves are *so* badly behaved, so cynical, so seriously amoral. An inebriated, naked stroll down a corridor doesn't seem to me to warrant dismissal. In one of the movies, beset with problems, almost the least of the problems took the form of a leading actress who, having completely flipped her lid, was discovered up a gantry with slit wrists dripping blood on the upturned faces below. Deprived of alcohol, she'd been drinking eau de toilette and had to be coaxed down and packed off to hospital. The more I saw of the movie world, the more astonished I was at the nonsense people got away with.

Audrey Hepburn (in *How to Steal a Million Dollars*) was so lovely. She was surprisingly tall and when we were introduced I was shocked to feel her tiny, fleshless hand – like holding a bird's claw or a small cat's paw. She lived a life of iron discipline that made me feel self-indulgent, watching the rushes twice; once alone and once with her make-up man, making notes; filming from noon till seven or eight p.m., eating only a little dry salad then going through every still photograph taken during the day (hundreds), rejecting all that weren't flattering, then home to the hotel, alone, for a little more dry salad and back to the studio in the morning for more rushes, more consultations and two hours in make-up before the day's work began. I realised that she was a woman playing a much younger girl and that the work behind this successful deception was enormous and gracefully embraced. It wasn't vanity on her part, it was attention to business. I didn't much like her husband at the time, Mel Ferrer. He installed her in Paris, sent her out to work and decamped, all over Europe having, as far as I could see, a fine old time.

When *What's New Pussycat?* was being shot, I spent my time at the George V and went sightseeing each day rather than go to the studio too often. Romy Schneider was a pillar of professional good sense, but I couldn't warm to Capucine who was playing 'my' part, though she was perfectly amiable. I thought she was a little dull. It was difficult to see how the director, Clive Donner, managed to keep the whole thing chugging along on schedule. The stories we heard told in the office back in London were alarming and Peter Sellers, whom I revered as an actor, went down rather in my estimation. Since his heart attack he was uninsurable and after the financial disaster of *Cleopatra* caused by Elizabeth Taylor's near fatal illness when she was shooting in England, film companies were very aware of the dangers of employing actors who were not in good condition. O'Toole, also a huge admirer and sympathetic to his plight, had pushed and pushed for engaging Sellers and finally the company had agreed to take the risk. At this point Peter Sellers, 'agreeing' to do the film which he desperately needed and wasn't wanted for, said he would only do the movie if he was given first billing over O'Toole. Executives reeled back, laughing feebly at this piece of madness and were totally nonplussed when O'Toole calmly told them that he didn't give a damn and Sellers was to be given anything he asked for. Jules was fit to be tied and even I thought it was a bit over-casual, but O'Toole refused to discuss the matter. So P. Sellers was given everything he demanded and he got top billing. Then when they started shooting he took against Woody, throwing out huge chunks of script and wiring music-hall entertainers in England for gags which were then inserted into his scenes. I was disappointed to see that O'Toole condoned this behaviour. They refused to rehearse with Woody Allen and I don't think Peter Sellers ever realised that he was dealing with a comic talent every bit as great as and even more complex than his own. Clive juggled the personalities and managed to run a very efficient, hard-working unit and produced a funny film.

Sellers came into my life some years later when O'Toole was filming *Man of La Mancha*. He pitched up in O'Toole's suite of rooms at the Excelsior Hotel in Rome and installed himself on the sitting room couch. He was having personal problems so he was depressed and couldn't return home to England because of taxation problems. Tiring of his guest, O'Toole urged him to go and stay with me in Hampstead, where he could be hidden from the Inland Revenue and would find the study day-bed much more comfortable than the Excelsior couch.

Our house, when O'Toole was away, centred around the activities of the girls; their diary was crammed with dancing classes, parties, visits to the dentist and oculist, homework, tests, sports and holidays. (I was amazed that they could fit so much into each day.) Now, we were told to expect the movie star and his chauffeur. I myself was also busy, so my mother made a wonderful Boeuf Bourguignon which would only improve as the hours went by and we awaited the arrival – time unspecified – of the Sellers team. When the doorbell rang I rushed for the door and saw more Louis Vuitton luggage than I had ever seen outside an antique shop (at that time there was no Louis Vuitton shop in England and it wasn't widely familiar). This was not luggage for a short stay I thought, with a sinking heart as I yielded up my study and day-bed. When '*Boeuf*' was mentioned, the two men started back, 'Didn't Petey *say* I was a vegetarian?' said Peter. 'No dear Petey didn't,' I said grimly. 'Well, he may have done,' soothed Mamgu. 'It's not a problem.' As we tore down to the basement kitchen she wailed in Welsh, 'What do vegetarians eat?' 'Vegetables,' I snapped. Liz the Nanny and I plundered our big cellars under Heath Street, returning with mountains of carrots and cabbages and potatoes and onions. 'Okay Siân, you upstairs to give them drinks and keep them distracted,' ordered my mother, back in charge. 'Liz, start peeling and fetch someone to help you.'

Within an hour Peter Sellers was exclaiming over the best home-made soup he'd ever tasted. 'Can I have this every day?' 'Of *course*,' said my mother, sweetly. Downstairs Liz and the au-pair and I cleared away mountains of peelings and began assembling the next day's pyramids of vegetables. When my mother came down, beaming, I held up a large cauldron and pointed at the dregs. 'What's that?' (In Welsh) 'Bones.'

'Vegetarians don't eat *bones*.' 'You can't make soup without bones.' I gave up the unequal struggle and for a month Peter Sellers thrived on what he thought was vegetable soup and glumly picking my way round the L-V trunks, unable to use my phone or get at my books, I thought, 'Oh, what the hell, it won't harm him.' Like many great comics, Peter was not much fun at home. He was depressed. At night, I would let myself in and try to tiptoe past the study and fly up the stairs unnoticed. On the nights when I was waylaid we would sit in the Green Room next door and Peter would talk of himself, explaining to me how impossible his life was and how sad. He had made a film with Sophia Loren and conceived an unrequited passion for her. Listening to him I couldn't believe that anyone so smart in his own field could be so stupid as to misunderstand the situation so utterly. How could he imagine that a practical, ambitious woman from a poor background – protected by Carlo Ponti, her powerful, film-producer husband who devoted his life to promoting her career – would, for a moment, consider endangering her position for a romance with a mere actor. I wasn't much use to him and I didn't become a close friend. As soon as I could I left the house and joined O'Toole at the Excelsior in Rome. The girls came to Rome as well and O'Toole laughed evilly when I arrived, worn out by my house guest and his self preoccupation. 'How *could* you?' 'Ah, get off. Don't make a fuss. There's no harm in him.'

Naturally, Mamgu became a confidante of Sellers and got to like Bert, the chauffeur. Peter had embraced an Eastern religion, we supposed, and she didn't much like the Eastern scrolls hanging over the bookshelves or the chanting which filled the ground floor from time to time but she liked looking after him. I stayed away till he was gone.

I'd been bumping up against famous people since I was a girl so it wasn't exactly difficult having to live with celebrities and I knew enough not to expect them to be fascinating when they were off duty, but alas, many huge stars were really heavy going. There is a kind of self-absorption that infects their behaviour and makes them less interesting than they might otherwise be. I'd been raised to have respect but not to be 'a respecter of persons' and I couldn't shake that off. There were glorious exceptions. I loved my time with Wilfrid Lawson, I would have given anything to know Ralph Richardson better, the time I spent with John Steinbeck and his wife, Elaine, is indelibly etched in my memory, as were the few evenings I spent with Jacques Tati and his wife. Laurens van der Post was even better than I could have imagined from reading his books and I was perfectly happy to be a kind of third hand-maiden on the left for Edith Evans because I admired her so much.

Kate Hepburn, whom I first met when she was filming *Lion in Winter*, was interesting and in many ways admirable, but I couldn't help feeling envious of the way in which she seemed to have her life organised so as to have things all her own way. Her seemingly simple life was in fact kept oiled and running by retainers of long standing. Her companion ('Phy-lisss!' would go the shout whenever she wanted anything) travelled with her and organised her living arrangements. She wore gorgeous, glamorous clothes all her life until, cleverly, realising that, no longer youthful, she couldn't compete with young actresses, she devised a marvellous uniform; colours of beige and red, black or white; slacks and smart gifted or purloined men's sweaters or jackets. Her years with Spencer Tracy suited her very well – a wife with none of the wife's boring jobs – and she admitted as much to me. When O'Toole, who was very smitten by her glamorous, unusual presence, was moved to say, 'My God – if I was thirty years younger I'd have given Spencer Tracy a run for his money', we looked at each other, slightly cross-eyed, wondering which of us had been more insulted; Kate for being considered too old to be desirable or me, who, all things being equal, would have been discarded in favour of a young Kate. It wasn't something to be thought about too closely, so we both smiled sweetly. When, in 1970,

Kate was playing in *Coco*, the musical, in New York, O'Toole and I dined at her house before leaving for South America. As we left, she grabbed me by the arm and hissed, 'You let him push you around – stop it. I'm spoiled. *Get spoiled!*' I nodded, smiling, and thought I'd like to see her try getting her own way with O'Toole, were she thirty years younger. Not a chance. I remember her as spoiled and selfish indeed but what wonderful common sense she had. And she took what she wanted and paid for it, and, I would hazard, has rarely had occasion to regret her choices.

On the whole, O'Toole kept me out of his professional life. Very few people were invited to Guyon House. We gave at the most two large parties and one tiny Christmas morning cocktail party, distinguished only by a very woozy Robert Stephens falling right through a rather nice chair. He was living with my friend, the remarkable and beautiful Pat Quinn (whose mother I played in *Shoulder to Shoulder*, the TV series about the suffragette movement). They married subsequently and were perfect for each other. An Irish friend of mine went to them for lunch one day and round about teatime Pat – not quite herself – served some meat, then a little hors d'oeuvre, then a pudding, then said, 'Oh God, I forgot the veg,' and left the room never to return. 'Please excuse Patricia,' murmured Robert. 'She's frightfully unhappy today.'

It was so mightily encouraging when Robert made a return (almost from the dead) to play Falstaff and get knighted. The most extraordinary things happen in our profession. I'm sure Anthony Hopkins would agree that he was, in 1978, the least likely candidate for international super stardom and respectable knighthood. Then he went to America, made some awful movies, temporarily renounced the theatre, nearly killed himself in a car, joined AA, and became one of our senior, respectable ennobled actors. Hepburn was one of Tony's first mentors in the movies. O'Toole, against the wishes of the American producers and the casting director, had insisted on engaging him for *Lion in Winter*. (John Castle was another of his 'finds' and Nigel Terry also – a remarkable, very Cornish actor.) When Tony played his first scene with Kate she took him by the shoulders and turned him away from her. 'There's the camera – over there. It needs to see you.'

Most of the actors I knew and liked were people I'd worked with but one actor, very close to O'Toole, became someone I treasured although we never worked together. Donal McCann was hugely talented. The son of a sometime Lord Mayor of Dublin, he'd been raised in the Big House and during his childhood had suffered an enormous tragedy. Entrusted with his younger brother's safety on the way to school, he'd looked away for a moment and his little brother had darted into the road and was run over. Donal never recovered, never escaped the demons that pursued him after this and he drank to excess for much of his adult life. He and O'Toole played *Godot* together many times, learning it holed up in the Shelbourne, sleeping in twin beds and working every moment that they weren't sleeping. They were wonderful together in the play, with Niall Toibin playing Pozzo. One day Donal came to visit O'Toole in Guyon House. His chum was spending the day in bed and not even for Donal could he be disturbed. We sat together till lunch time and Donal refused to come to the dining room to eat. I returned to the Green Room after lunch with the girls and we sat there as darkness fell. By this time Donal was into his second bottle of vodka and I, sipping cold tea, was getting sleepy. Nodding off, I jerked awake to dimly make out something odd about Donal's silhouette as he sat on the Green Room 'stage' with his back to Men's Surgical beyond the garden. He was on fire, having dropped his cigarette into his curly black hair which he was in the habit of teasing with his right hand as he talked. I crossed to the drinks tray and, picking up a soda siphon, turned it on to Donal and put out the fire on his head. He blinked a bit and held out his glass for a refill. Years later, when I was on location in Dublin a slim athletic figure darted across the road and embraced me. I could hardly recognise the teetotal Donal. His work, which had always been good, became even more wonderful. *The Steward of Christendom* at the Royal Court, not many years before his untimely death, was a never-to-be-forgotten piece of acting.

*Godot* is one of my favourite plays and McCann and O'Toole surely approached the intention of the author. The author . . . Sam Beckett. So beautiful, so vain. Blind as a bat and didn't wear glasses. Exquisitely dressed in cashmere polonecks and soft tweeds. A cross-Channel swimmer. And an opinionated bigot in some ways, I thought. I sat in a flat in Manchester Square and listened to Beckett and O'Toole, fascinating and good-looking, as they became drunker and drunker and through a haze of tiredness and boredom I heard Mr Beckett say, *Godot* can never be filmed. No film with dialogue has *ever* succeeded. Buster Keaton is the only film actor worth considering.' Sitting there, slightly outside the adoring throng at the great man's feet, I thought, 'Oh puhleez. Give me a break' and, aloud and unheard, said 'Excuse me,' and left. Standing in a fog-bound Manchester Square I began to laugh as I searched for a cab. Here I was wandering around W1 on my own because I was bored to death by a great playwright who I thought was talking rubbish about the movies.

In 1966 I worked for Sam, and it was an extraordinary experience. Jackie McGowran came to my dressing room at the Vaudeville Theatre where I was halfway through a long run of *Man and Superman* with Alan Badel. He was carrying a copy of *Eh, Joe*. 'We'll do it at the BBC,' he said. 'You will speak the "play" – a monologue lasting twenty minutes. You won't be seen and the camera will remain on me throughout.' What a lovely, easy job, I thought as I agreed to go the following Sunday to a flat on Haverstock Hill and work with Mr Beckett himself. There were very few preliminaries and I began to read for him. It wasn't an *easy* read but I thought I was doing quite well until, after about ten minutes, I caught sight of Sam's face contorted with what looked like pain. I ploughed on and when I'd finished there was a long silence. Then 'I don't know where to start,' said Sam, faintly. I was too sorry for him to be upset on my own behalf and I urged him to be as brutally frank as he wished and please to believe that if he *told* me what he wanted I *would* be able to deliver it to him. I don't think he believed me. It took two weeks of grinding work to get the twenty minutes anywhere near what Sam wanted. He banged his hand on the table like a metronome; three beats for a full stop, two for a colon, half for a comma. Three speak, speak, speak. Half speak speak. Two speak stop. I gave up trying to interpret the monologue and learned it like a piece of music, hanging on to that text like a stubborn dog with a bone. Finally came the moment when Sam nodded from the control cubicle. Michael Bakewell who was producing and Jackie who was hanging about looking anxious, both looked relieved. I had a bit of time to spare before going to the theatre and I asked Sam if I could try another take; one for me. He shrugged but maybe he thought I'd earned a small favour after all we'd been through, so off I went, hoping that enough of Sam's rhythms had become second nature to me because I wasn't thinking about them on this take. When I'd finished Sam said, '*That's* what I meant all along' and I could have hugged him except I didn't dare. I could quite see why whole companies had gone on strike during rehearsals of his plays and refused to work if his time-beating hand wasn't removed. But I was glad I'd hung on; it had been quite an experience to remember. Patrick Magee and Jackie McGowran and Billie Whitelaw were Beckett 'naturals', the rest of us had to work quite a bit harder. And there's nothing quite as wonderful as having the author around. What would it be like to be able to pop up to Admin to ask Shakespeare what exactly did he mean on page 32?

A pattern of sorts emerged. O'Toole's work took precedence

over everything. His large office in Belgravia presided over by Jules was organised so as to keep him busy as much of the time as possible. Jules, who had spent his earlier life with some of the major players in the movie business, had a theory that work was the only thing that kept some of the more 'highly coloured characters' sane. And much as I would have liked to have been able to have more of O'Toole for myself and the family (maybe even to take a holiday), I had to admit that Jules might be right. While he was preparing for a big movie, O'Toole was an angel; hard working, moderate and a benevolent presence in the house. When he was actually filming he was quiet, self-disciplined, a little 'absent' even when at home. Once work was completed, very often after a six-month work period, he became a different person, erratic and unpredictable, turning night into day. Then he would sleep and sleep and wake penitent and chastened and spend days being attentive and charming – overwhelmingly charming. I never saw anyone fail to forgive him completely, no matter how badly they'd been hurt and I was as susceptible as any of them. This roller-coaster life would continue only until his attention was engaged by a new job and then quiet times would be resumed. It was my good fortune to love and be loved by this extraordinary man and it was my deep misfortune to be as incapable as the next person of expressing my anger at his unfair, unjust behaviour. No one else in my private or working life had ever been able to treat me as he did. I was part of a huge conspiracy directed towards protecting O'Toole from the painful consequences of his behaviour. It didn't make me feel better that bigger, stronger, cleverer people than I shared the urge to protect him.

Walking out on him was not an option. Unbelievable as it may seem, life in Guyon House was happy; it was a big house and the children, my mother and Liz led busy, enjoyable lives in very comfortable, beautiful surroundings. They took holidays in Ireland in a cottage we had acquired in the Sixties, and we began to plan an Irish home, on the large piece of land O'Toole had acquired. Taking a meat-cleaver to all this seemed pretty selfish. And there was so much of our life that I loved. Trying to figure out how to proceed, I decided that the only truly awful thing that could happen to me would be for me to become sour and resentful. I had *truly* to get over my feelings of hurt pride. I also had to stop identifying with O'Toole, feeling embarrassed or guilty when he behaved badly in public, and above all I had to learn not to accept as truth his icy criticism of me as – when drunk – he ordered me out of the car or restaurant or our house. 'Who owns this house?' was the frequent Dr Jekyll challenge. I never liked to point out that we owned it jointly. On the whole – with a few mutinous lapses – I managed to embrace survival strategy and in the process I became harder and rougher around the edges but it made the bad times bearable. Someone asked me, 'How do you manage to combine your busy private life with your career?' O'Toole answered for me, 'She doesn't have a career. She has jobs.' No, I thought, but let the moment pass without comment.

I didn't show my hurt over my summary rejection from *What's New Pussycat?* and I got my reward almost at once. A few years previously I'd been asked to be in *The Night of the Iguana* by Tennessee Williams. Vanessa Redgrave, who'd made a *very* good start to her career and had great support from her husband, Tony Richardson, was to play Hannah Jelkes and I was asked to play a part I was totally unsuited for – Maxine – the character that Bette Davis had played when Margaret Leighton had done the play in America. I fell completely in love with the role of Hannah and felt bitterly frustrated not to be asked to play her. I was so right for the part. So was Vanessa, of course, but that wasn't my concern at that moment. I'd turned down the offer and in the event the production didn't take place. Now the play came to me again; Richard Shulman and Philip Wiseman had acquired the rights and were going to mount it in Croydon. Croydon . . . the

Ashcroft Theatre in the Fairfield Halls complex wasn't exactly the most appealing of theatres. I said 'Yes', of course. I just wanted to play Hannah Jelkes but it was a damned shame that it was going to take place for such a short run in one venue.

I'd seen the movie of *The Night of the Iguana* with Richard Burton, Deborah Kerr and Ava Gardner and hadn't thought much of it. It was given wisdom that once a play had been filmed it could not be mounted as a West End production, so I was lucky to get Croydon. And I would be able to commute.

As I read the script I realised with dismay that it wasn't the same script I'd read when Woodfall Productions held the rights, before the film was made. The cuts really bothered me and I began to ask if I could reinstate bits of the play that for no reason I could see had vanished. I became a terrible nuisance, bargaining for a line here, a speech there. Philip and Richard were patient but firm – we *had* to perform the new version. Gradually I discovered that some of the cuts had been made at the insistence of Bette Davis who hadn't been too happy with the way her part was received as they began touring (Maxine just isn't as good a part as Hannah). Tennessee, I was told, was obliging beyond belief, chopping away at his play with a will. I was astonished; the playwrights I'd met were touchy about altering commas, let alone brilliant chunks of text. Temporarily deflated (I'd seen myself as the author's champion), I began rehearsing the new version but as the weeks went by I began to slip back the bits I couldn't bear to be without and Philip turned a blind eye.

This was the best part I'd been given for years and I became over-enthusiastic and probably tiresomely obsessed by the play. Philip Wiseman, a quiet, bookish American in English tweeds, was a marvel of discretion. Somehow he reined me in – he admitted afterwards that directing me was a bit like handling a jumpy, highly strung race horse – and we arrived safe and secure at our opening night. I fell in love with the Ashcroft auditorium. Philip had 'placed' the production so well in it that it felt wonderfully comfortable. I enjoyed going to the stage in a lift that also carried boxers or wrestlers (half-dressed muscular men, raring to hit something) on their way to the sports arena. It was very relaxing to be in a dressing room that totally defied one to pretty it up. There were half-pint glasses of half drunk beer on the dressing table with its layer of dust and grease. I didn't even bother to make a 'place' for myself. I don't know if anyone sent flowers; they certainly didn't make it to the dressing room. Mark Eden was the Reverend Shannon and I was lucky again that he also possessed the temperament of a gentleman. As I nagged and altered things and rehearsed and re-rehearsed and over-rehearsed, he got on with his own work and helped me where he could and resisted what must have been a justifiable temptation to take me by the shoulders and shake me until I quietened down. I think I was as much of a nuisance as is possible to be within the walls of a theatre.

On opening night the play went wonderfully well. The following day I got up early and went off to model some clothes for an Irish designer. I was in the middle of a long photographic session when Philip tracked me down and asked me if I'd seen the papers. No, I hadn't (I hadn't thought the national press would come to Croydon). 'Well,' he went on, suppressing what even on the phone I could tell was huge excitement, 'we have rave notices across the board and our pick of five London theatres into which to transfer. Be at the theatre early and we'll talk.' I went back to my photo session more thoughtful than excited. Already I was worrying about the transfer; would our show work as well outside the confines of what had become to me the 'dear Fairfield Hall'? The phone went again. Audrey Wood, Tennessee's agent, sent a message of congratulations and said that 'Tom' (Tom? I didn't know that Tennessee wasn't called Tennessee) would be coming to London for the West End opening. Back to the clothes and the posing. 'Chin down, eyes up, button the jacket.'

Eventually I'm through and dash home to see the girls and then take the train to Croydon. The journey gives me time to think. My mother says the phone has been ringing all day with requests for interviews and photographs, the house is full of bouquets; she's quietly pleased. I feel odd. It's four years since I was the subject of this kind of attention and something has happened to steal the joy from the moment. I feel – what? Apprehensive. A bit of me seems to have broken and I don't have the confidence to enjoy all this fuss. It's as though I'll wake up to find that a mistake has been made. 'Not you! Whatever made you think we meant you?' And what if it *was* a kind of mistake last night at the theatre? What if I can't do it again? Keeping these fears hidden I put on a brave, bright face and join the high-spirited gathering at the theatre. It is wonderful for Richard Shulman and Philip and I'm genuinely happy for them. We'll choose a theatre tomorrow. What larks! I'm glad to get to my dingy dressing room and put on my dingy clothes. The only way I can maintain my equilibrium is to think about nothing but the play from now on. Let the rest wash over me. See to the children. Attend to the play. This unexpected turn of events has thrown into sharp relief how badly I've reacted to the events of the last few years and how low I've been brought. For whatever reason I've arrived at a state of mind where I cannot feel that anything I do is of any consequence whatever and I'm worried how this success might affect my relationship with O'Toole. Might this change? If it doesn't, is it something I might be able to turn to my advantage? Or will it always apply a little brake to my efforts?

# Chapter Twenty-one

Playing eight times a week really suits me. Many of my friends hate it and they hate being in a run. Not I. To me there is no greater pleasure than steering a good production of a good play through the different circumstances that occur each night. Each night is different and not different. Flops are another matter. I've had more than my share and can get fed up with a bad play in a week, but even then, there's a kind of perverse satisfaction in getting a bad job done well. I've been stage-struck since I was six, and sat in Swansea Empire watching a pantomime. Will I go on feeling like this for ever, I wonder.

At the moment I'm as happy as can be, ensconced in the Savoy Theatre. Tennessee – Tom – did arrive and stood on his seat in the front row and over-did his enthusiasm. Richard Condon (the novelist and Debbie Jupp's father) rushed a massive basket of flowers down the aisle and had a noisy row with an usherette who wouldn't let him hand it up to the stage (for fear it contained explosives?). There were flowers everywhere and I remembered that on my last opening in London, just a few months ago, someone had thrown copper coins on to the stage and there had been the noise of booing and hissing, rather than cheers.

Nothing had happened to alter my reservations about opening nights. I'd worn a nasty, mustard-coloured old frock to work so that I wouldn't be tempted to go out to celebrate afterwards; straight home as usual, a relatively early night and up early with Kate. Later, when the play settled down, I began going out to parties with my new best friend Tom but I think I was a bit of a disappointment to him as a date. My neuroses were far too well submerged and I could have only a flimsy grip on his attention. As we entered a room I would watch him as he prowled around for a while before homing in on someone who, a surprising number of times, would turn out to be in the throes of a breakdown, or recovering from a failed suicide attempt or about to do something disastrous. Nose to nose, they would chat for hours.

On other levels, we got on very well and corresponded from time to time after he returned to America. He sent me a poem he wrote for me. I got to know Audrey Wood, his agent, as well and they sent me all his new material for many years to come. I admired him above all the authors I knew so I suppose that pre-disposed him to like me too.

Soon after we opened, O'Toole returned from France where he was filming and when he came to see the play he was generous about my performance. To Ken Jupp he said facetiously, 'Blimey, they'll be calling me Mr Phillips in a minute. I'm off!' and hopped back to Paris. When the film finished he went into rehearsal for a new play by David Mercer, *Ride a Cock Horse*. It was long, very long, and had a difficult shape. In two parts, it consisted of six duologues between the hero and his wife, his girlfriend and his older mistress. It was a marathon part for an actor. It was also, I was given to understand, a '*pièce à clef*' about well-known contemporary writers. It was so well written and so depressing. (My life, in comparison, seemed peachy, I thought gratefully.) The ladies of the company were Wendy Craig as the girlfriend, Barbara Jefford as the wife and Yvonne Mitchell as the unhappy mistress. Rather them than me, I thought as I made my way to the Savoy.

David Mercer began to visit the house to work with O'Toole. A great deal of alcohol was consumed. Then, when O'Toole began rehearsing and cut out the drink, David would arrive and drink alone and finally O'Toole would retreat to the bedroom to work, leaving my mother to cope with the brilliant but very touchy playwright. I, thank God, was out of reach at the theatre. My mother spent hours listening to David talk about his parents so one night when he arrived dressed in a railwayman's overalls, mourning the death of his railwayman father, my mother ministered to him and finally he spent the night on the Green Room couch. When it was revealed later to her that his father was in fact alive and well, my mother – endlessly patient – was *almost* annoyed with him.

Between shows at the Savoy on matinée day. A knock and then the door opens before I can say 'Come in' – O'Toole, followed by Michael Codron the producer. Drama. At rehearsal, they've lost (or shed) Yvonne Mitchell. Can I open in Nottingham next Tuesday? I open my mouth to say 'But what about my play?' and they say they'll buy me out of the last two weeks of the run (Bernie Delfont, a friend, is one of the producers). I don't want to miss two weeks of *Iguana* but it doesn't occur to me to deny O'Toole. Also, it's a challenge. I don't like the David Mercer play and I don't think that, at my age, I'm very well suited to a part based on Penelope Mortimer in a bit of a decline. All the more reason to try, I think perversely.

So I'll travel to Nottingham the day after I close Tom's play on Saturday and open on Tuesday. 'When will I rehearse?' O'Toole considers. 'Well, now, let's see. Learn it and go over the moves with the stage manager and we'll rehearse you *after* we open. We have four weeks on the road.' Heavens – this *is* a challenge. I've never opened a play without rehearsing it. It's an endless part; two duologues of over half an hour. If I pull it off, O'Toole will be so grateful. And I'll be doing him a favour. Michael Codron is strangely silent. I wonder if this is O'Toole's harebrained idea and he doesn't like to object. We're all going along with the idea. Gordon Flemyng, who had made such a good job of directing the TV play *The Other Man*, which I did with Michael Caine and whom I introduced to O'Toole, is directing the Mercer play. I didn't know he worked in the theatre at all.

Nottingham is a nightmare. O'Toole has decided that we will only play the biggest of theatres and, confident of doing good business, he will clear all production costs before we come into town. There are banners reading 'O'Toole' all over the streets and the run is completely sold out before we begin. I've never seen anything quite like this and I've played with some of our biggest theatre stars. I learn my lines and write down my moves from the prompt copy. I share a suite with O'Toole but hardly see him. He's deeply involved with David Mercer who is drinking heavily. Every night we have dinner with him and Gordon in a private dining room in the hotel. I still haven't rehearsed. I haven't dried on stage and I haven't stood in the wrong place but I haven't the faintest idea what I'm doing. It's utterly horrible. The little bit of confidence that grew during the months of success at the Savoy drains away now in the first week of playing *Ride a Cock Horse*.

They cut chunks of the play. Every night the stage manager comes round at the half and says things like, 'Take out pages twenty-four and twenty-five, the top of forty-five, two lines at the bottom of fifty, this section on fifty-one.' I barely know the original text, learning cuts every day as well is torture. The play is down to about four hours long. Now O'Toole declares, 'Go faster. Top all the laughs and let's see if we can't cut fifteen minutes by playing faster.' 'Topping' laughs means coming in at the crest of the laugh and moving on smartly; it's a struggle, in a huge theatre, to be audible without shouting when you're speaking over a huge laugh. We all manage. Floundering about a bit, I catch O'Toole on stage looking at me quizzically. 'Are you going to *do* it like this?' he mutters sardonically in the middle of the scene. I'm fashionably flat-chested. Message from the management: 'Get her some falsies.' This is hell.

'When do I rehearse?'

'Tomorrow.'

'Oh, thank God.'

At seven o'clock I wake, alone, in the suite. At nine thirty a.m., walking through the foyer to go and rehearse with O'Toole, I meet him and Gordon Flemying coming *in* after a night on the town.

'Hello, darling, where are you off to?'

'To rehearse with you.'

'Ah, sorry about that, darling. Bye. See you for a spot of late lunch?'

Each day I go to the theatre and go through my lines but I'm no nearer playing this part properly. I hate this play now. I hate the dinners at which D. Mercer gets drunk then gets on the hotel phone and recites soliloquies from it to someone who must be driven mad. It's all so depressing. But the money is flooding into the box office. Who is in charge? 'I'm going to complain to the Management,' I think and then, remembering that this is a co-production with Keep Films, I realise I *am* the Management.

The torment continued. Being confused, nightly, in front of thousands of people may not rank high in torment on a global scale but it *is* major nastiness on a personal scale. Gordon, the director, managed to avoid me, Barbara and Wendy had their own problems and O'Toole never did rehearse with me. We opened to a sold-out, limited run in London. The big Piccadilly Theatre seemed quite cosy after our huge touring theatres. Production costs had been paid off. I supposed that, as usual, O'Toole was not taking a salary. I don't know how the play was received by the critics (I'd recently stopped reading reviews), but it was a huge commercial success. People – Kenneth Tynan notable among them – came again and again. I hated every minute of it. O'Toole and I had completely different timetables. I would rise early, see the girls, see to the house while he slept. Seething with resentment, part of me longed to have a huge row with him. Who else, I wondered, would treat me with such colossal disrespect? No one I could think of. But he was marvellous in the play and he loved it and he had a huge job to do each night: how could I have a row with him? And if I did, how would he torture me on stage? I didn't delude myself that I was smart enough to cope with an angry O'Toole, certainly not in front of a packed house. Each day at five o'clock I would eat a plate of scrambled eggs, go to the West End, walk about a bit, go into the theatre and go up to my dressing room, call home unnecessarily to check everything was still all right, throw up, get made up, do the show, afterwards descend to dressing room Number One if we had mutual friends in to see the show, occasionally I would go to dinner (always if the Bucks or the Jupps were around). The rest of the time I went home alone. It was odd. And faintly embarrassing.

And yet O'Toole gave me one of the best opening night presents I ever received. He remembered that, many years ago, fleeing from a failed relationship, I'd had to leave behind my mother's complete set of Charles Dickens which I'd been reading since I was a little girl. He bought me a lovely edition of the complete works. The boxes were delivered to my room just as I was throwing up and hating him and I was overcome with gratitude and love and misery all at once. Fancy his remembering something that had happened so long ago. Fancy his knowing how much I missed those books. He always knew things about me that no one would guess at.

It felt as though the whole town flocked to Dressing Room One. One regular visitor – and he didn't even watch the show – was Robin Douglas-Home. He irritated me hugely and was for ever insisting that we should go with him to a gaming club in Mayfair. O'Toole, son of an unsuccessful gambling bookmaker, liked gambling but had successfully disciplined himself not to indulge. Week after week, day after day, Robin Douglas-Home haunted the theatre and, finally, we went with him. I watched, impassive, while O'Toole lost almost £10,000 in half an hour. We smiled and accepted a glass of champagne and drifted into the night, still smiling, but I couldn't speak for fury.

The play and O'Toole's pace of life are taking their toll. He begins to bleed from the nose on stage. Night after night there's blood everywhere but the audience doesn't seem to notice. I never cease to be amazed at what the audience simply doesn't see. No one can understand why he's losing blood every night but Gerry Slattery says it's time to stop. The play, which is only slated for a limited run, could actually run for ever but everyone has been paid and a profit has been made so it's decided to close the show two weeks early. There is a God, I think. I'm just about as low in spirits as it is possible to be. One of my teachers from RADA and a friend of O'Toole's as well sees that I'm in a bad way despite the bright smile after the show. The following day he sends me one of my unread notices for *The Night of the Iguana*; only months ago W.A. Darlington the senior critic of the *Daily Telegraph*, it seems, had written, 'If she never acts again she has proved she is a great actress.' I look at it in stupefaction. I feel that I've now spent months acting badly and doubt that I was *ever* any good. The review gives me no consolation. Going about my daily business; dealing with the domestic details of our life, occupying myself with the children, listening to my mother and my treasured daily help, Manolita, writing letters for O'Toole, I am well aware that the way I do my job doesn't matter to anyone except me. But it does matter terribly to me whether I act well or badly.

We never worked happily together, sadly for me. *Ride a Cock Horse* was a push-push experience – all bad but usually there were good aspects as well as painful ones. *Goodbye Mr Chips* was an example of a pull-push engagement. I was cast in a roundabout way and felt that O'Toole was not pleased that I'd been given the part of Ursula Mossbank (which Terence Rattigan based on Tallulah Bankhead). I spent some time during the student riots of 1968 in Paris, marooned in the

George V with Herb Ross who was to direct the film and Nora Kaye, formerly a prima ballerina and now Herb's wife and collaborator. We got along famously and Herb asked me if I'd like to be considered for the part of the actress – along with half a dozen of my contemporaries. When we were able to return to London I duly presented myself at the studio and read for Herb, who had never seen me act. He gave me the part and, to our dismay, when we came to film the party sequences O'Toole declined to rehearse with me, leaving me to walk the set with Herb and with Ossie Morris, the lighting camera man.

I retired to my dressing-room and stayed there alone, going over the scenes until I knew them backwards, sideways and upside down. I was terrified of the ordeal ahead but determined not to be found wanting. Called to the set, I sat on my own, waiting. O'Toole sat alone, some distance away. Afterwards, Herb said it was like sending into space astronauts who didn't know each other. He was nonplussed and I didn't know either why O'Toole behaved as he did. I guessed that maybe he was overwhelmingly concerned that I might not be any good and simply couldn't deal with his nerves. But that was my guess. In the event the scenes worked like clockwork without the usual preparation and despite the complex set we 'got' the scenes in one take. No mention was ever made afterwards of the tensions of the day. 'What was that about?' asked Herb. I shook my head, as mystified as he was. O'Toole was affability itself when he returned home. I loved watching him work on that film and thought that he gave a great performance in a so-so movie. When he was made up as old Mr Chips I looked for him in the canteen and, not recognising him, walked past him. He made a lovely old man. We rented a house in Cerne Abbas in Dorset where the bulk of the film was shot and the girls and I spent wonderfully happy weeks there.

Trials, like the hateful first day of filming, served me well in the long run. There was very little I couldn't handle and very few actors who scared me, however 'difficult' their behaviour. Surviving O'Toole in a bad mood made me very self-reliant. When in 1970 I came to work with Rex Harrison on *Platonov* I was aware that he had a fiendish reputation for being ungenerous, to say the least. His behaviour didn't alarm me at all. Interestingly, in Wilfrid Lawson's opinion he had the edge on his contemporaries: Sir Laurence and Sir John and even Sir Ralph. 'Took the wrong turning,' Wilfrid said sadly. Rex's rages were apocalyptic and strong men paled as he tore a phone from the wall one day and threw all the furniture off a set he didn't particularly like. Watching him, I could imagine what a great Lear he would have made. Knowing him to be ruthless in appropriating whole scenes for himself, I was determined not to be eclipsed and once he saw that I had more than done my homework and that I wasn't frightened of him, he let me 'in' and although it was always as dangerous as acting on sheet ice, acting with him became truly thrilling and rewarding. I admired him almost more than anyone I had ever worked with.

# Chapter Twenty-two

Meanwhile, our domestic life was going through one of the welcome, quiet periods. O'Toole and I were working hard and my mother became the point of refuge for neglected guests. O'Toole was lavish in his offers of hospitality and equally protective of his working time (easily bored, as well). People would arrive and find themselves adrift and alone in the Green Room. A great deal of the time I didn't know who was in the house and if I returned late from the theatre to find a party in full swing I shot through the hall and up the stairs to the bedroom before my presence was registered. I really liked getting up early and seeing the children in the morning.

My mother actually enjoyed staying up and talking, especially to the writers. For instance, she was the one who scooped up and took down to the big kitchen a figure that I'd stepped over in some exasperation as I left with Kate early one morning. He'd obviously been asleep on the hall floor for hours. I called her later to find out who the derelict drunk was. 'Oh a lovely boy,' she replied. 'Yes, but who?' 'Wait a minute now, James – James *Baldwin*, that's it. I've just ordered his books from the High Hill Bookshop. He's had a wash and eaten a good breakfast. *Brilliant* man.' She guarded O'Toole's privacy ferociously and was known as 'The Dragon' by some of our more frivolous friends ('They've got nothing but time to waste, that lot,' she sniffed). I felt a little faint one day when I heard her on the phone saying, 'No Sir Laurence, I'm afraid it is *impossible* for me to disturb Peter. He is *working*.' 'No' (more emphatically), 'it is *impossible*.' 'Mummy, are you sure about that?' She turned, wide-eyed and shocked. 'He's *working*.' She worshipped him and the two of them would sit up late into the night playing Scrabble and talking, talking. She got rid of our cook and catered for his every whim – surprise lunch for eight, midnight snack for him, endless pots of tea at all hours, breakfast for people who hadn't been to bed.

It was a big house and because of the increasingly valuable art collection, it couldn't be left empty. Even so, with constant vigilance, dozens of internal locks, alarms and bars, we were still burgled twice; once very audaciously through the bars at the front of the house, well lit by a lamp post in Heath Street. It was a rather Hampstead-type break-in: the (very slim) burglar left with a valuable painting cut out of its frame, leaving behind a comb and a bloodstained copy of that week's *New Statesman*.

Good daily help was crucial but finding it wasn't my great talent, especially as I tended to muddle up the people I'd interviewed. I must have been more dozy than usual the day I engaged Miss Statema; Dutch, almost six feet tall, stately in sombre clothes. 'What d'you think, Mummy?' Mamgu, who would have been the one to perceive the softer side of Genghis Khan, enthused, 'Wonderful choice. Immaculate.' When Miss Statema became ill, almost at once, my mother tore down the hill to her basement room, bearing flasks of hot soup and home-made bread, and Miss S. was back at work in no time, but looking subtly different. It was the clothes! No longer sombre; many shades of pink and the apron had been discarded. She looked almost modish. The following week she appeared in a dated but very dressy light wool 'afternoon frock' and the following week I was halted in my tracks in the front hall as she sashayed by in a lilac taffeta dress with a sweetheart neck and puffed sleeves, ballerina-length skirt, the ensemble finished off with elbow-length lace mittens and silver, open-toed dancing slippers.

She had a bad habit of throwing away a Hoover bag every week and I'd narrowed my good housekeeping down to the task of curing her of this wastefulness. Now, not quite daring to remark on her sartorial tribute to Christian Dior circa 1947, I overtook her, stood barring her way at the top of the stairs to the basement and began, 'Em – Miss Statema, once again I must *insist* that you reuse the Hoover bags.' Towering above me malevolently, she stretched her right arm out behind her and, swinging it round, whacked me accurately across the face. As I reeled sideways into the (mercifully) closed door, she drew back and waited, strangely serene, as I gathered myself sufficiently to say, rather feebly, 'Em – I rather think you're going to have to – er – leave.' She nodded graciously and swept out saying, 'Send on my National Insurance Stamps.'

Determined not to share the house with any more sinister people, my very next choice was a small, round and cheerful, apple-cheeked woman who looked down to earth and healthy, as though she worked out of doors.

O'Toole was reading in the ground floor study so I asked her to work very quietly as she moved around the hall and Green Room. She nodded cheerfully. Descending from the nursery that afternoon I heard the lusty strains of music from below. 'Come and join us! Come and join us!' she sang and as I peered down the stairwell I could see her, duster in one hand, bucket in the other, not doing much in the way of work, *marching* up and down outside the study as she sang. Running down the stairs, I hissed, 'Hush! Hush!'

'Oops,' she beamed and disappeared down to the basement. I knocked on the study door and went in to apologise. O'Toole was sitting in his wing chair and looked amused. I joined him and while we chatted our new daily left by the front door and as we glanced out of the window we saw her put down four bulging plastic bags and open up the doors to the big dustbin enclosure. She began riffling through the bins, singing to herself. I opened the door. 'Where exactly did you say you lived?' 'Oh, here and there,' she said breezily. I realised I'd employed a lady tramp who'd fancied a day or two indoors.

Mostly I left the interviewing to my mother and it was she who found Manolita, one of the nicest women I'd ever met. We became close; she did her job perfectly and a lot more besides, and I became godmother to one of her children. We never discussed anything personal or intimate but she knew more about my life than anyone else in the house. Her discretion was absolute and I was grateful for her.

I used to tease O'Toole for acquiring what I called 'Petruchio's servants', charming, feckless people, hopeless in any job. Now, *he* got lucky as well and in fact the whole family benefited when Lionel Bryant was appointed as O'Toole's chauffeur.

One of his previous jobs had involved driving Montgomery Clift while he was filming *Suddenly Last Summer* and rendering everyone mad with confusion and exhaustion (and a young O'Toole was interviewed with a view to replacing him, should he fall apart completely). His drivers came and left on a regular basis. He never went to bed. He never told them where he was going – or why – or where he might be going next. They hung about all night and sometimes all day and, overcome with fatigue and deafened by wifely complaints, they resigned. Young Lionel Bryant heard the horror stories at the prestigious car hire firm where he worked and became intrigued by the challenge. He liked Monty Clift's acting so why not have a go, he thought, and volunteered his services.

Warning his wife, Margaret, not to expect him home much, he told her, 'I'm going to drive Monty Clift and I'm not quitting.' And he didn't. Monty, with a drink or two taken, liked to travel lying on the floor of the limo with his feet out of the window. This raised eyebrows as they pulled up at smart restaurants, so Lionel always shot round to open the door, addressing him as 'Sir', daring the doorman to be disrespectful. He liked to tease at five o'clock in the morning, going round and round in the revolving door of the Dorchester. No one could use the door, he was impossible to catch. The staff liked him and were tolerant. Lionel found him to be as congenial as his acting was wonderful and, enduring nights in the countryside tramping through fields, looking for 'cows to stroke', he stayed with Monty and grew to like him more and more. He didn't quit, but Margaret Bryant was rather pleased when the movie finished and Monty went home to America. Driving Judy Garland, he felt sorry for what he saw as her under-privileged children and gladly spent days playing with them in Battersea Park. 'But you know, the little girl – she never talked. Just sat in the back of the car, singing, singing all the time. Drove me mad, all that singing.'

Now some benevolent act of fate directed him to us. It was Jules who engaged him and it was the most perfect piece of casting he ever accomplished. He was part of our family for thirteen years. He was O'Toole's driver but when O'Toole was away he drove me or Mamgu or the girls (Liz, the Nanny, had her own car). A Leo, he was an organiser and a bit of a bully, in a quiet way. No use getting into his car and saying 'Shepperton'. He really needed to know why Shepperton? Was it a nice visit, or an ordeal? Did we need to be dead on time or keep them waiting a minute or two? And how was I feeling? I learned to tell him what the day held; how easy or difficult it was going to be and then he would work it all out and it would always be to perfection. I was surrounded by Leos: Jules, O'Toole, Lionel, Derek Coombs (O'Toole's brother-in-law), and they all had to be top dog.

Lionel wore Rolls-Royce livery at times but he knew I was unimpressed and cared nothing for cars. I overheard him outside my dressing room at Pinewood, standing next to our brand new Rolls. 'So what's the Boss's wife think of it?' asked his friend. 'Her? All she wants to know about a car is "Where's the ashtray?".' He was like a brother to me and loyal to O'Toole and fond of my mother and protective of the children. Sometimes, when O'Toole was hard on me, these feelings were in conflict with each other and reconciling them put years on his life – literally, sapping his strength. While he remained at his post, I remained at mine. Does this seem absurd to outsiders? I suspect that only Lionel and I would fully understand the situation.

My mother, Manolita, Liz and Lionel formed a protective shield around me. I might have had difficulties at work but I had more security at home than I had ever before experienced and I had no fears for the girls. Even so, I never forgot the need for caution and I took nothing for granted. The balance achieved was delicate and I prayed we could all maintain it.

# Chapter Twenty-three

At last, the closing night of *Ride a Cock Horse*. I've been writing lists for a week at home and I've packed the bags and they're ready at the theatre. During the last show I clear out the dressing rooms. Lionel drives O'Toole and me to Heathrow and we catch a plane to Venice – just the two of us for two weeks. All the ugliness of the preceding months drops away and we move on to a level of total harmony, total happiness. His nose stops bleeding. I stop throwing up. We beam at each other, hold hands. This is what our doctor, Gerry Slattery, calls 'Time out of life'. But surely this is the problem. 'Out of life', above the humdrum, on journeys, in crisis, in danger even, we are in perfect accord, and happy, ecstatically happy a good deal of the time. Faced with ordinary life, surrounded by people and obligations, we become stiff, disjointed, dysfunctional, resentful. Nervously I put in a bid – can we try to make work a *part* of ordinary life, not something divorced from everyday life? He looks at me with those old eyes and nods as though he knows what I mean but that's as far as it goes. He knows how hurt I am, how much I've hated him over the last months and effortlessly he makes it all better. I don't understand his magic. So how am I ever going to make sense of my life? I don't think anyone could ever know me the way he does and I do have this urge to be wholly known. So does he. We know things about each other that we never articulate or share with anyone.

Cold, misty Venice. Unpoetically I think of it as the great poultice; the badness is drawn out of both of us, everything is healed. I grow smooth and soft and stop protecting myself.

Familiarity with Venice has bred more and more love for the city. We have been coming here every year since we met. This time we've brought James Morris's book on Venice. We walk all day carrying his book and find Othello's tomb, with strawberries carved on it and as we approach the district called the ghetto, (I think the word *getto* means metal works), we hear the clink, clink of hammer on metal. One morning we meet a lovely American (there are very few visitors in this weather) and he says would we like to explore the lagoon with him? Of course we would, and we set off in a small boat to look for the island where the dug-up bones are put when the city graveyard is full up. 'It doesn't exist,' we've been told. Following a slim Edwardian guidebook, we cross and criss-cross the lagoon, finally bumping up through the mist into a bank of reeds. Pushing in, we reach solid ground and in the silence, hear the rustling of tall dry reeds stuck here and there with bones. It is an island of dry bones pierced by grasses. Sam Beckett talks of a 'bone orchard' and here it is. We don't want to walk on the bones so we push off again into the mist, cold and silent and glad when we get 'home' to the bar of the Danieli where we're staying and the company of Gastone de Cal, the head barman, who has now become a friend.

We're building a little family in Venice. Gastone began it all and introduced us to the four-star gondolier of Venice, Gino Macropodio. He's doubly endeared to me because he has a wonderful tenor voice; Welsh tenors sound like Italian tenors and Gino makes me feel at home. We sing duets. Then we meet Gastone and Gino's friend, Buzz Bruning Jr, who is American but has become a Venetian resident, owning a house next to the Frari. He is writing a cook book with his friend, the Cavalieri, who is a great gourmet and a war hero. We all dine out with the Cavalieri's sister, Maria, who is in her late seventies and is hugely admired by all the young men for her sprightly gait and terrific appetite. 'Look at her eating,' says

Gino to the young waiter. The gaze in fond admiration as tiny Signora Maria tucks into a dinner that would satisfy a bricklayer. Sometimes Norma, Gastone's wife, brings their little children along for dinner as well. Each night we are three or four generations at one table, all having a good time, enjoying each other. A generation gap is maybe the first sign of a sick society.

Gastone, Buzz and Gino finally introduce us to their friend, the Great Toio, 'Toio Piazzetta' as he's known. He has a restaurant on Giudecca – a restaurant? It's a room with one table and the people at that table eat whatever it is that Toio's wife and mother-in-law are cooking for the family in the room beyond. Toio feels that he was meant for greater things and at night he escapes from the bedroom window and makes for the piazzetta next to St Mark's Square and there he spends his time hanging out with his friends, moving slowly from bar to bar. He doesn't speak Italian, only Venetian, and even Gastone and Gino have trouble understanding him. I spend entire evenings sitting next to him, desperately trying to get the drift of the stories he tells – he never stops talking. Many of the stories are to do with the war and bunkers. The minute we hear 'bunkers', pronounced 'Boonkerrs', we know we're listening to a joke and in time the word is enough to start us laughing – which inspires Toio to tell *more* funny war stories. Never in my life have I spent so many hours genuinely laughing at stories I don't understand at all. Dear, exasperating, rotund, bellicose Toio.

For years, as I got to know the city, I felt more and more that there was a deep reserve within the Venetians and even O'Toole, usually adept at nosing out secret places, admitted that there was something he could not penetrate. It was as though, overrun by and living off tourists, the city with its great past resolutely kept something of itself to itself as at the same time it entertained, cosseted, cheated, spoiled and took advantage of the hordes that invaded it except in the depths of winter; hordes without whom it could not live. In a city where the inhabitants live with an awareness of the past ('So we all clubbed together and built this.' 'When was that?' '1732.'), tourism must be a bit of a come-down. Our feeling of being politely excluded lasted until our visit following the close of *Ride a Cock Horse*. It was winter. We flew to Venice but in fact we were diverted to Milan, landing in torrential rain. There, we were put on a bus to Venice and when we arrived – it was still pouring with rain – the driver said, 'Okay, everyone back to Milan. You cannot go into Venice.' O'Toole looks at me and jerks his head towards the exit. Without hesitation I make for the door. 'No, you cannot disembark. There is nowhere to go.' 'Thank you. All the same—' pushing forward. 'No, madam. I must insist.' 'Keep going' (O'Toole from behind). 'Frightfully sorry, I have to get off. Thank you, goodbye. Just need the bags.' O'Toole, following, stuffs a bundle of notes into the driver's hand and he releases the bags from the hold.

Well, here we are. It's so quiet, unusually quiet, in Mestre. There's a lamp outside a deserted building and underneath it we pile up the bags and I sit on them. O'Toole gives me a book and says, 'Look after the bags and have a read. I'll be back. Just wait.' I read. It's still raining. When he returns – there is still no one about – he says, 'Okay, I think we're on,' and we manhandle the luggage to a jetty which is in pitch darkness. The bags are loaded into a little motor boat. We speak in whispers. Why? Off we go. Why does the trip seem so strange? Well, for one thing it's dark – totally dark. It is the middle of the night but there are no lights at all. We go down a deserted Grand Canal and encounter no other traffic. Here and there windows are lit by candlelight. This is a view of Venice no one has seen since the nineteenth century; Venice lit by candles alone. We turn off the Grand Canal and see a bridge ahead. The driver turns round and motions to us to lie down. Obediently, we lie down on the floor. So does the boatman. He cuts the motor and as we approach the bridge which seems dangerously near to our heads, he lifts his legs and begins to 'walk' slowly along the underside of the bridge. He gestures to us behind and we follow suit, pushing the boat down in the water. We have to 'walk' with bended knees and, emerging the other side, we straighten up and look at each other. The boatman raises a thumb. We nod. What on earth is going on? We're in a dark, empty stretch of water and there are *things* bumping into us. What are they? As we approach the Danieli Hotel I realise that we are working our way through broken masonry, bits of timber, and drawing close to an unfamiliar looking jetty. It's the top of a balustrade and there, back-lit by a huge, flickering candelabra, is the massive bulk of Bruno, the doorman. He looks amazed and, arriving at the boat, lifts me over his head and, reaching the top of the mahogany reception desk, he sets me down on it and returns for O'Toole and the baggage.

The Danieli is under water. I walk along the top of the desk and begin to hop and skip through the flooded foyer on stepping places made of pieces of furniture. Gastone de Cal, the head barman, hasn't gone off duty and is standing on a little island of tables, looking amazed and overjoyed. No one has managed to get into Venice for twenty-four hours. Traffic is not allowed on the Grand Canal after dark. There are no guests in the hotel, they've all left. What do we do now? 'Have a drink!' Normally, O'Toole would be only too glad to sit down and celebrate our feat in getting into the forbidden city. Tonight – this morning – he can see that things are bad; the staff are trying to save the ground-floor furniture. 'Come on, Siân,' he says. 'Get some wellies. Let's get to work.' They find waders for us and we spend the next few hours carrying chairs and tables up the main staircase, rolling up the staircarpet and hoisting everything that can be moved up to the first floor. I never had such a good time at the Danieli as I did that night. Finally, at dawn, we take our pick of the empty rooms. Gastone explains that we'll have to move from bathroom to bathroom as there's no plumbing and there's no electricity and are we *sure* we want to stay. Are we sure? What could be more fun than to camp out in this beloved, familiar, romantic hotel.

We've been coming to Venice for years unremarked among the glitterati of the world, avoiding high society and any occasion remotely smart. Now, we are famous in the nicest way. Wet and shabby in our waders, we seem to be the only guests in the city. As the water subsides we have our own brooms and we help sweep out the filth from Florians and the little shops around St Mark's Square and, finally, after years of being visitors we discover real, hidden, secret Venice. It's a rich reward for a bit of discomfort and no running water. The Venetians let us in and we spend weeks of pure pleasure, getting wet and dirty and sitting in people's back parlours and being entertained in their favourite wine shops, far off the tourist track. All our new friends are 'experts' on their city and we're dragged to and fro, sightseeing all day long from the eye-opener of grappa first thing in the morning to the nightcaps at the Danieli.

A member of the hotel staff who has become a companion and guide in his off-duty hours shows us paintings, dirty and unlit, in small churches where he produces a torch so we can stand and admire silently with him. He's as proud as though he were the painter. We go into little bars serving food, which we have passed by dozens of times on earlier visits. 'No tourist has ever walked in here. Good wine – *our* vineyard.' The wine is alarmingly robust but very welcome in the cold morning air. It's also purple and stains our tongues and lips an ineradicable, lurid but rather fashionable Mary Quant colour (it looks better on me than on O'Toole who looks as though he's in some louche Carnival scene). Our friend's father is a painter – a very special painter. Sworn to secrecy, we visit his studio in an unremarkable apartment in an unfashionable street. The sprightly, elderly Venetian is busy grinding his 'colours'. All around are astounding eighteenth-century paintings. After a few hours of sitting around and admiring and drinking tiny beakers of wine ('I know the vineyard – very good', I read in our good guidebook that the Venetians don't drink; I'll be lucky to get home with half a liver intact), and after a spot of lunch – blissful home-made pasta with tiny, almost transparent, brownish shrimps (I also read that Venetian food isn't up to much!) Sr X confides that his business is forgery.

This doesn't pose an artistic problem for him as it does for many forgers who feel their 'own' art, just as skilled, is unappreciated. He lives for paintings, loves Guardi, in whom he specialises. 'It's only embarrassing,' he says, 'when I have to go to authenticate something for a museum, sometimes in America. I see it is mine and I hate to disappoint them. I have some Guardis in most of the big museums. Not too many.' He has been busy during the last few days. The high tide has 'liberated' eighteenth-century paper from a basement around the corner and his flat is festooned with washing lines of drying paper. 'So good to have the real thing.' He prepares his paints exactly as Guardi and Canaletto did, but the paper and canvas is always a problem and now the flood has brought him a rich windfall. As we leave, he presses a small canvas into my hand and gives me his cousin's address. When I go there he is busy making eighteenth-century furniture. His family has, for countless generations, been making furniture in the same manner. He gives me an eighteenth-century picture frame. He's so *proud* and so he should be; this isn't reproduction, this is top of the mark deception. Our time here is becoming more and more splendidly unreal.

At night we have to wait in an improvised bar until the night staff come on because the night electrician at the Danieli is the best tenor. We learn Venetian songs and I improvise an alto line. We sing until dawn. High tide is a horrible thing but the Venetians are behaving like blitzed Londoners and we have the time of our lives.

I think we love travelling because it stops us from thinking about ourselves. Ourselves – oh, so difficult. Armed insurrections, hunger, thirst, danger – oh, so easy. To move ahead. To move. Interesting. Binding. We never failed to have a good time while engaged on the many journeys we made together. Neither of us was a passive tourist and life, while we moved about together, was arduous and exhausting and exhilarating. Some of our journeys, marooned in provincial railway stations or stranded in unpromising, unpicturesque spots would have bored and frustrated many but we always found something interesting to keep ourselves amused. Most of our journeys were, however, more exotic; some were dangerous. Tedious, uncomfortable, glamorous, perilous; it didn't really matter what the conditions were, I think we both travelled for the sake of travelling and consequently we travelled well – almost always.

My trip to Cambodia in 1963 was unexpecedy brief. I arrived in a daring skirt made by a new designer called Mary Quant. It was demurely box-pleated but it rested an inch and a half above my knee (a bit like my school uniform, which I detested). I had square-toed, stubby-heeled shoes and a modishly straight hair cut. O'Toole was appalled. We had a vehement, all the more intense for being whispered, exchange when he suggested I went home on the next flight. 'What have you come as?' he asked in horror. Fortunately I was able to reassure him that my luggage contained below-the-knee skirts and ordinary shoes and on the spot I was able to shake my hair into a less fashionable shape. I hated him for greeting me in such a way but understood by now the tensions of reunions and – I hated to admit it – he was quite right about the clothes. Skirts were getting shorter and shorter; the one I wore to Cambodia was a restrained version of the London fashion. I had to agree with him when he asked rhetorically, 'What is a tall, thirty-year-old, mother-of-two doing dressed in clothes that would look well on a twelve-year-old?'

We may have been good at travelling but we were bad at reunions and, rather embarrassed by our own behaviour, we made for the hotel and a soothing bath. A spider, larger than any I had ever seen, fell out of the beautifully folded towel. 'They wear hob-nailed boots here,' said O'Toole, glumly. 'Clump, clump, all over the place.' At the night shoot the film lights sizzled with large, dead, fried night bugs. This place was all snakes and bugs. The loo was a wicker contraption on stilts. the prop-man – prop-men are always my favourite people on a film set – said, delicately, 'Siân – now, not to worry, but we had a really nasty snake in the ladies' tonight and they always go in pairs, so be really careful when you – you know.' There was a snake called the Two-Step. You got bitten and then two steps later you fell down dead. O'Toole sent me on a trip round Angkor Wat. 'Wear boots because of the snakes.' I set off into this amazing place and spent the day there. There were soldiers hiding in the bushes, guarding the bits of art that might get chopped off and taken home. Good for them. I wondered if O'Toole had been thinking of 'liberating' a little art.

That same week, news came that the political situation was rapidly worsening and American and British nationals were advised to leave at once. The film unit was disbanded and dispersed quite fast. O'Toole ignored the official evacuation and preferred to trust to his own wits and I had no doubt my best bet was to follow him. 'Let's go to the airport,' he said. There were no planes. I was installed in the ladies' lavatory. No luggage (the contentious skirt was now in the possession of the attacking army). How do I know what I'm going to hear next? 'Here, read this and *wait here*, darling.' I had a guidebook to Angkor Wat and nothing else except my passport which seemed strangely useless in what appeared to be an armed insurrection. I sat on the floor in a cubicle in the ladies' lavatory and read about what I'd seen during the day. It kept me busy for over an hour until a familiar hand appeared under the door. I touched it. 'Open up,' breathed a voice and I opened the door and O'Toole crept in. 'We've got a plane.' (There were few left in the airport.)

'Oh, good.'

'But not for five hours.'

'Oh hell.'

We sat on the floor of that horrible lavatory, alternately whispering and reading and actually having quite a nice time (I learned a lot about Angkor), until the appointed hour when we straightened up and cautiously moved out and on to the runway. O'Toole thought he recognised our small plane. 'OK, run!' he whispered and we belted out across the airfield and up the staircase. It was the right plane. Money changed hands and we were off. Where to? 'Don't ask.' We landed in Hong Kong where O'Toole had been filming before arriving in Cambodia. O'Toole hadn't trusted the film company to get us out of a war zone but once in Hong Kong he summoned the might of the company to get us an hotel. They may not know about politics but film companies sure know hotels. We were directed to the newly built Mandarin and rolled up – dirty and hungry, no baggage – to inaugurate the Presidential Suite. There was a lot to play with; lying on the vast bed I opened curtains, raised televisions, altered the temperature – I'm not sure I didn't run a bath while lying down. O'Toole proved surprisingly adept at acquiring toothbrushes and paste and combs and shampoo and also summoned tailors to the room to measure us for clothes. I ordered a modest frock (skirt on the knee) and a jacket and coat and O'Toole ordered a few pairs of slacks and shirts and a jacket or two.

He showed me around the Hong Kong he had become familiar with and into the bar frequented by 'Hot Pants Molly Malone' (a bit of a disappointment), whose card he'd retained. Who wouldn't? Then he ventured into more interesting territory. 'There's this square mile owned by a feudal war lord.' 'Ah yes.' 'But no one goes there. The police don't dare. Let's go and have a look.' 'Sure.' I was in my new Chinese 'Chanel' coat

and dress, still clutching the Hermès handbag (the only thing
I'd brought out from Cambodia). Our taxi driver said, 'No!
No! Please!' as he set us down. 'Just wait here,' said O'Toole
sweetly. 'No, sir! You cannot go there. Not the lady.'

'Be all right, old son,' murmured O'Toole as we ducked into
a dark alleyway, the entrance to the forbidden city. So this was
the place where criminals went, knowing the law could not
pursue them. 'Now, are you sure . . . ?' 'Come *on!*' After a
few twists and turns I felt horribly conspicuous. There wasn't
a lot to look at, either. My Hermès bag seemed to be sending
out signals. 'O'Toole—' 'Yes?' 'This is very interesting but do
you notice how the women are taking the children indoors?'
'Yes.' 'D'you think this is a bad sign?' No reply. The dark,
narrow, foetid alleyway ahead was now deserted, save for a
few moody-looking young men.

'Mmm, don't look frightened. Just turn around casually,
make a left and *stroll* back – no, *STROLL* dammit.' As we
turned around we saw that the street behind us had emptied as
well. Was this prior to some act of violence? Or did they think
*we* were dangerous? We strolled, God, how hard we strolled.
I have no sense of direction and couldn't think how to get
back to law-abiding, everyday Hong Kong. O'Toole sauntered
confidently, his casual amble at odds with the vice-like grip in
which he held my hand. Light ahead. Daylight. Not quickening
our step, we made for what turned out to be a version of
Oxford Street, and our taxi – thank God O'Toole had a great
sense of direction. The driver practically wept when he saw us.
I suppose it would have been very awkward for him if he'd
reported back to Columbia Pictures without its star.

'Yeah, well – you can't think about all that,' said O'Toole,
recovering his high spirits as we made for the Mandarin. 'You
go back to the hotel. I've got a chance to buy a little bit of
Korean something or other. Bit dodgy. Tell you what – have
a read and just *wait for me.*'

I waited for a long time in that huge suite before he returned with a lovely bulky piece of bas-relief – horsemen rushing into battle.

'Excuse me, but I'm awfully itchy.'

'Well, so am I.'

'How strange.'

Strange indeed that the first guests in the Presidential Suite should be lousy from their spell in the public lavatory at Phnom Penh Airport. They fumigated the rooms – and us – and O'Toole said, 'Let's go to Japan.'

# Chapter Twenty-four

As we walk down a Tokyo street, nasty as the Edgware Road and twice as noisy, I glance into a small sandwich bar and see an empty piece of Formica countertop and on it, in a jar, a single branch of flowering cherry. Behind the deep-fryer is an open door leading to a postage-stamp of garden – cool and quiet. It's a tiny, powerful piece of calm and beauty holding its own against the tumult. Pressing forward into the unbearable over-congestion of the street, I feel excitedly that once again I am in a truly foreign place – already I've encountered ten things I do not comprehend. I decide not to try to understand anything and begin to review the contradictions of the day. Mrs Kawakita is our contact as head of Toho Films. She is tiny, dressed in traditional costume, perpetually smiling and polite. I'm told that grown men have been known to cry after bruising business encounters with her. When things get really tough voices remain low, but terrified underlings in the outer office fancy they see Western blood seeping under the door before Mrs Kawakita emerges, head nodding, smiling and eyes lowered, a favourable contract completed.

I tower over her in my Hong Kong pretend-Chanel and feel, as I try to gauge my bows to correspond with and not exceed hers – otherwise we'll be here all day – that she looks quaint and a bit odd in that get-up. It takes only a week for me to begin to marvel at the beauty of her hair and make-up, the complexity of her dress, the delicacy of her movements and the subtlety of her expression, while feeling more and more like a clod-hopping land-girl; too big, too loud, too vulgar of face. Even my perfume – that year Mitsouko by

Guerlain – seems too obvious by half. I feel *ugly*, is the short word.

We have elected to stay in a Japanese hotel. Walking up the white-lined corridor to the suite, we notice tears here and there in the paper walls. 'Looks as though someone bad with props, like Johnny G, has been here,' remarks O'Toole. He is great with props. I am not, as I demonstrate within minutes of entering the huge, empty, beautiful set of rooms. Exploring what might be a bedroom, I withdraw the wooden bolt in the wall in order to open a window and find that I have the entire wall in my hands and am precariously balanced, leaning outwards over a lovely moss garden one floor below. I dare not move. I breathe, 'Pete – Pete! Help! Help!' It seems an age before O'Toole, thinking he hears something, drifts into the room and, anchoring me around the waist with one arm, takes possession of the wall with the other and, shaking his head resignedly, much as he does when I mess up a bit of business on stage, replaces the wall and leaves me to unpack while he goes in search of a bar.

I tiptoe around the dividing screens. So much in the rooms is so light and breakable but at the same time the deep, narrow bath, the bedroll which is laid out at night only, the headrest, the dark wooden floor, are so confidently heavy and in their correct, immovable place that I am constantly wrong-footed as I move around, at one moment behaving rather patronisingly like a grown-up in a doll's house and the next submitting to an alien but mightily convincing arrangement of objects.

O'Toole returns, having discovered not only a bar (the Japanese are crazy about whisky, it seems) but a massage parlour below where a little lady *walked* up his spine. I settle for a shampoo and set but even so my little lady shampoo-er does something unprecedented to my skull. We're two Brobdingnags in paradise. 'I'll bet they laugh at us,' says O'Toole. 'Apparently we smell awful and they call us "the Big

Noses".' He's probably right. My nose – rather unremarkable I always thought – seems to be growing.

Sleep. Such sleep. My first night on a Japanese bed-on-the-floor. No book, no radio, no television, big darkness, the polished floor near my right hand and sleep that I can almost taste.

In the morning, film representatives come to call. They're discouraging about the possibility of buying art. 'You'd swear they don't *want* to sell anything,' says one. 'I've been rooting around for ten years – nothing.' O'Toole nods gravely and we promise to ring the office if we need anything in the way of restaurant reservations, cars and so on. This must be a horrible job, looking after movie stars and their whims. We have a couple of numbers we've found for ourselves. Eureka! Kurosawa rings back; he's filming *The Red Doctor* and we're invited to watch him. Our cups run over completely when the most famous of all Japanese actors, Toshiro Mifune, calls. It's going to be very hard to behave like rational beings around these two men. They're like mythical beasts to me. I owe my knowledge of them to O'Toole and am overwhelmed now by the magnitude of my debt to him. I don't actually want to meet these men at all. But I do want to *watch* them; however, meeting is a part of all that.

The set of *The Red Doctor* is wonderful. If this were movie making then I would want to do little else but make Kurosawa movies. He is a master, Kurosawa – and he's tall! He's a good-looking cowboy of a Japanese. His mother is tiny and she cooks and runs the kitchen on the film set. It's like filming in his parlour, except one is aware that he is one of the most illustrious directors in the world, but oh, the difference from anything I've seen . . . He doesn't act great. His mother doesn't treat him as great. The unit mills about like family retainers, the actors behave with modest dignity; no one is treated exceptionally well. But there it is – hanging over the ramshackle location – the impact of great quality.

Watching movies being made is low on the list of spectator sports but I could have sat on my orange box for months – and I didn't understand a word of text. It seems the financiers are exasperated by the length of the shoot; Kurosawa is being hounded and harried. His great talent and reputation don't save him from being treated badly. I make a mental note once again *never* to feel bad when I'm badly treated. Much better talents than mine are treated shamefully by people who are actually only trying to hang on to their jobs, trying to save a bit of money.

Toshiro Mifune appears! This is a star! He, also, is tall, another Japanese cowboy and when he walks he displaces a lot of air . . . It's a pleasure to see him and he and O'Toole fall on each other. O'Toole has adored 'Tosher' since he was a boy in Leeds; it must be wonderful to stand on Japanese soil and embrace one of the best Japanese actors, and to find that they like each other on sight! I hang back slightly and watch the meeting. They arrange to see each other later.

Where do we meet? I'm getting used to the unexpected and don't blink when we enter a huge, ghastly, dark, pleasure-drome where they serve – of course – many kinds of whisky. Toshiro loves whisky. O'Toole loves whisky only too much and becomes a mad person when he drinks it, so he's forsworn it and I'm impressed when he refuses one now. Whisky is a big treat. Toshiro is buying. O'Toole is choosing – who knows what? – it's not whisky and I'm silently overcome with admiration. He wants to make a good impression on Mifune but not at the expense of turning into a mad person. They talk through an interpreter and I sit, enjoying this meeting, hating the venue and only vaguely understanding what is being discussed. The noise is *tremendous*! This is worse than Annabel's.

We now have a longer list of phone numbers. I'm getting to understand that in this country, without a personal rec-ommendation, it is very difficult to reach anyone significant.

Kurosawa and Mifune between them pass us on to the best kimono maker in the country, the best antique dealer and the best lacquer man and we make calls and wait. Then we embark on a series of visits that feel a bit like auditions.

And in the interim the film company arranges visits to the theatre. They are touchingly eager to please a big Star and I think that they must be keenly grateful for an easy few weeks now that the Star has the Wife in tow. Nothing is required except visits to special monuments and trips to the theatre and they must wonder what we do with our time. 'This play goes on all day, you don't have to stay,' we're told as we go backstage at the theatre. Backstage is huge. Actors sit in front of cheval mirrors, hands on knees, legs apart. Silently they look at themselves as they are transformed into the character they will inhabit for the rest of the day. Old men become young girls. Young men become elderly. I believe it all. Here, in the ordinary light of day, the atmosphere is church-like. Out front, I settle into an uncomfortable seat next to an old lady who is sitting on her feet. On the floor in front of her is a primus stove and food and tea. The play opens with the most compelling entrance I've ever seen an actor make: slow, slow, lateral walk to the acting area but the acting, the diction are at first grotesque and after a mere ten minutes, totally believable and natural. The audience gasps and cries as one; red ribbons are as real as the blood in a Peckinpah movie, blue cloth is a believable, impassable river. The movie representative appears in the aisle to 'rescue' us. No way am I leaving. My old lady busies herself with a bit of cooking and I wish she'd offer me a bite, as we settle down for another couple of hours of drama. Eventually, shaken and exhausted and exhilarated, I emerge into the Tokyo afternoon. We have an evening appointment, otherwise I *could* have stayed there all day. Why? I find it quite difficult to sit through a long play in London. I've read about people sitting through a day of theatre in Ancient Greece and wondered how they could do that. Maybe there has to be this degree of mutually accepted tradition and commitment before the experience becomes possible. Come to think of it, I'm rarely convinced – this carried away – in a theatre at home. Back in my empty Japanese room I sit and wonder at the day.

Our phone calls lead us to people who are distinguished artists and not about to start making a sale to just anyone; not even at the say-so of their important and successful friends. Sometimes it's O'Toole's reputation and charisma that gets us by but sometimes it's my patience and sincere admiration that wins the day. We sit day after day in what looks like a council flat in North London (except our feet are dangling over a fire-pit under the dining table) and gradually the Lacquer Man brings out small objects for our consideration. Kurosawa has explained to me that this man marks a tree he will use in ten years' time and he waits and waits for it to mature and his output is wonderful and prized but tiny and he will never be rich but he is the greatest lacquer artist in Japan and, sitting in his dowdy living room and knowing nothing, even I can tell that he is great. My ideas are getting such a shake-up. Actually, I'm learning to forget what I've been absorbing over the last ten years. What was that? Style, I suppose. I'm unprepared for the person who lives in an unappealing house like this, wears undistinguished clothes like this, eats dull food such as this, but thinking back, I recall that Johns the Postman in Cwmllynfell, in my home in Wales, drank too much, looked like a cleaned up tramp, lived in a little house with a Mabel Lucy Attwell calendar on the wall and antimacassars on the uncut moquette chairs and wrote Welsh poetry, the complexity of which would bear comparison with the best Greek poetry. And now, I'm sitting in a little living room with nasty wallpaper and awful little ornaments and the man of the house is showing us great art, wrapped up in tea towels. O'Toole can see that I'm making an impression and he leaves the negotiating to me. Well – I don't talk about *money* – I ask about being *allowed* to *acquire*.

Eventually, we leave with eight superb bowls. I've had such an intense few nights with this man but I don't say, 'We'll be in touch'. What would be the point? He hasn't any idea of who we are but we have connected quite strongly. Maybe he can see that I will remember these few days for ever. I hope he can. I will.

The Kimono Man is a bit more of a showbiz character, more accustomed to visiting stars. We order kimonos that bear no relation to the ordinary kimonos sold in the shops here or in England. (When they wore out I tried to have them copied and no one could master the intricacy of their making.)

Art is so much more difficult to find. The film people – Westerners who live in Tokyo – are almost right when they say that the barrier between 'us and them' is as good as impenetrable. We sit, night after night, drinking tea in suburban houses. Occasionally, our host says 'Let's go and visit X' and off we trundle to another little sitting room and drink more tea. Still no art appears. A week goes by before a bundle is produced and, unwrapped, proves to be an actor's mask from the eighteenth century – holly wood, painted for the Old Man's character. The owner gestures to me to put it on and I do and I am very moved by the gesture and, taking it off, I sniff a bit, and pass it to O'Toole. He puts it on and the company roars with laughter to see the beautiful star face transformed to decrepit old age. He lays it reverently back on its cloth and we drink tea for hours. As we leave, the mask is bundled up and pressed into O'Toole's hands. Our interpreter must have agreed to pay; these negotiations are always rather lordly.

The Mask Man hands us on to another dealer and after many nights in back rooms we buy almost my favourite object of all, a terracotta head, so simple it is scarcely formed at all.

When I say 'we', that is of course completely misleading. O'Toole chose to spend a major part of his earnings on art and I was an enthusiastic helper but he was spending *his* money, not mine. I spent a large portion of *my* earnings on antique furniture but I never felt a great sense of ownership except in a few, emotional, instances. I rarely bought art. Here, in Japan, I'm becoming acquisitive. I buy an eighteenth century scroll – I want to live in a low, Japanese house. I want a garden of mosses. I'd like to be smaller, quieter, less scrutable.

# Chapter Twenty-five

B ack in Heath Street in Hampstead, fitting our acquisitions into this lovely fortress of a house and our life in it continues to be workable, as well as intermittently ecstatic or unbelievably dreadful. We've acquired a family of cats who live downstairs and a bulldog called Scobie who lives in the basement and in the Green Room and who absorbs a great deal of household energy. O'Toole bought him as a protector for the houseful of girls he has to leave behind when he goes filming. Fierce to look at, Scobie became a well-known feature of street-life in Hampstead, plodding out twice daily on what looked like a glum walk, occasionally slipping his lead on the Heath and once, during such a moment of freedom when the fair was paying its Easter visit to Hampstead, charging up the steps of a fairground caravan – he wasn't named after a jockey for nothing – and, unable to stop, smashing his way into a china cabinet. 'Very good china,' said the vengeful and formidable old fairground woman when she visited us and her eyes alighted on O'Toole's name here and there in the Green Room, and then, taking in a poster on the wall, 'Royal Doulton mostly – and some *Limoges* as well, and then there's the *crystal*!' 'Yes, yes,' I said soothingly as I pressed bundles of notes into her hand.

Scobie had already been in a spot of bother with the law and I didn't feel he was well placed to survive more trouble. Although every time one of the many burglar alarms in the house went off at night, he greeted the police, tail wagging, dribbling affectionately on their trousers, he'd taken against being loaded into a Black Maria when he, along with his young walkers, had been arrested on an apple scrumping expedition and hauled off to Rosslyn Hill police station. The schoolboys obediently trooped into the sinister van but Scobie exerted all of his not inconsiderable strength, summoned up the indomitable spirit of his breed, and would not budge; policemen overbalanced and sat down suddenly on the pavement, helmets rolled down the road and as passersby clutched each other, crying with laughter, Scobie glowered at everyone and phone calls were made to the house to 'Get this damned ferocious beast out of here. NOW!' It was my mother who hurried down the hill and murmured reproachfully, 'Oh, Scobie!' and he trotted over and sat at her heels. She apologised to the recovering officers, glared at the boys cowering in the van, and in the voice that could still make me jump with fright said, 'And as for you. Just you wait . . .'

At home, when he inadvertently knocked someone to the ground, he stood there mournfully, breathing hard, bestowing the odd wet lick on the prone figure until, to his evident relief, it righted itself. He arrived 'toilet-trained' but he'd got the message wrong and would stand for hours on the Heath, longing to pee, legs crossed, practically hopping with anxiety. Then, once back in the house, he would lean against the closed door in the hall in a 'Thank God' position and the floodgates would open. He had to be sent back to school to re-learn the lesson but he was never entirely sure that he'd got it right. Nor had he when he appeared in the film, *Great Catherine*, as the dog belonging to the British Ambassador, played by Jack Hawkins. He rode to Shepperton in the Rolls, sitting motionless up front and dribbling steadily on the upholstery to Lionel's frustrated fury. 'I'd like to *murder* him,' he muttered. He lived for thirteen years and was the longest lasting of O'Toole's Petruchio's servants – adorable and totally useless in the job for which he'd been engaged.

Scobie personified our home life – sweet and slightly cockeyed.

In spite of my earnest efforts, there were times when I found it almost impossible to contain my frustration over work. Time and again I failed to embrace my hero Sydney Smith's dictum, '. . . If my lot be to crawl, I will crawl contentedly; if to fly, I will fly with alacrity; but, as long as I can possibly avoid it, I will never be unhappy.'

Desperate to be 'flying', in a place where it counted in those days (and London seemed to be the only place that really signified), I jumped at the chance to play Cleopatra at the Vic. O'Toole wanted to know all the details of the production (none of which I knew), saying that a 'true professional' would not embark on such a job without making sure that all the conditions were perfect, down to the smallest piece of casting and costume. (He added that the play rarely worked.) Very differently situated from him, I was not in a position to make demands and exhaustive enquiries. Nor was I convinced that a guarantee of perfection was any guarantee of a successful outcome but as the arguments raged at home and they became more concerned with my character and less about the job, I withdrew from it and domestic harmony was instantly restored, but I was sick at heart as I resumed a modest crawl.

I lost *The Cherry Orchard* in much the same way. When I began to quiz my old friend, director Frank Hauser, about the casting he was outraged that I should be interfering in his production plans. That was the reaction I expected and I wasn't surprised when he withdrew his offer and didn't work with me again for a good ten years. I was disheartened to see how little courage and confidence I was able to muster at home. Defiance was out of the question.

Almost at once, in 1966, I came near to losing *Man and Superman* as well. This time, the order from O'Toole was not to play it without acquiring a major star for Jack Tanner (a role that O'Toole had played brilliantly at the Bristol Old Vic). Philip Wiseman, the director, and Richard Shulman, the producer, were bemused but obligingly, as requested, offered the part to a few movie stars who they knew were never going to accept the job (and who took months before they bothered to reply). Finally, reality overtook everyone and a list was compiled of major theatre actors who might reasonably want the huge part as well as being able to perform it. As we looked down the impressive list the crumpled, exhausted production team, *longing* to get on with the job, paused at one name and we read no further. Everyone wanted one of the most exciting actors in the country, only too infrequently seen in the great parts he was born to play. It was just as well that Philip and Richard and I were equally enthusiastic because it became clear that Alan Badel was as reluctant as any Hollywood tyro to respond to letters or to return phone calls. Weeks and months went by and in despair I called Alan's wife, Vonnie. (Their house was more of a fortress than ours.) Vonnie lifted the phone and there was a very guarded, 'Yes?'. 'Vonnie, it's Siân and I'm desperate. Do you think Alan will do the play?' 'Well, I think he should.' 'But *will* he?' 'Leave it with me.' I did and within days we had a message of acceptance. O'Toole approved. Well, how could he not?

When Alan turned up to read the play with a good but hastily assembled cast, Philip and I were only slightly put out when we slowly realised, chatting with Alan over coffee, that he had turned up to rehearse *Arms and the Man*. A copy of *Man and Superman* was hastily but casually slipped on to the table where Alan would sit. I watched him touch it, his face revealing nothing, as he made a mental readjustment and prepared to sightread Tanner. It was the beginning of a long, incident-packed journey which culminated in one of the longest commercial runs of any Shaw play. The highs were glorious and the lows difficult to look back on without shuddering.

The opening night at the Arts was, on the whole, a low. Alan, busily teasing Philip because he belonged to that hated breed –

directors – neglected to thoroughly learn his part. Philip was exhausted from directing the play while keeping out of Alan's sightlines. I was dazed with fatigue from keeping the peace between the two of them and was far from having figured out how to play Anne. Also, I couldn't help noticing that Alan – my friend – having summoned up all his formidable resources in order to get through the long opening duologue with me was playing it brilliantly but also was playing it pressed up against the backcloth while I (his friend and protector against the wrath of the management) sat, pinned in my chair, down stage. To the uninitiated this is called 'upstaging' someone. I loved acting with him and forgave him completely. O'Toole, in England for a while before leaving for Warsaw to film *Night of the Generals*, arrived at the theatre in a state of mixed emotions and passed out drunk in the corridor backstage, so we made our entrances stepping over his curled-up figure in the corridor. What little stock of embarrassment that remained to me evaporated for ever that night. Alan went on a few weeks later to be superb and although the long run threw up its share of weekly crises, it was for me one of the most exciting, if erratic, of jobs. During the year Alan and I worked on *Antony and Cleopatra* in our spare time and hoped to mount a production of the play and when that collapsed I thought I really wasn't *meant* to play the part, except in my head.

My mother in the play was played by Marie Löhr who, despite the disparity in our ages, became one of my closest friends. Marie, well into her seventies when I met her, was stately, on the stout side, and beautifully dressed in the grand clothes of an earlier time. In spite of a streak of sheer naughtiness which she retained from a youth studded with some startling romances and adventures, she had the air of a grande dame and it wasn't difficult to see her as the actor-manager she had been in her heyday. Living alone now in a small flat, she had developed a few idiosyncratic habits but her awareness of the absurdity of a great deal of daily life – her own included – quite exempted her from being perceived as eccentric. Lest she should miss something interesting, she kept both radio and television running softly as she dealt with her correspondence and, in order to keep her beloved canary near her when she released him from his cage, she sprinkled bird-seed on to the crown of her head so he was never away for long, returning to peck away among her shiny, white curls. This seemed very sensible to me and I would forget about the seeds and it was Marie who would lift her hand halfway to her head, as we sat down in a restaurant, raise an index finger, mouth pursed in comic disapproval, and sail majestically into the Ladies to remove her hat and shake out of her hair the forgotten remnants of Joey's breakfast, before returning to further enslave an adoring bunch of waiters who would never have seen her act, but who knew she was Somebody, all right. Her exquisite manners were camp in a ladylike way and fragments of advice she passed on to me were all too few and so lightly produced as to be in danger of passing unnoticed. She never talked about herself or of the past except when, knowing her better and better, I would press her to look back.

There were great gaps in the story always, but I pieced together enough to make me wish that she'd kept a journal. She'd been an actress since she was sixteen or seventeen and described the scene up and down Shaftesbury Avenue or the Charing Cross Road as dozens of young actresses ran from theatre to theatre to be seen or to audition for jobs. There is a wide walkway along the side of the Garrick Theatre where we were playing at the time and she remembered it being full of girls – young ladies – all in hats and gloves and carrying little bags with their spirit heaters and curling tongs for smartening up the hair before they went on stage. She became Sir Herbert Beerbohm Tree's leading lady in *Faust* when she was eighteen. He was an actor-manager who was a law unto himself and when Marie lost her voice he suspended rehearsals and sent her and her mother to Brighton for a week with his own recipe for throat medicine and instructions that she was not to speak until she returned to London. She did as she was told and the play opened triumphantly when he felt that it and she were good and ready.

Marie's mother (I never heard her speak of a father) was an actress called Kate Bishop and Marie was utterly devoted to her. They were living together when Miss Bishop died and when Marie described her last illness her jauntiness deserted her and the sense of loss was fresh in her voice. Her mother loved and had a way with birds and as she lay dying, small song birds sat on the bed-head and on the piled-up pillows and even on her hand where it rested on the coverlet. 'She smiled and smiled at the end,' said Marie.

She herself made a glittering career, becoming an actor-manager and ran a fine house, somewhere on the river. When she took one of her own productions from her theatre in Shaftesbury Avenue to New York, she re-cast the play and an actress called Margaret Bannerman was given her star part. The play did not do well in America and she was obliged to come home, where she found that her husband had taken up with her replacement. She lost everything – jewels, furs, grand house – and even saw Miss Bannerman wearing her jewellery. An excruciatingly painful divorce followed and in court the judge – an admirer of Marie's – asked plaintively, 'Who *is* Margaret Bannerman?' 'I could have kissed him,' said Marie, her eyes glistening with malice.

When she toured she – an expert player – travelled with her own custom-made, collapsible billiard cues, along with a great deal of luggage. She loved the company of men and she acted with most of the matinée idols of her day; occasionally when certain very renowned names came up she would look a little absent and the conversation would halt and I guessed at a *tendresse*, to say the least, but knew better than to ask her to reveal more than she had already volunteered. She was a lady.

Her beloved mother had been a contemporary and a colleague of Ellen Terry and as small children, Kate Bishop and Ellen Terry had both been engaged as fairies at Bristol, where Mrs Kendal (Madge Robertson) was actor-manager of a stock company. It was awesome to me to realise that some of the voice exercises passed on to me by Marie had been taught to her mother in the middle of the nineteenth century.

After playing my mother for about nine months in *Man and Superman*, things went well for a while; she played in a film and on television with O'Toole and was made much of by visiting Americans who were inclined to whisk her off to the Connaught which she loved. Then she had a few falls at home and decided that it was dangerous for her to live alone. Lacking family to live with, a good friend, with the very best intentions, moved her from London to a nursing home in a quiet, prosperous part of Brighton. Lionel moved her in our Rolls and the trip was, he said, hilarious. She was completely disorganised and he did most of the packing before they set off, hours late. They had lunch on the way and he installed her in her nice room in the large, soundless house. Then, I think, the laughter ended for Marie. She sat in her room, with some of her own good furniture around and whispered, 'I don't see anyone here. They're all *old*, I think.' She became slim again, and then thin and all her lovely clothes had to be given away. She went on dwindling and very soon she was gone, and I miss her still.

Philip, Richard and I worked together for a third time. We missed acquiring the rights to *A Streetcar Named Desire* by a matter of hours only, but Tennessee sent us a re-written version of *Summer and Smoke*. He called it *The Eccentricities of a Nightingale* and we tried it out at the Yvonne Arnaud Theatre in Guildford. Our doubts about the reaction of the stockbroker belt to Tennessee were dispelled in the first few days. Our reception and favourable press led us to believe that we would have no problem in finding a home in the West

End after one month in Surrey. London was however packed with plays and we grew anxious as the days went by and every play in town seemed set to run and run for ever. Then, like a miracle, we were offered one of my favourite theatres, the Vaudeville. It was a rush job; closing in Guildford on Saturday, we had to open in the Strand on Tuesday. The revolve at Guildford on and around which Nicholas Giorgiardis had devised a beautiful, elaborate set, was as wide, if not wider, than the proscenium arch at the Vaudeville. Catastrophe. We needed to borrow five thousand pounds in order to move the set and re-jig it to fit the new theatre. I turned to our company – Keep Films – and, to my surprise, I was told that 'they' ('they' included me, surely?) needed to inspect the management's fiscal health and to 'think' about the transaction. Clement Scott-Gilbert and Richard Shulman, the producers, went to the office armed with their bank statements and balance sheets, confident that all would be well. The following day we were all mortified to be told that in Jules's opinion, Tennessee Williams was too 'chancy' a playwright to merit such a loan. To general stupefaction, we closed the play and sent the set to be broken up. Of all the blows Keep Films dealt me over the years, that one was the most difficult to overcome.

During this time I made infrequent forays into the London that was called the 'Swinging' London of the Sixties. From time to time I read with bewilderment that we were part of the set that embodied it. Nothing could have been less plausible. When I wasn't working I was usually at home with the children and O'Toole was far too busy working or doing the crossword to meet most of the film stars who came to London and called on Keep Films. As a director of Keep Films, I was occasionally deputed to pick them up from the Dorchester or the Grosvenor House and get them in to Tramps or Annabel's, the first places they wanted to visit. I would have done one, sometimes two, shows before I picked them up. Once installed inside, we would make conversation for a moment or two. 'And what do *you* do?' 'Oh, I work in the theatre here in London but I have small children – do you mind if I leave you now?' For me to spend an evening in Annabel's was torture; the ceiling was too low, the music too loud. Twice I went there with Jules and Joyce, sat on the banquette, ordered a drink and fainted clean away.

One night after the show, my dresser gave me a message to go to Tiberio – a lovely restaurant off Curzon Street – where the acoustics were so bizarre that from certain tables you could hear every word spoken at some of the other tables (since deals were made at each table at lunchtime it really paid to know exactly which were the vulnerable spots). I couldn't get a taxi from the Garrick Theatre and sprinted over to Mayfair, where I joined a large table nearing the end of dinner. They were all beautifully dressed in the fashion of the day: soft silk shirts for the men, stiff, beaded frocks for the women, hairpieces, false eyelashes, false nails. I sat down recognising all the famous people – nods and kisses. Peter Sellers! How nice – yes; hello, yes – all round the table. There was one little woman I didn't know – not an actress – speak to her later. Later was a bit too late. The one person I failed to recognise was Princess Margaret. It was only when she switched suddenly into HRH mode and tremors ran around the gathering that I realised my mistake. I rather admired her in her wrath. Lord knows what had inspired it on that night.

# Chapter Twenty-six

London – the end of the decade. Another film offer, to be directed by Peter Yates who had recently made *Bullitt*. I was to play a doctor, working opposite Warren Beatty. 'I absolutely can't. So sorry. But thanks.'

At home, O'Toole said, 'Are you *sure* you don't want to do this film?'

'Oh, absolutely. South America! With the girls coming up to their entrance exams. Not a chance.'

'But South America,' he kept on insisting, 'a wonderful place. Oh, you should go. The girls could visit after their exams.'

Eventually I said, 'Well, maybe. And Warren Beatty is a nice man, they say. And South America does have wonderful vegetation . . . oh well, all right. *Murphy's War* it is.'

After I accepted, O'Toole stopped talking about the film. I went off to the medical centre and was jabbed in dozens of places. I went off to the Quaker Centre in the Euston Road to learn about their attitude to foreign ministries (I was to play a Quaker). I concentrated on life at home, especially on Kate's entrance exam to a school I had chosen above all others – the North London Collegiate. Visiting, I had embarrassingly dropped a little curtsey to the Headmistress, Madeleine McLauchlin. My mother was also besotted by the school. We *had* to get both girls in, somehow. (We entered them for Camden and Francis Holland as well, just in case.) My mother was appalled by the results of the new methods of teaching: classroom walls being torn down; grammar despised; mathematical tables not to be learned, nor poetry memorised;

the children measuring the walls of their classroom and shaking powder from cocoa tin to cocoa tin and doing unbelievable things with empty egg boxes. Not only had Harold Lever advised Harold Wilson to close down every legal tax avoidance scheme so that high earners like O'Toole now paid nineteen shillings and sixpence in the pound in income tax ('Go abroad at once and stay there,' was the advice. O'Toole refused and elected to stay), but the Labour Government that we fought for was now – it seemed to me – also destroying the education system to which I owed my present life. The National Health Service was still intact. But for how long? At the moment it was the education system that worried my mother and me. She went to a few PTA meetings and I watched in awe as she rose to speak against the new system. The hostility and derision were palpable. After one meeting, a man sought us out; ignoring the headmistress, he talked to my mother. 'I just want to thank you – I didn't have the nerve to get up but thank you – I'm a Maths lecturer at London University and I'm appalled at the ignorance of incoming students and the rot begins right here at primary level.'

'I *know* that,' said my mother, grimly. Unsmiling, they looked at each other and parted, too upset to say goodbye.

'I'm taking them out,' said my mother. 'How d'you mean?' 'They have to know how to read and write and add up and subtract and multiply and divide or they'll never get into a decent school.' I envisaged scandal and endless newspaper attention. 'Just say they're not well. Get a note from Gerry. I'll teach them at home.' 'For how long?' 'Give me four months.' Feebly, I begged sick notes from Gerry and wrote letters describing fictitious family dramas. My mother held classes in the dining room and I took grammar and literature in the Green Room then, feeling like a deserter, I left for South America and my mother was left with the task of getting the two little girls into a *decent* school – the sort of school that, thanks to Rab Butler (a Tory), had been mine by right. The world turns.

\*       \*       \*

'So I'm going to do this job?' (To John Miller, my agent.)

'Yes, dear. Oh, by the way, Warren Beatty isn't doing it.'

'Really?'

'No, he wanted too much money. The producers are being a bit careful; even your part now incorporates three others – a man and two women.'

'I see.'

This is a week before I leave for South America and I say, 'So who *will* be playing Murphy?'

John looks amazed and embarrassed. 'Oh, don't you know? Er – well – O'Toole is the star of the picture. It seems he's mad about South America.'

I return to Hampstead, hatchet faced. *Ride a Cock Horse* had been a never-to-be-forgotten, horrible experience. How would we get through a four-month movie together?

'Aw, come on – it'll be *great*,' he smiles. The study desk is piled high with books about Simon Bolivar, Eldorado, Pre-Columbian art, Spanish primers, dictionaries. I look at him, quivering with excitement, all his attention directed at the desk.

My mother appears, beaming. She's been won over. So much to *learn*, how lovely.

'Don't worry about anything. Sort everything out when we get there. This is going to be a *great adventure* – just you wait.'

Caracas, Venezuela. The Caracas Hilton, isolated in what is a large, hot version of the new Spaghetti Junction in Birmingham and no possibility of going out for a walk. There's a grand welcoming party to wish the film well. The big garish reception room is full of the most beautiful women I've ever seen congregated in one place; their skins range from black to brown to café-au-lait to olive and the effect is devastating. I remember that Miss Venezuela is usually a starry presence in the Miss World line-up and am astonished to realise that the dazzling good looks that are so extraordinary in London are the norm here in this part of South America. And there's something else, as well, the rich pungent smell of expensive perfume and leather and cigars adding up to – what? Later, unwrapping the beautiful piece of jewellery nestling in my bouquet, the gift of a stranger (no address, thank goodness, or I'd have to return it), I realise that the smell is the smell of extreme wealth. Caracas may have been beautiful once. No longer. The slums, a huge shanty town a stone's throw from our smart hotel, are large and appalling. I'm glad to get away to start filming. Our base will be Puerto Ordaz and we're to live on a Greek boat and travel by Hovercraft to our locations in the huge delta of the Orinoco. 'No!' shriek our new acquaintances. '*Nobody* goes to the Green Hell.' I've brought all the wrong clothes, as usual, and leave almost everything in Caracas. The delta will be sulphurously, stiflingly hot.

It was. We tried to settle in on board the rather run-down Greek cruise ship. It wasn't a success. The cabins were cramped and, making a stab at running a happy ship, a nameless person put out cheery messages over the ship's loudspeaker. There was a lot of 'Wakey, Wakey! Savoy Grill now open' at breakfast time. Within a week we were all desperately trying to get away from each other – and there was no means of escape. I tried to learn some Amerindian, laboriously compiling a phonetic dictionary of useful phrases I might use in the film in my role as doctor. We got on with wardrobe fittings and make-up tests and grew more and more restless – no filming in sight. On our first outing in the huge Hovercraft we encountered very rough water (no one had realised that the Pacific meets the Caribbean hereabouts and the waters are always rough). All the windows smashed in and we took on a great deal of water. My hairdresser, who was calm about most things, shrieked that this was *it*. No more Hovercraft! There was rumbled, sea-sick assent from the unit and we limped home to the accompaniment of audible prayers. So, no way of getting to work and, on board ship, a mutiny. We were taken off and housed in the Rasil Hotel in Puerto Ordaz and helicopters and trucks were ordered to get us into the rain forest and deeper into the delta. All this was desperate for the company and for Peter Yates, the director, who couldn't begin filming. It was decided that it was by now cheaper to continue than to abandon the film. Not having any responsibility beyond knowing my lines and staying upright in the killing climate, I was loving the beginning of the adventure. O'Toole was still up to his eyes in books about Simon Bolivar, the liberator of Venezuela and the difficulties – the near impossibilities – brought out the best in him. Our companion was Philippe Noiret who, until fairly recently, had been a senior member of the Théâtre Nationale Populaire, the TNP, in France. We ordered ourselves brightly coloured cotton pyjamas and bought identical straw hats and called ourselves the Theatre Nationale Orinoco, the TNO – The tay en oh. We divided our leisure time between the only two restaurants and our sitting room where Philippe unveiled his cache of champagne and I contributed a large Cheddar cheese and Branston pickle, sent from Jermyn Street by Joyce. Philippe had packed *A la recherche du temps perdu* in French and we looked at each other in amazement as I opened my trunk and revealed my complete Proust – in English. Working conditions were appalling but we had a high old time. Peter Yates was kindness and forbearance itself and somehow, slowly and painstakingly, the film got made. It wasn't a 'smart' film but it was a really good adventure story and how else could we ever have lived in such an outlandish place, for so long?

On my last day I'd been filming alone, and was one of only a few people waiting to be lifted off by helicopter. The chief of police, an unpleasant man who'd been a heavy presence during the last few weeks, treating the movie as a holiday, was fooling around in one of our dug-out canoes on the Orinoco. A few of his men stood on the bank and as we waited there, barely paying attention, tired after a long day, one of the policemen on the bank took out his gun and shot his disliked superior. As my mouth opened, the unit member standing alongside me clamped his hand on my arm and hissed, 'Shut up. Turn your back and look inland.' I obeyed and we stood there for what seemed a very long time, ignoring the cries (of joy? protest? who could tell?) behind us. The helicopter approached, my friend pushed me into it and we lifted off from the delta for the last time. The scene below was quite calm. I'd learned a great deal in four months and knew enough not to talk about what we'd witnessed. I didn't discuss it with anyone when I returned to the hotel. I was scared and fascinated in equal measure by the absence of anything resembling law and order as I'd been raised to perceive it. It was a lesson we'd had to learn quickly: that the so-called absolutes, the codes of behaviour we'd learned to live by, meant nothing here in the remote corners of this continent.

# Chapter Twenty-seven

'Everything that can go wrong, will go wrong and at the worst possible time.' So says Murphy's Law and the months of filming on the Orinoco convinced everyone that the Law contained an incontrovertible truth. Even after we moved to the comparative comfort of the Puerto Ordaz hotel, the Rasil, the company still faced the problem of transporting the large unit to work each day. Tracks were cut through the rainforest, tracks which within a week would become impassable under the rampantly returning vegetation. We were soon made to understand why 'nobody goes to the Green Hell'; almost invisible, clouds of small insects bit or stung every scrap of exposed flesh and the steady drip, drip, of sweat drove the sound operator mad. One night the river rose fifteen feet and our set disappeared and once, at three in the morning, I was awakened by an Irish crew member who'd been sent to fetch the all-important barge which figured hugely in the film (as Philippe Noiret's home and O'Toole's torpedo carrier) in order to sail it to a new location. Maybe no one else answered the phone or maybe he was too nervous to confide in anyone more important. 'Siân?' he whispered urgently. 'Siân – THE BARGE IS SUNK.' He'd encountered treacherous waters in the sea to the east of the delta and, alive and not too shaken, was making his long way back to base in the casual manner peculiar to those men who like working in inhospitable places. It was left to me to pass on the dreadful message which galvanised the set department into heroic, round-the-clock work as they reproduced the eccentric vessel. I worked alone for a week with 'my' Indians who played my patients in the film, all of us running for our lives day after day, while enemy planes bombed us and shot at us and the village burned all around. I returned to base thinking that the climate was beginning to get me down and that, moreover, I'd pulled a muscle in my upper back and was having trouble breathing and maybe I should let the doctor have a look at it. 'Got a few days off?' he enquired. I nodded. 'Good,' he said. 'Stay in bed. You're just recovering from pleurisy.' He understood completely that the symptoms of pleurisy could seem like part of the rather poorly feeling that afflicted us all as we struggled to get through the day. Life on the ground was difficult but the movie was largely about aeronautics and the Frank Tallman team of American aviators had been engaged to do all the Second World War stunts. They purveyed the glamour of danger and they were such stars! Their wives – blonde and glamorous – were never seen, except at night, dining with their dashing husbands. Of course, not everyone realised that Gilbert Chomat, with the camera strapped to his helicopter, had to do everything the Tallman team did. We became fast friends with Gilbert (he *wasn't* starry) and the three of us made trips over the rainforest every weekend. One day he told me, 'You know, this job is too dangerous for a family man – all my helicopter pilot friends are dead. I have four small boys and a beautiful wife in Brittany. I will do only one more movie after this – *The Blue Max* in Ireland.'

Gradually, it occurred to me that O'Toole had a purpose behind all the flying around over the massive delta of the Orinoco. We had been collecting Pre-Columbian art for some time and had been assured by a Venezuelan government official in London that there was none to be found in Venezuela. This seemed improbable, if not impossible, so he began to scout about for likely settlement areas. Sheltered spots on rivers seemed favourable and indeed when we were able to touch down and walk to the waterside, we occasionally saw signs of past occupation. One day we arrived at an unusually pleasant curve in a river tributary. We stood there breathing in the calm of the place, when O'Toole whooped – a ghastly Irish sound – and darted to the mud bank. He extracted a beautiful parrot-head handle which must, once, have been attached to a big bowl. The Pre-Columbian art was surrendering to us, falling out of the soft earth. Gilbert and I tentatively joined in the 'dig' and loaded the helicopter with twenty-five beautiful 'bits'.

After that we made frequent weekend forays, not always fruitful, but I can't remember spending more pleasurable times. We found a great many objects – almost two hundred in all, including one entire pot, very precious. I thought that the existence of art was denied through ignorance but our visit to Angel Falls opened my eyes to a darker purpose and frightened me.

O'Toole: 'Angel Falls! We've got to go there.'

'It's hopeless. They're invisible most of the time.'

'We've got to *try*, though.'

Gilbert said, '*I'd* like to try.'

Bob Willoughby added, '*I'm* in!'

Bob Willoughby, the famous prize-winning photographer, had worked on foreign locations with O'Toole before. He contributed to all the major picture magazines and now, frustrated by the physical difficulty of travelling to our locations, he made it his mission to get us to Angel Falls and then to attempt to travel to the remote reaches of the Orinoco, where it flows through the Amazonas territory, not far from the border of Venezuela and Brazil. He was preparing a book of portraits of women and was desperate to photograph the Waika tribe. He went to work to obtain permission from the government for an expedition.

'But *when*? *How*?' I asked, disbelievingly.

'Oh, later,' said O'Toole, cagily. 'Maybe not at all. Forget it.'

I knew better than to try to question him further so I *did* forget all about these wild plans until, with a free weekend ahead, I was told to pack a few toothbrushes and a change of knickers and socks and be ready to leave the Rasil Hotel at dawn. I knew we were going to try to land on top of Angel Falls. I also knew that the film company would knock us out and lock us up rather than let the four of us do anything so foolhardy. I spent a sleepless night, guilty and pleasurably excited in equal measure. We were on the little airstrip at daybreak and found Gilbert waiting at his helicopter. He explained to me that we didn't have enough fuel for such a long trip but that I wasn't to worry because O'Toole and Bob had learned from someone called 'Jungle Rudi' that there was aviation fuel stored nearby his place in Guiana. It had been there for years and the metal drums were all rusted but *no doubt* it would get us to Angel Falls and then home again. No doubt. Oh, yes. But this was no time for doubts. We were off.

The Guiana Highlands lie in a corner of Eastern Venezuela, Bolivar State. This is El Dorado, the Terra Incognita between the Orinoco and the Amazon. Sir Walter Raleigh was here; one hundred men and five rowing boats and no luck at the end of the journey. Of course, there *has* been gold here. Until the discovery of the Rand goldfields of 1886, Venezuela was the largest gold producing country in the world. We're after water not gold. Angel Falls, named after the great aviator, Jimmy Angel, whose plane got stuck on the summit.

'Going down,' shouts Gilbert over the noise of the helicopter and we land in a landscape unlike anything I've ever seen. The river and the trees where we stand are dwarfed by the *tepuis* all around; massive, squat, sheer-sided, table-top mountains that seem to belong in a work of fantastic fiction. An unkempt figure appears. Somehow, Gilbert, after flying for hours with no sign of human being, has located Jungle Rudi, who greets us. They confer and Gilbert says we'll be back later.

'Now hold this.' I'm given a small piece of helicopter and see that Gilbert seems to be taking his machine apart and the men are neatly piling up everything that can be safely detached and soon there's nothing left but the frame and the seats – no doors, no sides, nothing to hang on to except the frame of the seat in front. 'Okay,' he says cheerily. 'Let's go.' He and O'Toole are in great high spirits. The summit of Angel Falls is more often than not out of sight, blanketed in thick cloud, so it had been far from sure that we would be able to land there but now, it seems, Gilbert thinks we have a good chance. Bob and I scramble into the back seats and hang on as we whoosh up and away and the ground, only too visible beneath our dangling feet, recedes and at the same moment the rain begins. We're drenched in minutes and that, coupled with the unaccustomed, terrifying feeling of naked vulnerability in a foreign element so disorients me that it is moments before I realise that the shrieking noise I can hear is coming from me. We fly into cloud and that is calming but as we emerge from it I realise that we're going to put down on a piece of flat ground that to my fevered, disturbed senses doesn't seem to be much bigger than a grand piano. I clutch Bob's arm and scream, 'I can't look! I can't look!' 'Nor can I,' he shouts, 'and I'm taking the pictures!' As we make a perfect landing I open my eyes. 'Get out carefully on the *left side only*,' says Gilbert. 'We have no more than five minutes, then we must lift off before the cloud descends again.'

The summit of the *tepui* is spongy (no wonder Jimmy Angel's plane got stuck there) and it's covered in mosses and ferns which, so I've read, grow nowhere else. I've got gloves and pruning scissors and plastic bags in my pocket and I begin collecting. I believe Gilbert when he says that there's nothing but emptiness on the right-hand side of the helicopter and I stay on the left as I'm told, too frightened to look anywhere except at what lies directly under my feet so, standing where No Foot Has Trod is somewhat wasted on me; I'm seeing very little. The sound of water is deafening but I can hear O'Toole laughing at my RHS gloves, or my cowardice, or both.

'That's it,' calls Gilbert. 'We have to go.' We obediently

jump in and rise sideways and then, dropping slightly and moving in close to the side of the *tepui*, we come face to face with the falls as they emerge from rock and I realise that Gilbert is going to descend *with* the sheet of water thundering down the side of the mountain. I've heard of down draughts (or is it up draughts?) and the dangers of what we are doing, but after the trials of the morning I have no fear left and I am able to admire both the beauty of the sight before me and Gilbert's skill as we gently drop three thousand, two hundred and twelve feet to the ground below. Purged and quiet, we disembark weak at the knees, floppy like rabbits and smile our gratitude at Gilbert who is looking very pleased, as well he might. We return to the fuel dump and re-fuel, Bob filtering the precious stuff through a nylon stocking while Gilbert spoons it off.

The adventures were not over and the day ended on a sombre note. After reassembling the helicopter, we flew a short distance, O'Toole and Gilbert conferring and searching around – for what? Suddenly they spotted a lone figure standing on a piece of level scrub near a small shack. It was Jungle Rudi's home. We put down, switched off the engine, and I followed the group making for the little house where we sat drinking brandy and Jungle Rudi told us a fantastic tale of plots, of genocide, of danger. As he talked on and on, directing his attention to O'Toole only, speaking in an urgent, low monotone, I tried to separate the real, the probable, the believable from the improbably fantastic. I was tired and the brandy, taken on an empty stomach, was distorting my reason while at the same time in a way enhancing my acceptance of this strange scene. Rudi, his shotgun close to his right hand, talked of the destruction of huge tracts of land, flooded in the service of hydro-electric power. 'You think it is physically possible that they have warned Indian tribes impossible to locate even by expert anthropologists?' he asked rhetorically. I remembered that the student revolt I'd seen begin in the capital when we first arrived had been quelled in record time and when I'd asked how it had been stopped our Caracas friend, Mr Perez-Canto, had airily replied, 'Oh well, they shot quite a few.' I looked down at my precious bag of plants on the ground between my feet. This was a terrifying, beautiful, unruly place. I tried to rearrange my ideas of fair play and justice and my notion of the way things should be done. The intolerable was only too possible. But why was he telling this to O'Toole? 'They'll get me soon,' he said. 'They'. I began to withdraw. He could be just a lonely man, deranged by isolation. 'If you have art made by these so-called inartistic, ignorant, valueless people be very, very careful.' We had been digging and collecting for months, and yes, everyone *had* said that the Venezuelan Indians produced no art worth speaking of. That was the official line. I began to feel depressed, too tired and too inadequate to evaluate what was going on. Rudi and O'Toole walked together as we returned to the helicopter. I looked with relief at Gilbert's healthy Breton face and Bob's slightly sceptical, confident American sideways glance.

We were too tired to shout above the noise of the helicopter and sat silently as we flew over the seemingly endless rainforest. The last quarter of an hour of the journey found us sitting up, very alert and tight-lipped, while the red light on the chopper's panel glowed red for empty as we headed for the makeshift airfield. O'Toole kissed the ground when we landed safely and we headed off to the café to toast Gilbert and his dazzling skill. Back at the hotel, we sauntered through the coffee shop as though we'd been on a short taxi ride. I felt shaky but I swung my plastic bags of plants as though they contained a little shopping. O'Toole sat down and ordered a coffee. No one was to know what we'd been up to but Bob couldn't suppress his elation as he took off at speed to develop his pictures in his makeshift dark room. 'Nice day off?' asked someone. My eyes felt as big as saucers and I was sure I didn't look normal after the wonders of the day, all too much too absorb and digest, and I could do no more than nod and smile as I headed to bed and oblivion.

The Spanish Conquistadors had left behind forts which, unlike any subsequent buildings, caught the breeze and made the days bearable. The hospital scenes in the movie took place in such a building and while we were shooting these sequences the girls and my mother came to join us in Puerto Ordaz and made the long journey through the rain forest to watch the filming in the fort. Watching people filming is not a spectator sport and they were relieved to be let off to explore the pleasures of the American oil company compound which had, glory of glories, a swimming pool and a Coca-Cola machine. Even the Caracas Hilton was more fun for the ten and seven year old girls. So good to see the three of them; my mother had done a terrific job in my absence and under her coaching Kate had passed the entrance examination to three good schools and was all set to go to our first choice: the North London Collegiate School for Girls. My mother had a determined gleam in her eye as she talked about Pat's future. Pat, blonde, immaculate – a stranger to bad hair days – shrugged and smiled non-committally. My mother permitted herself a half-smile and I could see that Pat had a date with my mother's classroom-for-one in the big kitchen in Guyon House.

When they left, we embarked on the last phase of the movie. Fate was kind to our director, Peter Yates, who had struggled so hard against awful odds and filming was almost uneventful. When it was over, there was a concerted, mad rush for the exit. Our cases remained unpacked, however, and I assumed that we were to make a leisurely departure, returning via Caracas, the capital, where we had friends to visit. The telegram from our lawyer, Denise Sée, puzzled me. 'Poor Kate and Pat,' it read, 'to think of them as orphans . . .' Orphans? 'What does she mean?' I asked O'Toole. He looked at the telegram and tossed it into the wastepaper basket with a laugh. 'Good old Denise.

Nice try,' he said. 'Try? What?' I persisted. 'Oh, everyone is behaving hysterically,' he said, soothingly. 'Pay no attention. We're going to make that little trip I was talking about and Dr Inga Goetz is coming down from Caracas to help us on our way.' Dr Goetz was an anthropologist and I'd read her book about the Yanomama Indians. I'd also read about the difficulty of reaching the head waters of the Orinoco and I'd thrilled to the accounts of head-hunters and abandoned missions and missing travellers. It had made exciting reading, all right, and I was rather inclined to leave it at that, but already Bob was organising water purifying tablets and was all set for the trip. O'Toole's contribution to the packing was a couple of bottles of brandy and a few gifts of tin kettles and machetes and sheets of Yanomama words he'd been given by Dr Goetz. 'You could learn these,' he said encouragingly. I didn't waste time arguing. It was very clear that O'Toole was going up the Orinoco and if he was going then I was going. I visited the only store in town, and found three plastic ponchos, folded small. I couldn't find anything else to buy. And it was difficult deciding what to wear, so far from the Army & Navy Stores or Tropicadilly in London. In the end I wore a cotton Yves St Laurent safari jacket and a Herbert Johnson cotton bush hat (they qualified as suitable because of the words 'safari' and 'bush'). My trousers were stuffed into a pair of Charles Jourdan 'riding' boots. I remembered buying an anti-bug burning device from Harrods. It lay unopened in my trunk along with the complete set of *A la recherche du temps perdu* which I'd intended to read and hadn't. I slipped it into my little rucksack along with the brandy and a toothbrush. It didn't seem enough somehow, so I added some chocolate bars.

Even so, we seemed to be woefully unprepared but I could see O'Toole's reasoning. We only had two or three weeks at our disposal. If we loitered, trying to make adequate prepara-tions, we simply wouldn't make the trip at all. 'Remember,' he said, 'Englishmen once went up Everest in tennis shoes with a packet of sandwiches.' I supposed he was exaggerating but I rather agreed with the notion that anything was possible until it turned out to be impossible. 'Okay,' I said and bought more chocolate.

Dr Goetz arrived; German, tall, middle-aged and very sprightly. We were in business. The four of us flew in an alarmingly small plane to the small settlement called Ayacucho (I could have done without being told that this meant 'corner of death'). There, she helped us find a suitable small boat (the soapdish, O'Toole christened it) and a pair of guides. They were incredibly uncharming and shook their heads gloomily whenever Dr Goetz addressed them. We only had room for one man but they were adamant that they wouldn't accompany us alone and conveyed to Dr Goetz that they would only go 'so far'. It seemed that most of the missions along the river had been abandoned and only two remained. Dr Goetz would accompany us to the first one and persuade them to let us stay overnight. As we began our journey the following morning, sun shone and the river was alarmingly wide, as it had been where we'd been filming hundreds of miles to the east. The noise of the outboard was deafening and we were silent as we stared at the 'green wall' which was the vast rainforest on both sides. At least the river had a shine on its mud-coloured surface. O'Toole had decided that he wouldn't bother with water purifiers so we were to start drinking river water as soon as possible 'to get our systems going'. Bob looked incredulous. He was weighed down with the latest thing in camera equipment and water purifiers.

It took us a day to reach the mission; a day spent looking at not very much. It seems absurd but remote jungles and rain forests viewed from the river do present dull, almost blank, high 'walls' of green. I began the journey sitting up straight on the bit of bench that was to be mine during the entire journey, eagerly looking about. After about four hours I sat slumped, wishing I could at least identify the trees which made up 'the wall'. It looked impenetrable and I wondered uneasily how we'd manage when we pulled in.

The landing place looked very small when it appeared, protruding into the immense river. We tied up and Dr Goetz, who was familiar with the place, led us through the trees on to a serviceable pathway which led in turn to the clearing and the somewhat ramshackle mission building. The nuns were welcoming and indicated that they would be very happy for us to eat with them and to stay overnight. We were ravenous and fell on the food which was laid on a trestle table in a dilapidated room, bare of furniture save for a few benches. The meat was wild pig and was delicious. We were shown to small cells containing narrow wooden-framed beds with straw mattresses. I scarcely remembered undressing and the sun was high in the sky when I woke and scrambled to get ready to leave. Dr Goetz sat with us and gave us a last briefing before she returned to Ayacucho and then to Caracas. The bad news was that one of our guides refused to come any further. It seems he was now voluble with horror stories of the dangers ahead but I couldn't understand a word he said. Dr Goetz said that we should of course be careful but that in all probability we wouldn't find any native Indians. She had made thirteen properly organised expeditions and not all of them had been successful in this regard. She wished us luck and reminded us to use our Yanomama words, especially *Shori noji* (good friends) and to be as cheerful and as amusing as possible, should we be fortunate enough to find ourselves surrounded by the Yanomama.

Rested and fed, we were in high good spirits as we set off on our own and the rain began to fall. It didn't just fall, it leapt on us and jumped up and down. I fished out the plastic ponchos and we each retreated into a little brightly coloured tent. We were wet by the time we arranged them over our little places (Bob draped his over his cameras) and then the rain penetrated the neck fastening and ran up our arms as we tried to smoke. We couldn't even look up, the rain was blinding and the noise was deafening as it landed on the metal soap-dish and bounced off our ponchos. There was now a wall of rain between us and the wall of the jungle. There was nothing to do except stare silently at the floor and occasionally glance sideways. The remaining guide was malevolently fed up, as well he might be. I'd given him my chocolate bar, which he accepted with palpable disdain. I wished I could speak to him; we might have enjoyed a bit of a moan together. We seemed to have been travelling for a week already and I thought I sensed him wondering where we would sleep and would there be anything to eat except chocolate. Bob and O'Toole were full of high resolve and in no mood to be bothered with trivial details.

Out of the corner of my left eye I see something – the first *different* something I've seen all day. On a smooth outcrop of rock shining in the rain, backed by the dark green jungle wall, stands a person – a small, stocky figure, legs braced, arms raised, holding a huge bow, taller than himself, the arrow poised for flight. Snuggled under my pixie hood I figure the bow is six feet high, so the man is only four feet something. The arrow is trained on the soap-dish. I nudge O'Toole with my foot. He's sitting opposite me, staring at the ground. He looks at me through the rain. As subtly as I know how, I indicate the bank to my left. He looks and sees the naked figure. As he stiffens, Willoughby, behind me, follows his gaze and automatically his hands tighten on his camera. 'No,' breathes O'Toole. 'Leave it.' Our guide is oblivious, thank God, and we pass up river – oh, so slowly – and the arrow slowly swings around to follow us until we pass out of sight into the rain-soaked dusk. We can't discuss what happened, conversation is impossible, and we plough on. In a way, that little incident has made me less afraid. We've gone over Niagara in a barrel and there's no going back and that makes everything simpler. I no longer have any hope of knowing what time of day it is, or indeed what day it is, but suddenly the rain stops and we see a lawn – I swear – a lawn. It's like a vision, too Pre-Raphaelite bright to be real, and there, standing on the edge of the lawn is a figure in black robes with a huge white Old Testament mane of hair and long, spade beard. It says something for my state of mind and the amount of brandy I'd ingested that I have no recollection in what language we communicated with this priest. But we dined with him in a ramshackle shed and he showed us his work. He was making a dictionary. Yanomama to – what? I'd never make a decent explorer. I don't remember. I fancy it was Armenian. He looked Greek. There was no one left in his mission. And there were no missions left up river. He told us there had been trouble with the Yanomama – there was danger and we should turn back, now.

We ate bits of meat picked from small rib cages (what *were* we eating, I wondered). Now that we were at rest and the rain had stopped, we could hear noises again: birds shrieked and later frogs croaked and crickets filled the air with their sound. We slept in hammocks. I wasn't worried about what lay in store. Only later did I realise that I was living entirely in the present.

Onward up river. Against advice, we are not carrying guns (just as well, I think – my aim is probably as bad as my sense of direction). The rain is intermittent now and the boys have thrown away their red cloaks. Mine is stuffed under my seat, just in case. It's so incredibly boring, this trip up the exotic river. I'm now thinking of the jungle wall as green concrete. Where are we? How far have we come? What will the source of the river – miles away – look like, if we get there? Is it worth it? Plod on. Drink brandy and river water. Smile at guide a lot. He doesn't smile back once. I'm half asleep most of the time. There's a hallucinatory quality about my waking moments.

A small girl appears in a tiny clearing in the forest wall. O'Toole shouts at the guide to pull into the bank. The water is high but he manages to moor near a small spit of land and we disembark. Reality intrudes as the small child grabs O'Toole's hand and begins pulling him into the forest. Bob and I fluster out of the boat and set off at a run after them. The guide doesn't budge. Waist-high branches and creepers slash across our bodies as we try to keep up with the pair ahead. The little girl is so small that she can run under the impediments. How is O'Toole coping? We're slowing down to a trot and, breathless and scratched, we reach a clearing. Ahead is what looks like a huge, blond ski-slope and I realise it's a massive thatched roof made of palm leaves yellowed with age – it must reach from forty feet down to a little wall-opening just four feet high. The small girl drags O'Toole through the opening. Keen not to be left behind, we half crawl, half stumble after them. We are in a big *shabono*. I've never seen one from the air but I'm told that from above they look like doughnuts. From ground level they are much more elegant, the roof rising to an open circle, and below as many as forty families occupy a segment each of the circle; hammocks swing in two or three layers over fires which can be reached by hand from the lowest hammock. Behind the hammocks against the wall are makeshift shelves, holding little more than baskets, it seems, and on ground level, pet birds and parrots play. Babies are at all times attached to their mothers. Dusk is falling, it's raining again. The noise of the rain on leaves mingles with the shrill noise of female voices. *That's* what's so odd. There are no men here. And Willoughby and O'Toole have disappeared. I remember what Dr Goetz had told me, 'Say "*Shori noji*" – often! Smile! Lift your eyebrows as often as possible. And allow them to explore your body. They need to know what you are.'

There must be fifty small, small women pressing around me, not one reaching my diaphragm. Tiny hands pull at my St Laurent shirt. The buttons give (well done, back at the workroom). My black silk trousers give way at the waist and rip down the length of the zipper. My hat is torn off and my hair detached from its rubber band. They scream with laughter – these small, big-breasted women – I'm revealed as an androgynous, flat chested, wide shouldered, slim hipped, flat stomached – what? So much exercise, so much disciplined dieting to a perfect catwalk size 8 to 10 has resulted in hilarious entertainment for the ladies of the upper reaches of the Orinoco. I tie my clothes back on – I'm not enjoying this much but am trying to keep smiling – and hope that my genuine goodwill is going to get me through the ensuing night. O'Toole and Willoughby appear from the side of the *shabono*. It seems that most of the men are away on a hunt. I'm so dazed I don't ask how they *know* this. 'This is quite lucky for us.'

'We're to be taken to sleep now.'

A little group of women walk us back into the forest until we come to another clearing and there we see a group of nuns. Now, I do feel I'm hallucinating. I'd read that some of the Yanomama, while not accepting Christianity, quite like to live near a mission in order to trade goods. This must be the second of the last remaining missions. These sweet-faced women lead us to a trestle table and yet again we eat unidentifiable bits of meat attached to small ribcages. After much nodding and miming of gratitude we retreat to snug hammocks under a broken-down barn roof. I remember my Harrods anti-bug coils. I light the coils and place them under our hammocks and I lie there listening to the forest noises, looking up at the broken roof, wishing I hadn't read so much about vampire bats.

All night the air was filled with music. The women, alone in the *shabono*, ululated and sang for the success of the hunt. I made that up. They sang all night but I don't know what they were singing about. The men were away hunting. They may have been wishing them success or just enjoying a hen night.

In the morning we thank the nuns and make our way back to the *shabono*. The women are having a kind of lie-in after the musical efforts of the previous night or maybe this is how they spend their days. They lie in their hammocks playing with their babies, decorating them with paint and feathers. The older children play on the floor with the family pets. One woman is working; she is weaving a basket, lying down in her hammock, using her two hands and one foot. The vine is held away from her by her huge big toe. I notice that they all have large big toes that stand away from the other toes. A few men appear and try to engage O'Toole and Bob in some kind of game. We can't work out what they want but we do a lot of eyebrow work and smile obligingly. The women roll out of their hammocks and we follow them as they all trot a little way away from the *shabono* (they never seem to move at walking pace; everything is done at a run). Ah – it's to be a contest of strength. They're producing the huge bows and arrows we saw the young man holding on the river bank. O'Toole is almost twice as tall as these men, the contest seems unfair. Everyone is in huge good humour. Some of the men are laughing so much they can barely stay standing. They're calling O'Toole something and I write it down so that Dr Goetz can translate it later. The men give O'Toole a bow and arrow and stand alongside him. He's not a bad archer and now he good humouredly prepares to shoot with them. Their arrows fly into the air and O'Toole is left struggling. He cannot release the arrow no matter how he tries. They now lie on the floor, they're laughing so much. These tiny men have shoulders and arms like heavyweight boxers at the peak of fitness. We are now *loved*. O'Toole is patted on his bottom and is obviously being told what a great fellow he is. We trot out our bits of Yanomama and throw in lots of '*Shori noji*'s; greater harmony could not be imagined. The women have got used to me and stroke my clothes and my flat chest, fondly amused this morning. We can't stay, fearful that they might feel they have to feed us – and they don't seem to have anything in the way of food. Almost all of them accompany us (at a run) through the rainforest and down to our boat. The 'guide' and boatman looks appalled and stands apart, hatchet-faced, as we indulge in a prolonged leave-taking and O'Toole produces gifts from our little store of machetes and beads and tin cans. I've never had such a social success anywhere.

As soon as we set off up river it begins to rain again. I can tell that the river is very high. Today, we're seeing things. They were there before so have we only now learned to notice them? I can't believe that but we are now seeing birds as they sweep across the water: macaws, I recognise; dark green kingfishers also – although they don't look much like the kingfishers of Carmarthenshire. As I look at the jungle wall, I see an ibis, high up, miss its footing and fall gracelessly down four or five 'floors' of tree. It finds a landing place and, effortlessly elegant again, sits there, pretending nothing embarrassing happened. I catch O'Toole's eye and see that he has been observing the same comical scene.

The rain stops and we are able to look around again. I don't know what time it is – my watch became waterlogged days ago – and it is very hard to be sure how many days we have been travelling. There is a smooth rock and a piece of beaten earth alongside it that could be a landing place. We are very tired and very hungry and quite disoriented (probably a bit drunk as well). Pulling in, we set off into the rainforest. There *is* a path of sorts. The vines and branches lash cruelly across our waists and chests. We're too tall for this vegetation. On we go, each sunk in our thoughts, and suddenly there is another *shabono* but the drama is *outside* this time – we gradually realise we have walked straight into a hallucinogenic ceremony. There are no women in sight. The men are naked, save for the belt which holds the foreskin tucked up in its correct 'public' place. We freeze on the spot and no one acknowledges our presence. Squatting down, one man, clad only in a loincloth, is about to blow the hallucinogenic dust into the nostrils of another man. I've read about this often so I know what to expect but nothing prepares one for the explosion of mucus; the eyes, the nose, the mouth – everything runs violently. As I'd read, this pain seems to go on for half an hour; then, for the next half hour, the shaman (the wise man) receives auditory instructions and advice for the tribe, then he goes to the river and washes and takes another half hour to recover. So we watch the full one and a half hour experience.

Instinctively, we felt that we shouldn't linger in this place. There was none of the friendly curiosity we had experienced earlier. We laid our gifts on the floor, machetes and tin kettles, and while they were unsmilingly picked up and examined we nodded and smiled, said, '*Shori noji*!' and tried to melt into the forest, backing away as casually as we were able. I had found the ceremony alarming. Bob, of course, had snatched some photographs and O'Toole, who prided himself – with reason – on his nose for trouble, murmured, 'Don't hang about, my dears. Back to the soap-dish.' Once we were out of sight of the *shabono* we turned and ran back to the river and continued towards the source. We didn't make it but we stopped after travelling a very respectable distance. The BBC was in Venezuela making a documentary that year. They were making a proper expedition in a Hovercraft with guards carrying submachine guns and it seems that we managed to get four hundred miles further up river than they did. And this gave us a good deal of childish satisfaction at the time.

The return to Ayacucho dragged. We had none of the excitement of the beginning of the adventure and time was running out and we ought to be thinking of returning to England where, in a few weeks, filming would be resumed in the studio. O'Toole was in a 'Let's push on' mood and we took only brief rests on the long journey. The guide was handsomely rewarded for his pains. For an unguarded moment he looked surprised as he swiftly counted the notes O'Toole thrust at him. He hadn't realised that he'd been working for one of the great over-payers of the Western world. We hired a Cessna in Ayacucho and flew to Caracas. Coffee and beds and baths and a spot of scrambled egg were just beginning to feature in my thoughts when we flew into a violent storm. I was too tired to be frightened and looked at the men in disbelief as the little plane was thrown about and the pilot began to shout incoherent bits of advice to us over his shoulder. It was obvious that we had to escape from the storm so down we went – all the way down, in fact. The pilot managed to land and we stood in the middle of nowhere with our bits of luggage – mainly Bob's equipment – until the pilot succeeded in raising a local taxi who was startled but game when we asked him to drive to Caracas, five or six hours away. Bob and O'Toole pressed a great deal of money into the pilot's hand and off we lurched – it was a *very* old car; all of it rattled but we slept like infants and it got us to the Hilton, pulling up with a noisy flourish alongside the Bentleys and the Rolls-Royces.

Bob's wife, Dorothy, was waiting for him. 'We're going to Machu Picchu,' they said. 'Not without us,' said O'Toole and I went upstairs to pack and change the air tickets and telegraph London to say that we were safe and *almost* on the way home. I called Dr Goetz before we left Venezuela. She told us that the name O'Toole had been given was 'High Mountain'.

We rendezvoused with the Willoughbys in Cuzco and obediently followed all the rules for acclimatising to this altitude; no alcohol and a four-hour sleep, then very slow movement for a while. In the 'best' hotel our sheets were grubby and I took them off and we fell asleep under the rough blankets. (Why should we assume that the blankets were cleaner than the sheets, I thought lazily, and at the same moment thought, 'What does it matter?')

Awakening, we strolled – slowly – around Cuzco, marvelling along with all the other visitors at the wonderful stonework. O'Toole and I have a special interest in stone. Connemara in Ireland is a land of granite, the drystone walls of Ireland are beautiful and varied. Looking at the massive drystone walls of Cuzco, we decided that we would try to build a drystone house in Connemara. Like all the visitors, we wanted to go to Machu

Picchu. In 1970 it was still an uncomfortable trip and along with a cartload of other tourists we felt slightly adventurous. There was no place to stay, it was a bit like going to Petra ten years previously, and we were well able to rest curled up under a rock. Nothing can prepare one for Machu Picchu and nothing one can say can add to the descriptions or convey the wonder of it.

We moved on to Lima where O'Toole had a contact in the art world. Bob and his wife left us after the one conventional meal we were to enjoy and they also gave us money; we had run out but there was something called a credit card and it gave you money, no matter where you were. O'Toole and I were mystified and impressed and grateful. Lima was the noisiest city I had ever been in – or was I now unused to urban din? O'Toole went off to 'meet a man – don't ask' and I 'Wait here'. To pass the time, I pressed my dried plants (my mother would be fascinated to see them) and repacked our luggage and sat looking at the dark street. This city scared me somewhat, though I didn't know why. At four in the morning O'Toole returned, exhausted, bearing a few plastic shopping bags. 'Pack these – don't look. God, I'm tired.' Fully clothed, he stretched out on the bed and slept. This man slept better and longer than anyone I knew. Dutifully, I didn't 'look' and I packed the objects in the luggage. When O'Toole woke, we left for the airport and home. In Bogota we landed unexpectedly and the plane was kept on the ground for hours. 'Sorry, love,' he said. 'I think the game's up. Don't forget you really *don't* know what's in those bags.' I tried to read and not contemplate the punishment for the unlawful liberating of works of art. Suddenly we were off! I couldn't look at him. It was the luck of the Irish, dammit. I felt sick.

In the Green Room of Guyon House, my mother and Kate and Pat and Liz and Manolita unpack and drink tea. 'Oh, thank God for a decent cup of tea,' groans the Irishman. 'Where's the jewellery?' 'What jewellery?' 'You *know* – the jewellery from Lima.' 'Was there any? You said not to look.' 'Oh Jaysus – I'm surrounded by eejits.' 'Wait, wait,' soothes my mother and goes to search through the rubbish. 'Is this what you were looking for?' she says, holding up a ratty plastic shopping bag. 'Could be,' and he drops the most beautiful old necklaces over my head. The Pre-Columbian masks are put aside to be sent to our British Museum friend who will 'blow' the flattened gold back into shape and then they will be sent to Claude de Muzak in Paris to be mounted. We all look at the beautiful, battered, soft gold faces. The girls stroke them and I can't feel too guilty about any of this.

We leave for Ireland almost at once. Arriving at the cottage in Connemara, I unpack my plants from Angel Falls and see the *Irish Times* on the table. 'Air Tragedy', I read and before I pick up the paper I know it will tell me of Gilbert's death on *The Blue Max*. A small piece of something or other fell from above and cut Gilbert's rotor blade. It only takes a little something to destroy a helicopter and in this case five lives in Brittany. We look out over the fuchsia hedges, down to the Atlantic; the never far-away melancholy of this piece of Ireland rises up to chime with the desolation we're feeling.

# Chapter Twenty-eight

Since my schooldays I had never had anything much to do with people of my sex and age. I spent the most interesting times working with adults where I was 'the girl'. Then as I grew up and played leading parts, I worked largely with men. The other women I worked with were usually considerably older than I was. In private life I was a wife – a wife obliged to keep her private life very private and defined to a large extent by the identity of a husband. As a young mother I felt redefined by my children. Was it my imagination, or were young women years ago constantly in some kind of competition with each other? Certainly there were, as always, too few jobs for too many of us actresses so that competition was understandable. Those women whose ambition was to marry well seemed also to pursue a solitary path to their goal. As the wife of a rich, talented, glamorous man I was from time to time painfully aware of the unabashed, predatory behaviour of the women we met. From time to time I was astonished to observe that even women whom I regarded as friends were not above making a barely veiled attempt at seducing my husband.

Safe within my small circle of women whom I liked and admired, women whom it was not possible to define especially by their gender – well behaved, hard working, amusing, clever, good looking – I looked out somewhat nervously at the liberated woman of the late Sixties and early Seventies.

So when I was asked to play Mrs Pankhurst, the leader of the Suffragettes, in *Shoulder to Shoulder*, a six-part series that Ken Taylor had written about the movement and the women involved in it, even as I unhesitatingly accepted the producer

Verity Lambert's offer, at the same moment I thought, 'Oh, this is going to be hell on wheels – six months, virtually living with fifty women.' Half the plays were to be directed by Moira Armstrong, the other three by Waris Hussein – how would he cope with us all? – and even one of the camera operators was female. I could imagine the rows, the tears, the gossiping, the cliques, the jealousies that lay ahead.

The range and diversity of the personalities cooped up together in close quarters for long hours each day as we worked six, sometimes seven, days a week gave rise to amusement and absorbing interest rather than irritation. I realised that I'd turned some kind of corner when I found myself polishing Patricia Quinn's skin-tight leather dress – which she was wearing at the time. It had been bought in a shop in the King's Road in which I wouldn't have been seen dead but I could appreciate that it looked terrific on Pat. I played Mrs Pankhurst, the leader of the Suffragette Movement, Patricia was my daughter, Christabel, and Angela Down played Sylvia. Angela was as reserved as Pat was extrovert, I hovered somewhere in between and we became the little family which was the nucleus of the drama. Georgia Brown developed the idea for the series along with Midge McKenzie and Georgia played a leading part as well. Ken Taylor was the writer and as we all became experts on the politics of the turn of the century he grew to dread our pleas for extra scenes – especially 'good' bits of the story that we didn't want left out. If he'd listened to us the series would have been fifty hours long. Verity Lambert, the producer, presided effortlessly over the huge undertaking, helped by the best of buccaneering company managers (shortly to become a producer himself) Graham Benson who, on our first early morning filming call in the damp, grey countryside outside Halifax (which was playing Manchester, 1890), appeared in the makeshift make-up room bearing trays of champagne and orange juice 'to cheer things up a bit'.

We stayed cheered up for the next seven months, all of us running more or less complicated private lives, and no one pleaded tiredness or illness or heartbreak or buckled under the worries of organising homes and husbands and parents and children by remote control. There wasn't one woman who gave less than her best and I was buoyed up like a cork on the ocean. The men in our lives were a trifle bemused, as well they might be. Many of them found themselves at home while we worked late. This was a different kind of life we were leading and it made us all a little different. Waris Hussein, who shared the directing with Moira Armstrong, accompanied us when we let off steam occasionally and went out on the town, dancing for hours, and Graham Benson made sure we were all packed off home in good order. This was all quite unlike working in a more usual mixed-sex show where the men went out on the spree and the women rushed home to catch up with the housekeeping. I'd never had such a good time and my confidence began to grow. Observing how other women struggled to reconcile the many demands made on them with varying degrees of success and often with utter failure, I began to realise that it was impossible to do everything properly; that feeling slightly inadequate and very guilty all the time was a state common to us all. The current wisdom was that it was easy to Have it All, to Do it All. I had been photographed many times in my 'perfect' room in my 'fashionable' clothes with my clean, 'adorable' looking children, 'successfully combining my busy working life with my beautiful domestic existence', as the caption would read. What a lie! I thought, with relief. I knew now that I wasn't alone in finding the effort of running three or four lives almost impossibly difficult. It was comforting to feel part of a huge, struggling, largely silent sisterhood. Men weren't expected to help at all; if women wanted to work they had, somehow, to manage everything so as to inconvenience no one and many of us learned for the first time to admit failure and to ask for and give help.

More than a few of us had health worries as well. 'Pains peculiar to ladies', as I'd seen them quaintly described, were ignored, as were minor illnesses and even major illnesses were overcome with a minimum of drama. Both Verity and I were hospitalised with suspected breast cancer. When we went to visit our producer after her exploratory operation, she was holding an IV fluid bottle in one hand, a telephone in the other and gesturing at the champagne with her foot.

The moment that there was an indication that I might have breast cancer, Gerry Slattery whisked me back from Bristol where I was spending the weekend with O'Toole, who was doing a season of plays at the Old Vic. I was booked into the London Clinic at once, pausing only to tell Verity that I'd be back at work as soon as possible. She was reassuringly matter-of-fact; with fifty women on board for six months, these crises were depressingly frequent. The watchword was 'Don't get excited; just deal with the situation minute by minute.' O'Toole was more fearful than I was but he went on rehearsing.

It was winter and before I drove down to Harley Street for surgery, I went to one of my favourite Hampstead places, the High Hill bookshop, to order the Christmas books for the girls and for my friend, Ricci Burns and his mother, Lilian. Standing there, suddenly I wasn't able to maintain my chirpy attitude and I wondered morbidly if I would *be* there in Guyon House at Christmas time. I trailed back up the hill, feeling sorry for myself. There was no one at home in whom to confide. My mother most certainly wasn't to know; not many years past she'd survived a double mastectomy and I didn't want her to have to confront another, frightening cancer episode. It would be silly to worry the girls and I had waved them off to school as casually as I was able. As usual, my only confidant was Ricci Burns. I called him and he didn't let me down. 'Oh, my God, I can see it all! You're sitting in that house and you've convinced yourself you're going to die! Stop it! Don't be a drama queen!' I took his advice and stopped organising my funeral service.

O'Toole came to London from Bristol to receive an award and called in to the hospital on the eve of my operation. I think that hospitals and illness distress him beyond measure and am glad when he hurries off. As I'm on the brink of feeling alone and sorry for myself, the nurse comes in bearing a massive, magnificent bunch of red roses; it looks incongruous in this expensive but spartan room. When I look at the note I rejoin the land of 'normal', functioning people. It reads, 'Wear these in your hair tonight, love Ricci'. Ricci – thank God for him. I feel like Frida Kahlo in a Buñuel film as I snuggle down to sleep, broadly smiling, surrounded by red blossoms.

After the operation the next day when I came round, they give me my 'Permission to perform a mastectomy' form to tear up because the papilloma which had bled so alarmingly had proved to be benign. My first thought is to call the BBC to say I'll be back at work the following day. I call home. Lionel isn't available to bring me home; he's picking up actors and bringing them to Guyon House before they all set off for another week's rehearsal at Bristol. A little groggy, I thank my nurse and go out into Harley Street to look for a taxi. I feel lucky, standing there, listing slightly to starboard, under the weight of my roses. At home, the Green Room is alight with laughter and story-telling – there are some expert raconteurs in there, sitting and then jumping up to take advantage of the small stage. It's lovely but it's not for me today. O'Toole and I have a short, relieved moment together but I can tell that I'm expected to have moved on. That moment when I was at the centre of the domestic stage is over. Downstairs, Lionel looks mightily relieved when I flash him a grin. (He would have wanted to pick me up and bring me home, I know.) My mother, knowing nothing, looks a bit disgruntled that I've been away for a night for no good reason. Climbing the stairs from the basement kitchen I meet the troupe setting off for Bristol. I have another brief moment with O'Toole, then they're gone.

As the big Georgian door closes a profound silence descends on the house. Thanks to Manolita, everything looks beautiful. The big hall with its black and white tiled floor glows with the dull brass of the Persian chest, opened to reveal a tumult of oriental silks. The Bró paintings with their violent, vivid mop-headed trees are startling against the grey walls. The stairwell is hung with a large stone bas relief from China and rubbings from Angkor and deceptively quiet Picasso etchings. Turning into the bedroom with its big bow window shuttered against the winter light and, beyond the garden, the men's surgical ward of New End Hospital, I know that three floors below me, Scobie, the bulldog, is plodding to and fro under the fig tree, mute and mutinous; willing someone to let him in. Not I. Not today. My mother and Manolita will be clearing away the cups and glasses and ashtrays in the Green Room. Liz is in the nursery, the children are at school and the bedroom is extra silent. I drop my bag and sit on the bed facing my treasured Louis XIV bureau plat. The walls of cupboards are shut and behind them, I know, there is perfect order; hanging cupboards filled with clean, pressed clothes, blouses filed in order of colour, trousers, all black and white. Shoes, polished and lined up on brass rods – all fitted with their shoe-trees – everything rising unseen to the high ceiling. Gloves are neatly arranged – leather, cotton, suede, string. There are monogrammed handkerchiefs and underwear in scented bags. I know exactly what lies, invisible, behind the blank walls, the multitude of potentially chaotic garments which could fill the calm room, unfurling themselves, filling it with colour and confusion. Manolita's devotion and my anxiety keeps everything at bay, subdued and in its place. There is nothing in this beautiful room to indicate that I live here. Turning back the dark tapestry spread on the bed I switch on my bedside lamp. Lying down, I think gratefully that when I am alone, there are no surprises in this room, Manolita has seen to that, and I am comforted by our unspoken stand against the misrule and chaos that threaten to engulf me and this house. Yea, though I walk through the valley of the shadow of death, my folded clothes, my shiny shoes, my gloves and my clean handkerchiefs shall comfort me.

Lying there, I know no one will disturb me until the girls get back from school. Few people know this ex ex-directory line and anyway, who would call me in this fortress? I realise that I *had* said goodbye to all this, thinking of my own mortality in a way I had not done since I was a little girl, much preoccupied with death.

The next day I was back at work, feeling terrific.

I was on the whole blessed with rude good health but illness dogged much of our lives together. When I first met O'Toole he was living with Ken and Doriah Griffith in Belgravia and Doriah confided in me, half-admiring, half-scandalised, 'He sits there drinking alternate gulps of white ulcer medicine and Scotch. *And* he's smoking Gauloises!' During the Stratford season his ulcers got worse and he was urged to go into hospital. More or less organising his own treatment, O'Toole ordered gallons of white 'stomach medicine' and the kitchen was piled high with Complan. Naturally, he continued to stay up late and drink and smoke prodigiously. When he returned to London after the season, he was completely well again. His extraordinary restorative power, aided by a huge capacity for sleep and a healthy appetite, continued to stand him in good stead. My mother and I worried quietly and were mightily relieved when he underwent a cure before each job. And of course he emerged at the end of a job tired but healthy, after a prolonged bout of discipline. It was the in-between times that were difficult.

# Chapter Twenty-nine

In the early Seventies, inexplicable episodes of bad health began to occur. A few years earlier we had acquired the small cottage with a piece of land in 'O'Toole country' on the West Coast of Ireland. Our plan was to acquire yet more of the adjoining land and to build ourselves a family home. As we planned the new house we all squashed into the one-storey croft with two bedrooms and a living room, lean-to bathroom and kitchen, an attic bedroom for the girls under the roof, one turf fire for heat and a Calor gas cooker. Even when I was working and couldn't accompany them, the girls and Liz and my mother spent all the school holidays in Connemara. The girls were given a life that almost duplicated my childhood, disappearing after breakfast and returning at night to a house where there was no television or radio; just talk and books by night and freedom and security by day for girls who had at one time been on the receiving end of kidnap threats in London. In her seventies, my mother was returned to her youth. Her country skills were recollected and became useful again. Isolated and a bit out of our depth, we were dependent on her store of knowledge and that, I suppose, is what ought to happen in a family, but modern life is rarely conducive to this happy state.

The cottage boasted a garden which had been neglected for years. Brambles and sycamore seedlings, twenty-foot-high thickets of old hydrangea bushes, flowering green-white in the shade, stands of bamboo thickening over the kitchen garden. The soil was superb; friable and dark, chocolate brown (obviously this garden had once been beautifully looked after) and everywhere in the small front garden and in the copse at the side of the house, fresh, green-leaved plants in among the montbretia, all increasing healthily inside the overgrown boundary hedges of fuchsia. I admired the plants and looked them up in my gardening dictionary. My mother and I looked at each other in dismay; 'Bishop's Gout-Weed, Devil's gut,' we read, 'otherwise known as *ground elder* – the most virulent of weeds. Almost impossible to eradicate.' What to do? It was everywhere. We couldn't poison the whole garden – we wanted to start replanting.

Depressed, my mother flew back to London with the children and O'Toole and I, with some time off, stayed behind, for a few days as we thought, and I fretted over the monstrous weeds – the smallest piece of root left in the earth would grow into another plant and it would even go on growing out of earth thrown on the rubbish tip. It was like something from another planet and I began to regard it as a personal enemy and was sitting on the doorstep, wondering moodily what to do about it, when I realised that O'Toole, sitting behind me in the house, was distinctly unwell. Unwell enough to go to bed without argument. Unwell enough not to object when, the following day, frightened, I called the local doctor. He was also worried. O'Toole had dreadful stomach pain and there didn't appear to be an explanation for it. He was too ill to be moved and so began a month of misery. Our patient seemed barely conscious at times and lay there – just enduring pain. The local doctor came and stood, worried, at the foot of the bed. He spoke to Gerry Slattery in London. There was nothing to do but try to keep him as comfortable as possible. Eventually the pain diminished somewhat, and, exhausted, he lay there, drifting in and out of sleep, too weak to move. Twice a day I hand-washed sheets wet with perspiration and laid them out on the brambles to dry. I left the bedroom window open and a few feet away from the bed inside, and sick at heart with worry, I began to work on the ground elder, gently uprooting it by hand. All my misery and fear went into that weeding. Every few minutes I glanced at the bed through the window and for three weeks I worked my way slowly through those innocent-looking, monstrous plants.

When O'Toole was able to stand and walk, I felt that, together, we'd conquered something mysterious and dangerous. The garden also had been tamed, the ground elder banished, the beautiful soil sieved and checked over again and again for a fragment of evil, white, fleshy root. Powerlessness in the sick room had given me the tenacity of an animal, working out there on my hands and knees by day, while at night I listened for his breathing until I fell asleep, exhausted.

Back in London, we were none the wiser. What had it been, pondered Gerry and a few of his friends from the Royal Free Hospital. Well, no sign of anything now. O'Toole went back to work on *Rosebud*, a movie that would take him to seven or eight countries. 'All over for good, let's hope,' said Gerry. But it wasn't over. In Paris, O'Toole became very ill indeed and his make-up man, Bill Lodge, called a halt to the unequal struggle to go to work every day. Otto Preminger, the director, stopped the film without a murmur, got O'Toole into the American Hospital and sent for me. I did little except loiter, worried, in the hospital and spent the rest of the summer days of 1974 alone in the hotel, never straying far from the phone.

There is always a professional need, shared by all actors high and low, to keep illnesses a secret from the press and the public. In my case, this created an additional divide between me and the girls and the outside world as well. O'Toole's parents and his sister were not to be told anything but good news – Jules and Joyce and my mother (up to a point) and I were isolated in our falsehoods. The girls were asked not to talk about their father. And I wasn't told what was wrong.

Otto Preminger was capable of being a difficult director, but he was what Joyce Buck called a 'six o'clock pussy cat', turning into the nicest person imaginable once the day's work was done and certainly, to us during our troubled month, he was kind and considerate over and above the call of duty. I did see the other side of him once during the filming of *Rosebud* as for no good reason he demanded take after take from Richard Attenborough. There were actors of every nationality in the movie and I was very proud to be, if only by similar training, on Richard Attenborough's 'team'. Throughout the trying day he remained polite and calm and solid as a rock, never allowing Otto to affect his work adversely.

Script writer, Roy Clarke, had been co-opted and flown to Paris to improve O'Toole's dialogue (in a script written by someone else). I met him at the hospital and he gave me the few bright moments I enjoyed during that sad, worrying summer. We shared a coffee after one of our visits to the American Hospital and were sitting silently outside the Café de la Paix, watching the crowds go by. It was 14 July. Roy, in his North Country voice, broke the silence. 'D'you know what day it is today?' 'No.' 'Ah, well, at home tonight they'll all be asking "What did *you* do for Bastille Day then?"'

When O'Toole recovered from his mystery illness and we'd spent some time quietly in the hotel suite while he convalesced, he packed me off home. I was loath to leave him; he looked frail to me, but as usual he hated to be seen to be looked after and I knew Bill Lodge, his make-up man, would watch over him. Before I left I visited the set as they shot a street scene. The only actor I met that day was Peter Lawford, who looked appallingly ravaged. We sat together in a café and I had to make my excuses and leave; there was something unbearably distressing and depressing in his manner and conversation.

I flew home, low in spirits, and the film dragged on in an undistinguished fashion all over Europe. I had finished work on *Shoulder to Shoulder* and then played Mrs Patrick Campbell for the first time in a TV series about Jenny Churchill. Richard Shulman and Philip Wiseman and I tried to reunite to do Tennessee Williams's *Camino Real* but our plans failed.

Sara Randall, the most creative of agents, had commissioned a treatment of the story of Frieda, D. H. Lawrence's wife, and was beginning to negotiate with the BBC who were interested in producing six hour-long plays, each dealing with Frieda's relationship with a significant man in her life, beginning with her brother, Baron von Richthofen, the First World War flying ace. I began to read all the material available and my enthusiasm grew in spite of an encounter with Sir John Gielgud in Sloane Street. We were on opposite sides of the road, both dressed identically (except he was in brown and I in black) in long, Yves St Laurent trench coats with Herbert Johnson fedoras. John, who seemed to know *everything*, even in the planning stage, called across to the underground side of the road, 'Shawn, Shawn' (he never mastered 'Siân'), 'why d'you want to play that boring German cow?' Taking all my books and Tennessee Williams's new short plays, which his agent, Audrey Wood, had sent me, I left for Connemara and some serious gardening and building. The children were at school and my mother and Liz were left in charge.

Moving swiftly through customs, I located the driver and began the long journey up the West Coast into Connemara. I had a house to build!

'You throw your hat into the air and where it lands, there you build your house.' Leo Mansfield, the architect, told us this and we had stood solemnly on a hill above the vanished village of Eyerphort, which was where we'd bought the land and the small cottage we'd been staying in, and up went O'Toole's hat and we scrambled to the spot where it landed before it disappeared, borne away on the wind over the Atlantic. 'Is it always as – er – as – breezy as this up here?' I enquired. 'Pretty much,' was the reply. All the other houses in Eyerphort, past and present, were built down below in the southern shelter of the hill. Even the Castle near Clifden was sheltered (but nevertheless, all its trees had been destroyed in a famous, vicious storm). The cottage nestled down below the inhospitable spot where we were – barely – standing. But what a place on which to perch! We seemed suspended in air; Atlantic to the south and west, an estuary to the north and to the east Clifden, out of sight, and the Twelve Bens beyond. It was a difficult site from every point of view. It was high and obvious above the coastline and I racked my brain to think of a way of building an unobtrusive house. It was not going to be easy to get planning permission. I asked Leo to draw an elevation of the house. Soon discarded were all my ideas of a long Japanese house ('Yes,' said Leo, 'those low, over hanging Japanese roofs are very nice-looking. First bit of a storm and your house would be up in the air on its way to New York'), or a Roman house built around an atrium ('Have you ever looked inward week after week at an atrium under driving rain?').

Leo was an expert on the Irish vernacular and he persuaded us to build a low house of stone that snaked down the hillside, like a Welsh long-house, its stone walls merging into the granite boulders everywhere. Granite. Ever present in the west. Not far away to the south in the Gaeltacht there were fields as small as dining tables surrounded by lumps of stone taller than a man and beautiful drystone walls; works of art everywhere. The first thing to be done was to level a piece of ground and that meant calling into town for a few experts in the art of handling gelignite. The explosions were dramatic and swift and accurate. In the grey, bitterly cold, wet afternoon, I looked at the flattened site – looking much the same as it had a few hours earlier but without the big outcrops of living rock. There was no water, no electricity, no refuge from the violent wind. Would we ever be allowed to build where the hat had landed?

Winning permission took a long time and I became versed in the arts of patience and very un-English diplomacy. In Wales, I remembered, petitioners came to Uncle Davy's door at all hours but there was a faint effort to abide by a set of rules formulated in Westminster. Here in Ireland, I couldn't make out what the rules were that I was trying to bend. I wrote letters, submitted plans, tried to convey my good intentions, went to meetings, submitted to interviews and waited and waited and waited. And then, one day over a year later, it was over. Permission was granted to begin work on 'The O'Toole House'. Aware of the great favour extended to enable us to build this high above the spectacular coast, I redoubled my efforts to make a tactful house. Leo Mansfield was the perfect architect for this project and he not only designed the house but he taught me about stone and weather; the effect they had on the life of the inhabitants of the west and how they determined the style of the houses. I came to see that there was nothing random about the little crofts; every feature was there for a purpose and it became an absorbing game to build a house with six bedrooms, almost as many bathrooms, central heating and plumbing, while incorporating as many aspects as possible of the traditional Irish house. There was the huge hearth in the main 'room' where the turf fire was never allowed to go out and over which hung an iron pot where we could cook all our meals, should the need arise. Near the fire was a recess and a day-bed where the oldest (or sickest) person could sleep near the fire, the floors were made of slabs of stone cut from the cliffs of Moher, each one bearing the imprints of fossil remains of worms. Indoors we used them convex side up and outside, on the wide walkway surrounding the house, we turned them and showed the concave side. The roof was made of the Bangor blue slates of my childhood home, shipped over from North Wales. The doors and stairs and roofs were of pine, the door furniture was a cheat – I bought all the 'traditional' black iron from Beardmore's in London – but the outer walls were the real thing and gave me a thrill of pleasure every time I looked at them. It wasn't easy, finding someone who could drystone an entire house but I had seen writer Richard Murphy's barn in Cleggan which he'd had built by John Cosgrove, a local mason who spent a large part of the year odd-jobbing for the Council.

The Harbour Bar at Cleggan had become a centre of my activities as I searched for local craftsmen to work in the house. Eileen O'Malley was my ally in this. She had inherited the bar from her father, Matcher O'Malley, whom I had met on my first visit to the West as a girl when O'Toole and I had spent the entire day sheltering from the driving rain and mist, huddled next to the turf fire in the empty bar while Matcher leaned on the half-door looking out. Two cars passed through the village that day. When night fell and we decided we had to make a move, a lone customer, soaked to the skin, joined us in the bar and uttered a greeting. 'Ah,' said Matcher. 'A wet day and nothin' but cars goin' wesht wesht wesht all day.'

In this same bar I sat and tried to beguile the local building talent (O'Toole called me the Mata Hari of Galway County). Their expertise was hidden under a veneer of jovial insouciance and the menial work they did for the local Council mending roads, flinging up breeze-block bus shelters. Eileen O'Malley arranged a meeting for me with John Cosgrove. It was inconclusive and another was arranged. After a day's gardening I would clean up, shake out my black St Laurent skirt and sweater and set off for Cleggan, praying that this time I could persuade Mr Cosgrove to build me a house. 'No. No. No,' he demurred again and again after we'd skirted around the subject for an hour or so. 'I've only ever made barns – a few auld walls.' 'But a house is a few old walls,' I pleaded. After weeks of to-ing and fro-ing to Cleggan, he agreed to 'have a go' and began to order stone from a quarry nearby. He brought his son of nineteen with him and I spent hours watching as he selected the granite blocks he needed for each course and asked his son to fetch them and make more 'shtwff' with which to bind the narrow gaps (shtwff – stuff, was a mixture of straw and mud). Miraculously the walls rose.

To ease John's mind, I'd promised that the builders would

build a cavity wall inside the stone wall so that, as winter approached, we would have an independent shell to the house but, as it turned out, John and his son ascended at the same speed as the builders with their breeze-blocks. It was beautiful. I remembered the morning in Cuzco when we had looked at the dramatic pre-Columbian drystone courses at the base of the Spanish buildings and determined to try to make a smaller, Celtic version of this Inca marvel. After the house was completed, someone complimented John and said he must be very proud to see his work. 'Ah, Jaysus no,' he said. 'Every time I pass by I'm afraid to look at the yoke in case it's fallen down.' Nothing could ever overcome the modesty of this man whose skill was of such a high order.

Our first, small cottage, which we now called Mamgu's cottage, drew water from an old, small well on a nearby meadow. It was known as a well that had never been known to go dry, not even in the worst droughts. Now, we needed a much bigger well, high up on the hill. Matter of factly, Leo said that he'd order along a dowser. This was a magical development in the building process and on the appointed day, O'Toole and myself, Mamgu, Liz and the girls were out on the meadow waiting – for what, we weren't sure. The ordinary looking man in flannels and a sports jacket and a mac walked about with his home-made dowsing rod and we watched, entranced, as it occasionally kicked upwards between his hands. 'Just about *here*,' he said finally, as the hazel twig almost flew out of his hands. 'Have a go,' he offered. 'Have a go?' We looked at each other, wide-eyed. The man had just made our house possible (a house without water is no house at all). On his say-so, we were about to spend a great deal of time and money. Were we, also, capable of this extraordinary feat? Well, I wasn't, nor was Mamgu, nor Pat. Liz said she thought she felt something but O'Toole and Kate walked about, their hazel twigs twirling like things possessed. It was still a mystery but it was all systems go for building.

The artesian well was sunk and quite soon we accessed a huge supply of water – we drank it in wine glasses standing in the rain. Halfway through the building the well ran dry after a quarry across the estuary indulged in some over-enthusiastic blasting; we suffered panic-stricken days until the dowser returned and found us another source. Searchlights were put up in the meadow overlooking the estuary and I stood alone in the shell of the house, watching the men drill day and night in the driving rain. The meadow looked like a Texas oilfield. 'If they strike oil I'll commit suicide,' I muttered to Mamgu as I crept off to bed in her cottage. Down and down they drilled into the rock and one hundred and seventy-six feet below ground they found water again. I've never been so relieved in my life.

I travelled between the building centres in London and Dublin and Connemara. I bought the *Readers' Digest* do-it-yourself-building book and learned as I went along about plumbing and damp courses and electrics and generators and septic tanks. Working towards moving the family in was like working towards a big opening night. The children, my mother and Liz had been living it up in an hotel in Clifden as we hiccupped our way towards completion. At last, we were ready. Everything worked. The family arrived. 'Fill every bath,' I cried. 'We have limitless water.' The men waved goodbye and drove their trucks and cars across the lower meadow to the road and off they went for good. 'How's the water?' 'It's grand but it doesn't go away.' The men had laid the pipes too near the surface and had flattened the whole system as they drove away. We now had a houseful of water and no means of getting rid of it. There was nothing in Liz, the Nanny's past to prepare her for this (her name was not Elizabeth de la Court Bogue for nothing – she was rather grand), but sending for more joints and bits of pipe, with the *Readers' Digest* book open at our side, we, together, re-built the drainage system and went to bed in a house with perfect plumbing. They say that building a house makes you a philosopher. I don't know about that, but it teaches you many things. The chief of which, in my case, was patience.

There was a time for the girls when, I suspected, they would have preferred to spend their holidays pounding the pavements of the King's Road rather than clambering up and down the West Coast. Temporarily, they had an uneasy time of it but I was sure it would soon pass. O'Toole and I went to Connemara, together or separately, whenever we were free of work and between 1970 and 1974 I spent every moment I could there, working on the new house, and often this entailed making the long journey for one afternoon on the site. I was as happy as a clam; rising at daybreak and spending the whole day out of doors, a piece of cheese in my pocket and the kettle and coffee situated nearby in an open window so that, filthy and often wet, I need not enter the house until it was time to come in and scrub myself clean and begin preparing dinner. Pat rode a bit and went visiting. Kate, on strike from country pursuits, read indoors whatever the weather. Occasionally I bribed them to help me carry water or push wheelbarrows of weeds to the bonfire, but this was not really how they wished to be spending their vacation. They were pathetically pleased when we drove into the town and were able to watch a bit of television before dinner.

Guiltily, I occasionally gave up a day's gardening and organised an outing. My excursions were cursed with bad luck (or bad judgment) and inevitably we found ourselves hopelessly lost, miles from anywhere, or trying to cross a huge bog in the pouring rain, or arriving at our destination to find that the castle was shut or the people we were visiting had gone away. The girls were remarkably patient and there was nothing in the way of outright rebellion but I did discover from Liz that they raised their eyes to heaven, shaking their heads gloomily when they knew that one of what they bitterly called 'Mummy's little expeditions' was being planned.

Our neighbours, Ann and Eddie Pryce, who farmed on adjoining land, called round regularly and we all sat drinking tea and chatting – 'wasting' time. Old Mr Feste Pryce, Eddie's father, lived with them and my mother always brought him a gift of black-brown, solidly compacted 'plug' tobacco, wrapped in silver foil. The gift was received with a gracious nod and a smile and little else. In fact, I never heard Feste speak until one day, as Liz was driving me back from a shopping expedition to Clifden, we saw Feste and his friend, Tommy, not doing anything as obvious as thumbing a lift but definitely looking hopefully in the direction of home some fifteen miles away. We stopped and they nodded and climbed into the back seat. As we drove along the coastal Sky road, high above the Atlantic sparkling in the spring sunshine and studded with the tiny islands of the West Coast, I heard Feste say to Tommy, 'You know, one life is too short to enjoy all this beauty.' He had lived in the same house, looking at this same view, for over seventy years.

The road that ran past our land, and in some places through our land, simply circled the peninsula and returned to Clifden, so visitors were few and far between. When the big house was completed, high on its hill, we could see cars approaching from a great distance and one night as my mother and I prepared dinner and O'Toole read near the big fire, the girls who had been hanging out of the gable window watched a car approach and then they saw it stop at our gate and, wonder of wonders, the occupants began the steep, stony ascent to the house. Callers! 'Mummy! Mummy!' they cried as they hurtled down stairs. 'There's an old tinker woman coming up the drive!' When I answered the knock at the kitchen door and peered into the dusk it took me a moment or two to make out behind the shawl wrapped around the raincoat and the scarf tied over the hat, the wonderful features of Kate Hepburn and behind her, looking considerably more respectable, her companion, Miss Phyllis, and film director,

Tony Harvey (who had directed *Lion in Winter*). Abashed to have made such a huge mistake, the girls remained mute for the rest of the evening, sitting at a respectful distance, gawping at the most unusual film star they had ever met. I felt a bit like Moley showing off his house in *The Wind in the Willows*, as I recounted the story of the building of the house and Kate was every bit as obligingly admiring as Ratty as she inspected and approved the arrangements. I think she really did like the plain, solid rooms. She had been to visit Brian Friel to talk about a script and she now wanted to talk to O'Toole, but first she concentrated on my problems with the drains and the septic tank – still so fresh in mind. 'D'you know,' she said, 'if I had a daughter, d'you know what I'd have her train to be?' We leaned forward. 'A *plumber*!' she pronounced forcefully. The girls, pop-eyed, looked nervous.

Not everyone liked my efforts. Robert Shaw, with whom I had a mildly competitive friendship, began building his family home at much the same time as I did. Robert had spent years being dissatisfied with his progress as an actor. Too long a period carrying spears and playing small parts had left him feeling disgruntled and unappreciated, and the on-off success led to his losing patience with the profession and he determined to be a writer instead. His first novel, *The Sun Doctor*, was a success and he was well reviewed. As is the way of things, he immediately became a star actor, the most notable of his movies being *The Sting* with Robert Redford and Paul Newman and *Jaws*. Rich and successful, he was rebuilding and converting a bishop's country residence in a much gentler part of Western Ireland. He bounded up the half-finished steps into the living room. I waited proudly for him to comment on the enormous flags I'd had cut for the floor and the great wooden 'upturned boat' ceiling and the walls, four feet thick against the constant winds. There was a long pause and he said, 'What are you *doing*? Where are the *carpets*? Where is the *comfort*? You can't live like *this,* from *choice*. You're *mad*.' We agreed to differ and turned our attention to the safer topic of gardening. He quite admired my plans and said, 'I'll bet I get mine up and running before you do.' I was delighted by the challenge and fancied my chances for once. I was desolate when, soon after, Robert died suddenly, and I always paused on the spot where we had stood outside the house, and thought of him looking down towards the sea and seeing a garden which had not begun to exist.

My life in Connemara was becoming dangerous. It was by far the best part of my existence and I became more and more obsessed with the huge garden I had in my mind. There was a massive amount to learn; for one thing it was difficult for me to learn to think Big. O'Toole generously called me Capability Phillips as I wrestled with walkways and woodlands and planned vistas and hired JCBs. One day, I thought to myself, I might just stay here when it is time to return to London. Then what would happen? Would I be able to change my life completely? Could I really live there in isolation except for the family visits? These faint, uneasy thoughts remained in the back of my mind but they were sad days when I was driven away to Clifden and then to Shannon Airport. Not since I was a small child in Wales had I felt such an attachment to a place. I looked out of the back window of the car, printing the scene on my mind, as though I might never see it again.

# Chapter Thirty

The four years spent building the house in Connemara had demanded such an investment of time and emotion and hard work that now, on its completion in 1974, I felt it to be the centre of my life. There wasn't a scrap of it from the damp course and the insulation to the material of the blinds and the drawer holding the teaspoons that I hadn't scrutinised. O'Toole had let me have my head and when he'd been in the country he had taken a keen interest, not in the furniture and door handles, but very much in the structure of the house; the thick walls, the roof and, above all, the huge fireplace and main chimney. We shared the intense excitement as the walls rose and we walked around the shoreline, learning to identify the spots where one could first glimpse the house. We stood, leaning on the west wall where our bedroom would be, and looked at the sunsets. I don't recall that we ever exchanged a cross word while we were in Ireland. But we didn't spend all our time in Ireland and life in London was very different.

It's hard to describe how fragmented life became when O'Toole was not working. Although he was protected by Jules and the staff at the offices of Keep Films, he was nevertheless besieged on all sides by people who wanted his help, his advice, his money, his company. The hordes of journalists who wanted to talk to him were often fascinating people in their own right and they had the time of their lives with O'Toole, who was a newspaper junkie. Once they'd penetrated the defences, O'Toole found it impossible not to throw himself wholeheartedly into whatever project they had in mind. When he was drinking, sober-sided writers would be whisked off on a pub crawl they were not to forget in a hurry or, stone cold sober, he would spend hours a day with foreign newspapermen, pouring his enthusiasm and energy into giving them a guided tour of Hampstead or Soho. It seemed mean to begrudge the fine time they were having but I *was* mean and resentful when O'Toole returned home too exhausted to do anything but rest. It didn't help that I was able to see that my problems were largely of my own making. O'Toole was what he was and avowedly had never intended to make any changes in his behaviour. 'If you don't like me, leave me alone,' he would say, wearily, taxed for the umpteenth time in his life with not behaving like a 'normal' husband or father.

More threatening and only half in jest was the question 'Who owns this house?' It went without saying that the owner of the house made the rules. He and I had both grown up at a time when male-dominated households were normal, so part of me enthusiastically embraced the task of being a 'good' wife; supportive, undemanding, avoiding censure, basking in approval (also, alas, atoning for my past). Few men would willingly give up such a delightfully agreeable domestic arrangement where clothes could be dropped on the floor and reappear washed and pressed, rooms tidied by unseen hands, children raised and fed. Men in those days were not ashamed to say they had 'better' things to think about, the implication being that women did *not* have anything better to think about. Astonishingly, this attitude held even when women were occupied in the same profession as their husbands. Some brave spirits protested against all this and altered the structure of their lives. They were regarded as strident, tiresome, unattractive. I was not a brave spirit. Had I been partnered with any of the other men I'd ever associated with I wouldn't have thought twice about moving with the times and staking my claim for equality. Indeed outside the house I found it only too easy to assert myself, had no qualms about appearing strident, tiresome, unattractive, but

I was linked with the most powerful man I'd ever met, whose chauvinism was equalled only by his attractiveness. 'If you don't like me, leave me alone', indeed. He patronised me; called me 'a silly girl' and there were times when I didn't like him at all. Did I want to leave him alone? No, I did not.

But I wasn't a masochist. I *was* loved – hugely. How did I know? Simple; if you *feel* loved, you *are* loved. There were times when I was thanked for my help. There were times when he asked for my forgiveness and pleaded for my forbearance. There were times when we just had fun. And we were bound by shared prejudices and shared likes in books (a shared fondness for P.G. Wodehouse, which we would read aloud to each other, is not a bad reason for staying with someone).

When, as a girl, I first left Wales and home and safety, Saunders Lewis wrote to me saying, 'You must learn to live your life on the knife-edge of insecurity.' I had learned to do just that, for a time, but now I was unable. I was standing in the 'small place' my mother had predicted for me all those years ago in Stratford-on-Avon and not only was it small, it occasionally shook beneath my feet. The measure of balance we had achieved was flawed; it was too dependent on my conduct. Were I to be 'difficult' or argumentative, the whole structure of our life would collapse. Then what, for example, would happen to my mother who had come to live with us? She ran the house, made up the accounts, painted the odd ceiling, did all the washing, but if I were dismissed there would be no house for her to take care of. And the children? I would think twice before depriving them of the kind of life they enjoyed in Guyon House. All the money I made was spent on the house, on clothes for the girls and my mother and myself. I saved nothing. Keep Films took care of our medical insurance and Jules said there were now trust funds set up for the girls in Ireland and that they would be

With Alan Badel in *Man and Superman* in 1966 (*London Life*)

With O'Toole before curtain up in *Man and Superman*

Marie Löhr, my friend and my mother in *Man and Superman* (*Vivienne, London*)

With Rex Harrison in *Platonov* in
1971 (© BBC)

As Ursula Mossbank in *Goodbye
Mr Chips*

With Patrick Barr in Tennessee William's play
*Eccentricities of a Nightingale*
(*Surrey Advertiser*)

Fashion shot with my best friend Ricci Burns

The edge of Angel Falls with O'Toole (*Bob Willoughby*)

Being explored by the Yanomama
(*Bob Willoughby*)

Enjoying the moment as Peter fails to pull the bow any
further (*Bob Willoughby*)

Making friends (*Bob Willoughby*)

The house at Connemara on the Sky Road

Kate and Pat laying the foundation stone

As Mrs Pankhurst in *Shoulder to Shoulder*
(© BBC)

As Hesione in the BBC production of
*Heartbreak House* in 1977, with (from left to
right) John Gielgud, Lesley-Anne Down and
David Waller (© BBC)

The BBC Television production of *How Green Was My Valley* in 1975 (© BBC)

With Brian Blessed in *I Claudius* in 1976 (© BBC)

With Dan Massey in *Gay Lord Quex* at the Albery Theatre in 1975 (*Zoë Dominic*)

'The last of the summer wine' – *Daily Express*

With O'Toole and the girls during the filming of *Caligula* in 1976 (*Jerry Bauer*)

As *Boudicca* in the Thames Television production (© *Thames Television*)

With Robin, just after our wedding, in 1979

In my first musical *Pal Joey* performed at the Half Moon and at the Albery Theatre in 1980

With director David Lynch in *Dune* in 1983

With Keith Baxter in *The Inconstant Couple* at Chichester (*Sophie Baker*)

As Mrs Patrick Campbell in *Dear Liar* – this is the John Bates costume which got its own round of applause (© *Catherine Ashmore* )

After delivering the Royal Television Society lecture, support from the inner circle of friends (*from left to right*) William Corlett, Kevin Moore, Bryn Ellis, Pat O'Toole and Edward Duke

In the sunshine with June Havoc in Connecticut in 1992

entitled to a cottage each on our land. But all that would be in the future – they were eleven and fourteen years of age in 1974. Could I start from scratch and provide for them in the manner to which they were accustomed? I didn't have any idea – I doubted it. On the surface all was well and everyone in the house took the future for granted and, much as I tried to stifle it, my resentment grew. 'She is my rock,' I would read in the newspaper, or 'She is his still centre.' 'Without her to lean on . . .' What sort of woman was this solid, immovable object? She earned her keep but what kept woman didn't?

Unable to bear the pain when love and approval were withheld, I began gradually to reduce my dependence, to loosen the ties that bound us so tightly, so lethally. Less ecstasy, less despair would make my life more bearable and I couldn't think beyond this.

In early 1975 it was as if all the small and inexplicable episodes of illness that O'Toole had suffered over the previous five years gathered themselves into one life-threatening attack, so large and frightening that it obliterated all other considerations for many months.

Coming home from a prolonged reunion with his friend, the writer H.A.L. Craig who had just returned to London after a long absence, O'Toole couldn't conceal the fact that he was once again in dreadful pain. Harry looked sheepish and left and I put O'Toole to bed. As usual, he didn't want to see a doctor but I was so worried by his state that I went against his wishes and called Gerry Slattery (also a friend of Harry Craig). As we had done so many times in the past, Gerry and I sat, one on each side of the big bed in the dimly-lit bedroom, and Gerry chatted calmly, trying to piece together the events of the last twenty-four hours. It was pitiful to see O'Toole attempt to talk, even to joke as he answered Gerry's questions. Almost apologetically, Gerry said suddenly that he thought O'Toole should go to hospital. Normally, this would have produced voluble objections ending in stubborn refusal. I was alarmed when O'Toole now remained silent, overcome with pain which was evidently greater than any he had endured and denied. Gerry indicated that I should follow him as he made his way down to the study. Always in the past we had stood in his room while he reassured me that there was nothing to worry about. Even after wild drunken episodes ending in collapse he had told me that all would be well in the morning.

Now, almost apologetically, he said that O'Toole should immediately be hospitalised. Within minutes, it seemed, O'Toole was taken out into the gathering dusk and I was left to collect together a few things he might need, then follow them by taxi. What was I thinking of? I packed the *Times* crossword, the book on the night table, a toothbrush and an extra night shirt. I couldn't get a taxi so I ran to the Royal Free in Pond Street. There was nothing for me to do at the hospital. Everyone – Gerry included – had disappeared into the business end of the place, where no 'civilian' may follow. I walked down Pond Street towards South End Green and the Heath and sat on a bench but I couldn't sit still and I walked back up the hill, past the hospital to the taxi rank on the main road, standing there where there were strangers for company. Eventually, I returned and sat alone in the hospital.

Finally, Gerry appeared, looking drawn and grey. I could tell that he was miserably unhappy not to be the bringer of good news and I asked him what I should do. He told me to go home and go to sleep. 'But I want to *be* here when he comes round.' 'Siân, it's not quite like that. It'll be some time before he can see you.' I didn't know much but I could see that things were as bad as they could be short of – no, that was unthinkable. I asked the Sister if she would telephone me if there was any change and climbed the hill to Guyon House, standing dark and empty. The girls and my mother and Liz were all in Ireland for the holidays. Manolita would come in at nine in the morning but no one else would come. The phones were silent. Only Scobie, the bulldog, rumbled and snorted, grumbling to himself in the garden. I went down and unlocked the garden door and he shot into the house and up the stairs to the ground floor, pounding into the Green Room where he liked to spend his evenings. I put the lights on for him and went to sit alone in the study. I couldn't go to our bed upstairs and it was dawn when I went up and, entering, saw the bed and the sheets thrown back where he'd been lifted out, and I sat in the chair near the door and wept. If he was allowed to get better, never, I swore, would I ever entertain a disloyal thought, never would I feel resentment, never would I complain. I would do *anything*, so long as he didn't die. Dammit, I thought, I shall *will* him not to die.

I don't know how long I sat there before I stopped crying, got up and made the bed. Going downstairs I fed Scobie and went up to my bathroom and took a bath and put on more make-up than usual. Then I called Jules who I knew would be awake in order to make his calls to California and told him what had happened. Jules, the fixer, the do-er was frustrated when he realised that there was nothing he or I could usefully do, but he had to do something so he drove from Belgravia to Hampstead to see me. When I opened the door he was surprised to see me dressed and painted and assuring him that O'Toole *would* be all right. He nodded obligingly but not very convincingly and said that he'd been talking to Gerry and wanted to go to the hospital to see for himself how things were. I wondered what Gerry had told him.

At the hospital we were allowed to enter the room where O'Toole lay motionless and connected to a battery of instruments. Nothing happened and we were ushered out again. Jules went to the office; he had somehow to withdraw O'Toole from public view without actually admitting that he was seriously ill. There are people in every court room, theatre and hospital who ring the papers with 'stories' (and are rewarded very poorly for their pains) and indeed by the time

I was home, the phones were ringing. 'Was it true that Peter was at the Royal Free? Was it true that he was terminally ill? Did he have alcoholic poisoning?' . . . and so on, endlessly. I explained to Manolita what had happened and left the house to walk around Hampstead until it was time to go to the hospital again.

At first, I found the papers relatively easy to deal with; I had had long practice in being evasive without being too infuriating but as the days became weeks and my will to stay optimistic crumbled, it became harder and harder to put on a brave face – or in this case, a brave voice. One night after I'd been sitting in O'Toole's room for most of the day, I went home and sat despondently on my side of the bed. Picking up the phone, I heard the voice of a journalist I knew quite well. 'Look, Siân, it's Peter here. I know it's late but you're a sensible girl, you know what I'm up against and I want to do a good job – could you give me a hand updating the obit?' I couldn't think of anything to say to him but 'No' as I put the phone down before bursting into tears.

As time passed in that side ward I learned to operate the system of tubes and gradually lost my terror of the paraphernalia which had so intimidated me at first. Sister was unhappy and Gerry was so worried that he could scarcely bear to speak to me, unable as he was to give me reassurance and hope.

And then one day it was like sailing into a calm dawn at sea after a stormy night. O'Toole opened his eyes and they were *his* eyes. He couldn't lift his head but he gave me a lopsided grin and my heart filled with relief and love. We held hands and didn't say a word. One by one the nursing staff popped their heads round the door and smiled and nodded. There was very little talking. 'Very good. Very good,' said Gerry, nodding vigorously, his eyes almost shut, his head tilted back. 'He'll outlive us all, kid,' said Jules brusquely and shook his head as if to wipe out the horror that was past. I felt like a different person. O'Toole was different. We went home thankfully and quietly, so quietly. He went to bed to convalesce. My mother and the girls returned. We had him to ourselves! We had him. I had him. His girls revelled in him. When I looked at him I saw many people, people he did not know who were him, the people who, high up in the Royal Free Hospital, had hated me, reviled me, pleaded with me, adored me, all while he slept. And now he was back. Let us rest.

'I need to go somewhere nice to recuperate. Not too much sun. Quiet. Nice.'

Oh, no.


I had been so reluctant to take him abroad but the month in Positano had been transforming. He'd been right again. Now we came home and began to consider the next step in our new life – a life that seemed like a gift.

# Chapter Thirty-one

'*P*lease let me come with you.'

For the first time, I was pleading to be allowed to accompany O'Toole on location. The response was a firm, dismissive 'No'. He looked surprised that I should even raise the possibility of such a change in our routine and saw no reason that he should break the habit of a lifetime. I understood that it was important to him to be alone and independent while he worked but I was far too worried about his health not to try to persuade him that he needed to be looked after. He had escaped death by such a narrow margin. Did he fully appreciate this? Or was he deliberately erasing it from his mind? Whatever the reason he refused any discussion. I couldn't bear to see him, frail but straight-backed, determined to be as he was before, rejecting sympathy and help. In a way, I thought his behaviour brave and admirable but of course I didn't want him to reject *my* sympathy, *my* help. My part in the grim struggle we had endured had made me feel that I was indispensable to him, that our partnership had advanced to another level and it was a crushing blow to discover that I also was expected to dismiss from my mind the terrors, the pain, the discovery of a new well-spring of love, the perfect happiness that had followed the despair. I tried to show how profound was my disappointment but the habit of not being a nuisance was too strong and I gave way to his decision with reasonably good grace. I couldn't conceal my sadness but it went unnoticed amid the usual flurry of preparation for departure. Someone asked me what was the name of the film that he was going to shoot and who was the director and I realised that for the first time in our life together I had no idea and didn't really care.

How to explain my feelings to myself? I could hardly believe the alienation that had occurred. Never, not at the lowest point of our relationship, had I thought of leaving O'Toole; I had hated him, resented him, wanted to smite him and never entertained the possibility that I wouldn't spend the whole of my life with him. And now for the first time since we met I felt totally separate from him. It was almost as though my O'Toole *had* died at the Royal Free down the road. How *could* he behave now as though nothing had happened? Near-death had happened, a new beginning had dawned and now another sort of death was happening.

I made plans to return to work myself. I had foolishly assumed that I would be away in Mexico – New Mexico? I wasn't sure which. Now Sara advised me to do a play in the West End, partly because it would be rehearsed in London and would preview there as well so, at least, I could be at home while I worked. The play, which was one of the scripts I'd read without great enthusiasm in Positano was *The Gay Lord Quex* by Pinero. John Gielgud was almost alone in loving the play but he *did* admire it enormously and had now persuaded Eddie Kulukundis to produce it. The Edwardian settings and costumes were hugely expensive and it was to be a lavish production. For the most part my scenes would be with Dan Massey (who played the eponymous hero) and Judi Dench, whom I'd never before worked with but admired enormously and wanted to act with, not least because I was told it was the greatest fun imaginable. I could do with a bit of fun, I thought.

O'Toole was to be gone shooting *Foxtrot* in New Mexico for three months at least. His movies often took a good deal longer than this and Jules was vague even now about the actual date of ending. It was strange to be leading a normal everyday life while grappling with such inner turmoil. And no one noticed;

life went on as usual for the girls and my mother and Liz. The house ran on oiled wheels, Manolita and I scarcely needed to consult each other as we began to pack the big trunk and the suitcases; assembling everything that might conceivably be needed during O'Toole's time away, pasting the list of contents inside each lid. And as the hours and days went by I felt my presence becoming more and more indistinct. It wouldn't have surprised me if one of the family were to have walked right through me where I stood in the hall, an invisible person, as doors opened and shut, telephones were answered, children ran up the stairs, everyone absorbed and full of purpose. Everyone except me. I knew with certainty that I couldn't return to the old life with its long separations and lack of shared experience. When the day came to say goodbye to O'Toole, I felt I was saying goodbye to him for ever. I had been incapable of making him understand what I felt, how urgently I needed to be with him now. He had a hard task ahead of him and I could read the determination in his face and in the set of his shoulders. He would not yield to weakness. He would survive whatever the cost. I admired him for that but I was admiring him as I would a stranger and that left me desolate.

It was May – a wet May. I went to work as he went to the airport. What did he feel? I had no idea. It was hard to be bright and cheerful as I met the *Quex* company for the first time. Dan Massey was an old friend and he made me laugh as we were photographed in the rain in the churchyard outside our rehearsal room in Piccadilly. 'Great start,' he said, looking at my wet, ruined hair-do. That night I sat alone in the study. Were it not for the presence of the girls, the house would have seemed very gloomy. As it was, when they climbed the stairs to their apartment all the rooms on the ground and first floors were very quiet indeed and save for my desk lamp in the study, unaccustomedly dark. I went over the events of the morning and our farewells to each other. O'Toole had no idea how I felt, I was sure of that now. His farewells had been as they would usually be before a long absence and he would expect everything to be as usual when he returned in late summer. And of course I would be here – why would I not be? The future had yet to be resolved and I had no idea what it would hold. How quietly it had come about, this revolution in my life.

When I had asked O'Toole if I should come to visit him should the play not enjoy a long run he'd responded, 'No, no, you'd hate it. Cabo San Lucas is the arse-hole of the world.' Now I rose and took down the atlas and looked it up. Baja California didn't seemed to be horrible at all. I had always visited him however awful the locations and I was puzzled by his determination to keep Cabo San Lucas out of bounds to me. What did I know of O'Toole's life in Mexico?

Before he became ill, he returned from filming *Man Friday* in Mexico and dumped the usual pile of unanswered mail on my desk, and there was one letter written in a neat, childish hand that especially caught my eye and for some reason I put it aside instead of throwing it away with all the other mail, much of it too fatuous to need answering. A girl called Anna wrote sadly that she had obviously misunderstood all that had passed and – God, save her – I thought, apologised for her presumption. There was a greeting-card type of poem as well, a pathetic little adieu. I remembered that a Mexican girl called Anna had been given a job on a co-production of a film we had made without O'Toole. Was it the same girl, I wondered, but only for a moment.

It had not occurred to me that he might have another reason for wishing to be alone when away on location. I had always been too occupied trying to burnish my tarnished reputation in his eyes, trying (in vain, I sometimes thought,) to convince him that I was trustworthy, faithful beyond reproach. He was quick to criticise looseness in other women also and loud in his condemnation of what he called 'fouling your own doorstep' and I had assumed that he applied the same stringent standards to his own behaviour as he did to mine and certainly, with the small exception of the sad note from Anna, I had never been confronted with a whisper of infidelity on his part. Nor had I ever read anything of the sort in the mass of newspaper articles about him. Nor had I ever felt that his affections might be engaged elsewhere. When he first became famous, O'Toole had been as taken aback as I by the deluge of attention from women and I was left to deal with the intemperate behaviour and the surprising outpourings of respectable young women who ought to have known better. He was pursued by every manner of woman and I was astonished that he was able to deal with the avalanche of flattery with such grace and restraint. His close friend, Kenneth Griffith, said to me, barely controlling his laughter, 'D'you know – he looked me straight in the eye and said, "I have never been unfaithful to her".' I wasn't sure how he expected me to react and he, sensing my confusion, changed the subject. Now, as I thought of it, I wasn't at all sure that I regarded it as any of my business what O'Toole got up to during those long absences, provided it did not affect our life together. It wasn't anything we'd ever talked about and now it didn't matter in the least. All the same, I was mildly curious about Mexican Anna – if she still existed in his life or whether she had ever signified in it.

During the remaining weeks of May I spent my evenings at home and went to work by day, scarcely registering the considerable storms brewing in the rehearsal room. Like most sad times, this was laced through with comedy, verging on farce. Dan Massey, the same dear Dan – who wrote such elegant, witty letters, who was such a tower of strength when I put my back out while we were rehearsing *Alpha Beta* together in 1972, who made a game out of our violent fist fight in Act One and laughed me out of my terrors that I was disabled for life, that same Dan was now despondent, black, bowed, scarcely speaking to anyone. He and John Gielgud did not get on. Worse, they scarcely spoke the same language. Dan, who had just played an acclaimed Lytton Strachey, his first 'character' part, wanted to apply the same principles of research and heavy appearance-changing make-up to Lord Quex. Unfortunately, *The Gay Lord Quex* was a jolly, young man-about-town, handsome as all get out and a devil with the ladies. Nothing much else to think about.

There was a huge cast, four sets, four changes of costumes – and at the end of it all not a great deal in the way of a story. Judi Dench was playing the little manicurist and John admired her as much as he disliked Dan. When I laid aside my personal unhappiness and began to look around I became fascinated by John who came to work each day with a completely new set of ideas. He and the designer devised sets, each of which had a round object in the middle (make-up display counter, table, fountain) and occasionally he would cry, in pain, 'Oh for God's sake stop going *round* and *round and round*! You look as tho' you're dancing round a maypole.' We were – there was nowhere else to go. Occasionally, he would get up and demonstrate how an Edwardian lady would enter, speak and sit and that was magic. Descended from the great Terry family, he'd kept his eyes open around all those Terry aunties when he was a youth and it was a privilege to be given a glimpse into the manners of another age. But the rest of the time we limped from bad to worse. 'No. No. No! Why are you doing that?' 'Because you told me to.' 'When?' 'Yesterday.' 'But that was another *life*.' He and Dan stopped talking to each other completely. John could not understand why Dan couldn't just bounce on and be a charming roué. Dan retreated further and further behind elaborate make-up drawings.

Judi Dench was the cleverest actress I'd ever watched working. While she wasn't 'getting' the part, she remained calm and cheerful and good humoured and then, after about three weeks, she came in and declared that *finally*, after puzzling and puzzling, she'd got hold of the end of a string and, with any luck, if she pulled on it – that would be the solution. And it was! More than anyone I'd known she had a formidable, a huge, actor's intelligence and the solid good sense to get her through the vicissitudes of production week. When she came on at the dress parade in her specially designed dressing gown, Gielgud shrieked, 'Oh God, you look like Richard III.' Many leading ladies would have been put out (Peggy Ashcroft would certainly have locked herself in the dressing room, weeping), Judi – secure in her performance – probably consoled the unfortunate designer who had to make another costume in a hurry.

Almost four weeks into rehearsal, Judi and I decided that maybe we'd better work out our own moves on our own (John's were getting more and more wild). It seemed almost sacrilegious to doubt him but we *did* have to open and soon. That night we went to see John in his play, *No Man's, Land* by Harold Pinter, which he was playing with Ralph Richardson. He was so sublime that, of course, we decided we *were* being sacrilegiously insubordinate and henceforth we would slavishly obey his every whim. 'Did you really like it?' he smiled when we went round afterwards. 'D'you think it's a good play?' (So patrician.) 'I'm frightfully lucky to be playing it, you know.' (Lucky? He?) 'It's only because poor Larry's dead – dying – I mean so much better, thank God.' He beamed at his own success in avoiding a faux pas. An awed hush settled over the dressing room. It isn't often you see a legend strut his stuff.

John thought I looked like Mrs Patrick Campbell and he taught me some lovely bits of what he called 'plastique', but when I came on in my ballgown – plumes in my hair – he wailed, 'Sit down, *Shawn*.' 'But John . . .' (common sense overcoming my reverence) 'I've only got to say five lines and get off. It'll take hours if I sit centre stage.' 'I know, but I want you to *sit* in the middle.' 'John, it doesn't make *sense*. I'll be trailing this costume around for minutes with nothing happening.' 'I know, I know, but you must *sit down*. You look so *tall* when you're standing up.' I think this gave Dan the only smile in a dire dress rehearsal.

John was so sweetly apologetic when we opened badly. He gave Judi and myself the most beautiful presents. Neither Judi nor Dan could face doing the obligatory radio interviews. We had all said from time to time – John – 'Wonderful, sublime actor but cannot direct *traffic*'. My old friends at the BBC said *someone* had to do this interview, so I went to Broadcasting House and was vague about the virtues of the play and confined myself to remarks where I could be truthfully praising of John. He sent me flowers and then a card, thanking me for being 'more generous' than he deserved. I turned it over and the picture was of a policeman directing traffic. My blood ran cold. It was a privilege to be in a flop directed by this complex, brilliant man.

The weeks went by. No word from Mexico. I didn't have a number where I could reach O'Toole and anyhow, he didn't like the telephone. And in a way, he had a point; the wires don't support emotion or need over great distances.

During rehearsals I had seen Judi – so much more observant and more caring then I – restrain one of the young men in the play when he made as if to strike John after a particularly tactless piece of direction. I hadn't been paying any attention at all but I felt sorry for the pretty youth who sat, mutinously pouting, Judi's restraining hand on his arm. At the same time I thought how callow to react to John in such a way. It was another few weeks before I could take the time to look around at other people and their problems. The young man should have been all right in his part of a glamorous officer but John had completely incapacitated him. 'Come on and *take the stage*!' he would cry. After four weeks of John's direction he could scarcely walk straight, let alone dominate a scene.

Not my problem, I had no scenes with him. Didn't even know his name.

Weeks went by and predictably the 'notice' to end was put up. Only a fortnight more to play. I had been to the BBC to talk to producer Martin Lisemore about playing Beth Morgan in *How Green Was My Valley*. Still faintly tanned from Positano I wore a beautiful pale, pastel Missoni dress. When I went to talk to him, Ronnie Wilson, the director, joined us and said, 'This is the part of a *mother*, you know.' 'Yes,' I said, thinking maybe my new Maud Frizon shoes were a mistake. 'Look,' I said. 'I am Welsh and I *am* working class. I may be thin but I *am* a mother. Thin, tall mothers do exist, you know.' They smiled and dismissed me. I've never 'gone for' jobs and now I think maybe one should *dress* for them? No. If they can't see I can act this part a change of frock isn't going to help. Ah well. The play was ending and I didn't think I'd got the television part, so what to do with myself? I would go to Connemara and garden and perhaps as I wrestled with that inhospitable, rocky terrain I would begin to see what I should do next.

# Chapter Thirty-two

The girls and my mother and Liz were already on holiday as usual in Connemara. July 1975 was the hottest in years. The theatre was as hot as Hades and I was grateful to get out of my sodden costume and hurry into the alley alongside the Albery Theatre. I stood there, looking for Lionel and wondering where he'd put the car.

'Would you like to go for a drink? I've got a friend in and we're both going for a jar.'

It's the young man who was at odds with John. I'm *so* flattered. No one asks Mrs O'Toole out. Not ever. 'Well, there's the chauffeur . . . and I have an appointment early in the morning. I don't think so.' 'Only a drink.' 'Well, all right. We could pop over to Macready's' (a really depressing actors' club in Covent Garden. Damp.). I was a member so that left me more or less in control of the evening. Lionel drove the three of us to Macready's and it was shut. I was at a loss. Whenever O'Toole was away I never went out unless escorted by Jules and Joyce and I only knew really expensive places. 'Look – both of you come back to Hampstead.' We piled, rather uneasily, into the Daimler and, arranging to meet him early in the morning, I said goodnight to Lionel, and took the young men into the house, to the ground floor Green Room, unlocking the door to the basement floor and the wine cellars reaching under Heath Street.

The drinks tray held only spirits so we all went down to the cellars for wine. The night was still unbearably hot and I opened up the door to the garden, as well. It was so strange to be alone and using the house in this way. It made me feel rather grand and powerful to be entertaining alone in it. It was *partly* mine, after all, this place I lived in. Drinks. Music. (I *never* played records at night.) We sat and chatted until I thought it was time to end the evening. One young man (what *was* his name?) left and the other helped me lock up the cellars and garden and before we'd made for the front door his hand was on mine and the key was thrown aside. I couldn't believe what was happening. I had felt myself to be in an aunt-like position to these men and had no wish to complicate my life. I was well aware that the solution to my problems did not lie in displacement activity and, hopeless with names, I didn't even know who this person was. Knew nothing about him. And I welcomed this happening. Even as I thought to myself that I was making a dreadful mistake, I could feel a smile forming on my face. A smile of approval to some submerged self. Accustomed all my life to untroubled, wonderful sex, the worries and heartbreak of the last six months made this coupling something more extraordinary than usual. I was asleep when he left in the morning. Descending to start the day I looked at my handbag, where I'd left it in the study the night before. My wallet had disappeared. 'Serves you right, you fool,' I thought without rancour. 'He callously turned you over and you deserved it – and it was, in a way, worth it.' I laughed and was abashed later when I saw my wallet, intact, on the Green Room table. I knew so little of this man that I thought he might be a thief.

I went through the motions of running my house, distracted by my extraordinary behaviour of the night before and surprised by my lack of guilt. I felt – almost exhilarated. No, maybe not quite that, but certainly elevated above the rut in which I'd been living. Going to work at the theatre was another matter. I was deeply embarrassed when I made my first entrance that night, feeling as though the audience was pointing at me and whispering, 'Well, there's a fast woman.' I didn't see Robin – I'd checked his name in the programme and discovered that he was the son of one of my favourite British film actresses, Eleanor Summerfield. His father was also famous but I didn't know him, Leonard Sachs, best known as the chairman of *The Good Old Days*, the City Varieties Music Hall. I also figured out that Robin must be sixteen years my junior. Well! That was something new. But the play would end soon and that would be the end of the matter. Just a few weeks of awkwardness to get through. The fact that it *wasn't* the end of the matter was every bit as much my fault as Robin's and I felt that 'fault' *did* enter into it, even as I took pleasure in the fault.

Robin and I spent a weekend together in the empty house, camping out in the nursery, and it was domestic in a way that was quite new to me. Robin could cook rather better than I could. He prepared meals and we cleaned up together and it was highly unusual – wrong, but intriguing. He was a bit forward, I thought. Cheeky, in fact, and disrespectful in a cautious sort of way. No one had ever been bold with me. Monstrous, maybe, diabolical even, but cheeky? No. I rather liked it. My pedestal was niftily kicked into touch and I assumed my place as a grubby, voracious creature, sweating in the August sunshine and praised, and flattered – I had never been so eloquently, endlessly flattered – just for being myself. Or rather, less than myself. When the play ended, we parted, he to Greece with his brother and I to wind up business in London before joining the girls and Liz and my mother in Ireland.

The unbearable heat of 1975 turned my head and before leaving for Ireland I spent a wonderful week with an actor whom I had known and admired for the last twenty years. I knew he liked me but we had both behaved so well until now when we didn't. What was happening to me? I felt that I'd burned my boats as far as O'Toole was concerned. There was no way in which I could pretend to be the person he'd left in May. I didn't even want to be. Behaving badly was making me happy. Of course, Robin would have been outraged by my behaviour after his departure and I didn't give a damn about that either (though I didn't tell him so). As I boarded the plane for Ireland, I felt terrific.

My brief time with Robin had stopped me shrouding my body in Celtic decency or shame and I gardened in my bikini, covering up only if I saw someone approach – I was a guest in holy, Catholic Ireland and had no wish to give offence.

Martin Lisemore actually managed to get through to Mamgu's cottage telephone, assisted by Miss Heffernan at the Post Office. Yes, they'd like me to star in *How Green Was My Valley* with Stanley Baker and could I get back to London quite soon for pre-production. I told my mother the news. She lifted her gaze from our gardening notes only to say, 'Well, let's hope it's better than that last try.' She was referring to the Hollywood movie based on the novel in which the parts were all played by American based Irish actors because the Welsh cast was unable to cross the Atlantic in wartime. We continued planning the next stage of the garden. Did she notice I was different, I wondered? *Was* I different?

Back to London, alone. Robin was back from Greece and it was entirely due to me that we met again. Well, maybe he would have braved the castle keep, but I rang him and arranged a meeting in Kensington Gardens. I still felt that there was something odd about us but there was also a growing sweetness. He was so incredibly encouraging. No man in my emotional life had ever been encouraging or helpful or paid one so much attention. I could tell Robin all my fears and difficulties and he didn't sneer at me or belittle my feelings. I was warily impressed. Part of me now identified with the previously traditional male figures in my life and I sometimes thought, 'This man must be mad. He's so nice, there must be something wrong with him.' Then, 'No, wait a minute, this is really agreeable, this care and attention.' Occasionally, I worried about his attitude to work. During September as I prepared for six months at the BBC he was recalled and recalled for an important series. He didn't get the part and said, sincerely, 'The man who's got it is *wonderful* – and I'm happy I've got *you*.' Well, such generosity of spirit was alien to me and what did he mean he 'had' me? This was proceeding too fast and yet – he was getting something very right and maybe I *was* his already.

Something strange had happened in August. I received the only letter O'Toole wrote to me from Baja California. On what was the night I had first slept with Robin, O'Toole had had a strange experience. I had 'appeared' to him. In the letter he pledged his troth to me anew, implying that he regretted what had drawn him to Mexico but he did not elaborate on that. He wrote things I would have been so happy to read even four months previously. I couldn't respond. But my silence seemed to go unremarked.

In late August O'Toole returned and quickly settled down to London life. He resolved to take more of an interest in the running of Keep Films, so every day he would leave with Lionel and spend most of the day in Belgravia. His energy was prodigious because he was no longer drinking. The doctors had been uncompromising on this – he must never drink again. Another bout of illness could be fatal. Gone were the days of sleeping until lunchtime, of feeling slightly under par until the drinking began again. I could scarcely imagine how he managed this revolution in his life. As he interfered in everyone's business, read, made notes, wrote poetry, looked at his mail for the first time, tried to understand balance sheets and filled every moment of the day with activity, a friend said, 'Only Peter would try turning not drinking into an art form.' As for us, his assumption seemed to be that everything had settled down as he wished it to. We chatted a great deal less though and he seemed as unaware as before that there was a change in me. I was in pre-production for *How Green Was My Valley*, seeing Robin occasionally for a brief walk, usually in

Kensington Gardens. I was astonished that no one ever asked me where I was or what I did. It was amazingly easy to be deceitful.

I left for location in Wales and O'Toole came down with me and dressed as a collier and for a lark appeared as an extra. Stanley Baker played my husband. I'd been wary of him, a tough guy among tough guys. He turned out to be professional in the extreme, courteous, well-prepared, so tactful when, drawing on a wealth of experience, he suggested an alternative, maybe a better way of shooting a scene. He held the cast and unit together in the most unobtrusive way imaginable. When he got to know and like me, he would share his lunch with me on production weekends. 'There you go,' proudly handing me a perfectly nice but unremarkable cheese sandwich. 'Ellen made these.' Ellen, his wife, was perfect in his eyes. We worked well together and people would suggest that maybe we'd become very close. 'You know that look, in that scene – come on. Tell.' Nothing could have been more absurd to either of us. My admiration for him grew and grew.

For six months we lived in each other's pockets, Ronnie Wilson directing this bunch of volatile Welshmen, Martin Lisemore, the producer, keeping a close eye on us all. I travelled from Hampstead to the BBC rehearsal rooms in Acton each day, ran the house, spent a good deal of spare time at the North London Collegiate School, saw the children at night and also Marie Kean, who was staying with us, and went through the motions of being Mrs O'Toole, a role which no longer had any credibility for me. Once Marie said suspiciously, 'What are you up to? Why are you more cheerful than usual?' But no one else noticed my altered state. Very occasionally Robin and I would manage an early dinner together and I discovered a whole raft of cheap restaurants that no one I knew would ever dream of visiting. My liking for being adored was gaining ground. I'd never in my life met a man who was so unafraid to show his feelings, who didn't seem to want to protect himself or take control of the situation.

*How Green Was My Valley* drew to an end. My actor friends from Wales, who'd been commuting to London for six months, declared that they now had to get jobs to pay for this job, during which they'd spent their salaries in the bar of the Paddington to Cardiff train. There had been a great deal of drinking. On the day of the arrival of Beaujolais Nouveau, Stanley had arrived with the first shipment in his car and the entire company, floating on a sea of red wine, had been sent home early with a severe reprimand.

We held the 'wrap' party in the basement flat of one of the designers. I took part in the cabaret playing Stanley, dressed in his flannel shirt, corduroys and boots. The room was lit by candles placed against the walls. I'd treated myself to a new St Laurent suit in shiny black ciré fabric and as I perched on a side table, talking to Mike Gwilym, who had played one of my sons, he said, 'Siân, don't move,' as he placed his arms around me and hugged me tight. My jacket, too close to a candle, was on fire and melting horribly. The room was packed and mercifully no one saw him put the fire out. Later, as we were searching for my new black raincoat and realised someone had taken it by mistake, Mike, thinking back to the cabaret, said, 'Oh, poor Siân, what a night you've had; you've lost your raincoat, burned your new suit *and* you made a fool of yourself.'

Before I went to the party, when I was still in my dressing room wearing my worn Beth Morgan dress and cracked boots and white wig, Martin Lisemore came in bearing a large pile of scripts. 'Here, have a look at these and tell me if you want to play the part I've marked.'

As I took off my ageing wig and make-up for the last time, I flicked through one of the scripts – 'nearly bald, ancient, she looks up at Caligula' – oh no, not *another* geriatric part. Turning back, I read a scene which made me laugh. Flicking forward, I realised that this was a very camp script, very well written by Jack Pullman. I got Martin on the extension. 'That was quick.' 'Yes, well, I'm obviously doomed to play old bags for ever and this does make me laugh – and we've had a *nice* time over the last six months – haven't we?' 'Is that a "yes", then?' 'Why not.' By the time I left the building I'd agreed to play Livia in *I, Claudius*.

The incessant activity meant that I had very little time in which to review my private life which was, frankly, absurd. It was also becoming nicer and nicer and that was absurd *and* bad. I had a husband with whom I was living what a cynic would call a 'normal' married life – not much in the way of communication and totally satisfactory sex. My lover would have been horrified, I realised, had he been aware of this. Young and romantic, he took it for granted that I would have broken off 'relations' with my husband. I didn't care to disabuse him.

For the first time in my life I had a life of my own which was nothing to do with either of these men and I had no intention of sharing it with either of them. I took good care of all our properties (we had now acquired a flat in the West End as well), went on working on the Irish garden, maintained the Irish house and two other Irish cottages and the house in Hampstead ('maintenance' was a major part of my life). And, my main, big jobs aside, I made broadcasts, wrote book reviews, appeared on television shows, went regularly to the girls' school, organised their weekends, went to the cinema with them and supervised lives which, more and more, ran like clockwork. Everyone was having a perfectly fine, busy time. Although I was a part of many people's lives, it seemed to me that I was still shadowy and superfluous. Except to Robin. To him I was becoming more real – more a possible, valid part of his life. To me, this seemed still ridiculous. There was no way in which our relationship could become 'real', it seemed to me that it could exist only in its present clandestine form. And what would be the outcome? I supposed that it would simply fizzle out. Then what would I do? I would be sad, I was sure of that. O'Toole, leading a completely sober life, was understandably preoccupied with his own problems. The drinks table across the room from his favourite chair was laden, as usual, with bottles. Drink was *pressed* on all our guests. Dr Slattery prescribed large quantities of vitamins and they were conscientiously taken, also valium something new, beneficial and harmless, it was said.

Pat became more and more locked into her life at school and with Mamgu and Liz, and Kate began to rebel fairly seriously and demanded to be allowed to leave school after taking her O–Levels, going instead to an A–Level tutorial college in town. She also demanded to be allowed to go on holiday with a mixed sex group. All this was tricky but pretty standard, I thought. Kate had always been somewhat beyond my control. I admired her independence of spirit and was amused by her escapades and there was very little I could do to alter whatever course she'd decided upon. Until I realised this, we'd lived at loggerheads. Now, I told her what I thought and left her to make her own decisions. O'Toole said he would have a talk with her but that she should be allowed her freedom. I didn't really feel I was in any position to *tell* her how to behave. I'd done everything my parents wished of me: stayed at school, gone to university, married – well, maybe I'd gone slightly wrong at that point – but eventually I'd settled down in a spectacular way. And where had all that got me, I wondered? My life was unravelling and I was endlessly postponing the day of resolution.

But at Christmas I decided that I had to end the affair with Robin. He was devastated and the scenes were prolonged and painful; I also was distraught and very unnerved to realise how attached I had become to him. However my problems were twofold and separate and it was impossible to deal with the difficulties of the marriage while conducting an affair. The parting lasted all of three weeks. We were reunited, feeling relieved but more confused and muddled than ever. We saw each other little, we walked in the park in the cold. We were happy and not happy.

In 1976 O'Toole went to Rome to film *Caligula* with John Gielgud, Malcolm McDowell and Helen Mirren. He rented a house on the Appian Way and began to study Spanish; Mexico still held a potent attraction for him and he determined to learn the language properly. I discovered, by chance, that he had acquired land there and was thinking of building a house. '*Another* house!' I thought indignantly – as though I didn't have enough to look after. Then, realising that I wasn't meant to know about it, I also realised with some relief that I wasn't going to have to look after it, either. So, what did this signify? The language lessons, the Mexican real estate? I remembered Anna and his strange letter describing my appearance in his dream, almost hallucinatory in character. Was it possible that he, also, was looking for a way to terminate or alter this seemingly unbreakable relationship? That would be too easy by half, I thought ruefully. There was a horrendous time ahead and no way of avoiding it.

Cowardly, I put it out of my mind and concentrated on *I, Claudius*. Robin was a constant on the periphery but I was beginning to realise that to my sorrow, the affair was going to have to end again. I was simply too busy and too involved in other business to move it 'centre stage' and it was scarcely fair to Robin to keep him on the sidelines. I postponed the moment. There is something so strange in living a life which is totally chaotic in one aspect and so completely happy and coherent in the other. *I, Claudius* was, after a bumpy start, one of the most pleasurable, carefree jobs I'd ever had.

I'd worked with Herbie Wise, the director, before at Granada when he was part of just about the best drama department in television. He and Jack Pullman and Martin Lisemore and the designer Tim Harvey, and head of costume, Barbara Kroenig, and head of the BBC's superb make-up department, Pam Meagher had been working on the series for a very long time before that first read-though at Acton. I'd worked with or known many of the actors involved: George Baker (not for the first time I was playing the mother of someone who was my senior), Brian Blessed, John Hurt (an old friend), Pat Quinn (my daughter in the Suffragette series), John Castle (whom O'Toole had 'discovered' for *Lion in Winter*), Patsy Byrne (whom I'd been with at Stratford). Herbie laid down the ground rules early on. I had all sorts of ideas about the subtlety of my character, Livia. Derek Jacobi, in one of his first big television parts, was still doubtful about how he was going to play Claudius; we all had our little private problems. After the readthrough – pretty dull – Herbie said, 'Okay, let's get up and try a bit.' We played a few scenes. He looked appalled. 'Look,' he said (in effect), 'we don't have much time and we are certainly not playing some kind of English costume drama. *This* is how we're going to do this show – BIG, up-front, poster paint. It's *my* decision. No negotiation.' Consternation and tears (men, as well). Reluctant performances at rehearsals, wails (very British) of 'But this is so *obvious*.' Remorseless, he whipped us on towards the first episode. It was a nightmare. One of my big scenes came right at the end of the last twelve-hour day. 'Sorry, Siân. We have ten minutes to get this. Get a move on.' Somehow, we got it done – on the run. And it was over. Episode One was finished and we were committed to this somewhat un-English style of acting. Would it be good or awful, we wondered? Herbie was confident. Martin was thinking hard.

# Chapter Thirty-three

During the rehearsals for Episode Two we all calmed down. Derek was still saying that he might give up the part, Brian was a bit mutinous, but then Brian always is gloriously mutinous. I sat there, rehearsing a scene with George and Brian on the main set (what we called 'the family parlour'). It was a family squabble scene and I noticed, at the end, that Jack and Herbie were smiling, pleased. 'Tell me,' I said. 'Is this a Jewish comedy?' There was a pause before they beamed and said that they hadn't wanted to say anything so crass but, yes, that was more or less what it was. After that I did as little 'acting' as possible. And the less I did the more approving Herbie was. After the first few weeks everything became terribly easy and hugely enjoyable.

Even so, we had no idea that we were making a classic. As new cast members joined the show, they were sent to a viewing room to see what we'd shot so far. Time after time they came back to the rehearsal room looking doubtful. Close friends said, 'Oh dear, this looks really *strange* – I don't think it's going to do well.' It was so lovely to be in that we stopped caring about the outcome, successful or otherwise. In the summer my character, Livia, 'died'. Martin and Herbie took me to lunch and said we might be on to something. Already, I had begun to worry about my 'life' again and didn't pay much attention. The girls flew back from Ireland and together we went on to Rome to visit their father.

The villa on the Appian Way – pretty enough – had become a 'Petruchio' house, staffed by typical O'Toole Petruchio servants. There was a pool, but it needed cleaning; the sitting room was festooned with wires and recording equipment (Spanish lessons were in full swing). Meals were provided by a small Italian who was prone to fits of hysteria and who was running a busy sideline in stolen jewellery. Where did O'Toole *find* these people? What did the gardener do? Why did the cook confine himself to frying aubergines?

Our visits to the set were even more bizarre. John Gielgud stood there looking grand and pretending not to notice that the girls flanking him were bare breasted and carrying dildos. In the trailer, Helen Mirren and Malcolm McDowell were beyond caring and very funny about their experiences. O'Toole was playing Tiberius and as I watched, he nearly drowned, swimming in a huge red robe, surrounded by up-to-no-good under-age boys (Tiberius's 'minnows'). It was so strange to leave the set of *I, Claudius* (which can't have cost much), which had been researched, old BBC-style, for a year before shooting began and to walk on to this huge set with all that *Penthouse* money behind it and where the actors were paid vastly more than any of us at home and to see it all going horribly wrong. The costumes and make-up and sets were a mess and as for the script . . . I said nothing.

Kate's boyfriend from Ireland pitched up and came to stay. Michael from Clifden was one of the nicest young men I'd ever met and I was sorry that they were meeting at sixteen, when neither of them had spread their wings. They seemed so perfectly suited (certainly *I* was perfectly poised to be *his* perfect mother-in-law), but they were very young. When they disappeared to her room I felt that maybe we should exert some kind of control over them and asked O'Toole to sort out their living and sleeping arrangements. Telling me that I was a little out of touch, he promised to deal with the situation and I was glad to leave it to him. As for us, we had very little to say to each other; my head was still full of *Claudius* (which I had to return to for a 'ghost' scene) and my infidelity; he, for his part, was preoccupied with his Spanish and only in bed did we come together easily, mindlessly, pleasurably.

Jerry Bauer, a photographer who always took our family pictures and who now lived in Rome, came out to take photographs and he released a strange, sad picture of us to the press. It was captioned 'The Last of the Summer Wine'. It looked just that – the end of something.

The girls and I returned to London, leaving O'Toole in Rome, and I began rehearsing a play about Janet Achurch, the actress who created Candida for Bernard Shaw and who ended her days, a great nuisance to him, in a fog of drugs and drink. It was a BBC/TV production, written and directed by Don Taylor. *Frieda*, Sara said, was progressing well. Although she had set up the series through Keep Films, James Cellan Jones, the head of drama at the BBC, would ultimately be in charge. I admired him enormously and knew I'd be in safe hands. It was a very big project, six hours of television, and I looked forward to working on it for the whole of the following year, with any luck. O'Toole returned and began to film for the BBC as well. Jack Gold, an old friend, directed him in an adaptation of a book by Geoffrey Household, *Rogue Male*.

It was I suppose a measure of the gulf that had opened between us that my duplicity, my unhappiness, my withdrawal of myself seemed to go unremarked for so long. Not having any clear idea what I wanted to do I did nothing and dreaded the storm which would surely break over my head one day. In the back of my mind I calculated that when everything was known, I wouldn't have to make the decision which seemed so beyond me, I would merely have to react to events – whatever they might be. That was more or less how things happened, but they seemed to happen in slow motion and time spread and lengthened as it does in dreams. Finally, when O'Toole noticed that something was seriously amiss – and why did he, I wonder? – he sprang into attack mode and began interrogating me, something to which I was only too accustomed and I reacted like a frightened rabbit, much as I had all those years ago when we were first married. I couldn't tell him about Robin at first, not wishing to unleash the eloquent and derisive reaction which I could hear before it was spoken.

Secondary to this selfish desire was a wish to protect Robin; the contest between him and O'Toole seemed painfully unequal. Even worse, the passion I had felt for Robin was diminishing; his violent reactions to our partings had made me realise that he in his youth couldn't fully deal with the situation we had created. My recurring concern was the effect of all this on the girls' lives. Robin couldn't be expected to understand this. He wasn't a parent and had never met my children. All he wanted was me. And I worried about my mother who was oblivious, it seemed, to all that was going on around her. Closed doors and raised voices were things to be complicitly ignored in a house in which alcohol figures so largely. The habit of not acknowledging unpleasantness continued now that sobriety reigned in Guyon House. I went as far as to make it clear that I was unhappy and that I would like us to part and eventually I confessed Robin's name. Useless to say that he was a symptom not a cause, useless to say that all I *really* wanted to do was to live apart, on my own.

Somehow, for months we managed to work, plan future work, live our lives without confiding our problems to anyone. We slept little, argued a great deal, advanced not at all. O'Toole still spent a great deal of time as a more active partner of Keep Films, putting in hours in the office when he wasn't working. He and Jules worked on *Frieda*, among other things, and one day as I sat waiting for a taxi in the car park at TV Centre, Jim Cellan Jones called out to me and told me that after all the work the BBC was abandoning *Frieda*. The BBC felt that the demands made by Keep Films were simply too expensive and our company wanted to retain too much control. 'The next time you want to do something,' said Jim, 'do your own negotiating.' It was the end of two years' work. Sara was aghast. I was disbelieving; no one at Keep Films called me to explain what had happened. O'Toole said nothing.

Janet Achurch's photographs featured heavily in Shaw's letters and the BBC went to a great deal of trouble to produce a good photograph of me as her. The play had turned out very well and the photograph was so good that it was decided to make it the cover of the *Radio Times*. Then *Rogue Male* entered the lists and they called me from the BBC to say I'd lost out to my husband. I wasn't surprised, or annoyed. By now I was old in the faith and nothing if not a realist.

Events accelerated. Robin turned up one day to meet me for a snatched coffee and said he'd told his parents about us. I wasn't pleased but said nothing. In the same week, O'Toole summoned Robin to meet him in his palatial office in Belgravia. Robin had called him and asked for an interview. He was glad to have things come to a head but I felt sorry for him and I feared for him. He seemed strangely unafraid and unaffected and as far as I could make out, he more or less asked for my hand. I don't know how O'Toole responded. The situation was careering out of control. I wanted my hand to myself. O'Toole told me to end the affair once and for all and I felt that ending the affair *was* inevitably the right thing to do but not so I could stay within the marriage. The cheap jokes and the scorn strengthened my wish to leave. To leave and live alone.

But once again I ended the affair and again I was surprised to be overcome with sadness, more affected than I had anticipated I would be. I gave Robin my most treasured small possession and said goodbye and went home to bed where I stayed, crying into my pillow like a foolish girl – as I never *had* done as a foolish girl. I couldn't believe that I was behaving in this way. No one seemed to notice that I wasn't up and about. Life at home became a torment. Autumn dragged into winter and I began to see Robin again. There didn't seem to be any reason not to and I did miss him frightfully. I missed having someone to put me first. It was as potent as any drug.

By Christmas of 1976, which was spent in London, O'Toole and I had both reached exhaustion point. Sidney Gottlieb, O'Toole's friend and a hypnotherapist, came to visit and said that something had to be done; we were living a life of unbearable tension. O'Toole refused to discuss a plan, wouldn't release me in a coherent way and I couldn't just jump ship. But, feeling desperate, I did once again terminate my affair with Robin – this time for good, I thought.

I'd become immensely fond of the ugly BBC Television rehearsal rooms in North Acton where I spent so much of my time. There were sometimes thirteen shows in rehearsal so the crowded canteen at the top of the building was like an actors' club. I began to rehearse *Heartbreak House*. Sir John – by far the most illustrious member of our profession in the building – seemed unaware of his status. He adored gossip and scandal and each day he began pointedly looking at his watch a good five or ten minutes before the lunch break began. Once in the canteen he would stand there holding his tray, transfixed by the 'famous' faces all around. 'Look, look!' he hissed one day and I followed his gaze to a table at which sat a very young actress/model/singer/dancer, mainly famous for going to other people's opening nights. 'So?' I said, 'what's so special about her?' 'Oh, *always* photographed going through airports,' breathed John, admiringly. So different from Rex Harrison. When we were embarking on a long rehearsal period for his first ever television play (*Platonov* by Chekhov), he entered the canteen on the first day, a glamorous vision in oatmeal tweed with a cream silk shirt. Startled, he joined the queue as indicated, helped himself to a little food, then looked disbelievingly at his tray and at the plain, noisy room and, setting down the tray, turned and walked swiftly out of the building in search of his chauffeur and the Bentley and disappeared to fetch a little light lunch from his house in Belgravia. He could be seen each day after that, moodily picking at a little cold salmon in the back seat of the car.

When I finished *Heartbreak House*, the bitch – reality – began to nip at my heels again. Life at home was grim for me, living as I was in a kind of limbo; not allowed to leave, obliged to stay – for how long? I didn't know. I felt like a fly in a web, only half alive, wrapped in barely discernible threads. I was lonely. It was unthinkable that I should confide in anyone and I missed Robin's company. Everything around us was beginning to disintegrate; Lionel left to take up another job. For me, this was like losing a brother; although we never ever discussed family problems, in his privileged position he saw and heard everything and was the only person who knew exactly how I was placed. Much as he might wish to, he never ventured to defend me but he was, I knew, deeply upset when I was treated badly. I knew that I could not see him again until I regulated my life. A regulated life seemed beyond our grasp. At one stage it was suggested that we might separate, divorce, and continue to live in the same house – we were thrashing around like animals in a net. O'Toole began to fall out with Jules – Jules, who had run our lives, arranged our finances, organised O'Toole's life in the movies, dealt with every manner of trouble imaginable. In my view, for me to confide in Jules would have been disloyal to O'Toole and worrying and embarrassing for Jules, so I kept my distance and, deprived of the company of Jules and Joyce – my 'family' for as long as I'd been married – I was completely isolated.

O'Toole announced that he was going to Mexico alone to recuperate from his illness. It says a great deal about my half-paralysed state that it never entered my head to quiz him about his life in that country or his possible attachment to someone there. I asked O'Toole if I might go and spend some time alone in Connemara. He pointed out that the Irish house was not mine and that my presence there was unacceptable. I realised that I had indeed seen the Sky road and the house on the hill for the last time. Ordinarily, I would have been heartbroken, but now it just seemed to be one more blow, much like any other.

The weeks of February dragged. Looking at my diary I see that I went to school to talk about Kate's future. I went to listen to a recording I had made of *Antony and Cleopatra* with Robert Stephens and Ronald Pickup, under the direction of Martin Jenkins at the BBC. I tidied my papers, filed everything to within an inch of its life, rearranged books, answered O'Toole's mail, avoided our friends. Why didn't I take some action of my own? My mind darted from one problem to the next. What would happen to the family if I left? Where would I live? I had never saved money – all my earnings went into the houses, furniture and furnishings, and my clothes. What would I live on? O'Toole warned me that the scandal, when made known, might mean I would find work difficult to come by. And what would happen to my mother? Would I be able to take care of her? There were too many questions to which I had no answer. I was immobilised with no one to talk to in my secret life. And worst of all, I didn't feel I had the *right* to do anything. My capacity for altering my life seemed spent and I waited to hear what O'Toole thought I should do.

He was away in Mexico for six weeks and I kicked my heels in Hampstead. We were not in touch. When he returned it was only for a day or two before he left on private business in Bristol. He had arrived at a solution during his stay in Mexico – it was just as well that one of us had done so. It was clear to him that I should leave Guyon House. I had no reason to disagree with this decision but I didn't know where to go and when he returned from Bristol a few days later I had made no plans at all. It was 21 February and I agreed with him it was right that I should leave home the following day at four o'clock. Still I did nothing, made no provision. I couldn't argue with his disdain at my paralysis; I rather agreed with him that such feebleness was despicable. Had he not helped devise a means of departure, I might have continued for months to sit, half dead, in that lovely house.

On 22 February he assembled the household; my mother, Kate, Pat and Liz, meeting in the Green Room; the girls and Liz sitting on the big couch, my mother in an armchair and O'Toole in the high Prides leather wing chair I had bought him when he had hurt his back. I sat in the most disadvantageous chair in the room, a Charles Eames chair I had given O'Toole after a particularly well-paid TV job. It was low and luxurious and in its embrace I appeared indolent and relaxed. Unbelievably, I lounged there and told the people to whom I was closest that I was 'exhausted' and needed to leave home for a 'rest'. The family looked at me, silent and uncomprehending. I'd finished what O'Toole called my 'Father Xmas version' of the events of the last two years. No one spoke. Finally O'Toole rose and said, 'Well, that's that then.' He was brisk and benevolent as he moved to the study. It was clear that I was dismissed.

I went to the bedroom, while the family dispersed over the other four floors of the house. I felt numb beyond tiredness as I began to pack, barely acknowledging to myself that the scene I had rehearsed and played had been deeply humiliating. I knew that I would never see O'Toole again; he prided himself on his resolutely unforgiving nature and I had no wish to expose myself ever again to being patronised in this lordly way.

Swiftly, I reviewed the situation. My mother would stay and run Guyon House – she did not know and was not to be told that I would not return. The girls' lives would continue uninterrupted. They went to school at Edgware, so it was important that they remained where they were. Liz was, by now, part of the family and I knew they would be looked after properly and enjoy all the benefits to which they were accustomed. On that day in February I had nothing to offer them. It would not have occurred to me or to anyone in our circle to question O'Toole's decisions. I had sometimes observed people formulate an unspoken question in response to some draconian pronouncement on O'Toole's part, but I never saw anyone defy him or question him. Not once.

I began to fill two suitcases – black things only, something to wear to BAFTA which was coming up, one pair of black shoes, one black bag, a few toilet things. Where could I go? O'Toole had told me that I wasn't to tell anyone that we were parting. He said there would be unwelcome publicity if anyone found out that I wasn't living at home. I accepted this and it worried me but in a way, in spite of my efforts to free myself, I was still identifying with him, even against myself. I was looking at the situation from his point of view, not mine; I realised that I wasn't going to be able to handle this change in my life on my own but I couldn't ask any of 'our' people for help – it would place them in an intolerable position. Everyone was nervous of 'The Guvnor'. The only person I could think of who would not be made nervous by helping me was Ricci – Ricci Burns. I called him at his hairdressing salon in George Street. 'I'm leaving home and I have to be out of here in forty-five minutes.' He asked no questions. 'Take a cab and go straight to my flat in Portman Towers. Leave the bags there and then come back here to the salon to see me.' I called a taxi on the bedroom phone and looked around for what I knew would be the last time ever. The room had altered a little and was not quite as perfect as it had been when Joyce and I first designed it. The bed now had its back to the bow window since the night O'Toole had set fire to it when it was placed against the wall, but the room was still beautiful; my 'things' lay behind closed drawers and cupboards.

The months of turmoil were over.

I lifted both bags and walked downstairs and out into

the street to wait for the taxi. I met no one on the way out; the house was sweetly scented, shining and quiet and, like water, the air closed behind me as though I had never been there.

# Chapter Thirty-four

Ricci was wonderfully, reassuringly flippant and dispelled the effect of the endless gloomy drama that had prevailed for so long at home. 'Silly cow, get over this nonsense. Say you're sorry and *go home*, for God's sake.' Lilian, his mother, said, 'Have my room. I'll go away for a week – but *listen* to Ricci, please.' She was fond of O'Toole and he of her and we had spent many happy hours together, the four of us but, like many people, she liked the *idea* of us, the O'Tooles, and knew little of our private life. 'So,' said Ricci when he came home from work, 'you *look* all right. Who have you left him for?' When I told him that there *had* been someone and that it was all over and I was planning to live on my own, he simply didn't believe me. 'I love you but you're lying. I know you.' Ricci and I were so different and so close. He understood me very well and his advice on most matters, even complicated professional matters to which he responded in a purely instinctive manner, was always good and I listened to him even before Sara with her experience, or O'Toole with his huge knowledge of the Business. Now, he was wrong and we bickered and argued as we cooked supper and we went on arguing for weeks to come.

He found me a small service flat in Curzon Street and I moved in and began to heal physically. I couldn't remember when I had last slept so well. I was still smoking as heavily as ever but I didn't drink at all and I lived a hidden life in the flat, seeing no one except Ricci and Lilian and my mother, Liz and Pat. In the evenings, I hung out of my window, watching people entering the Mirabelle restaurant below. My life had

329

changed utterly overnight. (The Mirabelle was probably a thing of the past, I thought.) Our joint bank account was closed and naturally my small allowance ceased; my medical insurance was cancelled; however I was strangely untroubled as I felt myself becoming rested, stronger and more contented. I had enough money in my own account to live on for the present and I went on working.

I hadn't seen Robin since before I left Guyon House and thought never to see him again. The madness that had possessed me was over. Now living at home with his parents, he found out where I was and asked if he could come to see me. I realised that it no longer mattered to me whether I saw him or not. When he arrived I explained that I had to go out and left him in the flat to wait – or not – till I returned. He was still there at midnight and we spent the night together and it was hugely agreeable but I told him that I didn't even wish us to meet again. He accepted this, remarking that it seemed such a shame that someone who liked sex so much should consign herself to a celibate life. For a moment, I couldn't follow his thinking. Then I remembered that he had no way of knowing that I had maintained a sexual relationship with my husband. Feeling only momentarily guilty, I assured him that celibacy was probably going to be just fine and we parted. For ever. I realised that I was mightily relieved to have simplified my life.

A few people had to be told where I was. They were sworn to secrecy. Sara (to whom I'd been introduced by Ricci), was wonderful to me. I'd stuck by her early on in our relationship when she'd been hospitalised with a mystery ailment – and now she repaid the debt of loyalty with interest. As a sideline she read scripts for Keep Films and developed projects for O'Toole. Now he told her to choose between Keep and me. Unhesitatingly she chose me. Not only that but she called me every morning to check that I was all right before she opened the office. My accountant, John Libson, the son of the Keep

Films accountant, the great Nyman Libson, also showed that he was not going to abandon me and between us all we tried to find a financial path forward. It was realised that since I didn't know what O'Toole might suddenly do with regard to my mother or the girls, I had better try to buy a house that would shelter all of them – a four-bedroom house, in fact. How to do this? Out of the blue I received two large cheques – repeat fees for lengthy serials – and John reminded me that, on his advice some years previously, I'd left some film money outside the UK and now it could be retrieved, legally and tax free. I could buy a house! I could hardly believe it. Ricci and I found a house for me in an early Victorian part of Islington.

Miraculously, we kept the story of my separation from O'Toole out of the papers but I now told my mother the truth. She knew better than to suggest we might patch things up. Marie, who was staying at Guyon House while filming, spent her evenings with me and she also knew better than to suggest that the rift between O'Toole and myself could ever be healed.

Islington in 1977 had not become fashionable; the Georgian bits were fairly desirable but the Victorian section I was to buy into – built on a square mile of old market garden – boasted not too expensive, solid, well-built, airy houses with decent gardens. I found the house through Peter Brooke in the King's Road, a firm I remembered from my undergraduate days and renowned for its blunt descriptions ('Horrible flat in a bad neighbourhood, in need of repair, looks for a loving, mad buyer', etc). John D. Wood and Chestertons were snooty and depressingly pessimistic. It was raining. At Peter Brooke they took me in, gave me some tea, told me to sit down and get dry and reassured me that I'd have no trouble buying a house with the money at my disposal. And I didn't. Sara knew that I now needed to make regular money and between us we saw to it that I didn't spend an idle day. Ricci found me a larger flat in Chelsea and it was easy to move my few belongings to this new, secret address. Only Sara, Marie, my mother, Ricci and John Libson had the phone number.

I was preparing to play Boadicea for a Thames Television series called *Boudicca* and was spending a large part of every week in Kingston-on-Thames in an indoor riding school, learning to ride bareback on the nastiest horse I'd ever met – Jasper, who knew that I was vulnerable and took advantage. At weekends, bleeding and barely able to walk, I saw Pat and my mother and Kate, who, I fancied, was rather glad to have got rid of the Wicked Witch of the West and, looking at it from her standpoint, I didn't entirely blame her. She was at a rebellious age and, no doubt, behaved better when I wasn't there. My mother didn't think much of my flat, after the splendours of 'home'. The girls rather enjoyed pottering around it – it was smaller than their nursery apartment. It seemed that they had deduced correctly that the marriage was over and no one reacted with regret or sorrow or surprise. Pat said consolingly that she only had one friend with two parents living together. There was no possibility that they could move from Hampstead while they were at school, even had they wished to but I assured them that very soon I would have a house large enough for all of us, should the need arise.

Organising the house purchase was eventful to say the least. *Boudicca* was shot on location all over southern England. I would repair, painted white – or blue – as the script demanded, to the nearest telephone kiosk to plead with my charming young lawyer at Harbottle & Lewis to speed things up. 'How can I *force* her to complete?' 'Oh, it's very easy.' 'Really?' 'Yes, you take hostages and every day when she doesn't do it, you shoot one.' I stopped nagging him. My life was complicated by the fact that, following O'Toole's instructions, I was pretending to everyone (except those in my small, close circle) that I lived in Hampstead in the family home. In order to be picked up at 5.30 a.m. by the Thames TV car, I had to rise at 3.30 a.m. in my Chelsea flat and then get myself up to Heath Street and wait in the street until the car arrived to pick me up and at night, after I was dropped off in NW3, I had to make my own way back down to Chelsea again. Tired and furtive, I felt like a member of MI5 on a dangerous mission.

Towards the end of March I went to the British Academy dinner and award ceremony. The organisers wanted to arrange a suitable escort for me when they learned I wouldn't be attending with my husband. I resisted this vigorously; I was really enjoying life on my own and didn't feel the need for an escort. (I had a small dalliance with a really charming writer but decided I couldn't cope with a relationship and firmly told him so with a new-found honesty that I, at least, found refreshing!) I had been nominated as Best Actress for Livia and Beth Morgan but hadn't really had time to think about the possibility of winning. Ricci pulled me together and organised my appearance – my dress and my hair – and off I went alone in a taxi. I sat halfway up the auditorium next to a well-known comedian who told me that my position in the auditorium meant that I was *not* going to be a winner. I rather agreed with him and we were both surprised when my name was called.

After the ceremony I found a taxi and went straight home to Chelsea, preoccupied as usual with the problems of the morning pick-up in Hampstead. As I paid off the cab and fished out my front door key, a figure appeared from the shadows. It was Robin. He'd watched the ceremony on television and had come round to congratulate me. How was it that he always managed to find out where I was and be there to do something really nice for me? I had not been planning to mark the occasion at all, but now we sat up and had a celebratory drink together. He still lived at home with his parents in their house in Bayswater. 'Mind if I stay over?' he asked, trying to sound casual. He *was* forward. And sweet. I would have preferred him to go home but it seemed a bit mean, considering the fact that he was the only person who'd bothered to say 'well done'. 'Okay, but just for tonight,' I replied. He agreed and went home the following day and I got on with my life.

The post arrived bringing a typed confession for me to sign. I called Sara, asleep in bed, to ask what I should do. 'Sign nothing,' she cried and gave me the name of a lawyer to consult. Now, I was not only trying to buy a house by remote control, I also had a divorce lawyer to see every week. Trevor Williams – the most gentlemanly of lawyers – became a fixture in my life and I met him regularly for the next three years. Having completed *Boudicca*, I was on my way to try on crinolines at Bermans for a BBC serial called *Off to Philadelphia in the Morning*, when O'Toole demanded a meeting where I was to hand over the signed 'confession'. We met on the pavement and I told him that my lawyer would not countenance my signing such a thing. When he learned I had engaged a lawyer he was enraged. Engaging a lawyer, it seemed, was as bad a deed as having an affair had been in the first place. 'Goodbye,' he snapped, turning towards his chauffeur waiting at the kerb. 'Goodbye,' I replied faintly but resolutely and turned into the costumier's fitting room. It was still only 10 a.m. and I *shook*. They laced me into my Victorian corset and slipped on my opera singer's dress – pale blue taffeta – I heard a buzzing in my ears and the faces around me approached and receded and the voices grew loud and then indistinct and I felt myself beginning to fall and mercifully for a while I was released from the dreadful day.

I came to, laid out on an elegant couch in the big fitting room, worried, sympathetic figures hovering around me. I wondered how on earth I was going to survive this battle with O'Toole. Obviously the first step was to get on with the fitting so I could do the next job. I apologised and began to get up. My dress felt strange and oh, *merde*! I couldn't believe it – as though things weren't bad enough, for the first time in my life I had wet myself (and ruined yards and yards of expensive silk). 'Oh Lord,' I began, confused and embarrassed, 'I don't know how to apologise.' 'Hah!' barked an elegant young man and deftly tore the soiled length of silk from its moorings at my waist and consigned it to oblivion. 'Think nothing of it,' he said firmly, and calling out 'More silk!' went on with the fitting, and on I went, one step at a time, with very little idea where I was heading or what I would do when I got there.

After about a month Robin telephoned me – we hadn't been in touch at all since the British Academy Award night – and asked if he might come round to visit at the weekend. I was still in hiding and welcomed the company. He stayed the night. The same thing happened the following weekend and a few weeks later he left some of his things in the flat and before long he began spending the greater part of every week there. I was out at work during the day so it made sense that we should stay indoors in the evening. But weekends were difficult. I was nervous of being seen in the street near the flat and it wasn't easy being cooped up indoors, especially when the weather began to improve. On the whole we got on reasonably well but already I could see that there were difficulties ahead. At weekends I cleaned and laundered and shopped and cooked. Robin loved sunbathing above everything and while the sun shone he lay beneath it, methodically 'working' on his tan. As I hoovered and struggled to come to grips with domestic arts I'd never before had to try to master except briefly at Stratford – which was a long while ago – I looked malevolently at the oiled, brown body on the balcony. O'Toole's words to me after he'd met Robin crossed my mind. 'Watch out for those small, brown eyes,' he'd said, 'and remember, you can't afford him.'

As I worried about the girls and my mother, saving as much money as I could and working all the hours I could, I thought to myself, 'This is very pleasant in many ways but it is going to have to stop,' and finally I plucked up courage to say to

Robin that he could not possibly move with me to my house in Islington, when my life would cease to be a clandestine, hole-in-the-corner affair and become 'real' again. 'I cannot see you in the road with my Pickford's removal van,' I told him, trying to make light of it. 'Oh I don't see why not,' he replied breezily. 'I can take care of the whole thing for you.' And he more or less did. When the mood took him he could get a lot done. I was fully occupied with work and my visits to the lawyers' office; mountains of paperwork arrived regularly from O'Toole's lawyers and I had to sit for hours every week, answering all the points and trying to distance myself emotionally, but I came away from each meeting distressed and shaken. It was comforting to have someone take care of me. Robin organised deliveries, took messages and actually moved into the house while I was away at work and saw to it that we had a table at which to eat, somewhere to sit, somewhere to sleep, a cooker and fridge. With a sudden rush of energy he even built me a broom cupboard, bought groceries, prepared meals and was charm itself to the girls and my mother, who was impressed by the broom cupboard. I had now accompanied Kate on her first day to Davies College where she would do her A–Levels and my mother was still at Guyon House to see Pat through her O–Levels (Liz would be in Hampstead as well). Pat couldn't possibly travel from my house in Islington to school in Edgware each day. It wasn't perfect but it was workable and now I *did* have a house in place, in case of emergencies.

This house was the first I'd ever lived in where I took care of everything myself. I cleaned it, did the laundry, struggled with the ironing and, book in hand, I began cooking in earnest. Meals for ten or twelve people became the norm. Robin's family and our friends and the girls sat around the big dining table and, ironing excepted, I began to enjoy the intense domesticity. There were still moments when I wanted to murder Robin as, if the mood took him, he rested while

I wrestled with a new job *and* put in long hours in the kitchen, but on the whole it had a great deal of charm, this new life. Robin acted very little but this didn't seem to bother him. (For how long? I wondered.) My mother gave us a small, cheap car and for my part I began to familiarise myself with public transport. My life could not have changed more completely and although my vision of myself had been of someone living alone, unencumbered by the demands and irritations of a permanent relationship, there was something rather wonderfully absorbing about living with someone with whom I got on very well indeed, although we had little in common. It was shaking me up in an interesting way and I did, for a while, adopt alternative ways of looking at people and events. And it was exhilarating to feel that I was in charge of our lives. I said what I pleased, did what I pleased, within reason, and nothing in my life made me nervous or afraid. If anything annoyed me I could walk away from it. A horrible thought gave me pause; I was behaving rather as middle-aged men behave when they abandon their wives and take up with a younger, good-looking bimbo with whom they appear to have nothing in common. If that was the case it didn't reflect well on me or on Robin – and there *was* genuine affection between us. Nevertheless, I read something which gave me food for thought. It seems there are two periods in a woman's life when she throws her bonnet over the windmill; one is when she is about twenty-four and the other when she is about forty. At more or less those ages I'd first flown against all advice and married O'Toole and, much later, taken a young lover. It was humbling to feel like a textbook case. But, best of all, I wasn't living in, and being reminded that I was living in, a house that belonged to someone else. The house was constantly filled with people, and I could invite whoever I pleased.

Gradually, the house which had begun as a pretty but empty shell took shape. Each time I completed a job I 'did' another room or carpeted the stairs or bought curtains or china. Like many only children, I had been over attached to my 'things'; pencils, pens, books. I liked to arrange my room exactly as I wished, not really wanting to share my time or my possessions, and very often preferring to be an observer rather than a participator. I had carried much of this behaviour into adulthood but now I changed my ways. I had lost this attachment to my possessions. I would never again see 'my' garden in Ireland and if ownership is 'that with which man has mingled his labour' then it surely *was* mine. The Irish house and all my books and notes and furniture were gone, but I realised now that it was the work of building that I most enjoyed, not sitting around luxuriating in the result of that work. As for the beauty of the place, it didn't belong to anyone and it was imprinted on my retina. Every so often I would wish to be standing there. I would feel blowing into my heart 'the air that kills', see in my mind's eye 'the land of lost content'. But those moments were few and I grew to love my bright, cheerful house in the busy, dusty streets of N1, off the unlovely Essex Road.

Robin began taking an interest in horticulture and together we improved the garden at the back of the house – he, learning to lay York stone and build steps. He had no way of knowing that nothing a man could do would impress me more. Everything that we had, we shared with friends and he helped me turn my private life outwards for the first time.

# Chapter Thirty-five

Denise Sée was our Keep Films company lawyer – poached by us from United Artists – small, like a pouter pigeon in a grey barathea business suit and shiny black shoes and briefcase, iron-grey hair cut short, in private life a cordon bleu cook, devoted to her husband and her dachshunds. She was content to let her appearance lull her opponents into underestimating her formidable mind and killer instincts, and she took me in hand when I was a young wife under considerable pressure from the paparazzi. 'Whatever the provocation, don't answer back. Never complain. Never explain and above all do not engage in litigation.' I thought of her words each week as I climbed the stairs to Trevor Williams's office in Holborn. It seemed now I couldn't avoid litigation. O'Toole had teams of expensive divorce lawyers who flew wherever he was filming and lengthy affidavits would then come winging to me in London and there was nothing for it but to continue to sit with Trevor and slowly refute them, point by point. O'Toole still had the power to make me laugh and Trevor was occasionally scandalised by my inappropriate reaction to a particularly ridiculous statement. At one stage, O'Toole's lawyers were changed for reasons I could only guess at, and we all went back to square one. There seemed no reason why this divorce business should ever come to an end.

Denise pointed out that she had years ago secured half ownership for me of one of our properties, the house in London. That was all I could legally claim from the marriage, but I requested the rest of my clothes, my grandmother's furniture, my mother's silver and a guarantee that the girls would be assured money for their higher education. O'Toole quite rightly supposed that nothing would induce me to embarrass the children by opposing him in open court publicly raking over my difficulties within the marriage. Also, I didn't feel like presenting such a simple and consequently incomplete picture to the world. In many, so many, regards our life together had been thrilling and happy and exactly what I wanted. And my high regard for O'Toole's many virtues remained intact. Of course, as Trevor pointed out, this would be construed by the opposing side as weakness; and it soon became clear that his lawyers *did* think that I was stupid, which I wasn't, and my lawyer incompetent, which he was not. Trevor suited me because he was not a thug and not combative but even he said that he was bound to point out that it was absurd that I should walk away with so little after twenty years. He added that he understood my reasons for leaving quietly and even sympathised with my stance. There was a moment when it seemed as though I would have to fight to keep the house I had just bought with my own money but the claim was abandoned. Even so, it took almost two years to reach an agreement by which I willingly gave up everything I might reasonably have laid claim to. It was a sad and sorry affair and I was to see all my jewellery – the accumulated birthday, Christmas and anniversary gifts – for sale at Sotheby's. I tried never to think about the divorce the moment I closed the door to Trevor's office and he found the case so depressing that he said he was disinclined to accept another divorce suit. By the time I was divorced, Keep Films had ceased to involve Jules. Naturally, Joyce and I resigned as directors and the Bucks began to think of returning to America.

Trevor took me for a farewell lunch near Chancery Lane. 'There you are,' he said. 'Free – free to make the same mistakes all over again.' I laughed uneasily. It was the winter of 1979 and I'd been working flat out since I'd left Hampstead in 1977. I was driven by the need to achieve some financial security but, or maybe because of that, the work had been variable in quality. The West End play I did, called *Spine Chiller*, was so bad that it acquired a cult following. Friends crept in to see it week after week – to laugh. In January 1978 we received a notice that pronounced confidently, 'This is the worst play of 1978.' It is difficult, going 'on' night after night in a terrible flop. My friend Fenella Fielding called and asked me to get her tickets for the mid-week matinée. I pleaded with her not to come, but she insisted. When the day came I forgot that she was out front and trudged back to the dressing room after the matinée to put my feet up before the next performance. There was a knock on the door and I heard the unmistakable Fielding tones. Opening the door, I moaned, 'Oh God, Fen, I'd forgotten you were in. Please don't say anything. I *know* what it's like.' 'No, no,' she reproved, 'persevering out there in a turkey like this is useful. It *builds muscle*.' And it does, but one wouldn't want to do it too often. My dear friends Edward Hibbert and Edward Duke – both unknown to me at the time – sneaked in regularly for the curtain to the last act where, dressed in Balenciaga, I sank down, centre stage, cradling the dying, very black murderer in my arms and he looked up and whispered 'Mother' as the curtain slowly fell on my astonished face. Not as astonished as the audience, believe me. George Baxt, the author, a witty, clever novelist, became a firm friend and ever after we wondered how we had sleepwalked our way into such a disaster.

On top of everything I went down with violent food poisoning the night before we opened that play on the road and I saw the truly sweet side of Robin's nature. He was keeping me company on tour (and that also was a first for me and very agreeable) and now he sat up all night, holding my head, wringing out towels, cleaning me up. I'd never been taken care of in this way – not by anyone – and of course I liked it. But not enough to entertain the prospect of marriage and that was being proposed more insistently and with greater frequency.

The mere thought filled me with fright. And there was the question of the age difference. Once again, I brought up all the arguments against such a lopsided union. What about children? It seemed unfair that he should be denied a family and while it was physically *possible* for me to have children, I didn't want a second family and couldn't see how I could fit a child into my already overcrowded life. He assured me that he had no interest in being a father and that he had thought through all the problems. All he wanted was that we should be married and he wasn't going to rest until we were. I persisted in saying that – like him and me in the street with the Pickford's van – I couldn't *see* it. He pointed out that we were having a perfectly nice time, living together, so why *not* get married? The argument went on and on. Well, it wasn't exactly an argument; he remained good tempered and rational – and adamant, and I shook my head and feebly waved my hands about. Of course, it was *hugely* flattering as well as worrying – and wrong.

The day my divorce became final he came home with a special licence. I was aghast. He'd arranged a party after the wedding ceremony and we'd tell our friends then. We would get married first thing in the morning on Christmas Eve to avoid the press. 'For the last time,' he said, 'give me one reason why *not*.' It seems feeble to say that I'd been ground down, but I'd run out of arguments and yes, we *did* get on better and better. Something was working, that much was obvious.

There wasn't time to do much in the way of preparation for the wedding. I prepared a buffet supper for about fifty people. My main preoccupation was to avoid publicity but I bought a new grey skirt from Browns and fished a nice old St Laurent coat from the back of the wardrobe. Robin's family attended.

The girls were on holiday and my mother didn't choose to attend. I wasn't surprised or upset. Ricci and Sara came to the Rosebery Avenue registry office, neither of them approving or hopeful of a happy outcome. At the party at home as the news slowly circulated, not a few people asked, '*What* do you think you're doing?' I said, 'Look, I'm not doing. It's done. Don't ask.'

I entered the Eighties, nervous, dreading the newspaper attention, but determined to keep a straight back and maybe Robin had been right – life at home was now more relaxed than ever. Ricci determined to try to be pleased for me. Sara said, 'Keep your own bank account.' Almost everyone was unexpectedly kind and understanding. Inevitably, in time the press became involved and the papers made a huge business of the age difference. I tried to keep my comments on marriage to a minimum, pointing out that it was people who'd been married only once who were in a position to be knowledgeable and wise about the institution. What did I know?

Reading the tabloids one day I noticed with amusement that O'Toole had moved a Mexican girl called Anna into the house. (He renamed her Malinche after Simon Bolivar's mistress but she could have been the Anna of the sad note and poem.) So I had after all been right to feel curious, had I? How did he manage never to relinquish the high moral ground, I wondered, unable to keep from smiling at his nerve. My mother completely astonished me. She was still running the Hampstead house and over Sunday lunch at my house she said, 'You know that Malinche has moved in. She had a *beautiful* pair of expensive, new boots yesterday. I said to Peter last week, "I will look after Malinche as though she were my own daughter".' Well! I was lost for words. I was glad that she was taking what could have been an awkward situation in her stride but did she have to be *quite* so enthusiastically generous towards my successor?

Robin and I were apart a good deal now. He went off on a provincial tour and I got ready to go away to film a TV series about Sean O'Casey in Ireland. Before I left I tried to find a new stage play. After the débâcle of George's *Spine Chiller* I redeemed myself slightly with *You Never Can Tell* at the Lyric

Hammersmith, the play that opened the new theatre there. Our first week was gruelling as the construction workers moved out and earnest efforts were made to clear away the drunks from their usual pitch outside the stage door before we embarked on four days of openings – for dignitaries, the press, fund raisers and, finally, Her Majesty the Queen (the drunks were back for that, I noticed). Smoke alarms went off, the sprinkler system was activated and there were police dogs everywhere sniffing at one's make-up. I love Shaw but Mrs Clandon is one of those heavy-duty parts that are all hard work and no jam. Paul Rogers was superb as the Waiter and it was a uniformly good cast, but even so, I wasn't sorry when we closed. The plays sitting on my desk weren't spectacular. The best script by far was not a play, it was a musical. But I'd never done a musical. I could read music after a fashion but I'd never sung alone in public, so I laid it aside and went on reading the plays. But I kept coming back to the musical. No harm in talking to the director, Robert Walker (what on earth made him think that I could do this show, I wondered). He was breezy and confident on the phone. I explained why casting me was a terrible idea. 'Nah, nah,' he responded. 'Give it a go. It'll be great.' I was beginning to think he was deranged. 'What's he like?' I asked around. The answers were uniformly favourable: 'talented, bit of a maverick, deeply attractive, law unto himself'. Mmm. I knew the score of the show because I'd been playing the LP at home for at least ten years. 'I'd better come and meet the musical director,' I suggested. If he says 'no' I shan't do it. 'Yeah, okay,' Robert agreed equably and so I found myself in a house in Islington nervously (and presumably very badly) singing through Vera's numbers from *Pal Joey*.

'Yah, great,' said Robert casually. He didn't seem to be paying a great deal of attention. 'What d'you think?' I asked John Fiske, sitting at the piano. 'You'll be all right,' he said, 'if you start taking singing lessons right away and keep at it. Call Ian Adam, he'll get you on.' I walked home through Canonbury hardly believing that I had just agreed to star in an American musical. Of course, it was only for a run of six weeks and the theatre was in the Mile End Road. No one I knew would be there to see me fall on my face. I bought a tuning fork and hoped that Robert Walker knew what he was doing.

Before I had time to begin getting nervous about my new job, I read a TV script that made me laugh so much I almost fell out of bed. It was one episode of a very long and successful Tyne Tees serial called *Barriers*. Unbelievably (in view of the nature of my role) it was targeted at older children. Over-riding the dampening comments in the production office ('She'll *never* do it.' 'It's only *one* episode.' 'It goes out late *afternoons*/early evening.') Malcolm Drury, the casting director, said, 'Nothing ventured . . .' and mailed me a script. Even as I finished it, I reached for the phone and accepted the job. I was to play a slightly dazed, glamorous middle-European, retired opera singer, a widow who'd been married to a very small, rich man called Mr Dalgleish who left her lots of money, a castle in Scotland and two Rolls-Royces and she employed two chauffeurs – very young and beautiful, in pasted-on trousers – 'Two – in case one gets tired, you know'. As it turned out, my contribution apart, the series was very moving. Who had dreamt up this extraordinary character? I turned back the pages and read 'William Corlett'. I looked him up. Former actor, theatre playwright, award-winning novelist, TV writer – award-winning TV writer – for some reason I had never come across him. Paul Rogers was the star of the series and Benedict Taylor was the juvenile lead. It would be lovely to work again with Paul, one of the best actors in the country, and I could just fit this in before *Pal Joey* and *Sean O'Casey*. What could William C. be like? Would I get to meet him?

I called Robin to let him know that I was off, picked up

a dress from St Laurent, negotiated the hire of a sable coat for myself and, with no time to fit a wig, packed a Graham Smith turban. I did *love* dashing around as and when I chose, answerable to no one. It occurred to me that maybe I was enjoying my freedom too much. Undeniably there was an element in it not only of making up for lost time, but of getting my own back on everyone who'd ever cramped my style. Robin might have more trouble to deal with than he could have anticipated.

In Newcastle, Maggie Bottomley, the producer, gave a lavish dinner for Paul, Patti Lawrence (who was playing his secretary), William Corlett and myself. It was a riotous evening and we ate and drank too much and I was in no mood to stop but Paul coughed gently and indicated the lift and bed. I couldn't wait for morning when we would drive to Bamborough Castle and begin shooting. Mr Corlett – Bill already – had made me laugh more than anyone I'd met for a very, very long time. We had a wonderful time, freezing all over Northumbria (thank God for the sables). Maggie provided real champagne for the picnic scenes and every night Bill and I thawed out, listening to *Pal Joey* and then, already replete with location catering food and sips of champagne, laid into huge dinners. By the time we took the train back to London we were fast friends and planning to do more work together. We were also a good deal fatter. I felt I'd acquired a brother and I blessed casting director, Malcolm Drury for sending me the script and Sara for encouraging him to do so.

It was March and *Pal Joey* was not due to start rehearsing until June. I knew all the lyrics and I took the tapes with me to Dublin where I would stay in Baggot Street with Marie Kean while I played Countess Markievicz in the Sean O'Casey series. Because there was a TV strike on I had a great deal of time off and Marie and I spent far too much time going to restaurants and staying up late at the Arts Club where she was a member. This was another aspect of my new life in which I was revelling – and far too enthusiastically; for the first time drink was a huge pleasure, with no worries attached. I could drink as and when I pleased because there was no fear that I would be setting a bad example or laying the ground for trouble ahead. If anyone became drunk and objectionable, I could walk away if I pleased. I no longer had to be the good caretaker and it was terrific – for a while.

Waking one morning with a terrible hangover, I looked at Marie and said, 'This, alas, has got to stop.' On the spot I renounced my brief career as a bar fly and began to *run* to Marie's masseur's clinic every morning for a treatment before running on to work at the TV studio in Donnybrook. Life in Dublin was just as much fun on tea and orange juice as it had been on wine and I began to get fit. I might not be any *good* in *Pal Joey* but I was determined to be 'able' for it. I loved working at RTE, and especially enjoyed working with the wonderful Irish actor, John Lynch, who played Sean O'Casey, and only disliked having to learn to handle a rifle. I don't think I managed to make it look more menacing than a handbag.

When I finished in Ireland I joined Robin on tour in Scotland and we spent a lovely week in Edinburgh before returning to London together. He was a skilful driver and I always felt safe with him. Driving down what Ralph Richardson used to call 'the backbone of England' was an unexpected pleasure. I was astonished to see that so much of this small island was still green, unpopulated and unspoiled.

London. *Pal Joey*. My life closed down to contain nothing but the show. I met my vocal coach for the first time and from now on I would see Ian Adam four times a week and every day I would practise his exercises at home. Without Robin I could never have done *Pal Joey*. Well, I *would* have done it, but with great difficulty. Ian, my music teacher, lived in Knightsbridge, I lived in Islington, *Pal Joey* rehearsals took place in the East End and there were wig fittings with Brian Peters in W1 and costume fittings in Soho. Without Robin's willingness to drive me all over London every day, to wait for me, to pick me up, to deliver me back to work and to have something prepared for dinner at night, I don't see how I would have managed. I was being paid sixty pounds a week with no prospect of earning more. It would have been ruinous for me to take taxis all over London and public transport would never have got me to my appointments on time.

I was on a strict diet again (I'd given up dieting when I met Robin). The script demanded that the clothes for Vera in *Pal Joey* had to be simply wonderful. The Half-Moon Theatre budget was £200 for six outfits. Impossible. Among my new circle of friends were two of the top British designers, John Bates and Bill Gibb. Lunching at John's apartment one Sunday, I tentatively asked if he might consider designing me just one outfit in which I could sing 'Bewitched, Bothered and Bewildered'. 'I'll do the lot,' he said, casually. 'If I don't have time, Billy there will do them,' indicating Bill Gibb. I was speechless. 'Mind you,' said John, 'no bra – no underpinning and you need to be *thin*.' 'Thinner?' I asked, standing up straight and breathing in. ''Fraid so, dear.' John set about making a breathtaking wardrobe and also took care of the hats, gloves, furs, shoes and bags. He made no charge. Whatever came after, I was going to make a stunning first entrance, looking confident and RICH. No trouble or expense was spared. John's best cutter was on holiday and he looked at the white silk jersey dress that his *second*-best cutter had made and in a fury tore it off and flung it to the floor, lifting the phone and summoning the 'genius-with-the-scissors' back to London immediately. Naturally I had to do my bit as well and, weight dropping steadily, I stood for hours in the fitting room, one eye on my watch, with hours of work ahead, worrying desperately if I was up to any of this.

Stuart Hopps had the daunting task of teaching me to dance. Denis Lawson, who played Joey, was a very good dancer and an experienced singer. They were both endlessly patient, going over my routines in corridors and unoccupied corners of the shabby little rehearsal building – rat poison everywhere – over-run with confident, noisy youngsters who seemed to know exactly what *they* were doing. It was, for me, a time of total confusion. Every so often Robert would look at this revered script ('book by John O'Hara') and he'd say, 'Oh, I don't know about this' and set about turning it upside down, enthusiastically tearing out pages and rewriting. The only things that got rehearsed were production numbers, we scarcely looked at the scenes or my songs and I grew more and more despondent and more and more certain that I would never get to grips with the show. A week before we began previews I sang 'Bewitched' for Robert. Stuart Hopps who was waiting to 'set' the song said, 'Why are you singing it so high?' I told him that that was how it was written in the script. 'Put it in a key that suits *you*,' he insisted. 'Can I do that?' I asked John Fiske, the musical director. 'Yes,' he replied and began to rearrange the orchestrations. My teacher, Ian, optimistic and encouraging, was sure I could sing soprano. Maybe I could have managed it but it would have been a dreadful worry each time I opened my mouth. All my keys were changed down.

We moved in to the 'theatre', the new premises of the Half-Moon in the Mile End Road, the conversion from Methodist Chapel barely accomplished. There was a block of seats 'raked' in the auditorium but they were wet with paint. The stage was just the flat bit at the end of the hall, the dressing room was a communal prefabricated building behind the chapel and there were Portaloos outside and duckboard walkways led to the Mile End Road. I realised that I would have to change for my first entrance at the front of the building under the stairs to what used to be the chapel gallery. They'd probably hang a cloth there later, I hoped. We were really short of funds. The production telephone was a red British Telecom kiosk on the pavement, and locals grew impatient as we received and made endless calls, and for a while our production company 'borrowed' electricity from the telegraph pole next to the telephone. Robert beamed, presiding over this mayhem like a prizefighter, hitching up his cotton slacks and executing a little shuffle from time to time, rubbing his hands with pleasure. I didn't doubt that he knew what he was doing but I had no idea what *I* was doing and he left me to get on with it.

It was hot July weather. Our first preview arrived. The paintwork in the auditorium was still wet. 'Send them away,' said Robert as a rather smart West End audience milled around in the Mile End Road. How *grand* he is, I thought. We still hadn't done a 'dress' run-through a few days later when we decided we *had* to open. (We simply couldn't keep sending people home.) As it was, we had to turn people away for lack of room. I'd tried to ignore the press interest in my involvement. I was playing a middle-aged socialite who'd taken up with a younger man. I was singing and dancing for the first time *and* I was past the great age of forty. The opportunities for column inches were limitless. By now, I *knew*, absolutely knew, that I was on a hiding to nothing. Only dour, dogged professionalism kept me chained to my post. I sat, wrapped in a shawl, eating sticks of celery and wishing I were dead. Outwardly, I smiled. My mother refused to attend the first performance. Sensing my mood (which no one else did) she said, 'I've no wish to be there to see her making a fool of herself.'

My mother . . . What I had feared had happened. My mother called and said she had to move out of Guyon House. She was shattered and could not speak of the circumstances. I told her to come and live with me right away. So, during the rehearsals of *Pal Joey* I had been making a flat for her on the garden floor of the house, buying furniture and making sure that the kitchen and the bathroom were in good working order. The big front bedroom was a half-basement, the large living room and kitchen at the back were light and airy, giving on to the garden. After work and at weekends, I obsessed over the floor, my worries about Pat and my mother and my part in the show projecting themselves on to this huge expanse of dingy tiles which were meant to be white. With a pail, soft wire wool and a sponge, I slowly scrubbed every inch of floor until it was blindingly clean.

My mother arrived at eight in the morning before we started previews at the theatre. She hated the flat. I looked at it through her eyes and indeed it was a far cry from the luxury of Heath Street. This normally rational, practical woman refused to unpack and I had to leave her sitting, disconsolate, surrounded by luggage. She was almost eighty. It took her a couple of weeks to adapt to her new life; nothing to run and organise, no accounts, no cooking to speak of. She'd lost her role and she, like me, had lost her life in Connemara. Kate was twenty and had flown the nest and for the first time my mother was separated from Pat, her 'baby', who was now seventeen. She'd lived in Guyon House for seventeen years and, curiously, the change was harder for her than it had been for me. She began to smoke. Gradually, we made her comfortable but I wasn't sure that she would ever be entirely reconciled with her new life.

And that was the background to the opening of *Pal Joey* – a smash hit, which transferred in September to the Albery Theatre in the West End and played there for over a year. There was enormous excitement, as is usual when one has a success, but I remember very little about the opening except the strange feeling of not being able to go on with the show and not knowing why (I had no idea what 'stopping the show' meant). Indelibly printed on my mind are the opening moments when, having dressed, hidden behind a blanket as the audience, inches away, filed into the theatre, I emerged into the empty foyer in brilliant sunshine and stood just inside the double doors, open to the street. As I turned to make my first entrance, unseen down the side of the steeply raked bank of seats, I was joined by an extremely drunk local who wandered in through the unattended front door. Smiling broadly, he attached himself to me. We scuffled noiselessly, unseen by the spectators above and to the side of us, who were all looking straight ahead at the stage. My cue was approaching and I was desperate. Hitching up my skirt I jabbed him in the shin with my stiletto and hissed, 'Fuck off! I'm IN this.' He went reeling back into the lobby and, adjusting my furs, I sauntered on down the aisle and into the acting area with an assurance I was far from feeling.

I cannot recall one time of success that has not been counterpointed by some kind of sadness or worry. Now, as I settled into a long run, I realised that with the arrival of my mother my time of kicking up my heels and living just as I pleased was once again at an end. Nevertheless, I felt pretty pleased with myself and with the way things were turning out.

# Chapter Thirty-six

There is something about being in a long run that stabilises one's life no end. My producer on *Pal Joey* was Ian Albery, son of Donald Albery who gave me my first West End job. We were playing at the Albery Theatre which had been run by Ian's father and before that by his grandfather, Sir Bronson Albery, and his great grandparents, Charles Wyndham and Mary Moore who also ran the Criterion Theatre, which dug deep into the bowels of Piccadilly Circus. Mary Moore was, to say the least, careful with money and a stingy employer. One day when workmen were seen digging up the pavement outside the Criterion and someone asked what they were doing, a disgruntled actor passing by replied bitterly, 'Disaster! Mary Moore's lost sixpence.'

When we were all young things in the fifties Ian, who was training in all branches of theatre management, came out on the road for the first time as company manager when O'Toole and I were in *The Holiday*. He was anxious and zealous and O'Toole's antics exasperated him beyond endurance. The company report book was full of remarks along the lines of 'P. O'Toole *laughed* on stage and made S. Phillips laugh, as well. *Spoke* to them.' There was a lot of *speaking* to. All these years later, he's a very grown-up producer and I'm a very responsible leading lady and we get along just fine. The favourite performance of the week for me is Saturday matinée when a small boy occupies the stage-right box and sings along with the whole show. He knows every word. Stage-struck as ever, I find it very moving to be playing to a small Bronson Albery in the theatre that until recently was named after his great great grandfather.

One always imagines that, once a show is up and running, there will be more leisure time in the week. The reality is that as the weeks go by, time shrinks as the need to stay fresh in order to keep the show fresh becomes paramount. Oddly enough, doing another job during the day can help to keep one fresh, but it goes without saying that there isn't a great deal of time left over for home life. However, domesticity – active, hands-on domesticity – was so novel to me that I shopped and cooked like a thing possessed. I was learning more and more about food and each Sunday I recklessly invited ten or twelve people to join us for brunch – lunch – dinner. Most of my recipes I learned from Bill Corlett, an expert in the kitchen. Every Sunday morning the telephone wires between Islington and the village of Great Bardfield rang with cries of '. . . but *how* do you get the bone out of the leg? Oh, okay – I've got it on the floor and – yes, it's out! – but it looks like a traffic accident.' 'How do I keep the stuffing from falling out? But my sewing's *terrible*. Oh Bill, it looks *awful*. Does it matter? Oh, yes what a good idea. I'll cover it with lots of parsley.' He more or less 'talked me down' from ambitious near-disasters for about two years.

It was one of the blessings of the early Eighties that Bill and I became fond of each other's partners. Grave, wickedly funny Bryn Ellis became as much my friend as Bill was and Robin was a treasured leavening and rising agent, egging us on to mild follies that we all loved even as we protested against them. We all went to Venice together and Robin very quickly cottoned on to the beneficial nature of an 'eye-opener' in the morning in cold weather. 'Spot of grappa to get us going, I think.' 'What? At nine in the morning? What are you thinking of? Oh, why not.' 'Another round of desserts?' 'Are you mad? But they *are* very nice. Oh, why not.' He was a mild lord of misrule and I loved being with him when we were with Bill and

Bryn. I loved it more, I realised, than I did when I was alone with him. We didn't have a great deal in common, now that the urgency of setting up home, getting divorced, and getting married had subsided. There was marvellous sex, of course, but I had never known anything less.

We did share some things; entertaining was a joint effort at this stage and it was enjoyable. Robin, having caught my passion for gardening, very quickly progressed from under-gardener to very capable, equal partner. Above all we shared a love of animals. He gave me my first Burmese cat, Spencer, a large, strong, blue tom cat with a loud, depressed voice. He was a present for me for the opening of *Pal Joey* but he bonded with Robin on their journey home from the breeder and he loved him evermore with ferocity. He was like the jealous cat in the story by Colette and I think that there were moments when he would have liked to murder me so he could have Robin all to himself. This didn't make me love him less and he, for his part, allowed me to feed him and love him and he grew to like me well enough, but passion he reserved for Robin. He came to think it was his right to sleep between us, so we decided to buy another Burmese so that he might spread his affections somewhat. And small, brown Barnaby came into our lives. Spencer 'mothered' him immediately. When Barnaby disappeared, we were frantic but our distress was nothing compared with Spencer's. He searched and searched for him, returning home dirty and dispirited, moaning loudly. Every day he led me around the house, pawing at closed doors, howling until I opened them so that he might check the interiors. He displayed all the symptoms of deep depression.

Barnaby had to be replaced in the hope of assuaging Spencer's grief. We found a breeder who could let us have a Burmese right away. So Rupert entered the house and took over, boxing Spencer's ears and appropriating the position of Top Cat in every sense. He sat high up on the tops of doors and bookshelves. He tormented us and Spencer. He was a force and he was wonderful, but he didn't replace Barnaby and Spencer became gloomier. For three weeks Robin and I spent all our spare time searching our neighbourhood and posting 'LOST' notes on trees and in shops and then I received a call from N19 (we lived in N1) from The Cat Protection League, saying that they had a very troublesome, noisy Burmese on their hands and it might be mine. A 'troublesome' cat, so far away, seemed an unlikely candidate for my small, quiet Barnaby, but off I shot with my cat box. There in the cat refuge, solitary in a cage, alone in a corridor, was a horrible-looking, screeching creature, his face all mouth, with a cut head and a misshapen leg. 'Oh no,' I began and then I saw a small defect on the right foot that told me that this unrecognisable creature had to be – 'Barnaby?' I said. The screeching stopped. The ferocity disappeared and the small cat quietly waited for me to open the cage, lift him out and take him home. He'd been screaming for help from home for three weeks and his screaming had worked or so he must think. As I thanked the staff of the N19 CPL and wrote the biggest cheque I could afford and carried him into the sunny street to look for a taxi, I thought how chancy were one's own hopes of a good result, of happiness, of getting what one wanted. It might seem as though we worked for things, won things, achieved things, but actually one's luck turned on being in when the phone rang.

Barnaby never spoke again. When I opened the front door, Spencer was waiting in the hall. I dropped to my knees, thinking I was going to witness a fantastic reunion. I opened the cat box and lifted Barnaby out. Spencer looked at the smelly, dirty, bloody animal, backed away and walked through the house into the garden. He never 'mothered' Barnaby again and became the slightly deranged outsider in the trio of cats dominated by Rupert. And they dominated us, as well. From this time on our lives revolved around that of the cats; we rarely went away at the same time. My mother, a dog woman, with her own dog in her flat, learned to become a cat person and took over Spencer's position in Barnaby's life. He demanded her undivided attention and gradually he won her over. At home, in Wales, cats were workers and lived outside. When Bill, on a visit to the farm, asked my small cousin, Mair, what the cat was called, she looked at him in astonishment and replied 'Cat'. My cousins were disgusted that the cats sat around in the kitchen, watching the cooking, stealing what they could (not Barnaby). Robin and I were slaves to these beautiful creatures – blue, brown and 'red' blonde – and we were completely at one in our care for them. Sometimes, animals keep a relationship flourishing more efficiently than children.

When *Pal Joey* ended I went to Ireland to film for television a play based on Jennifer Johnston's book *How Many Miles to Babylon?*. Ms Johnston, who came to visit us in Wicklow, was the epitome of my ideal Irish woman; independent, slightly racy, too stylish to be a victim of fashion or dietary whim. Meeting authors you admire is one of the big bonuses of being an actor *and* I was working in Wicklow *and* I was working for Moira Armstrong again (for the first time since *Shoulder to Shoulder*) *and* I acquired a new 'son'. Now that I'd begun playing mothers in earnest, my children were becoming a distinguished, beautiful bunch. Here was one of the most fascinating; Daniel Day-Lewis, whom I knew as Jill Balcon's son (Jill Balcon, so respectable and rather intimidating, who only a few months before, had along with me got the giggles so badly during recording of a Greek tragedy that we were both asked to leave the studio and not return until we could control ourselves). I hoped her son was as good, and as joky, as she was. He was playing his first decent part and within minutes it was evident that he was not only good, but very special (though *not* as joky.) Alec McNaughton was my husband (very joky). It didn't make me sad, being in Wicklow and Dublin. It was Connemara that had held me in thrall; I couldn't go west.

Afterwards, back in London, I went on working, slowly consolidating my financial position and continuing to improve the house. I bought myself a grand piano and made a second sitting room at the top of the house, next to the guest room; from there a staircase led to a roof garden that extended over the whole area of the house: white floor, white walls, it was like a Mediterranean garden. I was playing house. There was still something adolescent about my life during these years, in spite of the fact that I was taking care of my mother and seeing more of Pat and her friends than I had when we were living together in Hampstead. Kate I rarely saw these days. She was living with her current boyfriend in Islington, had decided against taking up a place at university and dropped out completely, but finally I tracked her down in Soho where she was working at Ronnie Scott's jazz club. I had made friends with Lynda La Plante while I was playing *Pal Joey* and I now persuaded her and her husband and Robin to come there with me on Kate's birthday so that I could deliver her a present. If there is such a thing as a star waitress, she was certainly it and I was sincere in my admiration as she whizzed around, placing well-heeled customers as far away from the bar as possible, thereby obliging them to tip her heavily as she made the long journey, carrying heavy trays to them. I was amazed and intrigued; she was good at her job and while I didn't think she should spend a lifetime being a waitress, it would never have occurred to me to try to divert her at this point. She was quick and smart and observant and sassy – all qualities I would dearly like to possess and never would. Now that I was no longer trying to influence her I found her totally enchanting; I didn't totally understand her but I really admired her. Nor did I have fears for her. Looking at her, only slightly put out by my presence, I realised that, bringing the whole of my personality to bear on her, I had made little impression on her. And that cheered me up enormously as I sat there in the dark, noisy club, wanting to leave for the relative quiet of the street. We made no plans to meet but I was sure that she would be in touch when the time was right. She got on well with Robin but I had a feeling that she found my relationship with him slightly comical, not embarrassing, not irritating, just faintly amusing.

Pat, on the other hand, may have been only too susceptible to the advice lavishly handed down by my mother and, to a lesser extent, myself. She was still the Good Girl that she had been all her life; school teachers, tutors, chaperons, nannies, all hated to see her go away from them. Her school reports were glowing, but she also decided against taking up her university place – and this hurt my mother, I know – and chose instead to go into the backstage side of the entertainment business. I wasn't displeased. She went on the road with her father as an ASM, and played a small part in *Pygmalion*. In very little time she was stage managing a West End show and I was amazed by her expertise in a field I knew nothing about. I was still uncertain in all things practical and one Sunday when I was making heavy weather of serving a three-course lunch for twelve people and standing in the kitchen, dithering, Pat, sensing trouble, rose from the table and joined me. Taking in the situation and speaking a theatre language she felt I might understand, she said forcefully in stage management speak, 'Okay! Go Roast Lamb!' Lunch was on the table in a trice.

I had believed O'Toole when he told me that when our parting became public knowledge I would find work difficult to come by but that hadn't happened and, looking back, I couldn't believe that I had been so credulous and so nervous. Weekends, as often as possible, were spent in Bill and Bryn's country cottage in Great Bardfield. There were more friends in my life than ever before and there was fun now along with all the hard work. The dancer and choreographer, Anton Dolin, whom I'd known slightly for years, became a staunch friend and he tried to teach me a little grandeur, which would be good for me – and then gave up and allowed me to be his *un*glamorous chum. John Bates and his partner, John Siggins, became firm friends and saw to it that, though I couldn't always afford it, I was decently turned out – spectacularly turned out, when the occasion demanded.

Lynda La Plante made me laugh more than anyone I'd met since Maggie Smith. She said to me while we were rehearsing something or other, 'I'm giving up acting.' (She was a wonderful comedienne.) 'I'm going to be a writer.' 'Oh, yes,' I replied, hardly listening from this point on. 'Oh yes, I've got this idea and I've written the story *here* – do you have one of these? You must. It's a Chisholms – from the stationers in Kingsway. Can't live without it.' 'It' was a smallish, leather-bound address book, notebook, account book, diary – combined. 'You organise your life with this.' I made a mental note to go and buy a 'Chisholms'; it did look lovely. 'Here, you want to see? This is called *Widows* and I'm going to put it on television.' I glanced at the notebook; huge writing with lots of spelling mistakes sprawled over the pages. I looked at her pretty features fired with excitement and felt a pang of sympathy for her. What disappointments lay ahead. How many actors at this moment were saying, 'I've written a film script – a TV series – a novel.' Poor Lynda. Why not stick to what she was good at. Then she told me the story and I thought, 'Heavens, that's good.' Even so, I was astonished when, within a year, *Widows* appeared on TV and Lynda became a star.

She and her husband, Richard, and Robin and I spent much of our leisure time together now. The men began to focus their attention on the gymnasium; on weightlifting, or karate. Neither Lynda nor I could summon much enthusiasm for this preoccupation, or for the spectacular, muscled results. She and I worked like beavers while the men perfected their physiques. We never discussed it but I think we were both relieved that they had something with which to occupy themselves. Lynda worked hard because she loved writing and I worked so hard partly because I, too, loved my job and partly because I felt I had to prove myself – not least as a bread winner – and I thought I had to make up for lost time. Sara was a friend as well as my agent and she knew and understood my need to be constantly employed and colluded with me on this. Wiser heads maybe said, 'Don't panic. Wait for the better jobs.' I couldn't and I did miss a lot of prestigious work because of my infernal drive to work all the time. I was so busy I didn't always pay attention. Maureen Duffy and I met for lunch at old Bianchi's (with Elena presiding) and she and I discussed the possibility of doing a show about Karen Blixen. I had loved *Out of Africa* for some time and thought the show to be a good idea but I wasn't really listening properly and the script wasn't going to be ready for a while and I wanted to get *on*. Fool that I was. I should have listened to Maureen and played that part.

Instead, I found a play which would come 'in' quite quickly. The director was Frith Banbury, a great name from the heyday of the West End in its glory days of Binkie and John and Ralph and Peggy and Edith. It was a play about Bernard Shaw and Mrs Patrick Campbell and it was *Dear Liar* by Jerome Kilty. A 'letters' play. Not too much acting, I thought, and nice to play Mrs Pat again; I had played her in a TV series about Jenny Churchill in the early Seventies. Robert Hardy would play Shaw, Bob Ringwood would design the set and John Bates would make me three outfits (one of which ought to get a round of applause for itself). We rehearsed in Knightsbridge and I turned up just before ten to be greeted by an immaculate Frith ('beautifully shod', as Coral Browne, the personification of elegance, would have remarked) who checked his watch, sat straightbacked and said 'Begin' on the stroke of ten. It was like joining a boot camp. Elegant, charming, polite Frith, associated with elegant, charming, polite theatre, was a bloody-minded slave-driver. No director that I ever met before or since expected so much hard work. The hours between

10 a.m. and 1 p.m. and 2 p.m. and 6 p.m. held nothing but work; no chats, no anecdotes, no breathers. He spotted my weaknesses very early on and was unremitting in his efforts to eradicate them. It was a wonderful experience, working for Frith. ('Frothy' Frith I had heard some acquaintance from the early Forties call him – Frothy? Hah!) He did a wonderful job on the play as did Bob Ringwood and John Bates (whose dress *did* get a round). Robert Hardy and I were pretty good too, by the time Frith had finished with us, but not all the elements for a success were in place. We came 'in' into the new Mermaid. Our producer became mortally ill, the theatre did not have permission to advertise its existence outside the building, there was no way of crossing the road near the theatre (Griff James, the famed company manager, used to go out into the busy highway to escort people across in safety). Frith had to go away on family business after the opening. We subsided quietly and Frith returned to a very sad scene. Good notices and a good show are not enough to ensure success in the West End. Without a well-managed advertising campaign and a good 'shop' one might as well not bother opening. But Ingrid Bergman came to see us one night with Ann Todd! And on the same night April Ashley blew in from – where? She was a vision. Sometimes the dressing room scenes should have been on stage. We came off.

Almost at once I was given a chance to work again with Peter Gill, now a great figure at the National, but I hadn't worked with him since we were at Nottingham Rep in the late Fifties. My room under the stage was next to Peter's stage manager's room, with the poisonous coke boiler, (renowned in repertory circles), between us.

'Next week we will give '*Amlet*. I myself will play the moody Dane and me wife will play Ophalia.'

'Your wife's an old whore.'

'Nevertheless, she will play Ophalia.'

Each night we would chant these ancient theatrical jokes

through the cotton sheet that divided us in our gloomy, noxious, underground booths.

Now – how smart – I would play Lady Britomart for Peter in his production of *Major Barbara*. And Penelope Wilton would play Barbara and best of all, Brewster Mason (my Petruchio from the early Sixties) would play my husband again. It all seemed too good to be true. Penelope was one of O'Toole's favourite actresses. I had seen her, wonderful in his *Vanya* and alongside him when he played a brilliant Darcy Tuck in *Plunder* in his season at the Bristol Old Vic which Sara had helped put together. Penelope was now married to my old friend, Dan Massey. I had longed to play at the National but none of the possibilities had ever worked out. I was delighted.

Rehearsals with Peter were so entertaining that I never wanted them to stop (they did go on for months). They didn't take place at the National because Peter didn't much like working there, so we rehearsed in Hammersmith at the Riverside Studio. I would have liked to have been at the National but Peter was a law unto himself and I was his willing slave. He must be one of the few 'teaching' directors of his generation. There was a time when almost all directors were able to teach actors how to play their parts. Then, as they relinquished lighting to lighting designers and sound to sound designers, many of them relinquished teaching as well, relying on casting directors to find actors who were 'right' for the parts. I watched Peter coax a great performance out of an actor that had neither the technique nor the natural aptitude for it. As for us girls, well, you can always spot a Peter Gill woman. He somehow reminds one of one's femininity and that confidence is retained long after the engagement is over.

We shifted over to the National a week before we opened and I found it very hard to 'learn' the building and never did become entirely confident that I could find my way to the right auditorium at the right time. I wished I had been able to rehearse there. (Subsequently, I fell in love with the confusing building and felt it to be the best place in the world in which to work.) Stage terror strikes at strange times. *Major Barbara* opens with a long duologue between Lady Brit and her son. David Yelland and I – both petrified – met each night before the show and ran the fiendish opening. We *never* felt confident enough to just come in and get on and do it.

Penelope Wilton was a wonderful colleague. Later, when the National went on tour, we both looked after Brewster who, by this time, was unwell and not good at looking after himself. She called herself Nurse Wilton. She and I went on a health kick and ran in the snow each morning before breakfast. And it was in Aberdeen, returning from our run along the riverside, that I learned that my friend, Marie-Liese Grès – John Hurt's partner – had died in a riding accident. We were friends and had been close neighbours in Hampstead. I had no idea how John was or where he was and I sat there, looking out at the bright, cold Scottish morning, snow on the ground, with no one to share my shock and I remember Liese and that view as if it were yesterday.

As we were about to open *Major Barbara* at the National, Sara had rung up, very excited, to say that a producer would like to see me about being in a major movie. As usual, at that time, I was stupidly underwhelmed by the prospect of the movies. Although I had been bitterly disappointed many years previously by the collapse of a plan to make *The Lonely Passion of Judith Hearne* and also very cast down when the director of *Ashes and Diamonds*, who had seen me in a play, failed to get finance for his film with me, I had never found it to be a problem turning down movies that didn't excite me. (Robert Atkins's command 'Don't go into the fillums' still sounded in my ears.) I asked the National for permission to go and see the producer. 'Not a chance,' was the reply. We were in the throes of technical rehearsals. 'Sorry,' I told Sara, 'can't go. We have to turn it down.' To my embarrassment, the producer and the director came over the river to see *me*. I slunk into the foyer with a white scarf over my wig and met – of all people – my friend, Silvana Mangano's daughter, Raffaella de Laurentiis. She was the big film producer! (I hadn't seen her since she was a typical naughty teenager in her mother's house in the South of France) and with her was David Lynch, the director ('*Eraserhead*,' I realised). 'Oh God,' I thought. 'This is the most embarrassing thing that has ever happened to me. I've dragged them all the way down here to sit on a window ledge and have a drink of water.' I apologised and apologised – I couldn't bear to think they'd had to trek over Waterloo Bridge. We parted, I still apologising. 'Have you got the part?' said Sara. 'Heavens, I've no idea,' I replied. '*I feel so bad* they had to come all this way.' 'Oh, be quiet,' she snapped and hung up.

We went on tech-ing. Days later, I remembered the incident in the foyer. 'Hey, have I got the part?' 'Yes, yes, yes,' said Sara, fed up with the whole thing.

'The part' in *Dune* took me to Mexico for almost a year off and on. Mexico. When Jack Hawkins was first diagnosed with throat cancer, after his surgery he and his wife Doreen and O'Toole and I had taken a cruise to Mexico and had fallen in love with the country. Later we had co-produced films at Churubusco Studio in Mexico City. O'Toole had made it his refuge when we were estranged. This was my chance to come to terms with another piece of my past. A thought: Was coming to terms with and overcoming my past taking up too much of my time? While I was playing *Major Barbara* I had time enough in which to review my personal situation and there was something not quite convincing about it. When one says 'Now I can be *me*,' what, exactly, is meant? In my case it meant being a person enjoying an absence of strain. Yes, that certainly. And freedom from the fear of disapproval. The subsequent increase in confidence, of course, but then ease and confidence tipping over maybe into complacency, self-indulgence, misplaced confidence – *over* confidence? Relaxation – verging on sloppiness, maybe? Simply getting rid of problems was not the answer to this great step forward that I had had in mind. And furthermore, who was this 'me' that I was now free to be? So many years spent trying to adapt to difficult circumstances not of my choosing had left me strangely diffident about realising 'my' personality. I was having no trouble at all adjusting to the massive change in lifestyle. I travelled by public transport and loved it. Robin adored driving and I bought him cars that reflected my gradually improving financial position, culminating in a BMW which gave him inordinate pleasure that I did not share. With a sinking heart, I realised that in a much more easy-going, pleasure-driven way, I was again adapting; this time to Robin's congenial idea of what our life together should be. And it wasn't his fault, not in any way. I had divined the scenario and, as well as I was able and without being asked to, I was living it out. There is more, however, to being yourself than changing your circumstances. If one is not careful a change of circumstance can be like a change of scenery; nothing much. ('*A groeso fôr Ni newid onid air.*' Crossing the ocean only gives you a change of air.)

Even work was slightly unreal. I now had to find a few friends who would help me with performances. Wilfrid Lawson used to say that one of the secrets to being a good performer was to 'find a friend'. Alas, not easy. People are very reluctant to be brutally frank and however self-critical you are, you can't see all the things that you're doing wrong, and the director is often too close to his part of the job to be able to help. I had been accustomed to long, fascinating debriefings at home with O'Toole and it was a two-way road, one of the few areas where I was free to speak my mind. No matter how well a show had gone, O'Toole and I spent hours the following day gently pulling the performance to pieces in order to reassemble it better. It was a totally absorbing, interesting process – occasionally painful but over-ridingly enjoyable. I learned more about acting from O'Toole than I had done from any of my teachers. Once, when I was playing mad Queen Juana of Spain in a play by Montherlant and was struck down by flu, he actually 'fed' me the performance on my sick bed, phrase by phrase, inflection by inflection and I got up and went to perform the play, virtually with no rehearsal and it worked a treat. I trusted him implicitly. Knowing I would never speak to him again (and neither he nor I would wish to attempt a meeting) I treasured the few words of advice I had had the sense to commit to paper; they proved to be the most useful pieces of acting advice I ever received.

The first time I saw Robin in a play I obligingly read the play carefully beforehand and made notes throughout. He was pleased that I'd liked the performance but looked aghast when I offered to go through the play the following day for improvements. I could see that the sight of my sheets of notes offended him, so I crumpled them up and hastily threw them away and we never discussed acting ever after. It was odd not to be able to share such a huge part of my life.

Now I was to spend the best part of a year in Mexico. Robin would not accompany me; he needed to find work in England. I knew I would be homesick for my house and my cats and our easy life and our friends, but I also wanted to get away. In the small hours of the morning I could not escape the fear that our relationship, Robin's and mine, was close to ending its course. Born in a series of random chances against a background of confusion and need, the attraction had been real enough but after seven years the differences between us were becoming more marked. I think it irritated Robin to find all the radios in the house retuned from Radio One to Radio Four as much as it irritated me to walk into a room to find, nine times out of ten, a quiz show playing on television. But these were small things, I told myself, and marriage was a big thing. I couldn't bear to be seen to fail again.

# Chapter Thirty-seven

Robin and I have a Venetian holiday with Bill and Bryn before I leave for South America. Bill and I have tried to acquire the rights to the E.F. Benson books featuring Mapp and Lucia and George and mad Irene. No success. London Weekend Television has the rights and is just sitting on them. It's maddening. I don't necessarily want to *play* in the show but I would love to be a part of getting it done properly – properly, as I see it, that is. Ah well. Our other attempts at producing are also unsuccessful. We both love a book by Russell Hoban called *Turtle Diary* but we miss the rights by a day. Our other obsession is J.R. Ackerley and we buy the rights to *My Sister and Myself* but it's regarded as too 'depressing'. It is, in fact, hilariously despondent. We spend a fair bit of money on this before we give up and go on holiday. It's good to share my insider's view of Venice. All the Venetian friends and acquaintances come through magnificently and we have a wonderful time. Then Bill starts a novel and I go to Mexico.

For a month I sat in my bedroom on the twenty-first floor of the Century Hotel in Mexico City waiting vainly to be called to work. The budget was so enormous that they could afford to call actors and pay them to sit in the hotel doing nothing for weeks on end. It was a bizarre experience living at the Century; the lift was out of order, so it took a long time to reach the street by the staircase. The building, like most of the fashionable Zona Rosa, was constructed of artificial fabric; nylon, vinyl, plastic, concrete – all totally unsuited to the climate. I walked to the Zocalo, the big square at the centre of the city, and wandered enviously through the

Majestic Hotel, made, Spanish-style, of wood and stone and marble, the deep-set windows catching every breeze. For the whole of that month I stalked through the city, visiting every art gallery and museum, speaking to no one. No one from the production office telephoned me and one day I felt so isolated and unnerved that twice I fell over from a standing position. Robin, in the interest of economy, had ordained that we shouldn't speak on the phone except in the case of emergencies. (It was *very* expensive calling England.) What constituted an emergency, I wondered? The fear that one was losing the power of speech? Driven in on myself, I kept my eyes open and watched everything around me. On Grasshopper Hill, below Maximillian's Palace, I saw a family, out for a Sunday picnic, with a bald turkey on a leash. He seemed very content. One very small obscure exhibition pricked my imagination into seeing Mexico City in a new light. It was an exhibit of drawings and watercolours from the nineteenth century, all executed by the wives and daughters of diplomats from Europe. I had no idea that Mexico City had remained luxurious beyond Parisian standards well into the nineteenth century, when it was still a city built on water – as it had been to a greater extent when the Conquistadors crossed the causeway to be greeted as gods by the inhabitants of the beautiful island. When I was there, Mexico City contained seventeen million inhabitants and the pollution was unbearable. At night I leaned out of my window and watched the smart streets gently invaded by beautiful Indian families who slept in the doorways of the expensive shops. One became sick merely by breathing the foul air but the romance of the location had gripped me, thanks to those watercolours and drawings, and I never lost my 'inner' view of the city and grew to love living in it.

I was, however, lonely for a few months, we worked very long hours and returned to the city too tired to go out. I spent long hours at night learning new songs, listening to Peggy

Lee and Mabel Mercer hour after hour. Why? I wondered. Just for fun? Maybe. Work was slow and the script was difficult to follow but director David Lynch and the actors were wonderful to work with and I learned something about being a lone lady traveller; I learned not to travel light. I had observed Kate Hepburn arriving in Provence for the filming of *Lion in Winter* with her books and her food and her companion and her record player and her easel and her canvases and paints and special china. At the time I'd thought she was being a trifle eccentric. Now, I saw the good sense of carrying one's world on one's back, like a snail. I acquired books and drawing paper and tapes and a recording machine and vowed never to be caught short far from home again.

During the year I was able to return to London a few times and Robin flew out for a holiday once. We had different ideas about how to spend a holiday, so it was only partially successful; he wanted to lie on a beach and I wanted to explore. I found it hard to spend days on the beach and Robin didn't relish the long, hot journeys in rickety buses into the interior. We compromised. Towards the end of that year Robin got his first really good job in a TV series with Terence Stamp, whom he came to admire enormously. It gave his morale a huge boost and I hoped it would be a turning point in his fortunes.

By now both my daughters had gone into the theatre. I, alone, was surprised by this which indicates that, far too much, I accepted things at face value; they displayed no interest in drama while they were growing up so I assumed they *weren't* interested. Now, belatedly, I realised that it must have been hard for them to declare themselves in that intensely theatrical household. Pat had got herself into a drama school in London (informing me of this after the event). When Kate came to the unhappy end of a love affair, her father took her to New York and she began a new life in America, first running somewhat wild in Manhattan and then, effecting a major change, entering Yale where she studied to be a dramaturge and was side-tracked into acting, leaving Yale to study in San Francisco and then in New York, where she began acting professionally at the Irish Arts Centre. She now came home to stay with me for the first time in years and I was mightily impressed by her appearance; drop-dead chic and, typically quirky, combining an elegant wardrobe with a startling punk haircut, and rolling her own cigarettes with flair and skill (one hand). I had watched Pat develop into the radiantly pretty girl she was and wasn't surprised by her control and her enviable insight and good sense, but now I *was* surprised to be getting along so well with this elegant creature whom I had spent so many years trying to alter. Thank goodness I'd had no success at all, I thought again, and counted myself lucky in my grown-up children. It did occur to me, not for the first time, that maybe I wasn't at my best trying to communicate with *small* children.

I was in a musical which was not a success but which was running in spite of its cool reception by the critics. It often happens that a poor show can lead to something wonderful. In this instance *Peg* led to two important friendships, one with musical director Kevin Amos, with whom I began an enduring musical collaboration and the other with an actor who became my very close friend and with whom I later shared my house – Edward Duke. At the moment when I met him he had been gathering praise and awards – and lots of money – for his portrayal of P. G. Wodehouse's Jeeves in a play he'd written himself, *Jeeves Takes Charge*.

A nice, eccentric man called Lou Bush Hager was obsessed with a show, which we always referred to as 'Peg-the-Musical'. (It was *Peg*, a musical version of the Laurette Taylor vehicle 'Peg o'My Heart'.) Lou was the scion of not one but two wealthy American families. Someone explained to me that innumerable people drink the Bush beer, Budweiser, and that every home has Hager's hinges on its doors and windows, so there was money raining down from all directions. His wife was sane and lovely but his mother gave one pause. She was called 'Poomey' (or 'Pumi' or 'Poomi'). We presented the show when it wasn't ready to be seen, because Poomey had flown over on her birthday with a Concorde-ful of friends. In the event, she passed on the opening but when she did decide to come she sat there, squat and bejewelled, occasionally, when pleased, letting out a loud whoop and exclaiming, 'That's mah boy!', compounding the confusion in the stalls of the Phoenix Theatre.

David Heneker was the composer and musically the show was first rate. Edward became, like Bill and Bryn and Ricci, one of my adopted brothers. We met on a nasty February morning in Pimlico. We'd already been rehearsing for a week and Edward had been detained in America. I'd obligingly written down his moves and what little dialogue we possessed from a threadbare book, which was to be whisked away and rewritten. He was hugely tall, jet-lagged and barely coordinated, long legs and arms and narrow patrician feet and hands shooting off in all directions. During the morning we rehearsed a scene and I told him I'd 'filled in' a script for him. He looked at it as though he'd never seen a script before. (Well, it wasn't *much* of a script at this point and already he'd realised that this was going to be a *sauve qui peut* job.) 'Don't think I want that, love pot. How about a spot of lunch?' Scarcely pausing to shake his head reprovingly at the nourishing grains and fruit generously provided by Lou, he took me by the hand and ran me from the gastronomic wasteland in which we were rehearsing in the direction of the only good restaurant for miles. 'If I don't have a decent lunch I get – unhappy,' he remarked, as we tucked into a large meal at Pomegranate. From that moment on we were inseparable, eating and drinking *far* too much each day, spending most of our salary at the Caprice at night. Never in my entire life had I eaten 'proper' food so regularly. Never in my life had I laughed so much.

When we moved into town the company manager, whom we cordially disliked, had appropriated what should have been his dressing room on the ground floor, so we shared my number one suite and our blossoming friendship made the whole trying experience bearable. Lou gave me orchids instead of the rewritten script and amazingly didn't take offence when, exasperated, I threw them down the corridor. Sir Ronald Millar, who for some reason was engaged to write a new version of a perfectly good book by Robin Miller, delivered bits of text after we'd actually opened on tour. Infuriated by one – as I thought – useless contribution written on the back of an envelope, I was panicked into yelling, furious and exhausted, 'This just won't DO!' He rounded on me. 'How many authors do *you* know,' he demanded, 'who drive a *Rolls-Royce*?' As I struggled to shape a reply I could hear the strangled noise of a hysterical Edward Duke going back to a darkened dressing room for a lie down.

It was an unusual experience in all respects but it had another happy outcome. By the terms of my divorce, the girls were to be supported until they'd finished their higher education. Kate's allowance had stopped when she left Yale and she was now living on a shoestring and also needed to pay off her student loan. I was happy to be able to turn over to her my earnings from a show I hadn't been proud of. Of course, if I hadn't spent so much time and money in the best West End restaurants with Ed, I would have had money left over for me as well. As it was, after my grand gesture to Kate and her current boyfriend who was also short of funds, I had to go back to work – fast.

Sara found a play for me that might be suitable for Robin as well and for that reason I agreed to try it. I was to play an older, professional woman who dumps her long-term middle-aged lover (wonderful Moray Watson) for a delivery boy on roller skates (Robin). I noted gloomily that it was *French* and what kind of luck did I ever have with French plays? None. Charles

Savage was to direct – very bright and very handy with rewrites so we might stand a chance. Edward, before he left the country, read it and said bluntly, 'Absolutely *no*, sweetie.' But when did I ever listen to reason? Too late now, anyway.

The play goes its long, predictable way. We try. We really do. Charles is valiant. In the end, after months of struggling, we fail.

The only nice things that happened during the latter part of 1984 were, firstly, that I was to meet Irene Handl and she came to the house for lunch – big hat and all. It so thrilled me, to see her sitting there, eating *my* food at *my* table, that I was struck dumb. I love her acting and her two novels and her love for Elvis Presley. The other was that I was able to do the best thing imaginable for my mother. The University of Wales made me a Doctor of Literature and I took my mother to the ceremony in North Wales and was able to invite her sister, Meriel, as well. The two old women had the time of their lives, seeing people they hadn't met for fifty years. No one paid much attention to me and I stood back and watched Sally and Meriel queening their way demurely around Bangor.

I was moved by the ceremony but as we were waiting to process into the hall and organs were playing and trumpets were beginning to sound, Sheikh Yamani reached under his Doctor of Law gown and, producing what looked like a medicine bottle, said, 'This is very special perfume – only for my family – made for *me* only, in *my* factory.' I was standing there with five or six distinguished academic gentlemen and we nodded and stood frozen by surprise as he liberally splashed the scent all over our robes, so that, when the doors opened, we marched into the great hall on a tidal wave of what smelled suspiciously like Jungle Juice.

A few weeks later I had reason to feel that my debt of gratitude for that weekend in North Wales could never be repaid. My mother was diagnosed with lung cancer and her doctor told me that she would not live more than six months. Meriel, her sister, was magnificent and navigated her way from Carmarthenshire all over the outer margins of North-East London to be with her sister as they waited for the results of tests and queued endlessly to be seen by a succession of doctors. The first hospital my mother went to was Dickensian and I came upon her, stripped and wrapped in a blanket, sitting up, cold and scared and confused after one of those painful, lung-draining injections. She was confirmed in her fear and dislike of hospitals and I noticed that whenever we drove past a hospice in North-East London – remarkable for its cheerful exterior – she pointedly turned her head away until we were well past it. I took the hint. Hospices were out. I began to plan her last six months. My sitting room was slightly raised above street level and caught whatever sun there was. Her bed could sit in the window. My National Health Service doctor put me in touch with the Islington Social Services and I had good reason to regret joining in the criticisms of the 'Looney Left' which abounded at the time. They asked me if I needed cleaning help – I didn't, or Meals on Wheels – no, or help with bathing and lifting – it might come to that later. Should someone help with shopping? No, but I outlined my plan to bring my mother's bed into the sitting room where she would feel part of our lives and have a good view of the street. The social worker's eyes lifted from her notepad. She looked surprised. 'Have you consulted your family about this?' 'No,' I answered, thinking what is there to consult about? She nodded and said that I was over-confident to think that I could keep my mother at home until her end but that she would monitor our progress and provide me with extra help, when it was needed.

After she'd gone, I thought again of her question about the reaction of 'the family' to my decision and realised that I was going to keep my mother at home for as long as possible, no matter what Robin's reaction might be. I could see that my decision would cause trouble in our relationship and I was prepared for that. My mother regarded him with a cool eye and he, for his part, seemed divided between fearing and patronising her. He was also anxious that we should move upward in the property market and our choices were limited by my insistence that any house we bought should contain an apartment for my mother and space for at least one daughter. For the moment she was able to live independently in her flat.

Christmas came, uneasy this year and for me everything was coloured by the awareness that it was Sally's last winter. I discussed my domestic plans with no one. There seemed no sense in precipitating a row with my mother who wouldn't wish to be dependent and with Robin who would not welcome the inconvenience.

February was a month of birthdays in the family. The women took turns in preparing the birthday dinners. It was my mother-in-law Eleanor's turn to prepare Robin's party at their family home in Bayswater. I privately commemorated my father's birthday and filmed some musical sequences for a *Life of Siân* that was being prepared by an independent TV company. But glittering and being gay did not come easily.

On 10 February, the day of Robin's birthday party, I got ready to leave for Eleanor's house. It was so cold. Robin went to the car and I ran down the side path to the garden entrance and knocked at my mother's apartment door. When she opened it I saw that she was looking very chic in a Jean Muir outfit; hard to believe that she had ever been chronically overweight. She was shivering, 'I don't think I should come. I'm *so* cold.' 'Oh, come *on*,' I said, bossily. 'Let me get you a warm wrap. You're coming, so there.' We got into the car. She was in the front and she took a long look at the house as we drove off, turning her head to keep it in her vision. Sometimes my mother's sense of drama really annoyed me. I thought to myself, 'I'll bet she's counting the times she'll drive away down Oakley Road never to see it again. *Damn* the drama!'

The Sachs's house in Kildare Terrace was brightly lit on every floor. I noticed my mother straighten her back as we climbed the steps. Glitter and be gay. We were nine for dinner and Eleanor – a wonderful cook – was busy in the basement kitchen. I went to offer help but she didn't need it. She was looking as pretty and as unruffled as if she'd just popped in for a cocktail. As usual I marvelled at her powers of organisation and her sense of perfect presentation. In the first-floor drawing room, Leonard was dispensing champagne cocktails and my mother, glass in hand, was deep in conversation with her favourite of Robin's relations, his Aunt Toffee – not in show business; bad legs, a slave to her cats, indomitably coping with her long, lonely widowhood. My daughter, Pat, arrived. Because she was taking drama classes in Bayswater she had taken to popping in regularly to Eleanor and Leonard's house. I sat next to Toffee and Sally in the first-floor drawing room. 'D'you know,' said my mother to me in Welsh, 'I don't feel so wonderful.' 'Would you like to lie down?' 'Maybe, for a minute.' There was a day-bed in the closed off 'L' of the drawing room and she lay down while I fetched a glass of water. Pat – devoted to her grandmother – began to say, 'Let's get a doctor.' 'Oh, don't be silly, Pat,' I said. 'Just make her comfortable.'

Pat and I sat on either side of the narrow day-bed and I began to think that something unusual was occurring. Robin and then Eleanor looked around the door and went away. Pat and my mother and I were alone in the room. Sally began to breathe more urgently, deep, rasping breaths. Pat became agitated and I told her to be calm and hold her grandmother's hand. Again she said, 'We should call a doctor.' I was sure that we shouldn't. Then my mother spoke for the first time. Her voice was strong and magisterial. 'Take off these clothes,' she said. I had a moment of not knowing what to do. 'Undress me,' she said in the same strong voice, the voice that as a child, I had obeyed without question. I looked at Pat and we both rose and began to take off the Jean Muir coat and blouse and skirt. Then the petticoat. Then the spotless white corset with its myriad hooks – how had she ever done them up I wondered. I had never seen my mother's bare flesh and I hesitated now before dealing with the straining hooks and eyes. Pat took the initiative and loosened the suspenders and rolled down the stockings. 'Go on,' said the voice – it seemed there was nothing of my mother except her voice – and I began to push and tug at the hooks and eyes. We discarded the bits of metal and rubber and steel and nylon and elastic and silk and wool. They lay on the floor and Pat and I stood one each side of the smooth, smooth white body. 'We're here. We're with you,' I repeated inadequately. I had a feeling that it no longer mattered to my mother whether or not we were here with her in this back room in Bayswater. Her breathing changed. I had never heard a death rattle but I recognised it now. I clutched my mother's hand and lowered my head. And after a while, knowing she was gone, I looked up and saw Pat staring, staring at her dead grandmother.

I looked at my watch. Barely fifteen minutes had passed. My mother's dying seemed to have taken longer, a great deal longer.

I did everything badly for the remainder of the night. It was as though I'd lost any sense of how to behave properly. Pat was now the person who needed attention and I didn't give it to her. Eleanor gave me a loose robe and I dressed my mother in it. I was all daughter, nothing of a mother. Unbelievably, after calling the undertaker, I said we should go ahead with dinner. Who knows what everyone wanted to do? I, in my distraction, imposed a form of behaviour on them all. Conversation was impersonal and polite. The men arrived to take my mother away. Sitting across from the dining room door, I saw the bound body as they carried it down and out of the front door. After dinner we went home. I find it hard to believe that we took Pat home to her flat and left her there instead of bringing her home with us. But we did. I find it painful to imagine how she got through the night. When I got home I began to weep for the first time. Robin patted me sympathetically. Later he reminded me that we were now free to move house. I felt a small canker of disdain for him which never went away.

In my mind I relived that February night in Bayswater and over and over again I picked and worried at that fifteen minutes. Something had happened that I hadn't noticed, something momentous had occurred when I wasn't paying attention and I'd missed it.

After the funeral in London, a tear-drenched, crowded affair, conducted partly in Welsh and attended not only by our small family, but by Kate's former boyfriend all the way from Clifden in Ireland (my favourite but never-to-be son-in-law) and undergraduates of Kate's and Pat's generation and staff from the North London Collegiate School, I was swamped with letters and, this being a Welsh occasion, poems written for the occasion. Meriel's bore a card saying in Welsh 'One small step behind'. Kate was back in America and unable to return but as Pat and I stood to say goodbye to the people who had attended the funeral I was surprised to find myself face to face with O'Toole. I hadn't spoken to him since we parted on the pavement outside the costumier Nathan and Bermans and now we shook hands and he left. We hadn't exchanged a word since we'd parted.

Pat and I went back to work the following morning. Robin had made all the arrangements, dealt with the technicalities of death in a city. There were times when I couldn't imagine how I would manage without him. Now he set me house-hunting. It was something to do when the acting stopped.

# Chapter Thirty-eight

Ricci got married! Consternation fought with rejoicing among his many friends, mostly women, to whom he was indispensable and to whom he was always available. Who could not wish him happiness? Nevertheless, it was going to be something of an exercise in timing and limiting one's phone calls and one's demands on his time and attention. House-hunting alone, I found a house on the day of his wedding and rushed on foot from Ripplevale Grove in Islington to the Registry Office in W1. Oh, I *was* unreservedly happy for him. His bride, Rachelle, was ravishing and as eccentric as he. Her small child was a dark beauty. After the brief service we lunched rather grandly and privately, and I was proud to be part of the small and select wedding party. Looking at the two of them, I had a feeling that they were going to achieve an unusual and successful union. Almost in passing, I noted that *my* third attempt at marriage seemed to be faltering. I put the thought out of my head and raised my glass to Ricci and Rachelle and J.J., their small boy.

And so in 1985 began the process of buying another house, a house which was at once a dream and a nightmare. Ripplevale Grove was one of those pretty roads, nestling in a conservation area, immaculately tended, always 'desirable' in the estate agents' lexicon. The houses were late Georgian, two storeys high, double fronted, like doll's houses, with front paths leading to neat front doors, fanlights intact. In fact, the houses were surprisingly intact inside as well as out. There were modern extensions leading into the large gardens overhung with tall, mature trees. It wasn't until I talked to Jack

Pullman, the writer of *I, Claudius*, that I realised why the house retained its windows and shutters and was very little affected by ugly 'improvements'. When Jack and his wife, Barbara Young, arrived for dinner in the new house Jack said, 'I have to sit down with a stiff drink. I haven't been back here since I was a boy.' I gave him a drink and he said, 'I swore I'd never come back. I was so glad to get out. This was the roughest area in Islington. Boy Scouts needed police protection to get to the club house.' I couldn't credit what he was saying and, seeing my astonished face, he said, 'When we left our house in Hemingford Road to go out and play, the last thing my mother would shout was "DON'T GO UP RIP!"' (which was what they called Ripplevale Grove). No one had been able to *afford* to improve the houses until they were slowly bought up by sympathetic people from the class of chatterers – of which I was one. I could only just afford to buy the freehold of Number 15 and I suspect that I was able to buy it – heftily mortgaged – only because it needed a new roof, new plumbing, new wiring, new floors, new walls in some rooms and there was dry-rot and rising damp as well. It was a gem but it was to keep me poor for the next five years as I worked incessantly and poured all I earned into fixing the house and garden. The constant work and the strain of living in a building site was also to put an intolerable burden on my marriage.

The house bought and the builders engaged, I went to Northern California to make a film about Ewoks. The producer was George Lucas. On the plane I developed acute sciatica. Surrounded by beauty and hospitality, courtesy of Edward Duke's incomparable address book, I was in such pain that I slept standing up for a month and suffered appallingly as we worked the long hours six days a week. Kate joined me for a brief holiday and on the day she nearly missed her plane back to New York I found that although I couldn't lie down or sit or walk, I could *run*. Thereafter I cranked myself up each day and ran around the quiet neighbourhood in Marin County where people didn't walk *or* run.

Painfully, I flew home and moved house. Having a 'bad back' didn't quite convey the pain of sciatica and I couldn't explain to Robin why suddenly I didn't want to carry heavy objects. My back had been giving out a few days before opening night for almost ten years and I had survived a couple of weeks of bearable pain and then snapped back to normal. Now, it took almost two months of truly severe pain before I recovered. I was worried. I had managed to get through a month's filming but I could never have opened a play in this acute distress. I saw doctor after doctor, got myself X-rayed, talked to chiropractors and surgeons and, having been told that I was stuck with this condition for life, '. . . look at the X-rays. Wear and tear I'm afraid, my dear' I couldn't accept it.

I baulked at surgery, bided my time. We moved, with an army of builders, to the new house and I began rehearsing *Gigi* in Chiswick. It was to move to the Lyric in Shaftesbury Avenue. I was not getting on with my director, John Dexter but, mercifully, I was on the best of terms with my 'sister', Beryl Reid, and Jean-Pierre Aumont and Geoffrey Burridge and Amanda Waring who was *Gigi* (and Dorothy Tutin's daughter). Although my sciatica had run its course I knew that, come opening night, I might fall ill again. I was desperate. Robin had been annoying me – playing at helping the builders when it suited him; slowing them up, entertaining them to breakfast. I stood drinking a coffee in what would, one day, be the kitchen while the men sat on the only chairs in the dining room and talked about 'manly' things before starting work. I could have done with a lift part of the way but our car sat in the street outside and there was murder in my heart as I left the house and ran past it on my way to the tube to Chiswick and to difficult John Dexter. Within a few weeks Robin and his brother were given a gift of money by their parents and decided to spend all of it going on a wonderful holiday. Robin left a list of things I was to make sure the builders finished before he returned and off he swept to Maui. His behaviour so embarrassed me that I couldn't think of anything to say to him. He didn't notice that I was less than chatty.

After he left, rehearsals became more and more unpleasant. John Dexter antagonised each member of the company in turn – I wondered when it would be mine. Every night I cleaned up after the builders, left a list of things I'd like them to do on the morrow (I had actually built a house so I could see what they were or were not doing) and tried to keep myself reasonably clean and tidy despite the dust and dirt that enveloped me and my clothes. When Robin returned after two weeks, tanned and fit and deeply critical of the lack of progress, I looked at him and wished him buried under the rubble that was the house, with John Dexter for company, but I didn't know how to confront him and could only back further and further away, hiding behind a veneer of good behaviour, implacably determined to keep my distance from him. Unfairly, I blamed him for not seeing that I was angry with him. Unreasonably, I blamed him for not being telepathic. Stupidly, I blamed him for qualities which had drawn me to him in the first place, a kind of sweet laziness.

By Christmas, the show was on in the West End. My turn to be worked over had come, so had Jean-Pierre Aumont's – I'll never forget the look on his face when he realised that he was being insulted. A polite, impenetrable shutter descended shutting out John Dexter for ever. I think John had an idea that breaking people down was in some way good for them and he was also patronising about the show, looking down his nose at its middle-of-the-road appeal. I met Alan J. Lerner in the wings as I was bracing myself to begin a dress rehearsal. 'You leaving?' 'Oh, yes, for good.' 'What do you mean?' 'Look.' He raised his hands; the nails had bitten into the palms of his hands and left a red, bleeding line. 'I have to clench my fists or I'll knock him out – and he's got diabetes, so I can't.' Dexter had just slung the great lyricist out of the theatre where his own show was to play and he was going, deeply, deeply hurt.

I was assured that John Dexter had once been a wonderful director. Right now I could only rejoice at the story that the opera star Julia Migines had chased him out of the Met in New York when he was running the theatre – she got rid of him for showing disrespect! I hoped I would meet the glorious creature one day. Jean-Pierre and Beryl both wanted to leave, but we all calmed down and I fell completely under Beryl's spell and had more fun on stage than I'd had for a long time. She improvised, flirted with the audience, doubled the playing time of our scenes if they were going well, cut out bits if they were going badly but never ever took her eyes off me to see if I was coping. I'd been a comic's 'feed' for six months when I was a young girl, so I was accustomed to a comic's lust for the audience's love and approval and laughter. I rather shared that feeling and felt privileged to be part of this great comedienne's nightly love affair with the house. Every weekend she bought presents of game and fish for me from Berwick Street and I bought fruit and veg for her and we couldn't have had a better time. And John Dexter never came near us after opening night.

Christmas arrived and the whole family came to visit me in the only-just completed house. I had Christmas day off and would have liked to have gone to bed for the holiday. The Burmese cats, Spencer, Barnaby and Rupert, sat high up on the tops of cupboards, fascinated by my seasonal efforts down below. As I was trying to stow away the dishes from the turkey part of the meal and tearfully retrieving my mother's Christmas pudding (injected with potheen, illicit, clear, raw Irish spirit) made the previous year, from its long, cloth-bound boil, Spencer decided to descend for a better view and somehow landed in the white rum sauce, at which I dropped the hot pudding. The three cats and I stared at the wreckage on the floor.

'Anything wrong?' cried someone from the dining room. 'No. No. No,' I responded, on my hands and knees, trying to rescue pudding and sauce and leave out the slivers of glass.

As I presented the dish to an unsuspecting table, I hoped I'd got all the glass out. I hoped. But I didn't really care, I was too tired and sadly I never exchanged a straightforward word with Robin after that year, 1985. The year of my mother, Sally's, death.

# Chapter Thirty-nine

How do people end relationships 'amicably'? I wish there were a manual. After all these years and all these liaisons I'm at sea, rudderless. The awful thing is I suspect Robin feels as badly as I do, but when I try to broach the subject he backs off and won't discuss it.

There is a practical problem. No matter how grand or carefree one might try to be, money can be a terrible source of discontent. Robin has always said that he doesn't mind that I am the breadwinner – and at first I was grateful for that. Now, after some twelve years, I'm less grateful. Occasionally, he says that if things don't pick up he's going to have to 'get a job' (meaning a non-acting job); this is offered as the most awful move imaginable, but I think that getting an honest job, *any* sort of job might help us both feel better. And he does feel awful, I can tell. He and Richard La Plante build their bodies to perfection. He learns karate and does well, and then stops at the point of gaining his black belt. Why? I feel sorry for him as he comes home from the gym and retreats to the garden room to lie on the couch and watch game shows. There is nothing I can do for him – or for myself. He's begun to gamble regularly; he really enjoys it so I have little objection. I think I understand this desire to have a smart car and be seen in smart clothes at the gaming tables. I may be harassed and overworked but I am doing a job I love and spend my days with people that are the best possible company. The life of a chronically out-of-work actor is truly awful. The spectre of unemployment terrifies me so much – a legacy of my childhood in Wales – and I can't discuss the problem but pick up the bills and cover the debts. Also, I did take the wedding promises seriously; this is worse rather than better and poorer rather than richer and there is sickness at the heart of our life, but this is what it is. The future seems hopeless.

A few things helped me along the way. Fenella Fielding, when I told her about my despair of ever curing my treacherous back, had suggested that I should consult a friend of hers from Israel, Lily Cohen, who had been a dancer and now taught T'ai Chi and the Feldenkreis exercise system and did a lot of voluntary work with old, disabled people. Feeling older than God's mother and twice as disabled and having exhausted all other avenues, I now embarked on a three-year course of treatment with Lily. We worked in her apartment in Bayswater three times a week and gradually my back grew stronger and I just knew that one day I was going to be completely 'normal' again. The regular exercise also improved my mood and, as an added protection against depression, I joined a drawing class so when I wasn't rehearsing or playing, I nipped into the Mary Ward Centre in Holborn and did a spot of bad but absorbing sketching – anything rather than sit at home. When I had a play to learn, I made that an excuse for going out of town; once I went to stay, alone, in a hotel near Lincoln Cathedral and another time Sara allowed me to use her country house in Norfolk where I learned lines and painted and became cheerful until my return home. I also got it into my head that the whole family should learn to meditate and that was an astounding success. Kate, who was back from America and now working in England, really loved the discipline but Pat was not so sure; Robin persevered and I added it to my cocktail of activities designed to keep me on an even keel. The garden thrived, the house improved gradually as I acquired well-paid television jobs. I was by no means out of the wood financially because our future seemed so precarious and the house continued to be a heavy drain, but when I got an unexpectedly large cheque, I was able to go back to St Laurent after a considerable absence and kit myself out grandly for the first time in years.

I was working really hard on the TV series, *The Snow Spider*, in Wales when I was asked to go and see Milos Forman and was delighted to have the chance to meet a man I admired so much. Trailing a lot of luggage and destined for Paddington, I made a detour past Blake's Hotel where he was staying. Would I read, asked the Czech fascinator; 'Well sure,' I purred, having rolled over on my back, charmed. And having read, I pushed off to mid-Wales. Sara was furious. 'You didn't have to *read*. You've *never* had to read.'

A few weeks later I was asked back. Again, on my way to work in Wales, I dragged my suitcases down to Blake's and had another enchanting meeting with Mr Forman. Would I read a scene *with* someone? 'Oh, of course,' I crooned, rolling over again. Sara was fit to be tied. 'What are you *doing*?' 'Well, it was fun.' I forgot all about it.

A few weeks later Milos wondered if I could assemble a kind of costume and learn a *scene* and do it with a few people and he would film it. This time I didn't dare tell Sara what I was up to. It was another Monday meeting and again I toiled down with my luggage and a token costume. This time Milos *directed* a scene and it was massive fun. I pushed off to Builth Wells again. Ages later I was told that I was the first person Milos had cast for the movie, *Valmont*. Never can a part have been obtained more light heartedly or more pleasantly (or more secretly).

So, it was to be Paris for six months. I hadn't been in Paris since I was a rich person, living at the Meurice or in our apartment at the George V, dining out every night at the best restaurants, the newest night clubs. This was a very different life. I no longer knew anyone there and I lived quietly, but I was ravished anew as, this time, I walked and walked around the city and we worked in the most beautiful locations. And I met Annette Bening (playing Mme de Merteuil). She was not only beautiful and talented but good and wise and lots of fun, and I learned a great deal from watching her. She was patient and friendly to everyone in that enviably open American way. When bad things happened she dealt with them by going for a long run along the banks of the Seine. She possessed formidable discipline and a huge sense of the ridiculous. We both loved and admired Milos Forman who, when he was working, was the most tactless person imaginable. He was so intent on the work in hand that his thoughts sprang from his mouth uncensored and uttered in endearing Mittel European. One day as we were working on an endless tracking shot in the Musée Camondo (which was 'my' house in the film), we repeated our scene over and over and over and over again. The unit grew apprehensive as it looked as though we girls were going to cop it any minute. Sure enough, an anguished scream from Milos: '*Why* are you behaving like ziss? *Why* are you talking in such a peculiar way? *Why* do you *walk* like zat? *Why* can you not be like *peeple*? *Why* not be *natural*? *Tell* me *why* you do it?'

Disconsolate, we turned to go back to our first marks and begin again, and Annette under her breath said to me, 'We do it like *ziss*, Milos, because we want you to hate us. And we do it like *ziss* because we want never to work again.'

I stored her in my mind as an example of good behaviour and there she stayed.

At Christmas, Annette's then husband, Steve Black, came to visit her from America and Robin joined me. It was an uneasy time. Robin was veering between low spirits and the sort of extra high spirits which none of us could match. The long separation was tearing apart the already threadbare fabric of our life together. When I returned to London, Kate came to stay and that helped somewhat. Robin was very well mannered and more good-humoured when she was around. Even so the atmosphere became more and more strained. I had very little idea now what made up Robin's daily routine. Where did he go in his BMW? What did he do when he wasn't at the gym or the casino? Once, in a family crisis, I needed to find him and I called the place where he'd said he was spending the day – he'd not been there since early morning. When he returned at night I asked if his day had gone well. 'Oh yes,' he replied and I found I had neither the will nor the inclination to question him further. Perversely, I felt guilty about the episode, as though *I* was the one leading a secret life. As I went through the motions of being a 'good' wife I wished that something or someone would happen along radically to alter everything. Since I lacked the courage to force a discussion there was nothing for it but to hope feebly for a theatrical, *ex-machina* solution. Something along the lines of 'with one bound she was free'.

Robin was marooned in a comfortable world, but dependant on me, where the phones rang for me, a world in which, at almost forty years of age, he was still referred to by journalists as a 'toy-boy', where strangers called him 'Mr Phillips'. He no longer kept my accounts as he used to. It was as though by distancing himself from the practicalities of life he distanced himself from all responsibility for the mortgage payments, the taxes, the insurance and the day-to-day task of maintaining a life.

Gradually, the house grew glossier and the cats thrived; when they weren't fighting each other, they lay on the most comfortable chairs, a beautiful heap of shining brown, grey and red-blonde fur but I looked at them and myself and felt that they, the house and I had all lost our lustre in Robin's eyes.

There was very little time for moping. I was always busy and the girls were both acting as well and when I went to see them I found, to my surprise, that watching them brought nothing but pleasure, with none of the fear and torment I used to feel when watching their father (or when I was a child, my father) on stage. Out of the blue I had been commissioned to write a book about needlepoint. Coral Browne had taught me the basic stitches in the sixties and I had made some large pieces;

now I struggled to complete the book (sewing to a deadline was much worse than writing) and continued to film the TV *Life of Siân* that had begun so many months ago. It was meant to be a story told without narrative or interviewer's questions; just pictures and songs, shots of me opening a play, rehearsing, performing songs. This was a difficult concept, made doubly difficult by my unwillingness to reveal anything about my crumbling private life and it seemed to drag on interminably. Edward Duke came to stay and developed a new hobby – cooking. It was a measure of my fondness for him that I didn't turn a hair as my immaculate kitchen became an impenetrable no-go area, piled high with blackened pots and dirty dishes and spilled sugar, flour and gravy. (The food, though, was spectacular.)

I piled on more and more work – besides writing and sewing and filming musical segments for *The Life*, I began to rehearse a play by Loleh Belon, *Thursday's Ladies* ('Another French play,' I thought with misgiving). The other Ladies were to be played by Eileen Atkins and Dorothy Tutin, the one handsome young man by Jeremy Brudenell. I was delighted to be directed again by Frank Hauser. It was too much to resist. We played ourselves as toddlers, children, teenagers, young women, switching from one age to another with no warning or preparation. Frank didn't want to help the changes by making lighting adjustments so we did our level best to age or rejuvenate in an instant, switching from one age to another with startling suddenness, concentrating like mad. The three of us worked hard – and happily – but the play which was so much fun to do, wasn't, we gathered, nearly as much fun to watch. One of my faithful fans said to me at the stage-door, 'Oh, Miss Phillips, some of these foreign plays you're in – I do *dread* them.'

It was a short run but one night I met a great friend of Eileen's, an actor whom I hadn't met since the Fifties, Ken Parry, a rotund, Dickensian figure, with shiny, round eyes that missed nothing and rosy, pursed lips that conveyed disapproval or disbelief in hefty quantities. We realised that we were neighbours and began to visit each other and became friends. From Wigan, but born in Wales of Welsh extraction, Ken's English was eloquent, sonorous and magisterial and I began to collect his more ornate tirades against the sheer bloodiness of life. Some of his pronouncements were startling. 'Albert Finney was on a bicycle as I came down the street with me teeth in, and there were six nuns passing.' 'I first met Charlie Kay with a parrot in the Edgware Road.' 'Gloria Swanson told me all those lies. For instance: she told me Rudolph Valentino wasn't gay.'

I moved straight from the play to a musical at the Donmar. Bill Bryden and Sebastian Graham Jones were going to write the show, called simply *Brel*, as we rehearsed the sixteen or so Jacques Brel songs that would make up the evening and Bob Crowley would design the sets and costumes and the company was to consist of two 'mature' voices to sing the songs of experience and a young man and woman to sing the love songs. In the event they failed to cast an older man so I sang all the 'mature' songs, including one for which I was totally unsuited though I struggled (manfully) with it, and Alex Hansen and Kelly Hunter sang the songs of youth. Dressed by Bob in leather, I walked on to his ravishing set (three full grown trees set on an empty stage and the walls of the Donmar painted Gauloise blue right up to the roof) and opened the show singing 'Amsterdam', a tough song about tough, louche sailors. 'Go on. You can do it! Don't fuss!' they cried and in the end I didn't fuss, although I wasn't convinced I could do it (I think the meditating was taking effect). I loved doing the show and during the run something inside me changed. Then, just before Christmas, I experienced one of my rare, strong, technicolour dreams.

Bob's set for the second half of the show was dominated by a vast dining table covered in a white tablecloth, with huge gilded dining chairs set around it. There was a picture of Brel propped on the chair at the head of the table, which was set with large crystal goblets. (One of the songs in Part Two was called '*Le dernier repas*'.) One Saturday night Robin picked me up after the second show and we set off to spend the weekend with Bill and Bryn, now living in Herefordshire. I strapped myself into the back and fell asleep instantly. Over an hour later I woke and saw that we were travelling very fast and that Robin was drinking from a hip flask. He was a responsible driver and this was very unlike him and for a moment I was speechless before finding far too loud a voice and demanding to know what the hell he thought he was doing. The 'Don't Drink and Drive' campaign was still in its infancy but, given my early experiences of being terrified in the car of a drunken driver, it was understandable that I should greet the campaign with enthusiasm. Absurdly, I demanded to be put out on the deserted roadside and Robin, refusing, insisted that he was perfectly capable of driving. The flask was, however, put away and we pitched up at the house silent and angry but unharmed at about two in the morning. Sizing up the situation, Bill and Bryn nervously suggested a quick bowl of soup and bed. I awoke from my dream at five in the morning. In it I had been singing and dancing Brel's 'Funeral Tango' which Alex Hansen and I used to do as a duet while Kelly Hunter looked on and at one point, dancing down the length of the dining table, as I looked down to check where I put my feet, I saw in the dream that all ten goblets were filled with salt instead of wine. The salt was as white as the tablecloth, and the chairs, upholstered in red brocade which was meant to echo the red of the wine, stood out shockingly as the only splash of colour in the 'room'. I lay there thinking that the goblets held the bitter taste of a souring marriage. I had no glimpse of resolution but at least I had been brought sharply to a state of awareness. My temporary solution was pretty useless: work harder.

Simon Stokes asked me to play Amanda in Tennessee Williams's *Glass Menagerie* – another of those parts, along with Hermione in *Heartbreak House*, that I was always being told I was 'born' to play. I'd had my fingers burned with some of the 'born to play' parts but the combination of Simon and Tennessee convinced me to accept the job at the Arts Theatre in Cambridge and after that on tour. Once again, I came to the conclusion that I appeared to do better in roles that seemed unsuitable for me. I never convinced myself as Amanda and also committed the ultimate sin of taking against my character. All my sympathy was with the boy, Tom, who escaped his family; Laura, the lame daughter, got on my nerves and I would have liked to shake Amanda until her teeth rattled. I just couldn't make a 'case' for her and that is a recipe for failure. I wasn't helped by the fact that I smashed my foot on a concrete block while I was running to have lunch with Colin Firth's mother in Winchester. By the evening my foot had swollen to double its size and we had to cut away half of my stage shoe (off-stage I wore a man's sock on my right foot). We were playing on a vertiginous raked stage – so fashionable in the Eighties – and I could scarcely hobble across it. What the audience made of the play in which the daughter's limp is one of the main features, when her mother's limp – never referred to – was much worse than hers, I can't imagine. The huge foot was extremely painful and showed no signs of subsiding.

The play ended in June and I had a few weeks only in which to pray that I got better soon because I'd agreed to do a play in London for Christopher Renshaw, with whom I'd been working on the score of a musical by Jerry Herman called *Dear World*, which we hoped to do together. Meanwhile, the play we were engaged on was a French comedy, set on the Avenue Foch, which meant clothes from Paris and *very* high heeled shoes. In the nick of time, the swelling went down and I managed to squeeze my foot into a smart shoe. Another French play, *Paris Match*. Will I never learn? Stephen Murray,

Leslie Ash and I bore the brunt of the action and we did everything to that play short of blowing it up and jumping up and down on the bits. The great Ray Galton came in to help and gave me some wonderful, sure-fire laughs which helped me, but nothing could help the play and a month after we'd opened in town I gratefully hung up my stilettos for the last time. But I couldn't take a break, unable to face the prospect of spending time at home.

Chris and I doggedly went on working on the musical (which never did happen) and at the same time I went into another play, *Vanilla*, this time an American play by Jane Stanton-Hitchcock which was to be directed by Harold Pinter. It was extremely incorrect politically and very funny and that, coupled with Harold's name and the prospect of working with a wonderful cast under the management of Michael Redington lured me on board against the advice of friends who now (rightly) sensed an element of panic in my choices. We came into the Lyric on Shaftesbury Avenue and as though doing the play was not enough, after the performances on Saturday night a car would pick me up and take me on the long journey to mid-Wales where I would work each Sunday and Monday morning on a television series, *Emlyn's Moon*, returning in time for the show at the Lyric on Monday night. During the weekdays I busied myself with broadcasts and recordings. The fact that I loved what I was doing couldn't disguise the fact that it was largely displacement activity. Taking on more and more responsibility at work was the only way I could hide from myself the truth that my life was out of control. The play did not succeed but I made enduring friendships with the author Jane Stanton-Hitchcock and one of my favourite Irish actors, Niall Buggy, with whom I shared a dressing room. We co-existed – I, pin neat and he, unbelievably untidy – without flying at each other's throats and continued to keep company harmoniously ever after.

After a long illness, Robin's father died and left him a

substantial sum of money. He genuinely forgot to tell me that he was proposing to go to Los Angeles for the period in the spring of the year, known in the television world as the 'pilot season'. For two or three months there is huge activity as innumerable new shows are cast and tried out. Most fall by the wayside but it is a time to see people and be seen and, of course, some people are lucky and get very lucrative work. Robin was comically mortified when he realised that he had discussed his plans with everyone except me. (I *was* out most of the time.) I considered this to be a good move on his part and helped him all I could, compiling a book of useful addresses and contacts. Ricci, when I told him the news, said, 'Well, that's the last we'll see of *him*.' I was so exasperated; such a glib, superficial, over-dramatic reaction, I thought. On 6 January 1991 I went to Heathrow and waved Robin off. After he'd passed through the barrier I stood unseen, watching his figure grow smaller as he descended a long ramp before disappearing from view. He looked vulnerable and very alone and I prayed that things would go well for him.

The atmosphere at home had been more friendly than it had been for a very long time and the parting had been easy because I was due to visit New York, Los Angeles and Washington within a matter of days, as a guest of Mobil Oil who presented much of our TV output in America. We were to celebrate the birthday of Masterpiece Theatre on Channel 13. We were flown to New York and went on to L.A. where Robin and I were reunited. He came to stay with me at my smart hotel for a few days. Waking early near Venice Beach, I stood on the balcony and wondered why no one had mentioned that the city was framed by beautiful pale purple mountains. Robin was unexpectedly sweet and affectionate, shedding a tear as we parted after a few days, he to resume settling into his life of flat and job hunting and I to do a dinner in Washington. He was due home in three months.

Our caravan moved on to Washington, where we arrived

on the eve of the Gulf War to be entertained by Mobil Oil in the beautiful reception rooms at the top of the State Department Building. There must have been some local doubt about the wisdom of this event but it was decided to go ahead and some thirteen of us British actors went up in the modern lift through the modern building and stepped out into the eighteenth century – it was *such* a coup de théâtre and we were suitably stunned into open-mouthed, silent admiration. The veteran broadcaster Alistair Cooke gave us a tour of the rooms and we sat down to eat, two actors to each table of eight Americans. The tables were charmingly decorated with appropriate 'props' from plays in which we'd appeared. Jeremy Brett was at my table and he shamelessly switched place cards so that he could sit next to me and, as he explained, 'that halves the talking I have to do'. He ate nothing, I remember, and when I urged him to taste something he muttered, 'No, no, no, this is much too impressive and I want to concentrate on it.' We were given a tour of the city late that night and there was a light at every window in every government building. It was overwhelming, being in a place that would see no rest, where the lights would not be extinguished throughout the night. In the morning the United States went to war and we flew home, subdued.

# Chapter Forty

I remained subdued until Edward Duke came to stay with me while we worked together at the BBC on a series of Noël Coward playlets, hardly distinguishing ourselves, alas, but having a lovely time at home cooking and watching incomprehensible Indian musical movies late at night, playing with the three cats, enjoying a spot of domesticity. We were juvenile, if not childish – and we were happy. Edward had become ill and I was aware that with the close of the pilot season my problems would reappear as urgent and as fresh as ever, so – so we ignored the future and took care to keep each other amused. When we finished the long job at the BBC we went our separate ways and for some time to come the laughter ended for both of us.

Before I embarked on another stage play I went to visit Robin in L.A. As I made my travel arrangements I found myself wondering why I was going on the visit; he was due home in a few weeks' time. He wasn't there to meet me when I arrived. I waited, feeling anew that this trip was a stupid mistake. My fellow passengers had all left when he appeared, eating. He explained that – waiting for me – he'd felt hungry and nipped out for some Mexican food. No apology. My uneasiness grew and stayed with me for the whole week. We were in an odd situation, partly estranged and partly over-familiar. I was genuinely pleased for him that he'd done an episode of a TV series and pleased also that he seemed so at home. He'd rented what I thought was a rather nice house which he shared with another English actor but he didn't like the neighbourhood, not smart enough, I gathered, and hadn't done anything much to brighten up his part of the house. He seemed to be abstracted, waiting for something else to happen. We made a trip to San Diego but he was anxious to return to L.A. We saw friends for lunches and dinners but I felt he was eager to resume his 'normal' life – whatever that might be. I couldn't work out what he did all day. I was uneasy.

It was a long week. My spirits rose slightly as he drove me to the airport. 'See you in a month's time,' we chorused too brightly. The plane was delayed. I suspected that neither of us could endure to be locked together in the intimacy of waiting for a plane and I asked if he'd mind if I went through so I could do a little work on the play, (an adaptation of *The Manchurian Candidate*.) Robin made a small show of reluctance and we parted. Miserable as I had been, now I fairly skipped through passport control and I imagined that he, too, must be happy to be driving alone through his beloved city. It really was dear to him. A few days previously, as we'd driven down a hideous road – gas stations, low, shoddily built shops, fast-food restaurants stretching for miles, disaffected youth lounging on the pavements – and I was wondering how this endless, messy sprawl had come about, Robin broke the silence saying, 'Isn't it *wonderful*?' I smiled, not speaking. It was charming and disarming, his genuine love of the place. As I pottered about in the airport, feeling better than I'd felt all week, I wondered again what form our future life could possibly take. Was he dreading a return to the poor weather and lack of excitement of London N1? Did London seem dull? Was the British actor's life of lower rewards, lower expectations, dreary in his eyes? When I tried to talk to him about the future he'd protested that London was 'his' town – his home. But I was sure that he'd fallen in love with Los Angeles. When he'd run out of money, would he want us – me – to maintain a home there? Should I embark on such a costly enterprise? How could I live in L.A. when I didn't drive? I had a score of questions and no answers so I settled down to work on the play until my flight was called.

The stewardess tapped me on my shoulder as I sat in my economy seat and asked me to come through to the first-class section of the plane. I was nonplussed until I saw Suzanne Bertish. I didn't know her but of course I recognised her. She was returning to London after doing a stage play in L.A. Forceful and authoritative, she'd just *told* someone to move me forward. I was impressed and grateful. I would never have thought of asking. As we talked, I mentioned that I didn't drive and instead of sympathising as everyone else did with my horrible experiences culminating in car-phobia, she reared up and said that it was *ridiculous* not to be able to drive and that doubtless my fears had nothing to do with cars or traffic and that I ought to *address* the problem and why hadn't I already *done* so? Losing interest in that, she moved on to other areas where I might smarten up a bit – chiefly, as well she might be, astonished that I'd never read anything by Robertson Davies. We talked and talked all the way across the Atlantic and it was one of the most lively and agreeable of long flights. But driving? Despite Suzanne, I couldn't see myself behind the wheel of a car.

The play to which I returned was a version of the novel *The Manchurian Candidate* by Richard Condon (father of my friend, Debbie). John Lahr had cleverly adapted and updated the book. I would play the hateful mother and Gerard Murphy, an actor I much admired, would play my son. We were to tour the play before bringing it to London for a season at the Lyric Hammersmith. Apart from anything else, I thought that this would give me a chance, once and for all, to perfect a good Southern American accent and I began to work with Joan Washington, my favourite accent and dialogue coach.

Neither the play nor the accent was easy and I had no time in which to worry about myself until, a month later, it was time for Robin's mother and me to collect him at Heathrow.

It was morning when we met him and Eleanor drove us back to Islington where I served a very quick lunch of pasta and salad. Robin exclaimed how wonderfully 'Californian' it was. It was evident that anything that might even remotely be considered Californian would be wonderful in his eyes. I felt a little defensive and was glad that it was a lovely spring day and that the garden, while not Californian, was looking very beautiful in its damp English way. Within days I left to open the play in the South of England, rushing home on the last train on Saturday night in order to spend the weekend there before travelling on to the next 'date' in Manchester. I was glad that Kate was staying at the house so that Robin – somewhat disoriented – wasn't all alone. I suspected that he hadn't wanted to leave California. He'd been gone five months, two months longer than he'd intended to be away. As I lunched at a friend's house while I was on tour in Manchester, Kate telephoned, very excited, to say that Robin had auditioned over the phone for a part in the mini-series of *Dynasty*. The actor playing one of the sons had dropped out for some reason and he'd got the part and was needed immediately in L.A. He'd gone while I played a matinée! It was like a fairy tale. Kate and I were beside ourselves with excitement. It was so *American*; the unexpectedness, the speed of it all. Although it wasn't long in duration, this job somehow justified all the time and money he'd spent in L.A. since January.

Later, I sat on my bed back at the little hotel where the company was staying and found myself writing a description of the room with its cheap bamboo furniture, cunning use of small space – the pretty bedside lamp just that bit too small and too low to make reading in bed comfortable, the little ornaments from Spain – noting the dull weather and the view from the window over the suburban backyards and knowing that this was the watershed of our life together. Nothing would henceforth be the same. I looked at the page and thought that maybe I was over-reacting. Robin's last message had been to wish me well and to say that he would be back for the opening of the play in London. I was unreservedly happy for him and if this job went well then it might follow that our lives might begin to make some kind of sense. It wasn't a job I would much want to do but it *was* a job and it might, with luck, help him on the way to a viable career.

As he dashed to the airport, returning to the balmy weather and the smart hotel, with his car waiting for him, I walked through the drizzle and caught a bus to the Opera House. My life was the usual combination of job satisfaction and anxiety and discomfort. It was not a life that Robin had ever truly embraced. And now he had a job in the beautiful climate that made him happy.

# Chapter Forty-one

Our set for *The Manchurian Candidate* – a huge piece of scaffolding – was difficult to work on and rather dangerous. Actors with vertigo had a particularly terrible time as they clung on to their moorings near the top of the proscenium arch. Clive Carter saved Gerard Murphy from plunging twenty feet to his death or horrible injury by grabbing at his waistband and praying that the wardrobe department had done a good job on the seams. We ran out of money in Cardiff. Our director had to leave to do another job. John Lahr was valiant (and generous with cash), and his friend Karel Reiz kindly stepped in to direct us. It was business as usual; part of the rough and tumble of putting on a play, but it was wearing and I was tired when we returned to London. The mini-series was soon over and Robin was expected back any day so I hastily organised a celebratory garden party for him. Then he called to say that although the show was over he was detained in L.A. I cancelled the party. His mother, however, was not pleased with him. After my opening night she and I went out for a small dinner with friends and I made excuses for him. In all fairness, I didn't totally disbelieve him. He might be evasive, protective of his privacy – I sympathised with that – but he had always laid great store by truthfulness and honesty.

Not only did he not return for the opening, he didn't return for the whole run of the play at the Lyric. There were 'people to see' hopes of 'another job' – it was all very understandable, I thought and moved on to another job, a television series called *The Chestnut Soldier*. One day I astonished myself as I lifted the telephone receiver and dialled a driving school that was offering a week's intensive, residential driving course, culminating in a test at the end of it. I arranged a place for myself the day after I finished the television series. I replaced the handset and wondered why it had taken so long for Suzanne's words to goad me into action.

Now as I nervously got ready for my driving course, I called Robin for reassurance and couldn't locate him. At last he called me and I was relieved to talk to him because he was a brilliant driver and I especially needed his encouragement and advice. I wasn't nervous – I was petrified; and what was propelling me forward? Was it Suzanne or a wish to make it possible for me to live in L.A.? I had no idea. Robin seemed bemused as well and wasn't quite as impressed and helpful as I'd hoped he would be. He seemed distracted. When I hung up, the phone rang and a woman from the driving school said that there had been a clerical error and my place was not available after all. I stood in the dining room in Ripplevale Grove, unable to move or think. If I couldn't begin this feared, dreaded venture and begin it at precisely the moment I'd planned, I didn't think that I would ever be able to begin it. It was established, like a challenging rock-face, in my mind and I couldn't imagine not climbing it.

Barely coherent, I called my daughter Pat and she, sensing that I'd lost my grip, told me to hang up and do nothing until she called me back. In less than half an hour she'd found me an alternative (non-residential) course, an instructor with whom I'd work all day and every day for a week and she had booked me into a small, quiet boarding house in Chester. She'd found the times of trains and I was to leave London in a few hours. I don't know that I thanked her properly but I did exactly what she'd told me to do. Before I left, I ran round to the shops at the Angel and my wallet was stolen. Back at the house, cancelling credit cards, I felt defeated before beginning; what if I sat in the car and burst into tears? What if I ran it into a wall? What if I killed someone? What if I simply couldn't move at all?

What if in twenty minutes I couldn't leave the house? I called Morag Hood and told her how bad I felt. She had a brain wave. 'Shall I consult the I-Ching?' she asked. This seemed to have a wonderfully calming effect on me and later she told me that she realised at that moment that I was fairly demented. When, before hanging up, I thanked her for her help and remarked that I had been quite sure she would be able to offer 'practical, down to earth' help, she had stood there with the I-Ching in her hand half laughing and half seriously concerned for the innocent people of Chester.

I don't recall what the I-Ching said but it should have told me that I was going to meet an angel in the guise of a driving instructor. He told me on the first day that there was no possibility that I could sit and pass the driving test at the end of a week; such boasts on the part of the driving schools were stupid. Occasionally a young man of around nineteen might pull it off but the rest of us didn't stand a chance. 'But you'll be driving in a couple of days,' he said matter of factly. It was a milestone week in my life. I was so anxious to live up to this lovely man's expectation that I became calm and methodical once I was behind the wheel. My feelings of unease were very near the surface the rest of the time. One day in the break between a daylight and a night driving lesson I went into a church and sat listening to an organist practising for a concert later in the day and found myself overcome with sadness and apprehension. Something was terribly wrong and I felt that if I sat there for another moment I would see clearly what is was that was stalking me. Drying my tears, I hurried into the narrow, busy street. I wasn't ready to confront the beast. Not yet.

I returned to London, having driven with my instructor to Warrington and back – at night! I felt that I *had* climbed the North Face of the Eiger. Bill Corlett, as he did many times, urged me to enjoy my accomplishment for a day or two but, as usual, I could only think how much more I had to learn and went to the BSM to arrange a course of lessons in London starting at once. I would never again find an instructor like my saviour in Chester but I no longer needed an angel – I was almost normal.

Robin was not in the flat I'd found for him (Gwen Humble's apartment – a smart address, more to his liking) and I had to wait to tell him the incredible news that I was actually up and driving. I had given him the address of an Anglophile with a lovely ranch in Santa Barbara, who had been married to a rich man and, parted from him, had fallen into a lucrative career doing voice-overs. Her ranch – the Red Rooster – was a haven for depressed foreigners, especially Englishmen. I had been urging Robin to call her and finally, after a lot of nagging, he did and was invited to spend a weekend there. He'd gone back to the Red Rooster for a last visit before coming home for good. He was still there when his niece was taken ill and I had to reach him a few days later. Morag Hood, who'd lived in Santa Barbara for many years, said that it was understandable he should linger there as it was one of the most beautiful, seductive places in the world. I urged him to make the drive up to San Francisco as well before returning.

It was October and Bill, Bryn and I made a trip to mid-Wales to visit a wonderful house where I'd spent some time filming in the summer. We always had a good time together but this visit was cold and dark and wet and we were in unusually low spirits. Robin was due back in two weeks' time and there were preparations to make for his return. Excepting a week at home in May he'd been gone for ten months during 1991.

I'd convinced myself that life in London would be dull for Robin, so I'd accepted some smart invitations I might otherwise have declined. On his return, as soon as he'd caught up on some sleep, we had a perfectly hideous night out at a smart charity ball, then we were taken to the Ivy by the producer of *Valmont*. I went on with my driving lessons and a dull week went by, during which I went to an award ceremony in Manchester. Understandably, Robin felt he needed some time at home to reactivate his London life so he didn't accompany me. I was nominated for an award for *The Manchurian Candidate* and Sara and I made the trip together. After a few hours of hilarity at the lunch, I realised how little light-heartedness there had been at home during the past week. Before I set off for London, I called Robin from the station in Manchester and he sounded surprised to hear my voice. I told him that I hadn't won and he seemed confused and confessed that he hadn't realised that I'd even gone to an awards ceremony. 'He must be very jet-lagged,' Sara said. It didn't occur to me that he might meet my train and he didn't. 'Are you all right?' I had asked him from time to time – too often to judge from his impatient reaction. I resolved to stop asking.

On the first day of the second week we arranged to meet a friend near Regent's Park and took a walk beforehand. He was abstracted and hating the weather. The day was just about as raw and as unpleasant as it ever gets in November in London. Everything compared unfavourably with California. I had run out of excuses but I felt protective towards the dozy waitress, the tepid coffee slopped into the saucer, the miserable geese in Regent's Park, the low, grey sky, the litter drifting about the pavement. I wanted to stand between him and them so he couldn't look down on and despise them. We met his friend, Clive. 'Are you looking after this lovely woman?' Clive asked, as he often did in his kind-hearted, unthinking way. Robin didn't respond at all. Usually, he made a joke in reply. I began to collect myself and grew quieter. Quite suddenly, I felt very uneasy indeed. The beast was coming close.

At home I made a simple supper which we ate on trays in the garden room, while watching a video of *The Bonfire of the Vanities*. 'You look very sad,' said Robin rather accusingly, and there, in that moment, I felt the thing which had been lurking about the edges of my life detach itself from the shadows, visible only from the corner of my eye, and emerge into the bright light. I looked at it and heard a voice – my own. 'Is there someone else?' Even as I spoke the little cliché, I began to feel the beginning of a surge of energy. The reply hardly mattered but it would come, after a move into the dining room and a great deal of displacement activity and huffing and puffing and bluster. 'Yes,' he said in the end and his relief was palpable. How long, I wondered, would he have gone on saying everything was fine and he was glad to be home?

As he grew almost elated after his admission, I grew despondent and my resolve to clean up this mess as fast as possible wavered. I felt weak and unconfident and it was common sense alone that got me through the next hour. Life, I reminded myself, had been unsatisfactory and unhappy for years. Since we moved house five years ago, after my mother's death, and since Robin had caught a glimpse of the promised land in America, our life had disintegrated beyond repair. He'd found a new 'family' in Santa Barbara, complete with stepson, dogs, cats, garden pond. We had been wretchedly unhappy. There was nothing to salvage, no loss to regret, nothing worth keeping. Better to end quickly. '*Llosga fe mas. Paid llusgo fe mas*' – 'Burn it out, don't drag it out', was the Welsh saying that came to my mind.

He was so excited now that he showed me snapshots of the ranch – very nice; himself and a very nice-looking woman in fine-weather clothes doing fine-weather things – very nice. I felt that he would like me to enthuse more. 'Very nice,' I said and told him that he should go back there at once. He looked alarmed. As a matter of fact, I told him, I had to be out of the house early in the morning and it would be a good move on his part to move to his mother's apartment before I got home in the evening. He began to protest that we should consider what we were doing and not do anything hasty. I told him I had no intention of taking the scenic route towards the divorce which loomed ahead and that was as nasty as I got that night.

In the morning I had promised to be at a press conference for the launch of the TV series I had made for HTV so I had to take my hopeless, fine hair to the hairdresser very early. There scarcely seemed any point in going to bed but I had a bath and changed and we sat up in the bedroom talking and now that all the ties had been loosened and we weren't *supposed* to be getting along with each other, I felt quite well disposed towards him. He was no soul-mate, not even a real friend, but I didn't dislike him at all that night.

In the morning I called Bill and Bryn and Sara and she said that Bryn Newton, her partner, would meet me and take me to the press conference for *The Chestnut Soldier*. I pasted a smile on my face which stayed in place until I saw Bryn and we went for a chilly coffee in Covent Garden. He was so whole-heartedly on my side, so unashamedly supportive that it shook my composure. At the press conference there were many of the usual questions concerning the difficulty of maintaining a marriage and a career. Bryn's handsome face was grim but he knew that I wouldn't falter in public. He and Peter Murphy, the producer, and I drank a great deal of coffee and I went for a driving lesson, surprising my instructor as I charged between the buses at the Angel with unaccustomed brio and resolution.

The day was far from over and I went home to change before joining Ricci and Rachelle for a dinner party we'd arranged for Robin in the Caprice in Mayfair. Robin was in the house; he'd almost finished moving out and he said he'd drive me into the West End. As we left, I asked him for the house keys and he seemed startled, but gave them to me without comment. And what would happen to his BMW? It had been an expensive purchase and he said he'd sell it as best he could and return me the money. Arriving at Ricci's house, he came in and asked if he could still come to the Caprice for dinner. He was navigating without a map and his responses were bizarre. Ricci explained to him that it would be quite inappropriate for us all to spend the evening together. He added that Robin would be much better off in California and that we should never have married in the first place and what a blessing it was all over. Robin looked more and more glum and finally left us and drove off. I was exhausted I realised but there was no doubt in my mind that I was experiencing a lucky escape. And there *had* after all been a *deus* – or *dea* – *ex machina*. I hadn't had to do anything except indicate the exit.

I had arranged a series of dinners at home for Robin and now I decided not to cancel them. I had better start getting used to entertaining alone – officially alone, that is. Robin came to finish his packing as I rushed around preparing dinner. I hitched up my skirt and realised that my waistband was hanging around my hips. I had unbounded energy and I'd lost a huge amount of weight in twenty-four hours. I was shocked when Robin made to embrace me and I flinched away from him, offended. I couldn't even muster a smile and realised that today I was disliking him rather. Was nothing going to remain the same for more than a few hours? He told me to 'go easy' on myself and not push the driving or force myself to go to all the Christmas parties we went to every year – and maybe cancel some dinner parties. He probably meant well but I was seized with rage and resolved to redouble my efforts to become a driver and that the stove at home should scarcely be allowed to cool between meals and that I'd get Ricci to find me a new wardrobe for gadding about. I kept my fury well under wraps as I wished him well and told him that he'd be free as soon as I could arrange it and that he shouldn't worry unduly about me. 'Anything you want to ask me?' he asked. I couldn't think of anything at all.

I never saw him after that. He went to America and six weeks after his departure – exactly a year after he first went to California – we were divorced. Ricci had been right, in principle, when he'd said in that January of 1991 that that was the last we'd see of him. Now he said, 'You'll never hear from him again.' I tried on my new wardrobe; I was almost two sizes slimmer than I'd been six weeks previously. Large mercies.

# Chapter Forty-two

After a roller-coaster life of much happiness and many troubles, a woman of a certain age makes a break for freedom. She makes a critical error of judgment and against all expectations enjoys some years of uncomplicated happiness but thereafter finds it very difficult to pay for this pleasure when the bill arrives, as it surely does. She is released from her impossible life with the minimum of blame, the maximum of sympathy, some hurt pride and public humiliation and a greatly improved financial situation and she recovers her health, not to mention her figure, and knows in every part of her being that what happened is for the best. She proceeds with life. She is content.

For a moment or two it seemed that that was the story but almost immediately in that winter of 1992, something went terribly wrong. My shiny new clothes hung in my dressing room where I had expanded into all the capacious cupboards. Now that I had only myself to think of, my hair and nails were expensively groomed and tended. The house had the air of 'my house', the phone rang constantly, I was surrounded by new friends as well as the group of friends that I called my 'family'. My real family was solidly there for me. Everyone was relieved for me. Everyone took care of me. The welcome-home dinners for Robin went on, although he was probably back in California. Sara must have called the girls and they both turned up unexpectedly during a dinner party, Kate all the way from Ireland where she now lived, blowing in, dishevelled. I was dangerously overwhelmed with gratitude for my daughters and I looked around the table at them and my friends and thought myself fortunate.

One of my chief tasks in those early days was to console someone who had become a close friend during Robin's absence in America. Kevin Moore's dismay was almost comical. He was the person who had provided me with the Santa Barbara address which I had given to Robin, with much urging to use it. Now he blamed himself for what had happened at the Red Rooster. I tried to convince him that what had happened wasn't his fault at all and that in any case it really was for the best. He had been helping me learn to drive and now he continued to do so. Tart of tongue, maliciously funny, he was also a man of principle and distressed to find someone he had thought to be a friend had behaved shoddily, as he thought. Missing little, he probably sensed that I was not quite as serenely over the upheaval as I thought myself to be. Bill and Bryn monitored my days by telephone.

Sara called me every morning before she opened the office and Bryn (Newton) called later in the day with a carefully prepared, hilarious piece of gossip. Kate stayed with me and was wonderfully, unfairly partisan. Pat was close at hand – all strength and health and sanity. Ken Parry summoned me to his flat and lectured me on how to live my life with the minimum of pain; evidently, and rightly, he wasn't one of the friends who anticipated a problem-free time ahead. I listened to his warning of trials to come without really understanding it.

Ricci and his mother Lilian were pleased at the turn of events and Ricci expected me to snap back to normal at once. For the first time in our friendship he made a misjudgment and it caused our only estrangement. It was temporary but it came at a bad time for me. He so wanted to see me happily established and looked after that he began to cast around for a new partner ('not necessarily to *marry*') for me. We didn't see each other until he promised to stop introducing me to strange men whom he considered 'suitable'. His childlike hope would have been to see me reconciled to O'Toole and it was very difficult to explain to him that such a thing was unfeasible and undesirable. In any case, we were unlikely ever to be in touch again. The divorce wasn't through when suddenly I began to feel bad. Very bad. For the first time in my life I couldn't sleep more than a few hours a night and would wake at four o'clock in the morning – three cats on the counterpane – and lie there shaking with fright. What was I afraid of? I didn't know. Weeping silently, I would ask myself what I was crying for? I didn't know. Kate would say, 'Why didn't you wake me?' But what would I wake her for? I had no idea what – fear aside – I was feeling. It was clear to me that something bad was overtaking me and I had no idea how to deal with it. By day, I was all right for a great deal of the time, then suddenly I would be overcome with sadness and fright. The hours between four and seven a.m. were hideous. Edward Duke called from San Francisco. He'd just finished a performance and his dressing room seemed jammed with *I, Claudius* fans. A stranger to economy at the best of times, he put them all on the phone to me in this worst of times. He had his own problems but he spent hours on the phone every week and knowing, somehow, that I wasn't doing very well, he drew me a road map for getting through miserable days. On his advice I bought a small note book and when I felt I couldn't continue some ordinary activity, like walking across the concourse of Waterloo Station, I would stop, duck into an empty doorway and write down exactly how I felt; after a few pages I'd find I could, as he'd promised, resume everyday life again. The only truly 'safe' time for me was late at night, when I returned home after an evening out or after work. 'Home to an empty house', words of misery and foreboding for many, was, and always had been, for me, a happy phrase of promise. Now, the moment of knowing myself to be completely alone for a few hours was one of the truly happy times in what had become an unhappy life.

I didn't know what to do but I began to realise what I must *not* do. I dimly understood that the perception of me by many was that I was good wife material. Wrong though that was, I could see how my industry, good manners, sense of responsibility, cheerful temperament and general deceitfulness would have brought about such a belief. Once again, as had happened when O'Toole and I parted, I began to receive proposals of marriage – mostly from people I had known years previously (and many of those were, I felt, polite gestures) but some, comically, were from total strangers. (One man enclosed a statement of his assets with letters from his bank manager.) It became obvious to me that people thought I *ought* to be married and looked after, partly, I suppose, because for over thirty years I had *been* married. I myself knew that no one needed less looking after in that married way than I, and I saw clearly that the one thing I must not do now was to fudge whatever was happening to me with the distraction of a close relationship. For the first time in my life I was going to stand alone.

Things took an unexpected and hateful turn and I struggled between genuine misery and true annoyance. What happened seemed monstrously unfair and I didn't like it one bit. Every bad thing I had ever done came back to haunt me. Every mean thought and malicious deed reared up as though it had happened only yesterday. At first I sat up in bed in the ugly, small hours and wrote notes about my sins of omission, my careless cruelties. After a few months of that, I couldn't bear it any longer and just lay there, appalled at myself. But it seemed so unfair, to be visited in this way. *Why* was this happening to me, I wondered, resentfully? I confided this to no one. Someone would be sure to say that actually I was quite a nice person and I wanted to be the one to decide that, sometime, maybe never. Conversely, during the days, memories of great *happiness* intruded, no matter where I found myself. I had lived in London for a very long time and had been happy and sad in almost every part of it. Every miserable moment forgotten, I was assailed by recollections of intensely happy times with the children when they were small, with friends, lovers, husbands – even with Robin. I was cursed with the remembrance of the happy years when we first met and the contrast with my present state was torture.

Everything went wrong at home; the vacuum cleaner broke, the washing machine 'died', the downstairs loo jammed and one rainy day a plumber came and dug up the yard and £400 later was about to begin taking up the utility room tiles, when a kindly builder across the road took pity on me, came in and fished out a small deodorant container which had lodged in the 'S' bend. I shed tears of self-pity and gratitude. I felt so *clueless*, and kept cutting myself accidentally and then, worst of all, Spencer, the oldest of the three Burmese cats, became very ill. It rained and rained and Kate and I went to and fro on foot to the vet. Finally, I took him to live in my bedroom, coaxing him to eat from my hand. He was the cat that adored Robin and now I fancied he must sense that Robin was never coming back and for the first time I was filled with real anger. Spencer spent the last week of his life in the vet's surgery, on a drip. He died on the night of 13 December. I asked for his body, not his ashes, and went to Upper Street to fetch him. It was raining when I carried the heavy burden back to be buried in the garden. The ground was hard and Kate and I had to use my mother's favourite gardening tool, a small pickaxe, to dig the grave. We were so cold and wet that we had to keep suspending work to come indoors for cups of hot tea. We cut ridiculous figures – dirty, laughing and crying and shivering and hacking out a grave. We buried Spencer wrapped in the cover of his favourite velvet cushion, broke his feeding bowl and put in the bits and added a few olives, to which he was very partial. He was twelve years old. Rupert and Barnaby slept, warm and dry, throughout the miserable afternoon.

I planted a rose on Spencer's grave. 'Isfahan' sounded good

and it was only after I installed it that I learned that its alternative name was 'Pom Pom des Princes' – just about as unsuitable a name as could be imagined for big, grave, humourless Spencer. The thought of Robin with his new family of cats, taking his ease in the sunshine while we buried Spencer in the rain, so infuriated me that I broke a lot of china that he'd been fond of and felt better immediately. I realised that I was teetering on the brink of very foolish behaviour.

Before Christmas I began rehearsing *Painting Churches* by Tina Howe, a play I had agreed to do before Robin's return. It didn't go well in any sense and Tina, whom I admired and liked enormously, didn't even stay in London for the opening, leaving for Paris in order to avoid what she was sure would be a disastrous production. We were underfunded and came very close to being forbidden by Equity to perform, which would have been a shaming experience. In spite of the difficulties at work, riding home from the Playhouse on the Embankment to Barnsbury and my 'empty house', I realised that I was content to be working, doing what I was meant to do. That was no small thing, I told myself.

Kevin and Kate and I went to the country to Bill and Bryn's for Christmas. People say that however bad things are, they seem worse at Christmas but I didn't feel that at all and we all had a lovely time. But even I smiled as I unpacked and laid my bedside reading on my night table and wondered how many people would have included *Living with Grief* along with the Christmas presents. Bill was one of the few people (Edward was another) with whom I could be totally honest and he bore the brunt as I talked and talked. He and Kenny and Kevin all let me ramble on and on during those months when I needed to be allowed to ramble and I could only hope that they had a mechanism which filtered some of the nonsense I must have been speaking. I had never before confided in anyone, had always had a horror of boring people or embarrassing them or being a nuisance and now that I'd begun to talk, the floodgates opened and washed over my closest friends. John Ehrman, the director, sent me books and advice from America. I clutched at everything indiscriminately and gratefully.

After months of this I wondered desperately whether I would ever again be free of fear. All the while I meditated night and morning and never missed doing the Feldenkreis back exercises I'd been taught by Lily Cohen, though I found I was at my most vulnerable and sad during the solitary twenty minutes of exercise. I longed to escape from the house but, ironically, work now kept me chained to London. Kate went home and before Edward returned, I schooled myself to live quietly with my unhappiness and to accept and come to terms with my own deficiencies, turning over and over in my mind the harm I'd inflicted on other people, the absence of kindness I'd shown only too often. My mother had never asked me for anything, but I knew what she would have liked to have and what mean-spirited arrogance it was that made me deny her a fur coat for her old age. I knew what she had in mind when she talked of fur; a musquash, no shape, grey, smooth and warm, as worn by the senior mistress at my grammar school. The coat of a woman who, though she could not afford a motor, went to Bruges for her holiday and once to Oberammergau for the passion play and who, if she chose, could go to see an Ivor Novello show in London. It was the coat of the woman my mother could have been. 'Fur? No, no liberal minded, caring person wears FUR nowadays!' My mother, transported from the Welsh countryside to the expensive shops of Hampstead, struggled politely with this glimpse of fashionable caring and nodded her thanks for the gift of a lovely and costly woollen cape. What mean impulse made me deny her the thing that would have made her harmlessly proud? It wasn't a small thing and it was one of a host of misdeeds that crowded into my mind, clamouring for attention. I was being brought very low.

My strongest resource, my reasonableness, was useful now, if only to preserve the framework of 'normal' life, enabling me to work and even to play a little. What I thought of as 'real' (hidden and secret) life was all tumult and confusion and I moved through the unfamiliar territories guided only by instinct; I neither questioned nor challenged the rhythms of this interior existence. As I sat alone with myself, I grew less appalled by myself and less interested in myself, but I knew that this miserable period was not over by a long chalk. Less and less I wished that I knew where I was going or what I hoped to achieve and I stopped worrying about my lack of purpose. The natural world exerted the same power over me as it always had and I didn't worry at my inconsistency in finding myself in a sad mood, then suddenly engulfed for a moment or two in happiness; a change in the weather, a trick of the light in the garden was still enough to surprise me into delight. The cats made me laugh. I laughed a great deal the day a blackbird walked portentously into the kitchen and looked at me and two inscrutable Burmese faces hanging over cupboard tops, before turning tail and walking out again.

The days began to lengthen and I vigorously reclaimed the garden for myself, uprooting without a qualm all the plants that Robin had chosen and which I rather disliked. It was deeply satisfying to be rearranging and replanting and learning the workings of the lawnmower (previously considered too 'difficult' for me). As I wrestled with the pond and its pump (also too difficult), I realised as well that I would never achieve Robin's way with animals. The fish ignored me; they used to feed from his hand. But it was deeply satisfying to see the garden looking just as *I* wanted it. I turned my attention to the house, which for a while had become an object of hatred, and gradually I came to like it again as I rearranged it and altered it. On impulse, one day I heaved the matrimonial bed into the front garden and bought a lovely new one from Heal's. Recalling Bob Crowley's set for *Brel*, I had the front hall and the staircase and the landing painted the colour of a Gauloise cigarette packet. Every morning I felt a surge of energy as I stepped into the wonderful blast of blue.

I still felt fear and pain but I had lost the wish to chatter and the need to validate everything I saw or did by sharing it. I was content to look and then stop looking and it didn't hurt me when what I did went unseen and unremarked upon, except in exceptional circumstances; when I passed my driving test I came home and telephoned everyone I knew, demanding astonishment and praise.

# Chapter Forty-three

Sara thinks it a good idea for me to accept a job in America. I think she's probably right but I'm scared. I've only visited New York briefly in the Sixties and Seventies as a celebrity wife, living in the grandest hotels, travelling by limo, insulated from the frightening city outside. I remember the terrifying wave of traffic surging down Fifth Avenue. Will I get around safely? Will I learn to live with the noise? The film is *The Age of Innocence* which Martin Scorsese will direct. Daniel Day-Lewis and Michelle Pfeiffer will play the lovers and I suspect they need a fair number of actors who will look comfortable in period clothes and appear and sound like well-heeled, turn-of-the-century Americans, as they munch their way through lengthy and complicated meals which feature so heavily in books of that period.

Early spring in Troy in upstate New York. Location catering is wonderful and I've eaten rather more than my period stays will allow. The leaves on the trees will soon be in bud and Alec McCowen and I are making our way back to our trailers. I can't help myself and I blurt out, 'Oh, isn't this all *wonderful*?' Alec, mildly surprised and mildly pitying, shakes his head and says, 'Oh Siân, you're *very* easily pleased.' I suppose I am – thank God. I'm so pleased that nothing awful is happening, that I'm actively *not* suffering what Edward Duke has christened 'NDs' – nameless dreads.

There's a rail strike so I'm put in a taxi to travel to New York where most of the filming will take place. My driver is appalled that he has to go to New York which is full of 'bad people', he says. He's so frightened that I become quite brave and when he gets lost somewhere in the Bronx, I take over the map and begin navigating and have no trouble in getting up safely to the Wyndham Hotel. I'm impressed by myself. He's too scared to say thanks or stop for a coffee and heads off to Troy, never to return if he can help it, he assures me.

The Wyndham is a smallish hotel, home from home for English actors. I walk around my 'neighbourhood' and very soon it begins to feel like home. Where is that intimidating city which used to scare me so much? Debbie Condon's friend from schooldays, Louise Emmett, calls me and takes me on a smart outing and teaches me a bit about the bus system. I feel as though I'm mastering demotic Aramaic as I board my first bus and then *change* buses.

The early rising and the long hours of work are familiar and soothing. When I'm not working I take huge walks and realise that I'm writing very little in my notebooks these days. It's also soothing to be with people who know nothing about me. This is most unexpected but New York is being just that – soothing. I begin to make friends. Meeting Louise was a piece of luck. She and Debbie attended a ladies' seminary here in the city. They wore white gloves and learned lovely manners, which have endured. I had not expected just yet that anyone would make me laugh uncontrollably, then I met Alexis Smith. We had to be separated because of bad behaviour during the party scene in the film. The first assistant was cross and I avoided Daniel's eye; I don't suppose he'd believe me if I told him that the last person to be evicted with me from a studio for laughing was his mother, Jill.

I loved watching Martin Scorsese at work. He wore crisp, rather military-looking cotton shirts and belted slacks and bounced through the day on the balls of his feet. Never did we see him looking doubtful or uncertain or even dissatisfied. From the first moment of the day's work, for twelve or fourteen hours, he knew exactly what would happen next and all precautions were taken to make sure that everything was exactly as he wished it to be. His sets had a cloister-like quiet – even his carpenters seemed to be able to hammer noiselessly. Occasionally, if there was an unauthorised snatch of conversation in the distance, he would stop what he was doing and, smiling, say, 'Did I hear something? Sh! Listen! No. Nothing. My imagination.' Those smiling moments were blood chilling but I liked and admired him.

Jane Stanton-Hitchcock, the author of *Vanilla*, invited me to stay with her on the Upper East Side. We were both wary of the venture. Jane was a full-time novelist and filming hours make actors unsatisfactory guests. Also, I wasn't at all sure that I wanted to *be* a guest; hotel life was undemanding and I'd become used to living in the Fifties. When I arrived at Jane's duplex on the East River, I realised that she lived in breathtaking style. I had my own entrance to the prettiest guest suite imaginable. I adjusted my ideas. 'Jane, I had no idea. Are you wonderfully rich!' Simple, sweet thing, she merely smiled. I stayed with Jane for the rest of my time in New York. She didn't want a guest and I didn't want to be one so we got on famously. Occasionally, Jane would stop writing and we'd chat. I told her about heaving the king-size mattress into the street. When she stopped laughing she asked, 'Have you ever been in therapy?' I saw what she meant. It *was* rather extreme behaviour. (I was blissfully Freudianly unaware of myself.) '*Don't* go into open-ended therapy,' she counselled. 'Do a sixteen hour course of *cognitive* therapy when you get home. It's called *CAT* and it will polish you up nicely!' I admired Jane for her chic, her industry, her expensive allure, her brains and her furniture. It would never have occurred to me not to promise to do as she told me.

Sara arranged for me to go and stay with June Havoc in Connecticut. Ageless at over eighty years, beautiful and gallant, she lived with her friend and assistant, Tana, in a wonderful farmhouse; the outhouses and fields full of the halt, the maimed and the blind of the animal world and in the barn stood her sister, Gypsy Rose Lee's, piano. It was all a bit too much for me and I lay on the grass and slept for a whole afternoon. June let me do some gardening for her and then took advantage of Tana's absence for a day, visiting her family nearby, to move a great deal of huge, heavy furniture from one room to another. Exhausted – I more than she – we had an early supper and went to bed. I woke very early, not knowing where I was for a moment and lay there looking at the New England sky, aware that something was different. I sat up abruptly and grinned broadly as I realised that for the first time in ages I wasn't scared, I was just awake. It wasn't a wonderful, exciting moment, it was lovely that something bad was absent. I went downstairs and sat with June and Tana and wished I could tell them what had happened but I couldn't because they didn't know my story and nothing *had* happened. Something had stopped, that was all. Tana took us to visit her enormous Italian/American family and for a moment I felt a pang of envy as I watched them cooking and playing and interfering in each other's lives but, standing alone on the verandah overlooking the sea, I reminded myself that my life was programmed to be very different and that we cannot have everything or do everything. Having It All had been too exhausting and time-consuming and finally it had defeated me. It was a relief to stop trying.

Back in the city, I begin to think about going back to London. I shan't be there for more than a few days because I've arranged to do a job in Austria. I've started packing. Walking along Seventy-first Street towards the park, I find I'm suddenly running from high spirits, as I can't remember running since I was a girl at home, but I don't have anywhere to run to and although I have a house in London, I no longer know where 'home' is. Since Central Park is ahead of me I run there and go on running until, winded, I flop down on a bench. Bending over, catching my breath, I'm glad to have a moment where my face is hidden because I can't stop smiling and feel I look foolish. Finally, I sit up, exhausted. Two young men passing by smile at me sitting there, smiling. As they pass on I realise that at this moment I am not merely *not unhappy* I am perfectly *happy* and secure, surrounded by strangers, my suitcases half-packed at Jane's and a sheaf of travel arrangements in my bag. I haven't any idea what will happen to me. Will I ever get another, 'proper', exciting job? Will I go on working? How will I live? What country shall I live in? Shall I live alone? Why do I feel terrific?

Rising and, still moving fast, going east towards the river and up towards Gracie Square, I realise that I don't really care to look for answers to these questions; I no longer have an impulse to look into the future, but there is a swing in my step that I had not thought to feel again as I continue my way through the smart neighbourhood; Seventy-fifth, Seventy-ninth, Eighty-first. Streets that are a world away from the places where I grew up but they feel as familiar and safe under my feet as the tracks across the low, Welsh mountains of my first home. The skies, the houses, the trees – green overnight in the swift astonishing New York spring – are improbably bright today with the Pre-Raphaelite clarity of a world seen with the eyes of youth – or of love.

When I was a girl, a moment ago, Saunders Lewis told me to 'Learn to live on the knife edge of insecurity'. It seemed to me an uncomfortable place to want to be but maybe that is where I have arrived and it begins to seem that maybe he was right; to live perilously is to live safely. Maybe. This is so undramatic, this afternoon in New York. So undramatic, so wonderful. No event has taken place. Nothing of significance has been said, but my life has changed. There is no solution, no resolution, no conclusion; but I am happy and I am at home and unafraid of what the future will bring.

# Siân Phillips

1959    *Siwan* (Theatre and TV), *Land of Song* (TV series), *The Garden of Loneliness* (TV), *Granite* (TV), *Treason* (TV and Radio), *The Tortoise and the Hare* (TV), *Game for Eskimos* (TV)
1960    *The Taming of the Shrew* (Theatre), *The Duchess of Malfi* (Theatre), *Strangers in the Room* (TV)
1961    *The Duchess of Malfi* (Theatre cont.), *Ondine* (Theatre), *The Lizard on the Rock* (Theatre)
1962    *Don Juan in Hell* (TV), *The Maids* (Radio), *Afternoon of M Andesmas* (Radio)
1963    *Gentle Jack* (Theatre), *This is not King's Cross* (TV), *Becket* (Film), *The Other Man* (TV Film), *Espionage* (Film)
1964    *Gentle Jack* (Theatre cont.), *Maxibules* (Theatre), *The Sex Game* (TV)
1965    *The Night of the Iguana* (Theatre), *Ride a Cock Horse* (Theatre)
1966    *Ride a Cock Horse* (Theatre cont.), *Man and Superman* (Theatre), *Man of Destiny* (Theatre), *Eh Joe* (TV)
1967    *Man and Superman* (Theatre cont.), *The Burglar* (Theatre)
1968    *The Beast in the Jungle* (TV Film)
1969    *Goodbye Mr Chips* (Film), *The Cardinal of Spain* (Theatre), *City 69* (TV), *Vessel of Wrath* (TV), *The Eccentricities of a Nightingale* (Theatre)
1970    *Murphy's War* (Film)
1971    *Under Milk Wood* (Film), *Platonov* (TV)
1972    *Lady Windermere's Fan* (TV), *Epitaph for George Dillon* (Theatre), *Alpha Beta* (Theatre)
1973    *Gloriana* (Theatre), *A Nightingale in Bloomsbury Square* (Theatre), *Shoulder to Shoulder* (TV series)
1974    *Shoulder to Shoulder* (TV series cont.)
1975    *Pilgrim Fathers* (TV Film), *How Green Was My Valley* (TV series), *The Gay Lord Quex* (Theatre)
1976    *How Green Was My Valley* (TV series cont.), *The Achurch Letters* (TV), *I, Claudius* (TV series)
1977    *Heartbreak House* (TV), *Off To Philadelphia in the Morning* (TV mini series), *Boudicca* (TV series)
1978    *Spine Chiller* (Theatre), *Clash of the Titans* (Film), *Oresteia* (TV)
1979    *Crime and Punishment* (TV), *The Doctor and the Devils* (Film), *A Woman of No Importance* (Theatre), *Tinker Tailor Soldier Spy* (TV), *The Inconstant Couple* (Theatre)
1980    *You Never Can Tell* (Theatre), *Sean* (TV series), *Pal Joey* (Theatre), *Barriers* (TV series), *Churchill – The Wilderness Years* (TV series)
1981    *Pal Joey* (Theatre cont.), *How Many Miles to Babylon* (Film), *Barriers* (TV series)
1982    *Dear Liar* (Theatre), *Major Barbara* (Theatre), *Smiley's People* (TV)
1983    *Dune* (Film)
1984    *Peg* (Theatre), *Love Affair* (Theatre)
1985    *Gigi* (Theatre), *Return to Endor* (Film), *'Life of Siân'* (TV documentary)
1986    *Gigi* (Theatre cont.), *The Two Mrs Grenvilles* (TV), *A Painful Case* (TV Film), *Lost In Time* (TV), *The Snow Spider* (TV series)
1987    *Thursday's Ladies* (Theatre), *Brel* (Theatre), *Vanity Fair* (TV series), *George Borrow* (TV), *A Killing on the Exchange* (TV series)
1988    *Brel* (Theatre cont.), *Mother Knows Best* (TV), *Shadow of the Noose* (TV), *Emlyn's Moon* (TV series)
1989    *Valmont* (Film), *The Glass Menagerie* (Theatre), *Dark River* (Film) *Paris Match* (Theatre)
1990    *Perfect Scoundrels* (TV), *Freddie and Max* (TV), *Red Empire* (TV), *Vanilla* (Theatre), *Landscape and Legend* (TV)
1991    *The Manchurian Candidate* (Theatre), *Emlyn's Moon* (TV series), *Tonight At 8.30* (TV), *The Chestnut Soldier* (TV series)
1992    *Painting Churches* (Theatre), *The Age of Innocence* (Film), *The Borrowers* (TV series), *Heidi* (Disney Film)
1993    Novello Concert, *Ghosts* (Theatre), *Covington Cross* (TV)
1994    *The Lion in Winter* (Theatre), *Marlene* (Theatre), *The Borrowers* (TV), *A Mind to Kill* (TV series), *Nearest and Dearest* (TV)
1995    *An Inspector Calls* (Theatre US), *A Little Night Music* (Theatre)
1996    *A Little Night Music* (Theatre US), *House of America* (Film), *Marlene* (Theatre)
1997    *Marlene* (Theatre US), *The Scold's Bridle* (TV), *Nikita* (TV)
1998    *Marlene* (Theatre cont.), *Alice Through the Looking Glass* (Film), *Aristocrats* (TV series), *Falling in Love Again* – Cabaret (Theatre Israel), *The Magician's House* (TV series)
1999    *Marlene* (Theatre cont.), *Falling in Love Again* – Cabaret (Theatre), *The Magician's House* (TV series)
2000    *Falling in Love Again* (Theatre cont.), *Coming and Going* (Film), *Ballykissangel* (TV)
2001    *Lettice and Lovage* (Theatre), *Falling in Love Again* (Theatre cont.), *The Leopard in Autumn* (Radio series) *Almost Like Being in Love* – Cabaret (Theatre), *Divas at the Donmar* – Cabaret (Theatre)

# Index

# Siân Phillips